Ken Sakamura (Ed.)

TRON Project 1987

Open-Architecture Computer Systems

Proceedings of the Third TRON Project Symposium

With 131 Figures

Springer-Verlag
Tokyo Berlin Heidelberg New York
London Paris

KEN SAKAMURA
Leader, TRON Project
Department of Information Science
Faculty of Science
University of Tokyo
Hongo, Tokyo, 113 Japan

ISBN-13:978-4-431-68071-0   e-ISBN-13:978-4-431-68069-7
DOI: 10.1007/978-4-431-68069-7

Foreword

Almost 4 years have elapsed since Dr. Ken Sakamura of The University of Tokyo first proposed the TRON (the realtime operating system nucleus) concept and 18 months since the foundation of the TRON Association on 16 June 1986. Members of the Association from Japan and overseas currently exceed 80 corporations. The TRON concept, as advocated by Dr. Ken Sakamura, is concerned with the problem of interaction between man and the computer (the man-machine interface), which had not previously been given a great deal of attention. Dr. Sakamura has gone back to basics to create a new and complete cultural environment relative to computers and envisage a role for computers which will truly benefit mankind. This concept has indeed caused a stir in the computer field.

The scope of the research work involved was initially regarded as being so extensive and diverse that the completion of activities was scheduled for the 1990s. However, I am happy to note that the enthusiasm expressed by individuals and organizations both within and outside Japan has permitted acceleration of the research and development activities.

It is to be hoped that the presentations of the Third TRON Project Symposium will further the progress toward the creation of a computer environment that will be compatible with the aspirations of mankind.

Kazuo Kimbara

Chairman, The TRON Association
Board Director and Group Executive
Electronic Devices Group
Hitachi, Ltd.

Preface

This volume is a compilation of papers presented at the Third TRON
(*the realtime operating* system *nucleus*) Project Symposium held in
Tokyo on 13 November 1987. The TRON project, now in its 5th year,
aims at establishing a computer system architecture for the 1990s.

Computers have become indispensable in the modern world.
Computers are now used in all walks of life and in the TRON project
it is assumed that the next decade will see an even greater and more
widespread application and that distributed computing will become
fully exploited. It is expected that many devices, including household
appliances, will come to utilize computers and become "intelligent"
in some way or other. These computer-controlled devices will be
linked to other devices for coordinated operation. When computed
coordination increases in the 1990s, it will become increasingly
important to have a consistent man-machine interface. It is thus of
prime importance that a man-machine interface for personal computers, mainframe computers, and computer-controlled devices be
designed based on a unified principle; otherwise, it will not be easy to
take full advantage of the highly distributed network of computers
and computer control.

The TRON project has addressed the problem of using different
languages with computers. Many languages that do not employ the
Roman alphabet are going to be handled on computers and it is
important to provide a framework for the use of such languages.
In the TRON project, an open architecture allowing free access to
the specifications is deemed necessary toward the construction of
a global network of computers. Most current computer systems are
"closed" in this sense.

Current computer system architectures are hindered by the need
to be compatible with older systems and future extension to current
systems is a main area of weakness. The TRON project was initiated
to solve the problems facing present architectures. The reader will

find here the current status of research and development on the TRON project and an examination of future trends.

I would like to thank the numerous people who have made the symposium possible. I hope they can continue to support the TRON project to its fruitful completion.

KEN SAKAMURA

Table of Contents

Chapter 1: Toward the Construction of Computer Architecture for 1990s

The Objectives of the TRON Project

Ken Sakamura

Department of Information Science, Faculty of Science, University of Tokyo
Hongo,Tokyo,113 Japan

ABSTRACT

HFDS (Highly Functionally Distributed System) is heterogeneous loosely-coupled computer network and generally has large number of computers including large number of intelligent objects.

The TRON project has been under way to bring the dream of computerized society, where HFDS's play important roles, into reality. The project will produce ITRON, BTRON, CTRON, MTRON, and TRON VLSI CPU when it is finished. ITRON is a realtime OS specification for embedded computer systems. BTRON is an OS specification for workstations, and it will define TAD (TRON Application Databus) data exchange standard. CTRON is an OS specification for servers and gateways on HFDS. MTRON is a network OS specification to control the operation of HFDS's. TRON VLSI CPU will run the TRON-based software systems efficiently.

The long-term objective of the TRON project is to realize an HFDS by utilizing the results of these subprojects.

Keywords: ITRON, BTRON, CTRON, MTRON, TRON VLSI CPU

1. INTRODUCTION

About 40 years have passed since the invention of digital computers. In these years, we have learned many things in computer science. What we have learned includes concepts like parallel processing, and AI. The advent of microelectronics has made it possible to build computers smaller than human body. We are now at the turning point of the computer technology. What steps do we take now?

For the next steps to take in computer engineering, some say AI is the way to go while others say supercomputers are important. These, of course, are very important.
However, I think the most important next step is the appearance of highly functionally distributed systems that span the whole globe. In this paper, for the sake of brevity, we call such systems HFDS's. HFDS combines many computer systems with different per-

formance in a loosely-coupled manner, and then let these systems offer more sophisticated services than these systems can offer independently. Implementing such HFDS is the final goal of the TRON project.

In this paper, the concept of HFDS is described, and then how the TRON project aims at implementing such HFDS is explained.

2. HFDS

In order to consider the future computer applications, we have to take into consideration the current applications fields, which have become widely available because of the microprocessors. One is the application of computers for embedded control systems. The other is so called personal computers.

2.1 INTELLIGENT OBJECTS

As microprocessors become smaller and cheaper, more electronic appliances and equipment have embedded computers for control. The examples are numerous: microwave oven, refrigerator, washing machine, camera.

One thing we should notice is that the control using microcomputers is not the indispensable part of these machines. Rather computers are used to make these machines capable of giving more sophisticated service than they can without computers. For example, automatic timer control, automatic focusing, and other nice features are now available thanks to the intelligence of the built-in control.

We call these machines which can give sophisticated services thanks to the "intelligence" of the small and inexpensive computers and sensors "intelligent objects".

2.2 COMMUNICATION MACHINE

The other important application of today, the personal computer, is for business-oriented users who have to process much data or for hobbyists. Personal computers are not for general laymen yet.

I believe the personal computers of today should evolve into communication machine for three purposes. The three communication tasks are; communication with the self, communication with others and communication with machines.

Communication with the self means the creation process by trial and error. That is, we regard the process of expressing one's thought and storing it into the computer as communication with one's inner thought. Such process is helped by computer software such as word processor, and graphics software.

Communication with the others means the ordinary communication task. The content of the messages passed around is the text or pictures created in the process of communicating with the self.

Communicating with machines means the control of various machines by computers. Recently, the two communication tasks here, namely creation and propagation of information attract most of the attention of the computer users. However, one important application of computers is the automatic control of machines.

The number of intelligent objects will increase and they will be used in a network structure. Controlling of these intelligent objects will become more important to deal with HFDS in the future.

So in a nutshell, we might say the true personal computers are really "communication machines." They are not general-purpose information processing machines, but necessary devices for three communication tasks, namely a sort of an "electronic stationery goods".

Providing dedicated machines as opposed to providing general-purpose machines has other benefits as well. The adoption of communication machines by the mass will bring about the reduction of price due to the merit of mass production. It is difficult to say which comes first; the price reduction or the mass production. The communication machines can offer dedicated services based on a small set of primitive functions. The simplicity of these functions make communication machines easy to produce. Hence the goal of mass-producing and reducing the price of such communication machines should be easy to achieve.

2.3 HFDS (HIGHLY FUNCTIONALLY DISTRIBUTED SYSTEM)

The two applications, intelligent objects and communication machines can become possible only because of the appearance of small and inexpensive microcomputers. When the two applications become widely available, the computers will (come to be) used in general households outside the offices where specialists use computers. This will result in the quantitative explosion of the computers. Before the introduction of microcomputers, one computer existed for every ten thousand men, and the numbers are increasing. Today we have one computer for every ten men, or possibly more.

If the trend continues, most machines in our surrounding environment including pieces of furniture will use computers. It is conceivable that 100 computers for a man will exist.

Some readers may think that the above scenario is impossible in terms of cost. It is true for the immediate future. However, if we take a longer view, the price of computers and sensors will certainly become a tiny portion of product cost. The micromachining technology to develop small sensors on wafers can be used to incorporate sensors onto the same chip on which CPU is fabricated.

The computerized society will incorporate the applications mentioned in an expanded way. Machines ranging from elevators to the air conditioners, furniture and parts of the buildings will have become intelligent objects with built-in computers and sensors. Every one will have a communication machine and use it for their information-related tasks. Machines in manufacturing plants will become intelligent objects, too. In order to help microprocessors with the added performance, specialized mainframe computers will be used to provide sophisticated services. The most important thing in the computerized society is that these objects will be linked in a network. (*Figure 1.*)

HFDS that consists of intelligent objects, electronic stationery goods, and specialized servers will make various things possible: people can call elevator cars by pressing buttons on their personal computers. People can work on manufacturing tasks as well using communication machine. For example, designing an automobile and then as design tasks controlling the manufacturing process of the car can be done from the personal computer.

Today, FA (factory automation) is pursued by many manufacturers. But it is rare that such system can give any clue about how a production of a new product affects the company management. FA implemented within an HFDS should give realtime information over such matters, and possibly can give information about the influence of one decision over the local economy.

The environment described above is the dream of the old-fashioned computerized society. The dream was thrown away and was not thought of as a practical achievable target when the limit of computing power was felt in the early days of computers. However, the advent of microelectronics and other technologies have enable us to take up the dream very seriously.

Let us summarize here the differences of HFDS from the conventional distributed systems. The differences can be described from the quantitative and qualitative point of view.

Quantitative difference is essentially the differences in the number of computing elements in the network. Conventional systems has usually several dozen computers that talk to each other frequently. The interaction among them is inherently local in nature. Network is viewed as an external environment.

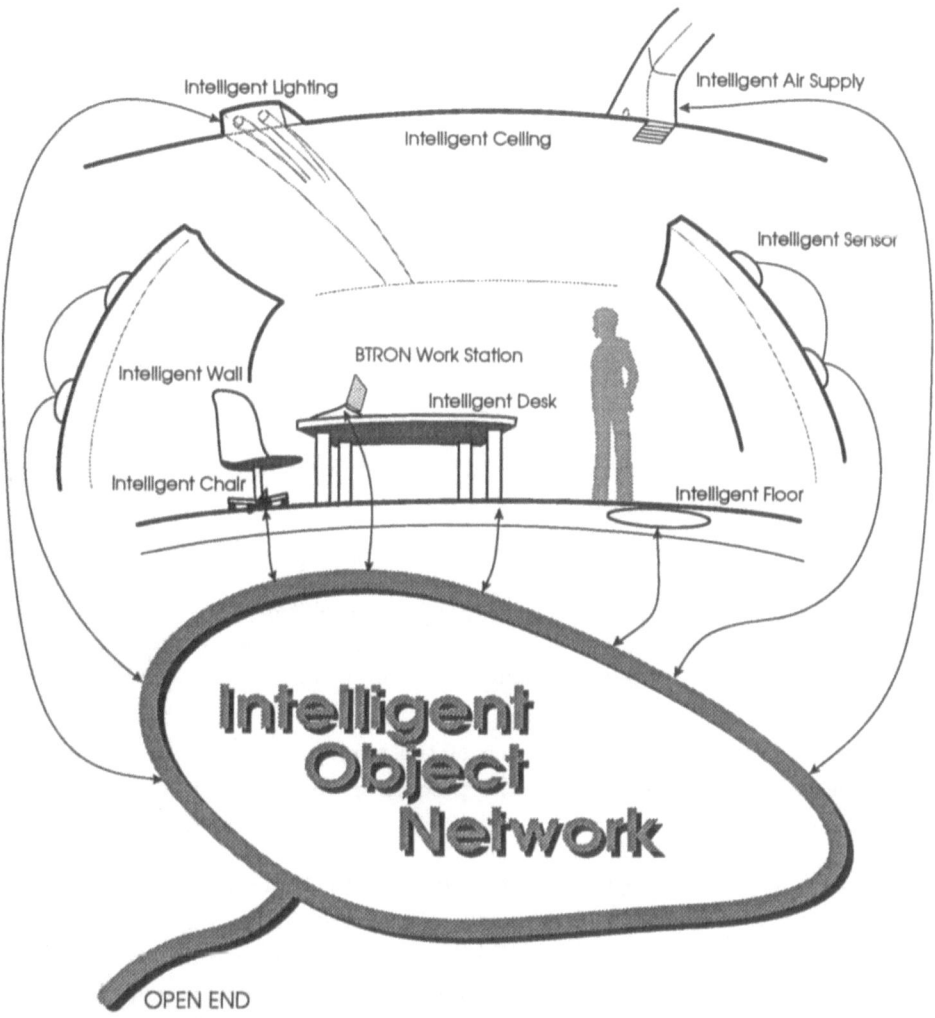

Figure 1. Highly Functionally Distributed System Environment

In a real implementation of HFDS, a room with hundred computers is likely, and buildings will have several thousand computers. Assuming that buildings will be grouped into HFDS, a city will have several million computers, and the nation or the HFDS that span the whole globe will have billion computers in it. We need a philosophy to handle such large loosely coupled computer network.

Qualitative differences of HFDS from the conventional computer systems is that the HFDS is inherently heterogeneous and that the interactions inside HFDS are much more varied than the ones in the conventional systems.

For example, the interactions among the following computers can exist in order to optimize the air conditioning; intelligent sensors in rooms, intelligent air conditioners, personal computers used by dwellers, and supercomputers that might be used to model the air flow of the room. The interactions are much more complex than the ones done in many local networks of today.

The router or gateway computers will also be the part of the HFDS. these will handle the load balancing, diagnose faulty computers, and reconfigure the network topology dynamically.

2.4 REQUIRED TECHNOLOGY

Many problems remain to be solved to implement HFDS in reality. For example, communication protocol is one problem. But it is just a start. New problems created by the quantitative and qualitative differences from previous systems must be solved.

There is very little that the present day computer science can offer to solve these problems since it has been almost impossible to imagine a society where many things have built-in computers. Hence these problems, some of which have something to do with the qualitative changes brought about by the quantum leap in quantity, have been seldom addressed. Only exception is the research of the parallel machine with thousands of microprocessors. But in this research, the processing elements are homogeneous and located in a close neighborhood.

In our approach, we put emphasis on the modeling of HFDS since it is a very new concept and having a model is important for constructive discussion. The physical environment must be modeled somehow as medium through which computer systems interact with each other. In existing systems, interactions among computer systems must be explicitly defined in details. However, in order to dynamically add/delete intelligent object to large HFDS, such detailed manual definition of the interactions are clearly impossible. Instead, by modeling the physical world surrounding the computer system, we should make it possible to define the system changes by means of the physical world description such as the distance, or direction among objects. Such description should be transformed into detailed definition of interactions among computer systems automatically. The models of HFDS should be capable of modeling the real physical world to some extent.

Using the previous example, staying in the same environment lets the air conditioner to detect the existence of newly installed mercury lamp because the real temperature distribution (sensed by a network of sensors) will be different from the one planned by the air conditioner. In a real HFDS, more complex interactions can take place. The system might have to use AI technique to offer flexible interactions among the components.

An action of intelligent object can affect the environment. The change in the environment, in return, will affect the actions of other intelligent objects. the interaction of intelligent objects through the environment can result in an unwanted behavior of the system such as divergence or unnecessary repetition. Such unwanted behavior can be dangerous at times.

In order to suppress such unwanted behavior of the system and maintain the cooperative nature of HFDS, it s necessary for each component to pursue its goals and to readjust its goals from time to time. In this sense, the concept of neighborhood where close interaction takes place is very important. The concept of closeness plays an important role in devising control.

The control models of HFDS have much in common with the real human society. The control of HFDS cannot be centralized and cannot be totally distributed. Each component has a set of given goals, has a priority assigned and can belong to multiple groups in the HFDS. In HFDS, many cooperating groups of components exist and interact in many ways. This is like a human society and we call it the "society of computers".

Intelligent objects must modify their internal models of the surrounding environment when new intelligent objects that can change the environment are installed. In reality, normal operation of these objects do not require such capability. Probably high-performance intelligent server will detect these changes and instruct affected intelligent objects to change their internal models. For example, air conditioners will have to switch to a new model of heat source distribution in a room when a mercury lamp is installed.

Of course, changes that can be anticipated can be announced by the newcomer. We must establish the standard format for such announcement. It is a good idea to let the manufacturers of intelligent objects to operate database servers to obtain various data of these objects to retrieve the necessary information to construct environment models dynamically. Instead of each object carrying large set of data, each object can possibly carry on an identifying code to access the data in the database.

When we focus on the role that locality plays in the control of HFDS, it is immediately apparent that the government structure is similar to the control structures of HFDS. It is impractical to recognize the billions of computers as individual units. Instead, some grouping of these computers are necessary to reduce the size of recognized components into a manageable one. Computers in a region of HFDS will be regarded as one component from the view point of control mechanism that handles wider area. In this case, the computers in a region are regarded as an entity that has some level of autonomy but at the same time dependent on other parts of the HFDS. For example, intelligent objects within a room will be regarded as one component in a building, the computers in a building itself will be regarded as one component in one district, etc. In principle, such recursive structure will be introduced to control and construct HFDS that spans the whole globe.

Aside from developing the model and control method of HFDS, the maintenance of uniform communication across HFDS is very important. Each component of HFDS must be capable of communicating with each other (possibly indirectly). In practice, this will pause many difficulties. However, the uninterrupted and unblocked communication among the components of HFDS is vital to keep HFDS running.

It is important that all components follow common communication architecture and that means having common communication protocol structure and using compatible data format. The compatible and yet specialized data format may be necessary to use advanced technology such as AI.

Humans are parts of HFDS and that man-machine interface or man-man communication interface play an important role. Thus the problem of languages used (computer languages as well as natural languages) cannot be ignored.

In designing computer network that can span the whole globe, the computer must be capable of handling many different language systems using different character sets. so the computer must support the features of languages including the use of different character sets, and different convention of printing, input, etc. This language handling capability was kept in mind when BTRON was designed. BTRON can, for example, handle input of Japanese characters nicely. BTRON, in principle, should be applicable to any language in the world.

Another feature of BTRON language handling is the portability of applications across country borders. For example, the software using English messages should be very easy to port to Japanese market on the BTRON workstations. It is very important to provide this portability feature in order to promote the exchange of software products globally. It is pure nonsense to force people into using non-mother tongue, say, English or Japanese, just to use computers. The language must be the user's choice and the computer systems should support such choices.

3. TRON PROJECT

The TRON project is under way with the final objective of creating real implementations of HFDS's. MTRON, one subprojects of the TRON project, aims at establishing the model and control methods of HFDS. TAD (TRON Application Databus) is a standard for the data compatibility. TAC (TRON Application Control flow) is a set of methods and design guidelines to pass the jobs among workers and how to write a set of programs to run across HFDS in order to support the division of labor across HFDS.

3.1 OPEN ARCHITECTURE

The TRON project has adopted the policy of openness. It is necessary to have an open standard of interface to allow anyone to hook into HFDS. Also, allowing many companies competing (with each other) to offer products that are compatible at the open standard interface is important to make the concept of HFDS popular.

HFDS must be a popular one in order to take advantage of the accumulated "intelligence" of its components. The more components it has, the better it becomes.

It should be noted that the research results will be disseminated for a nominal fee as the set of specifications of an open architecture of computer systems. We hope that this openness will ensure that the TRON architecture will be widely used by many companies.

In the TRON project, the standardization is "weak." The TRON Design Guideline is used to guide the designers into adopting a set of common design concepts. Standardization is done at the design concept level, Implementors are given much freedom to build real systems. Weak standardization is a good compromise to have both the adoption of emerging technologies and the compatibility of various components of the HFDS.

3.2 OVERVIEW OF THE TRON PROJECT

In order to implement HFDS's, we must implement its subcomponents one by one. The TRON project has the following subprojects to build these subcomponents. ITRON is to build the intelligent objects. BTRON is to build the communication machine. CTRON is to build mainframes and servers to be used in the networks of computers based on ITRON and BTRON architecture. MTRON is to control the cooperation in these networks. (*Figure 2.*)

From a different view angle, it may be said these subprojects are classified according to who the machines will talk to. ITRON will talk to machines, BTRON will talk to human users, CTRON will talk to computers based on ITRON or BTRON. MTRON will talk to all these computers.

The reason why the project has been divided into these different subprojects is the variation of realtime response capability necessary for different applications. The name TRON (The Realtime Operating system Nucleus) stresses the importance of realtime responsiveness of computer systems.

Application using ITRON typically requires the response time on the order of several milliseconds while BTRON system possibly can be built with the response time on the order of seconds. Human users will get irritated if the response time is longer than

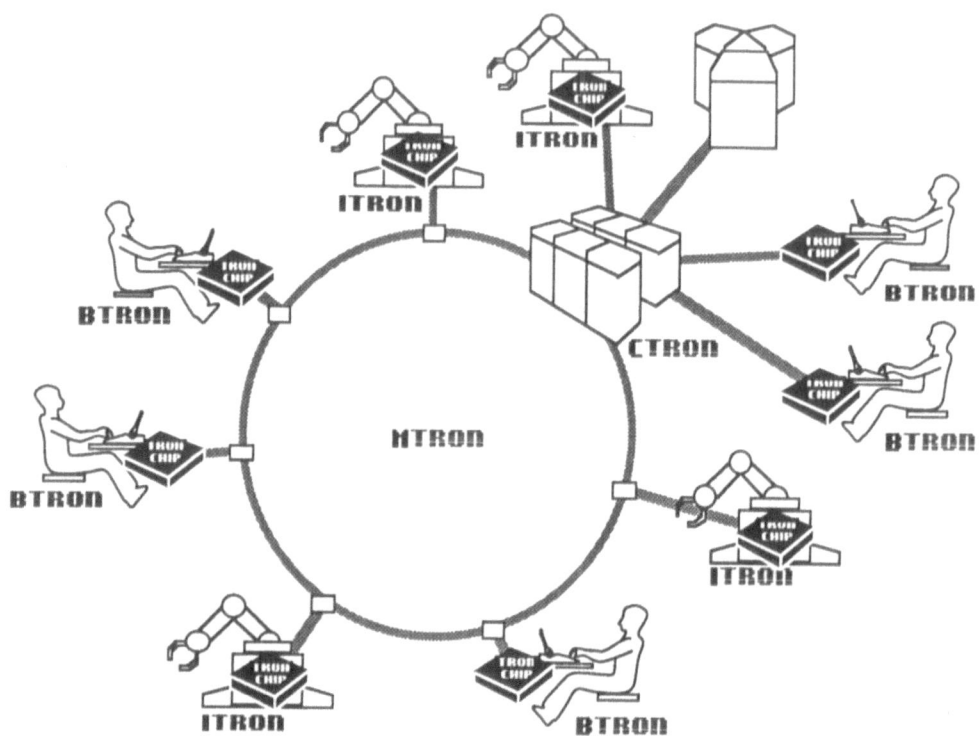

Figure 2. Overview of TRON System Architecture

several seconds, but programming technique can be used to make sure that the human user receive the acknowledgement of its instruction or some kind of message when the processing takes long time.

The nature of the tasks performed on these systems varies much, too. Tasks performed on computers based on ITRON require fast response and high degree of multiprocessing, but the each task is likely to be rather simple numeric task. Tasks performed on computers based on BTRON may not require very fast response, but the task itself is likely to be complicated and involves the text and graphics handling which has been handled clumsily on computers before.

We felt that single architecture cannot absorb the differences in the nature of application fields, and decided to develop a series of architecture to meet the demands of the real world.

3.3 SUBPROJECTS

Subprojects are summarized briefly below.

(a) TRON VLSI CPU

It is advantageous to have a series of general-purpose microprocessors in order to build intelligent objects and electronic stationery goods. TRON VLSI CPU is an originally designed VLSI microprocessor to support the components of HFDS.

The VLSI CPU is designed with extension in mind so that the semiconductor technology of 1990's will be well utilized. The first version is 32 bit, but extension to 64 bit is easy.

The instruction set includes special instructions to support ITRON and BTRON efficiently. Also, often used instructions are encoded in a compact manner and can be executed efficiently.

In order to meet various cost/performance requirements, there is a family of processors that can be used for products from inexpensive intelligent objects to high-performance engineering workstations. Also, the extra space reserved for sensors and others on the chip makes it possible to use the TRON VLSI CPU chips in ASIC-like manner.

(b) ITRON (Industrial-TRON)

ITRON is an architecture for the realtime operating system for embedded computers. It is used as the realtime, multitask operating system for the intelligent objects.

The major objective of ITRON is to minimize the task dispatching time. It can perform best in conjunction with TRON VLSI CPU, The implementation on currently available microprocessors are considered when ITRON was designed and these implementations can be efficient, too.

ITRON has many features. For example, task synchronization can be done using three different primitives. Only one of them is necessary, but users can pick up the best method to suit their needs. Unnecessary functions can be taken out of the OS to save space.

ITRON shares the same external data format as BTRON. Hence, it can be used as components in HFDS system and can communicate with other components without problems. Software development using ITRON OS can be done on workstations based on BTRON.

(c) BTRON (Business-TRON)

BTRON is an architecture of OS and man-machine interface (MMI, for short) for high-performance workstations. BTRON subproject will establish the TRON Design Guideline for the designers of MMI. The MMI thus created will be unified in a consistent manner so that users can move from one system to the other without running into difficulty with incompatible MMI's.

By providing uniform interfaces on BTRON-based machines, the users can have uniform methods to communicate with HFDS's. Also, the uniformity of MMI's across machines are expected to decrease the learning efforts.

In establishing a standard or a set of standards of MMI, we must have a very wide view. This is because MMI in the TRON project will be used on various machines from small FAX machine, electronic appliances, to high-performance workstations. MMI was usually meant to cover the man-machine interface through terminal devices before.

BTRON uses real/virtual data model as the base of its document handling system. It can simulate almost any data structure. This flexibility assures the compatibility among applications as much as possible. Communication which assures data compatibility is very important in HFDS's. Hence the real/virtual data model plays an important role.

We have made sure that computers as expressive medium is usable in the BTRON environment. The BTRON language handling capability features the highly sophisticated printing tasks that use multiple character font sets.

BTRON offers as its outer shell very high-level functions to support the features described above. The application programs can use these functions to minimize the development time and to achieve the high compatibility with other applications from the viewpoint of MMI and data format.

The keyboard is the most often used man-machine interface between users and HFDS 's. Hence special attention has been paid to the design of keyboard. Since the TRON project started in Japan, new TRON keyboard was designed according to the measurement of the human hands which was done in Japan and the analysis of the character distribution in Japanese documents. The new keyboard is easy to use and causes less fatigue than older keyboards. Electric digitizing pen is used as pointing device to draw figures or draw longhand characters.

The BTRON project will also produce a set of micro-BTRON specifications for very small specialized computers to be used as "electronic stationery goods". This is because the demand for such small computers has been very high.

(d) CTRON (Central-TRON)

HFDS cant be built using only machines based on ITRON and BTRON. Mainframe computers or specialize servers to handle very large database, very large and fast numerical calculation task, and complex network gate way services are necessary. CTRON is an operating system architecture of such computer systems.

The computers that CTRON controls will be aimed at applications currently handled by mainframe and superminicomputers. Although CTRON OS is multiuser, there is no direct man-machine interface in CTRON. Man-machine interface is provided by the BTRON-based machines and machines.

CTRON is aimed at specialized computers, and we have taken the approach of building application systems by having the designers extend the primitives offered in the kernel.

(e) MTRON (Macro-TRON)

The key to the realization of HFDS's is the MTRON subproject. MTRON is to establish a methodology to build an "operating system" for the large computer networks included in an HFDS. MTRON has become important recently since the results of other subprojects became gradually available. HFDS has become a meaningful target now, not a dream of computer scientists any more.

Currently, conceptual design and listing of subgoals in the design of MTRON are under way.

4. THE CURRENT STATUS OF THE TRON PROJECT

The first work which led to the TRON project started about 5 years ago. The project itself started in 1984. The TRON Association was formed on June 16, 1986 with a membership of 35 organizations including Fujitsu, Hitachi, Matsushita, Mitsubishi, NTT, NEC, Oki, and Toshiba. The membership now includes 85 organizations as of September 1987 and is expected to go over 100 at the end of 1987. Subsidiaries of overseas companies like AT&T and IBM have joined the TRON Association. The TRON Association is an open forum to promote the results of the TRON project.

The TRON project has been proceeding with the help from international computer community and paying attention to the needs of the real world applications. The current goal is to promote the results of the subprojects in the 1990's. From the end of 1990's to the beginning of the next century, we will try to connect various computer systems and make them work cooperatively. Building HFDS's is the long-term goal of the TRON project.

REFERENCES

[1]   TRON Project Special Issue, IEEE Micro,Vol. 7, No.2 Apr. 1987

[2]   Ken Sakamura, "New Concepts from the TRON Project," Iwanami-Shoten, Tokyo, 1987 (in Japanese).

[3]   Ken Sakamura, "Making of TRON," Kyoritsu Syuppan, Tokyo, 1987 (in Japanese).

Ken Sakamura is an associate professor in the Department of Information Science at the University of Tokyo. He initiated the TRON project in 1984. Under his leadership, several universities and over 50 manufacturers are now participating in the project in order to build the computers for the 1990's. In addition to his involvement with TRON, Sakamura chairs several committees of the Japan Electronics Industry Development Association and the Information Processing Society of Japan. He has written numerous technical papers and books. He received the BS, ME, and PhD degrees in electrical engineering from Keio University at Yokohama in 1974, 1976, and 1979, respectively.

The CPU to System Connection

James J. Farrell III
IEEE MICRO, VLSI Technology, Inc.
8375 South River Parkway, Tempe, AZ 85284, U.S.A.

ABSTRACT

For the ten year period that small, personal computers have been significant, the microprocessor has been the driving force behind the performance and function of the computer. The "solutions in search of a problem" approach of microprocessors is now taking different courses. This paper will briefly examine the current approaches that will effect the 1990's.

Keywords: CISC, RISC, Coprocessor, ASIC.

1. INTRODUCTION

During the mid-1970's, several "home" or personal computers made their way unto the market. Most were really quite capable, but lacked ease of use. Most required a good deal of both hardware and software "know-how" on the part of the user. The first really successful "personal" computer was the box produced by Apple. It was innovative, easy to use, and capable of solving real problems. It was also well-marketed. The central processing unit of the computer was the 8-bit 6502, which in many respects had an instruction set similar to the competing 6800. Another powerful 8-bit microprocessor was the 8080, which had especially good software and system support. Other very capable microprocessors, such as the 6800 and Z80 also appeared, and established themselves as significant contributors to microprocessor technology. Even with all of the technical enhancements from competing devices, the 6502 remained the volume leader for some years. The primary Reason for this was its acceptance and usage in the Apple personal computer. The other microprocessors were successful in a large and growing number of applications, although none had achieved a really major widespread computer design-in. For several years the the microprocessors continued to improve in performance and complexity, without a clear-cut winner, until a very significant event took place.

2. THE IBM PC™ [1]

The decision by IBM to select the 8086 family as the core CPU for its family of personal computers was a watershed event in the progression of microprocessors. Even though some IBM models sold much better than others, the overall IBM PC and PC-compatible family were an overwhelming success. A very large number of computers that run PC software are not manufactured by IBM. The "clone" manufacturers, taking advantage of demand and the huge PC software base, have, and are continuing, to produce an enormous number of PC-compatible computers. Virtually all have an 8086-type CPU at their cores.

3. THE APPLE MACINTOSH™ [2]

Following the IBM PC debut, the selection of the 68000 microprocessor family by Apple for their new Macintosh family of personal computers had an excellent effect on that family of microprocessors. The Apple Macintosh, with its high resolution graphics capability and small form factor, became very popular also, even though "clone" makers have not been a significant factor in this market. Other microprocessor families have also increased in complexity, and gained design-ins in several applications during this period, but none to the extent of the 68000 or 8086 families. All of the microprocessor families during the period from 1976 to 1985 gained in complexity and processing power. the age of the Complex Instruction Set Computer (CISC) and its connection to the personal computer had become well established. Four divergences from this trend will have a landmark effect on computers in the coming decade.

4. THE RISC

The first is the emergence and acceptance of a different type of microprocessor- The Reduced Instruction Set or RISC machine. Several different suppliers – both component and system – have announced new computers based on the RISC design methodology. All claim that RISC offers much higher performance than more traditional CISC devices. The common denominator among these suppliers has been a systems approach to the CPU design problem, in other words, the CPU is considered as a single unit. When multi-chip solutions are involved (as most are), interfaces are defined around performance and bandwidth requirements more than functional blocks, the partitioning found in most commercial microprocessors today. Component suppliers often partition their systems around functions, like scalar processor, memory management unit, and floating point processor. This allows each circuit to be used without the others, meaning that

---

[1] IBM PC™ is a trademark of IBM Corporation.
[2] APPLE MACINTOSH™ is a trademark of the Apple Corporation.

not all components must be available before some sales can begin. By partitioning around functions, the component suppliers may be sacrificing performance or requiring other system elements, such as memory, be faster than necessary at a given performance level.

As RISC technology moves from the laboratory into the commercial environment it is important for system designers to understand these new considerations. When new applications arise that cannot be addressed cost-effectively by CISC architectures, this new technology may provide the only solution. By examining the following system the designer will become familiar with this new, emerging computer technology and learn how systems can be partitioned around parameters other than functional blocks.

Higher integration in semiconductor technology brought down the high cost of logic and memory. Soon, computer architects found they could build an equivalent system cheaper, with lower power requirements, and having more reliability. Also, integration allowed them to add enhancements to the instruction set to improve performance of key customer applications for less cost than before. Assembler language programmers wanted more enriched addressing modes that moved some of the computing functions from software to hardware. In addition, it improved programmer productivity by reducing the number of lines of assembler language necessary to code programs. Less lines per function to code meant more functions could be coded in the same time thereby gaining higher productivity. High-level languages were available but generally were too inefficient to use except in the simplest level of problems. Hardware designers began adding new instructions and addressing modes to meet the programmer requests while remaining compatible with previous generations of software. Soon, system architects realized that they could provide more performance if they could sacrifice backwards compatibility and redefine their instruction sets to exploit new technologies. The instruction complexity had increased to the point where decoding multi-word, multi-format instructions was the limiting factor in processor speed. Unfortunately, customers had huge investments in software and were reluctant to change to hardware that could not execute their installed base. New architectures were limited to new customers and applications.

High-level language efficiency and hardware performance improved dramatically and became more useful for most applications. This helped two areas of concern in computer systems, programmer productivity and program transportability. High-level languages helped programmers write code that was hardware independent, at least in theory, as compilers stood between the programmer and the execution environment (physical hardware and operating system). Compiler differences and ambiguous language specifications caused some portability problems, but in general it was practical to port programs between machines. With more high-level language programs being written, hardware suppliers felt pressured to add even more complication to their instruction sets to support compiled code. Many architectures added hardware implementations of high-level constructs like FOR, WHILE, and PROC (procedure calls) directly into the instruction set. The problem arose as to which language to support because each is different, e.g. whether the conditional execution expression is evaluated at the beginning of the loop or the end. As a result, most architectures may support only one language well or are so general that the compiler cannot exploit them efficiently [3].

In the mid-seventies computer scientists began to investigate new methods to support all high-level languages more efficiently. It was becoming apparent that most problems were to complex to be written in assembler language and no one high-level language was sufficient to support all applications. From these development efforts came the RISC methodology for CPU design. What constitutes a RISC computer is yet another area of debate, but most emerging machines do have some characteristics in common. First, most RISC machines are based on single-cycle instruction execution. Unlike their Complex Instruction Set Computers (CISC) counterparts that may take up to 100 minor (clock) cycles to complete complex instructions, the RISC machines instruction set is limited to primitive functions that can execute in a single or extremely few machine cycles. Compiler writers have suggested that it is more efficient to provide primitives to build solutions rather than solutions in the instruction set. When instructions have too much semantic content, a clash occurs between the language and the instruction set [3] introducing inefficiency and increasing compiler complexity. In addition, single clock execution helps lower interrupt latency, thus making the system more responsive to the asynchronous environment of today's time-shared and/or networked systems.

Another common trait of RISC machines is a load/store architecture providing larger CPU register files. In a load/store architecture, the data processing instructions (logical and numeric functions) can only operate on the CPU registers. A separate set of instructions are used for memory reference that usually support a limited set of addressing modes. Streamlining the addressing modes helps simplify instruction decode, eliminate special-purpose address ALUs, and speed pipeline processing that can be slowed by multi-word address operand fetches. Recent improvements in the global register allocation problem faced by compilers have made efficient use of large numbers of registers possible. In response to compiler improvements, most RISC systems have added larger register files to improve performance. Two factors bring about significant performance increases from added registers: (1) register operations execute much faster, and (2) memory references are reduced because registers can hold temporary results.

In general, RISC machines are tightly coupled to their memory. The simple instruction set translates into a higher effective instruction execution rate, meaning the processors demand a high bandwidth from their memory systems to provide peak performance. In order to provide this bandwidth most, but not all, systems have implemented very sophisticated caching techniques which increase system cost and complexity dramatically.

The requirements for a small computer today, are very much different than even a few years ago. Now users expect a small computer to have capabilities that were only available in minicomputers. Full color displays at resolutions up to 640 by 480, real memory of 1M-byte, and networking support are common features demanded by end-users. The VLSI RISC system is "centered" around the memory, with each element designed to use the bandwidth efficiently without making outrageous demands that require premium memory components. The video display is integrated into the design to utilize the main memory for display area, eliminating the need for expensive add-on video cards. The system operates with a 24 MHz clock that yields a basic processor cycle of 8 MHz (125 ns). Even at this speed, the memory system uses inexpensive 120 ns access time page-mode DRAMs.

The VLSI RISC processor provides the computational element in the system. The processor has a radically reduced instruction set containing a total of only 46 different operations. Unlike most others, all instructions occupy one 32-bit word of memory. In keeping with the tradition of RISC methodology, the processor is implemented as with a single-cycle execution unit and a load/store architecture. The basic addressing mode supported is indexed from a base register, with several different methods of index specification. The index can be a 12-bit immediate value contained within the instruction, or another register (optionally shifted in some manner). The index can be used in a pre or post-indexed fashion for any method of specification.

5. THE COPROCESSOR

The second important development is the development of the coprocessor. Over ten years ago, when it became clear that a cohesive and orderly method of communicating between computer boards in file bus structures for microprocessor-based systems evolved. While there are many buses- and many proposals for buses, Multibus was one of the first. Multibus was—and is—widely accepted, and the bus has been upgraded with the current Multibus II. Multibus II is a high-speed synchronous bus capable of throughput that is greater that most boards require- 32M Bytes per second. Interfacing to this bus is no longer a 40 device design.

Multibus II is generally a single board that usually contains a microprocessor controlled, high-speed system with a non-multiplexed, local bus. This typical system consists of the CPU, memory I/O and bus interface modules. The system interfaces to the Multibus II Parallel System Bus (iPSB) by means of a large number of integrated circuits necessary to accomplish all of the interface protocols, or a single device called a Message Passing Coprocessor (MPC). The MPC provides a processor independent iPSB interface solution for intelligent subsystem boards. These subsystems can typically be intelligent peripheral controllers, file servers, data communications controllers, or graphics/image processors. Using the single-chip MPC component improves overall Multibus II system reliability by performing the error checking and reporting protocols defined in the iPSB bus interface specification.

Several microprocessor based sub-systems would interface to the iPSB bus of the Multibus II system. The bus is synchronous and runs at 32 megabytes per second. The subsystems run at speeds less than this, but information is moved on the iPSB at the 32 megabyte rate. Two types of messages are transmitted on the bus: solicited and unsolicited. Unsolicited messages are actually a form of intelligent interrupt. In addition to the signaling function they also contain a short data field with status information. This eliminates the need for further polling to establish the nature of the interrupt. The interrupt is thereby identified and fully self-sufficient. Support is provided on the subsystem side of the MPC by way of a register interface available to the local bus. On the Multibus iPSB bus side of the MPC resides a packet transfer mechanism. An unsolicited message is initiated by the subsystem CPU sending a message on the local bus to its resident MPC. The transfer is performed as a series of register writes to the transmit FIFO. An unsolicited message may be no smaller than four bytes, and no larger than 32 bytes in length, in four byte increments. Once the message is transferred to the MPC, the sending CPU is no longer required to retain it in memory. It may proceed with another task. In parallel to the sending subsystem CPU operating on a different task, the resident MPC requests the iPSB bus. When obtained, the MPC transfers the message as a single packet to the receiving subsystem. It is interrogated by the recipient by examination of the destination address field, which is part of the message. If the identification in this field matches the resident identification of the candidate recipient subsystem, the packet is stored in a buffer. Error conditions are then checked. Any detected errors are then signaled, on the iPSB bus, to the sending MPC. If error free, the recipient subsystem MPU is informed of the message's arrival by way of an interrupt sent by the MPC. The recipient CPU then performs a series of register reads to retrieve the message from the receive FIFO.

Solicited messages may be viewed as the Multibus II method of Direct Memory Access (DMA). Unlike the unsolicited message, the solicited message is expected, its transfer is negotiable, and its length may be very long as in the case of a large block of data to be moved. Before a solicited message is sent, the proposed transfer is "negotiated" by means of unsolicited messages. The initiating subsystem CPU sends a special requesting unsolicited message to the proposed recipient subsystem. The recipient then responds to the initiator. If the response is affirmative, the initiating CPU starts the solicited message procedure. A buffer request is sent to the sending MPC transmit buffer. The MPC recognizes the message as a buffer request, and saves the destination address, source address, requester identification, and the transfer length. The MPC will pad the end of the message by adding dummy bytes, if necessary, so that it will be a four byte word. The buffer request is then sent on the iPSB bus. The data transfer phase is handled by the sending and receiving MPC's and their DMA controllers. Neither subsystem CPU is involved in the transfer operation. They may be processing different tasks. The end of transfer is signaled to the receiving MPC by the last packet of data. Solicited message transfers are limited to a minimum of 32-bytes (plus header) and a maximum of 16 Megabytes. Any errors generate an interrupt and provide an error status. In addition the iPSB handles a large number of other control functions and the supports the Central Services Module (CSM), necessary for all Multibus II systems. In addition to the Message Passing Technique, the older and slower dual port memory techniques are supported also.

The VLSI MPC is a single piece of silicon design by Intel using VLSI Technology, Inc. design tools in order to completely implement the message passing protocol in a single part. The message address space in the Multibus II architecture has been defined to provide a high performance interprocessor communication mechanism for multiprocessor systems. By performing the message space interface, the MPC component offloads the local on-board CPU from interprocessor communication tasks which decouples the local bus activities from the iPSB bus activities. Decoupling these two functioned eliminates an interface bottleneck present in traditional dual-port architectures. The bottleneck is the result of dual-port requiring tight coupling between a processor and a shared memory resource. As the number of processors in the system increases, system performance degrades at an even faster rate. Message passing decouples these resources by allowing the local bus and system bus to operate independently without the need for wait states while awaiting arbitration for shared resources. Further, message passing allows transfer at the full bandwidth of the associated bus (or 32 megabytes per second, whichever is less). Previously, full implementation took 50 LSI integrated circuits and consumed a very large amount of printed circuit board space. An interim solution consisted of two gate array devices, the Bus Arbiter Controller (BAC) and Message Interrupt Controller (MIC). The MIC and BIC, while very useful in many applications, did not fully implement all of the functions required in the Multibus II system. Further this large device count adversely impact power supply costs as well as system reliability.

6. THE ASIC SOLUTION

The third significant innovation is the parts count reduction in parts count in personal computers. The PC/AT-compatible, being the most popular, materially became the first candidate for this comparatively new technology. A 5-device chip set from VLSI reduces the IBM PC/AT-compatible computer motherboard from 110 to 16 (exclusive of memory) devices. Each high-integration device has been designed as a specific entity in the PC/AT-compatible design. While each device effectively contains the ASIC Megacell of an existing discrete integrated circuit function, each device has a system character of its own:

The PC/AT-Compatible Peripheral Controller replaces two 82C37 Direct Memory Access Controllers, two 82C59A Interrupt Controllers, an 82C54 Programmable Counter, a 74LS612 AT Memory Mapper, two 74ALS573 Octal Three-state latches, a 74ALS138 3-to-8 Decoder, and approximately five other less-complex integrated circuits.

The PC/AT-Compatible System Controller replaces an 82C284 Clock Controller and 82C288 Bus Controller (both are used in iAPX286-based systems), an 82C84A Clock Generator and Driver, Two PAL16L8 devices (used for memory decode), and approximately ten other less-complex integrated circuits used as Wait State logic.

The PC/AT-Compatible Memory Controller generates The row address strobe (RAS) and column address strobe (CAS) necessary to support the dynamic RAMs used in the PC/AT. In addition, the device allows four memory options for the user, up to a full 1M-byte system. All four options allow a full 640 Kbytes user area to support the disk operating system (DOS).

The PC/AT-Compatible Address Buffer provides the system with a 16-bit address bus input and 41 buffered drivers. The buffered drivers consist of 17 bi-directional system bus drivers, each capable of sinking 20 mA of current; 16 bi-directional local bus drivers, each capable of sinking 8 mA of current; and eight memory bus drivers, also capable of sinking 8 mA of current.

The PC/AT-Compatible Data Buffer provides a 16-bit data bus input as well as 40 buffered drivers. The buffered drivers consist of 16 bi-directional system data bus drivers, each capable of sinking 24 mA of current; eight bi-directional local bus drivers, each capable of sinking 10 mA of current; and 16 memory data bus drivers, each capable of sinking 10 mA of current. The device is compatible with 256 Kbit DRAMs, 1M-bit DRAMs, and 4M-bit DRAMs.

This approach reduces the non-memory device count of the PC/AT from 110 to 16 devices. In addition to the "vanilla" PC/AT functions, specific, customer defined functions can be implemented in the devices Since the devices were designed using VLSI's design tools, the devices can be quickly modified for use as cores in user-specific designs. This allows original equipment manufacturers to offer unique features and special functions to serve their market.

7. TRON

The fourth significant development for the next decade is the TRON Project. Since this is the 3rd TRON Symposium, this paper will not restate the aspects of The Real Time Operating System Nucleus that are by now well-known to the overwhelming majority of the attendees. (For a concise tutorial on the TRON Project, in the English language, please refer to the April 1987 issue of IEEE MICRO.) By taking a different and open road, the TRON Project represents a significant and affirmative approach to the future of computing systems. The synergistic architectures of the devices, operating systems, and CPU chips open the door for a significant class of systems to come upon the world scene. While the established and developing IBM, Apple and other systems are most certainly here to stay, There is room and a need for TRON.

REFERENCES

[1]   Clark, D. and H. Levy. "Measurement and analysis of instruction use in the VAX 11/780," in Proceedings of the 9th Annual Symposium on Computer Architecture. ACM/IEEE, Austin, Texas, April 1982.

[2]   Hennessy, John L. "VLSI Processor Architecture." IEEE Transactions on Computers, Volume C - 33, Number 12 (December 1984), pp. 1221 - 1246.

[3]   Wulf, William A. "Compilers and Computer Architecture." Computer, July 1981, pp. 41 -47.

[4]   Sakamura, Ken "Japan's TRON Project" IEEE MICRO, April, 1987.

James J. Farrell III is the manager of technical communications for VLSI Technology, Inc., Application Specific Logic Products Division in Tempe, Arizona, U.S.A. He graduated from the U.S. Armed Forces Institute, LaSalle University, and attended New Jersey Institute of Technology. In addition to being the editor-in-chief of IEEE MICRO since 1985, he is a member of the IEEE Computer Society, a member of the Professional Update Committee of MIDCON'87, and vice-chairperson of the WESCON'88 Professional Program Committee.

Chapter 2: ITRON

ITRON: An Overview

Ken Sakamura
Department of Information Science, Faculty of Science, University of Tokyo
Hongo,Tokyo,113 Japan

ABSTRACT

ITRON is a specification of realtime operating systems developed in the TRON project. ITRON specification has been designed to meet the stringent cost/performance of embedded computer systems including intelligent objects. ITRON is highly portable across many processors. Many system services are available in the ITRON so that applications can easily build and the OS itself is adaptable to variety of needs. Ease of training was a major consideration during the design of ITRON specification. Already there are several implementations of ITRON-based OS's. Future extensions are already being designed.

Keywords: Microprocessor, Realtime OS, ITRON, TRON VLSI CPU.

1. INTRODUCTION

The price decrease of high-performance microprocessors has brought about the replacement of analog or relay circuits with microprocessor-based controllers in various types of equipment or household appliances. These include NC machine, robot for industrial application, washing machine, air conditioner, audio-visual equipment, and individual engines, or motors.

Microprocessor-controlled machines can decide on their own what actions to be made after sensing the outside environment. We call these devices with "intelligence" as intelligent objects. Intelligent objects will become major application areas of microprocessors.

Microprocessor used in various machines including intelligent objects is used as only a part of larger systems, not an end itself. It is used to control devices based on calculations it performs. External devices operate on their own, hence the computer must finish calculations before the results of the calculation are requested by the devices. For example, in controlling the electric plug to ignite combustion of an engine, it is necessary to finish the timing calculation before the next piston cycle begins. In designing these computer systems, it is necessary to pay attention to how quick the computer can give necessary service. The realtime response of computer systems is necessary for embedded computer systems. Operating systems (OS's for short) to support such fast response are called realtime OS's.

ITRON (Industrial-TRON, where TRON stands for The Realtime Operating system Nucleus) is a realtime OS specification. The design of ITRON was done with the following objectives in mind.

2. ITRON FEATURES

2.1 AVAILABILITY ON VARIOUS PROCESSORS

Embedded computer systems have to meet stringent cost/performance criteria. Hence, the choice of processors is often made from the viewpoint of cost. Hence, if similar OS is available on various processors, the designers can have freedom in choosing microprocessors. Even if the microprocessor used is changed to a new one in the lifetime of the system, transition to a new microprocessor will be easy if the OS based on the same architecture runs on the new microprocessor. One reason why the realtime application construction was difficult was the lack of a standard realtime OS. By implementing ITRON-based OS on various microprocessors, we aim at establishing ITRON as a de facto standard of realtime OS on microprocessors.

2.2 HIGH-PERFORMANCE

Realtime OS cannot help but become processor-dependent to achieve good performance on a given processor. Although ITRON aims at a de facto standard of realtime OS on various microprocessors, some parts of the ITRON specification, most notably interrupt handling and exception handling, are made processor-dependent. This is necessary not to degrade performance because of inter-machine standardization. Task dispatching and interrupt handling are designed so that minimum overhead is involved.

2.3 ABUNDANT FUNCTIONALITIES

ITRON provides many functionalities so that programmers can tune their applications using appropriate OS primitives and can write applications easily. For example, to support synchronization and communications among tasks, ITRON offers event-flag, semaphore, and mailbox mechanisms.

2.4 ADAPTABILITY

Embedded computer systems must meet the space requirement (the size of ROM and RAM) and the timing criteria. It is necessary to reduce OS overhead as much as possible. The ITRON specification has much freedom in various OS parameters in order to let designers adapt the OS to their needs. For example, designers does not have to implement some systems calls, can choose the number of registers saved/restored at task dispatch, and specify the extent of checking of incorrect parameters for system calls.

Adaptability goes hand in hand with the abundant functionalities of ITRON. The specification offers many functionalities from which designers can choose only the necessary ones in order to build tuned systems.

2.5 EASE OF TRAINING

The TRON project aims at establishing a computer system architecture that is easy to learn. The training is paid attention during the design stage. The name of ITRON system calls are systematically given so that they are easy to learn. System calls of ITRON have the form of "xxx_yyy" where xxx stands for operation and yyy stands for the target of the operation. That ITRON runs on various microprocessors will incur less training cost than different OS's on different microprocessors will.

The system calls of ITRON are shown in *Table 1*.

3. ITRON IMPLEMENTATIONS AND FUTURE PERSPECTIVES

ITRON-based OS's have been implemented on various processors by several companies. These include NEC RX116 for V20 and V30 microprocessors, Hitachi HI68K for Motorola MC68000, and Fujitsu REALOS/286 for Intel iAPX286. REALOS/286 uses the built-in MMU of 286 chip and follows the specification of ITRON/MMU. ITRON/MMU is an extended version of ITRON to use MMU. There is an experimental implementation of ITRON on National Semiconductor NS32000, which is called ITRON/32. No other realtime OS has been ported to so many microprocessors. Our aim of establishing ITRON as de facto standard of realtime OS has very high chance of success now.

In the ITRON subproject, the following works are now being performed; incorporation of file management functions, implementation of ITRON-based OS, called ITRON/CHIP, on the TRON VLSI CPU, and the development of micro-ITRON specification for single-chip or 8 bit microprocessors.

ITRON's file management system is actually a subset of object management system of BTRON and is capable of exchanging data with BTRON-based OS. BTRON's object

Table 1. System calls in ITRON Specification

1. Task Management

cre_tsk:	Create Task
sta_tsk:	Start Task
del_tsk:	Delete Task
def_ext:	Define Exit Routine
ext_tsk:	Exit Task
exd_tsk:	Exit and Delete Task
abo_tsk:	Abort Task
ter_tsk:	Terminate Task
chg_pri:	Change Task Priority
rot_rdq:	Rotate Ready Queue
tcb_adr:	Get Task AccessKey
tsk_sts:	Get Task Status
sus_tsk:	Suspend Task
rsm_tsk:	Resume Task
slp_tsk:	Sleep Task
wai_tsk:	Wait for Wakeup Task
wup_tsk:	Wakeup Task
can_wup:	Cancel Wakeup Task
cyc_wup:	Cyclic Wakeup Task
can_cyc:	Cancel Cyclic Wakeup Task

2. Synchronization and Communication

cre_flg:	Create EventFlag
del_flg:	Delete EventFlag
set_flg:	Set EventFlag
wai_flg:	Wait for EventFlag to be Set
flg_adr:	Get EventFlag AccessKey
cre_sem:	Create Semaphore
del_sem:	Delete Semaphore
sig_sem:	Signal Semaphore
wai_sem:	Wait on Semaphore
sem_adr:	Get Semaphore AccessKey
cre_mbx:	Create Mailbox
del_mbx:	Delete Mailbox
snd_msg:	Send Message
rcv_msg:	Receive Message
mbx_adr:	Get Mailbox AccessKey

3. Interrupt Handling (processor dependent)

def_int:	Define Interrupt Handler
ret_int:	Return from Interrupt Handler
set_int:	Set Interrupt Mask
dis_int:	Disable Interrupt
ena_int:	Enable Interrupt
fet_dat:	Fetch Data
get_dvn:	Get Device Number
get_vec:	Get Vector Number
iret_wup:	Return and Wakeup Task

4. Exception Handling

def_exc:	Define Exception Handler
ret_exc:	Return from Exception Handler

5. Memory Management

cre_mpl:	Create Memory Pool
del_mpl:	Delete Memory Pool
get_blk:	Get Memory Block
rel_blk:	Release Memory Block
mpl_adr:	Get MemoryPool AccessKey

6. Timer Management

set_tim:	Set Time
get_tim:	Get Time

7. Extended System Call Management (optional)

def_svc:	Define Extended SVC Handler

8. Version Management (optional)

get_ver:	Get Version Number

9. Input and Output Management (optional)

def_gio:	Define General I/O
req_gio:	Request General I/O
def_cio:	Define Character I/O
get_chr:	Get Character from CIO
put_chr:	Put Character to CIO
get_lin:	Get Line from CIO
put_lin:	Put Line to CIO
cio_sts:	Check CIO Status
cio_ctl:	CIO Control

10. MMU Support (ITRON/MMU only)

cre_spc:	Create Logical Space
del_spc:	Delete Logical Space
spc_adr:	Get Space AccessKey
cre_map:	Create Logical Mapping
trf_map:	Transfer Logical Mapping
sha_map:	Share Logical Mapping
del_map:	Delete Logical Mapping
set_prt:	Set Protection Code
mov_dat:	Move Data to Another Space
get_dat:	Get System Data (for system control)
set_dat:	Set System Data (for system control)
sha_seg:	Share Segment (segmented machine only)

management system supports the real/virtual object data model used in the BTRON man-machine interface. It has a very general directory path mechanism. It is possible to use BTRON-based OS as host to develop ITRON applications. The sophisticated BTRON MMI can offer an easy to use development environment.

TRON VLSI CPU is a high-performance 32 bit microprocessor to be used by many TRON-based systems. TRON VLSI CPU has special instructions to support BTRON or ITRON. For example, queue handling instructions and context switching instruction will help boost the speed of ITRON-based OS. ITRON/CHIP will run on chips from more than one manufacturers, thus increasing the program portability.

The development of micro-ITRON is under way to support low cost microprocessors. Micro-ITRON is a natural variation of ITRON from the viewpoint of adaptability. Micro-ITRON is meant for single-chip microprocessor that has very limited amount of RAM and ROM, or 8 bit microprocessor with relatively low performance. Although micro-ITRON is limited in its function, the compatibility with ITRON specification will be maintained as much as possible. The version of ITRON to run on hardware with multi-processor configuration is also planned.

BIBLIOGRAPHY

[1] K. Sakamura, *"TRON Project,"* Proc. IMAC 84, pp.203-208 (in Japanese).

[2] K. Sakamura, *"TRON Total Architecture,"* Proc. Architecture Workshop in Japan, Information Processing Soc. Japan, 1984 (in Japanese).

[3] K. Sakamura, *"Real-time Operating System ITRON,"* Operating System Study Group 24-10, Information Processing Soc. Japan, 1984 (in Japanese).

[4] K. Sakamura, *"ITRON Realtime Operating System,"* J. Robotics Soc. Japan, 1985, pp.41-48 (in Japanese).

[5] K. Sakamura, *"ITRON Real-time Operating System; Architecture and Future Perspective,"* Proc. Architecture Study Group, Information Processing Soc. Japan, 86-CA-61-1, 1986 (in Japanese).

[6] E. Yabe, *"ITRON/68K,"* Proc. Architecture Study group, Information Processing Soc. Japan, 86-CA-61-2, 1986 (in Japanese).

[7] K. Kudo et al., *"ITRON/MMU286,"* Proc. Architecture Study Group, Information Processing Soc. Japan, 86-CA-61-3, 1986 (in Japanese).

[8] H. Tsubota, *"ITRON/32000,"* Proc. Architecture Study Group, Information Processing Soc. Japan, 86-CA-61-4, 1986 (in Japanese).

[9] H. Monden, *"Development of ITRON on 32 bit CPU,"* Proc. Architecture Study Group, Information Processing Soc. Japan, 86-CA-61-3, 1986 (in Japanese).

[10] Y. Kushiki, *"Microprocessor Operating System Interface, MOSI(IEEE855) and ITRON as international standard,"* Proc. Architecture Study Group, Information Processing Soc. Japan, 86-CA-61-3, 1986 (in Japanese).

[11] K. Kuwata, *"ITRON - Realtime OS for V-series Microprocessors,"* Proc. 1st TRON Symposium, 1986 (in Japanese).

[12] T. Shimizu et al., *"ITRON/68K-based OS ITOS68K,"* Proc. 1st TRON Symposium, 1986 (in Japanese).

[13] K. Kudo, *"ITRON/MMU286 - ITRON for Protect Mode of 80286,"* Proc. 1st TRON Symposium, 1986 (in Japanese).

[14] H. Tsubota, *"ITRON/32 - Realtime Operating System for NS32000,"* Proc. 1st TRON Symposium, 1986 (in Japanese).

[15] K. Sakamura, *"The TRON Project,"* IEEE MICRO, April 1987, pp.8-14.

[16] H. Monden, *"Introduction to the ITRON: The Industry-oriented Operating System in the TRON Project,"* IEEE MICRO, April 1987, pp. 45-52.

[17] H. Tsubota et al., *"The Structure and Performance of ITRON on NS32000,"* Institute of Electronics, The Proceedings of the First Meeting of Information and Communication Engineers, Realtime-OS TRON Study Group, pp. 40-52, 1987 (in Japanese).

Ken Sakamura: see *"The Objectives of the TRON Project"* in this proceedings.

The Implementation and Evaluation of the RX116 Version 2.0

Hiroshi Monden, Tamotsu Iwasaki, Satoshi Fukui

Microcomputer Products Division, NEC Corporation
1753 Shimonumabe, Nakahara-ku, Kawasaki, 211 Japan

Abstract

The TRON[1] project is becoming well known in the World. The ITRON is one of the projects which forms the TRON total architecture. One of the authors had already introduced the abstract of the ITRON[2]. The RX116 is the first realization of the ITRON architecture.
This paper describes the implementation and evaluation of the newly developed RX116 version 2.0. The new version achieved higher performance than the previous one and fully supports for the V-series microprocessors.

Key Words

ITRON, RX116, Implementation and Evaluation, Task switching, V-series microprocessors

1 Introduction

The RX116[3] is the first realization of the ITRON architecture. It fully conforms to the ITRON specification. The OS runs on any system which equips tho NEC V-series microprocessors, the V20/30, as well as required minimum peripherals namely an 8259 type interrupt controller and an 8254 type timer counter.
Since we introduced the RX116 in 2H of the 1985, more than 100 customers adopted the OS. Being 2 years past, many customers require higher performance and supports for the V40/50. Therefore we decided to develop a new version.
In this paper, first, we will review the features of the OS including new features in the next section. In the section 3, we will explain the internal structure of the OS related to the new features. Then we will refer our testing method and environment. Finally, we will discuss its performance and evaluation.

2 Features of the RX116 version 2.0

The main purpose of this version up is execution performance improvement. After some re coding of bottle necks by carefully chosen assembly codes, we achieved less than 70 microsecond of task switching using V30 CPU at 8MHz. Therefore we can expect less than 60 microsecond of task switching time at 10MHz clock rate.

As the task switching time of the previous version was 99 microsecond at 8MHz
V30 CPU, we got 30% improvement by the version up. We believe in spite of the
restriction of the CPU architecture, the RX116 is the one of the fastest real
time operating systems based on the ITRON specification. At the same time, the
authors do believe that we should define exactly what does the TASK SWITCHING
TIME mean ? Let us discuss later in the section 5.

From the specification or functional point of view, the RX116 version 2.0 is
upward compatible with the previous version. Only small adjustments are added to
conform the latest release of the ITRON standard specification. These modifications seldom cause troubles for users because they are the option switches
rarely used.
On the contrary, the advantages of the version 2.0 are very significant. There
are two major points.

1) Memory Block Size
 In the previous version, the upper limitation of memory block size was limitted
to 64K bytes. We expanded the limitation up to 1M bytes. This allows the full
use of the CPU addressing capability.

2) Full Support for V40/50 integrated microprocessors
 The V40/50 integrates many standard peripherals such as an 8259 type interrupt
controller, an 8254 type of timer counter, an 8251 type serial controller and
uPD71071 DMA controller. The Rx116 version 2.0 can fully take these advantages
of the integrated peripherals. The OS can utilize the on-chip interrupt controller and the on-chip timer counter. The serial controller also can be used when a
console handler task is specified in the system configuration.

There are other user interfaces which we should refer. They are structures of
the internal control blocks. We have been showing them for users in our (so
called) technical manuals in order to make effective use of the OS. We have
slightly changed the TCB(Task Control Block). As for the other blocks, nothing
was changed.

3 Basic control structure of the RX116 version 2.0

 In this section, we will show how the kernel works in accordance with the advantages of the version 2.0.

3.1 The System Initialization

 Receiving the cpu control after system reset, the initialize routine of the
kernel initializes hardware, system management tables, free memories and intializing tasks successively. During the initialization operations, the V40/50
support is fully considered.
 Information for the initializations are provided by the SIT (System Information
Table). A conversational utility named System Configurator generates the SIT of
use's system configuration.

1) hardware

According to the SIT, the kernel initializes these things bellow in succession.
*coprocessor: The kernel issues the reset instruction to a coprocessor.
*cpu: If the V40 or V50 is specified as a cpu, the OS assingns proper I/O addresses and pin configurations to internal peripherals corresponding to usages of them.
*interrupt controller: First, the kernel initializes slave controllers if specified, then a master controller. If the V40 or V50 is specified, the kernel sets address values to I/O relocation registers of the controller. Finishing the job, the kernel masks all the interrupt inputs until the whole initial operation is over.
*timer counter: The kernel sets adequate values to a timer counter. If the V40 or V50 is specified, the kernel sets address values to I/O relocation registers.
*serial controller: If the V40 or V50 is specified, the kernel sets address values to I/O relocation registers.

2) system management tables and free memories

*interrupt vectors: The kernel sets address values to interrupt vectors.
*SBT (System Base Table): The kernel uses about 2K bytes of memories from the lower address of free memories as the SBT area. Initial values are set according to the SIT information.
*free memories: The kernel creates the #0 memory pool and its management table. The free memory area become as FIG.1.

3) intializing of tasks

The kernel creates two tasks at the beginning, a user defined initial task and the idle task. The role of the initial task is to create an execution environment of the user own system. The idle task is invoked when no other task is ready for execution.

3.2 The Memory Management

After the initalization by the kernel, The OS manages all free memories as a #0 memory pool. The OS puts management blocks such as TCBs created by associated system calls to the #0.
Users can use memory pools #1 and after. When the cre_mpl is issued, the OS creates specified size of memory pool out of the memory pool #0. Then the OS puts a memory pool management block to the top of the pool.
The block contains a memory block queue header which is used for free block chains, a pool ID number, an upper limit address of the pool, a lower limit address of the pool, a wait queue header which points to a TCB where the associated task is waiting for memory allocation, a memory block size in 256 bytes per unit and option information.
A task should issue the get_blk system call to get free memory blocks. The OS allocates specified number of blocks in the specified memory pool to the caller task. In the FIG.2, the relation ship among control blocks are illustrated.
Thus, the RX116 can offer the full memory management support.

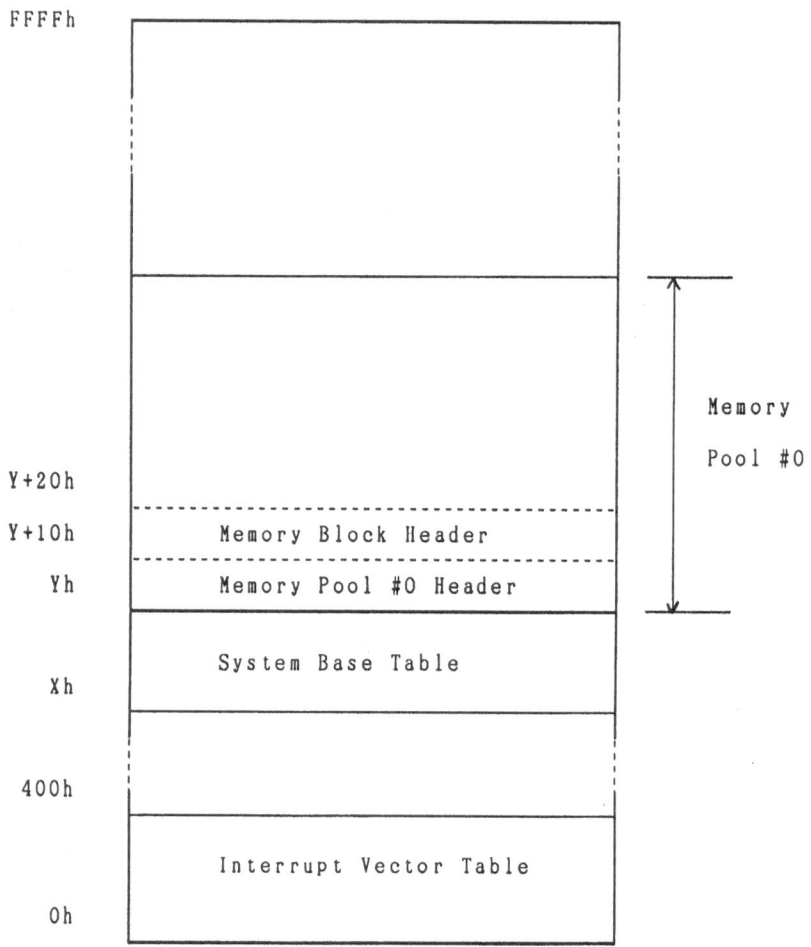

FFFFh

Y+20h
Y+10h   Memory Block Header
Yh   Memory Pool #0 Header
               System Base Table
Xh

400h
               Interrupt Vector Table
0h

Memory
Pool #0

X,Y are offsets

Fig.1   The Memory Configuration after Initializing

3.3 The task switching

The task switching flow is shown in the FIG.3. As the algorithm is rather simple, coding technique determines the performance of the routine. We chose proper instructions considering code sizes and execution clocks. Finally, we achieved less than 70 microseconds of task switching time defined in the FIG.3.

4 Testing

Generally speaking, testing of software causes heavy head ache. Even if the software is static one such as a compiler which does not communicate with exter-

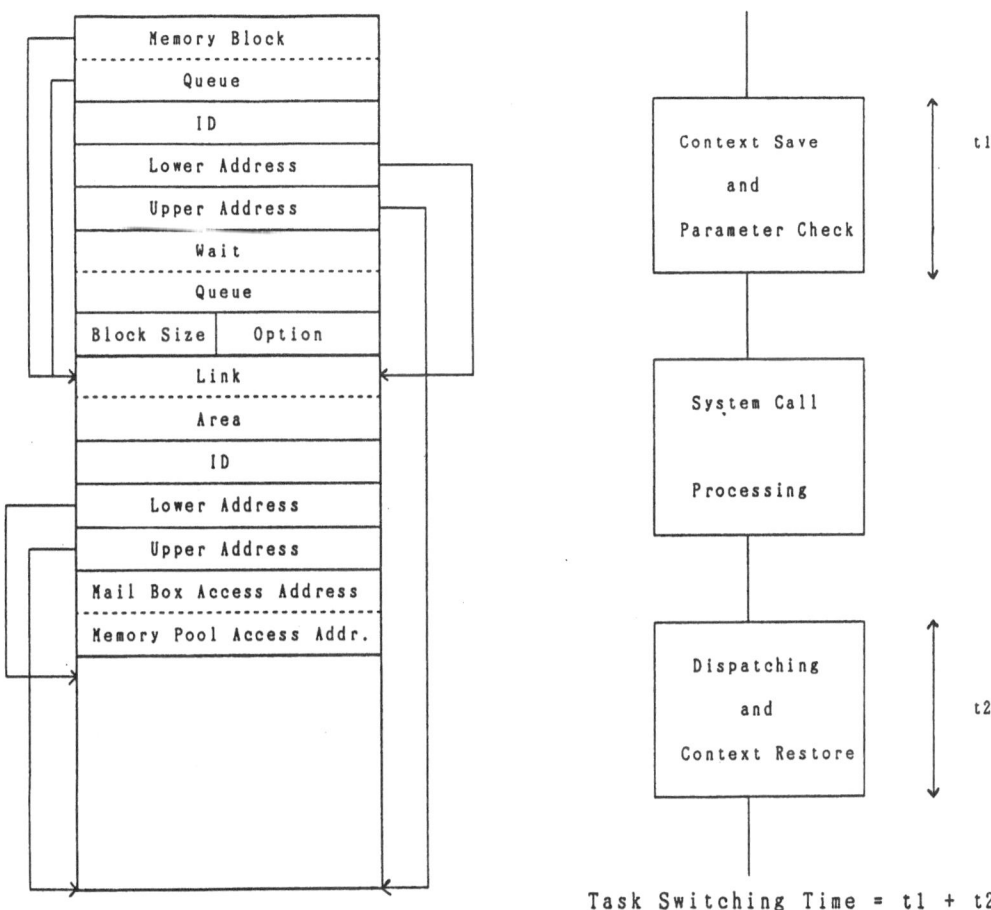

Memory Block
Queue
ID
Lower Address
Upper Address
Wait
Queue
Block Size | Option
Link
Area
ID
Lower Address
Upper Address
Mail Box Access Address
Memory Pool Access Addr.

```
Context Save
    and
Parameter Check          t1

System Call

Processing

Dispatching
    and
Context Restore          t2
```

Task Switching Time = t1 + t2

Fig. 2 Free Memory Management Scheme

Fig. 3 Task Switching Flow

nal world except the operating system where it runs on. Testing of real time operating systems may be much difficult than that of static software since the software itself is an operating system and handles external events as well as internal events. One can imagine exhaust and elaborate test programs. We adopted 2-step testing method to reduce testing costs. The first is called quiet(or functional) testings because they test specification features without any external event. The latter is called dynamic(or non-syncronized) testings as the tests examine dynamic features of the OS with external events.

4.1 Testing environment

Corresponding to the 2-step testing method, we prepared two kind of testing environments. At the beginning of the test phase, we used an NEC personal computer model PC-9800vm4 as a testing machine. The personal computer is connected

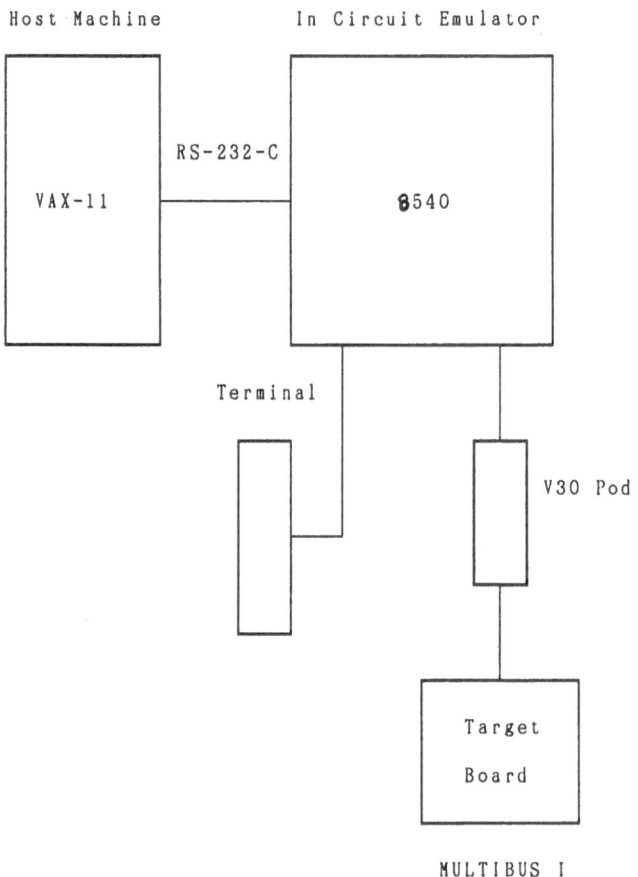

Fig. 4   The Evaluation Environment

through a LAN to a VAX machine runs UNIX(4.3bsd). Test programs are written in c
and compiled by NEC cross c compiler for the V20/30. After that, object programs
are sent to the personal computer which equips the V30 CPU and runs MS-DOS.
  In the second phase, we used the environment shown in FIG.4. In this case, an
8540 of Tektronics is a control machine. The machine is also connected to the
VAX through the LAN. Actual testing is performed on the cpu board which equips
the V30. In the second phase, first, testing programs are loaded from the VAX to
the 8540. Then The 8540 loads them to the target cpu board. For the dynamic
testings,the system can generate random or programed interrupt signals to the
target cpu board.

4.2 Quiet testings

  At the beginning, we ported the OS on to the PC-9800 personal computer. For the
porting, we wrote a dedicated console driver and rewrote the timer routine of
the OS. Then we generated more than 5,000 test programs. Each test program is a

task runs on the RX116. Each task is stored as a MS-DOS file and can be loaded by MS-DOS commands. Test tasks issue related system calls to be tested. After issuing the system calls, then a debugging task compares expected data with resultant internal status parameters. The test results are also stored in the MS-DOS disk file of the personal computer for test result analysis.

4.3 Dynamic testings

Instead of the MS-DOS loader, we used an ICE for test program loading. This method of loading is much faster than through an RS-232 serial line. The circuit associated with the cpu board is for interrupt signal generating. It can be programed by the use of a programmable oscillator.

5 Performance Evaluation of the RX116

Among the indexes which indicate the performance of real time operating systems, task switching time is the most significant one. We will focus our discussion on the task switching time.
Before starting with the discussion on the task switching time, we need the definition for the parameter to be measured. In FIG.3, our current definition of the task switching time is shown. The measurement was done in the environment in the FIG.4 already shown in the previous section.

As the task switching mechanism is very simple, it is difficult to improve the performance. If we can change or modify the CPU architecture, we are able to expect higher performance. For example, if we can utilize banked register files, context save/recover time will be drastically reduced. In such a case, the overhead of context save/recover may be within one or two microsecond. We have another V-series named V25 . It is a single chip microcomputer which integrates 16 register file sets on the chip. Taking the advantage of on chip register file set, we can expect around 50 micro second of task switching time. Therefore our next target of the RX116 family development is the V25 single chip microcomputer.
Apart from the discussion above, we have proposed a standardization of performance measurement[4]. Although people often claim task switching time is XX microsecond by their operating system, most of the case without showing their evaluation environment and even though definitions. The authors believe such kind of figures make no sense.
In general, it is difficult to define any kind of standard for operating systems of different specifications. However, we have now the ITRON as a common specification. We should take a first step.

The idea for the standardization is as follows.
1) The viewpoint should be that of users.
2) A user can get the figures again by himself.

Our rough conclusion of the proposal is ;
1) Benchmark programs written in c should be defined. The c compiler should be available in public.
2) Anyone can get measurement hardware such as cpu boards or a logic analyzer in public.
Of course we proposed some benchmark test programs written in c. If we can take another opportunity, we will discuss them in detail.

6 Conclusion and acknowledgment

We have been promoting the ITRON. We are convinced that the RX116 has much contributed. Now that functional features are well known among users, our next job is to establish how to define its other characteristics such as execution environment or performance as well as implementations on 8- or 32-bit microprocessors.
The authors wish to acknowledge Dr. Ken Sakamura of Tokyo Univ. for his useful discussions and Dr.Kenji Kani of NEC corp. for his helpful suggestions.

References

[1] K. Sakamura, "The TRON Project," IEEE MICRO, Vol.7, No.2, 8-14, April, 1987
[2] H. Monden,"Introduction to the ITRON," IEEE MICRO, Vol.7, No.2, 45-52, April, 1987
[3] RX116 Use's manual, IEM-911C, NEC Corp., March, 1987 (in Japanese)
[4] H. Monden and T. Iwasaki, "A Proposal to Performance Evaluation for the ITRON," Proc. of the TRON real time system Study Group, the institute of Electronics, Information and Communication Engineers, 1-4, Oct., 1987(in Japanese)

Hiroshi Monden is an engineering manager of the Development Tools Department in the Microcomputer Products Division of NEC Corporation. He received his MS degree in electronics from Kyoto University in 1973. His interests include software development environments, realtime systems and computer architectures.

Tamotu Iwasaki is a chief engineer of the RX116 project in the Department. He received his BA in material science from University of Electronics and Communications in 1983. He is particularly interested in realtime systems and software development environments.

Satoshi Fukui is an engineer of the RX116 project in the Department. He received his BA in computer science from Kyoto Industrial University in 1986. He is interested in personal computer software. He wrote most of testing programs in the 1st stage.

REALOS/286:
An Implementation of ITRON/MMU on 80286

Akira Shimohara

Microcomputer Development Division, Semiconductor Group, FUJITSU LIMITED
1812-10 Shimonumabe, Nakahara-ku, Kawasaki, 211 Japan

ABSTRACT

REALOS/286 is the realtime operating system based on ITRON/MMU, which is an extended specification of ITRON adapted to a processor having a hardware memory management unit (MMU). The most significant feature is the provision of memory protection for a realtime system. It is especially useful for a large multitasking application system because it improves system quality and reliability.

KEYWORDS: Realtime Operating System, ITRON, Memory Management, 80286, Logical Address

INTRODUCTION

REALOS/286 is the REALtime Operating System which is executed on the 80286 in Protected Mode. This paper introduces the features of this operating system, focusing on the MMU support of REALOS/286.

REALOS/286 is the first commercial product based on ITRON/MMU specification. ITRON/MMU is the extended specification to support MMU functions. Recently, processors have achieved high performance and application systems including embedded industrial systems are becoming larger and more complex. There are many tasks in these systems and a task sometimes destroys data for other tasks or an operating system. Under the circumstances, it is more important to improve reliability. Using MMU functions is an effective method to achieve high reliability. The original ITRON specification did not support a hardware memory management unit. MMU Support Functions have been added which allow application programmers to use MMU functions. Based on ITRON/MMU specification, REALOS/286 supports the 80286 on chip MMU. As a result of MMU protection application systems are more reliable.

1. REALOS/286

1.1 STRUCTURE OF REALOS/286

The product REALOS/286 consists of three main parts. The first is the Realtime Operating System Kernel, which controls execution of tasks, logical address spaces, definition of handlers, and so on. The second is the Debugger. It reports status of the processor and the operating system and controls system execution. The last part is several device drivers for the FM-16β(personal computer provided by FUJITSU LTD.) which was selected as the standard hardware system for REALOS/286. The product provides other support programs. The C language Interface Library is available for programming tasks in C. The Setup Support Utility, using the system configuration, reports the initial state of the system.

Figure 1 illustrates the structure of REALOS/286 and the specifications are shown in *Table 1*.

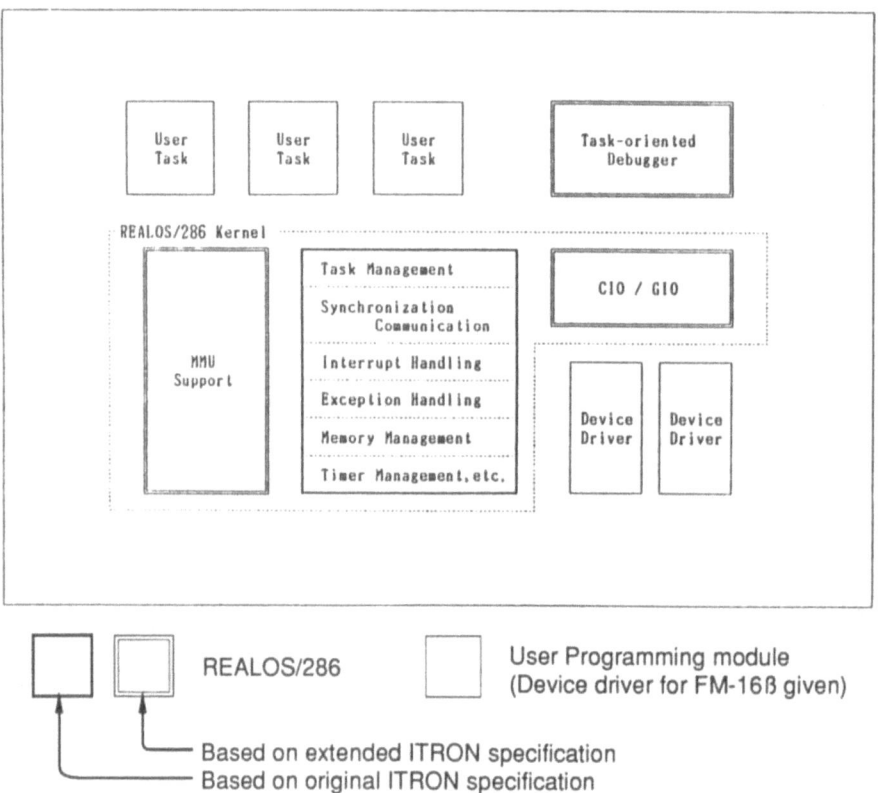

Figure 1. Structure of REALOS / 286

Table 1. REALOS / 286 Specifications

Processor	80286 (Protected Mode)
Specification	Based on ITRON/MMU
Program Size of Kernel Code	13.5 KB
Scheduling	Priority Based Scheduler
Dispatch Time	70 μs
Memory Protection	Yes (Use of 80286 MMU)
Number of Task (Max)	255
Number of Priority	0 - 255
Synchronization, Communication	Event Flag, Semaphore, Mailbox
Support Handler	Interrupt Handler Exception Handler Expanded SVC Handler Exit Routine
I/O Interface	CIO/GIO Interface (Based on ITRON Specification)
Programming Language	C or Assembler
Support Software	Task-oriented Debugger (Based on ITRON Specification) Device Driver for FM-16ß (RS232C, Printer, Keyboard, CRT)

1.2 ITRON/MMU SPECIFICATION

The essence of REALOS/286's features is due to the ITRON specification. It includes most functions which are necessary for an operating system used in embedded industrial systems. It includes most functions which are necessary for an operating system used in embedded industrial systems. In addition, achieving high performance was taken into consideration, especially rapid response to external events. Virtual machine designs afford portability of application programs but do so at the expense of performance. In contrast, ITRON allows the machine dependent designs only if performance gains are realized in areas such as interrupt handling. This ITRON feature is called the System Adaptation Mechanism and includes selection of the system calls and implementation methods for high performance and compactness.

The fundamental ITRON specification defined fundamental functions for embedded industrial systems. It is illustrated in *Figure 1.* where there are thick lined boxes. Originally, ITRON was not designed to use functions of a MMU. When REALOS/286 was designed for the 80286, the original ITRON specification was extended to support the features of the 80286, including the MMU. This extension is called ITRON/MMU.

The other paper in this Proceedings shows [1] system calls of ITRON and REALOS /286. In many instances the calls are the same. REALOS/286 are added Special System Calls for 80286. (See Table 2.) ITRON specification is described in other papers [2] [3] [4] . The following is an outline of the functions.

1) Task Management: In this category, system calls which directly reference a task by task ID (or Task Access Key) are classified. Task management includes controlling of task status, defining the task exit routine, and controlling the cyclic wakeup task.

2) Synchronization and Communication: ITRON provides many interactive functions between tasks. The Event Flag is for simple synchronization, the Semaphore is for general purpose interaction and the Mailbox is for data transfer between tasks.

3) Interrupt Handling: Interrupt handlers are written by users and there are defined by a system call. When the interrupt occurs, interrupt handler is directly invoked by the processor. The execution of the interrupt handler is supported by system calls.

4) Exception Handling: ITRON defines two classes of exceptions. One is a CPU Exception caused by a processor execution error. The other is a System Call Exception which is caused by system call error. The exception procedure is user definable.

5) Memory Management: With regard to ITRON, memory management means the management of free spaces as memory pool for memory assignment by software. Memory management helps users use memory resources efficiently.

6) Timer Management: There are only two system calls in this category, but many timer operations are manipulated by system calls of other categories. For example, cyc_wup offers cyclic wakeup and wai_tsk offers alarm clock wakeup operation.

7) MMU Support: MMU Support functions allow use of hardware memory management. These functions are described in more detail below.

8) Input/Output Management: REALOS/286 supports input/output operation based on ITRON specification. These calls are classified as GIO, that is General Input/Output, and CIO or Character Input/Output.

9) Others: Other system calls include, Extended System Call Management, Version Management and so on.

Table 2. Special System Call for 80286

cre_spc_ldt	Create Logical Space Information from LDT Information
cre_tsk_tss	Create Task from TSS information
chg_iop	Change I/O Privilege Level

1.3 REALTIME OPERATING SYSTEM KERNEL

The Realtime Operating System Kernel is a main part of REALOS/286. The features of the Kernel are based on ITRON specification and the 80286.

Via the System Adaptation Mechanism of ITRON, REALOS/286 provides two program modules. One, called the Debug System, is used during application development. It invokes complete error checking operations of REALOS/286, including execution and programming errors. The other, called the Running System, is used to execute the program. Its error checking operations do not include checks for programming errors.

Numbers are used to represent objects such as Tasks or Semaphores. When an object is created, the ID No. or logical number is used as a reference. After the object is created Access Key is used instead of ID No. In REALOS/286, ID No. and Access Key are the same number. This is useful because the same number can be used to reference an object.

REALOS/286 offers many functions for initialization. Creation of Memory Spaces, Tasks, Event Flags, etc. and definition of various sorts of handlers usually implemented with system calls can be accomplished with the initialization functions. If desired, a SetUp File can be created for definition of the initial state. Using initialization functions, a task which initializes the system can be omitted and essential system operations can start as soon as system initialization of REALOS/286 is finished.

1.4 INPUT/OUTPUT MANAGEMENT

It is necessary for embedded industrial system to control various input/output devices. If control of an external device is the programmers responsibility to provide, it restrained the portability of software. It is difficult to define rules for all devices, but possible and useful for some devices which are thought as standard. In response REALOS/286 provided input/output specifications and rules based on ITRON. There are two categories. One is called CIO which controls character input/output. The other is called GIO and provides for general input/output. REALOS/286 includes some device drivers for FM-16β based on CIO/GIO.

1.5 DEBUGGER

In addition to the ITRON specification, a system debugger command set has been supplied. The similar nature of debuggers makes this an attractive feature. The REALOS/286 Debugger is based on this command set and is executed as a task of REALOS/286.

The Debugger reports operating system information, such as task status, and can control task execution according to system status. For example, system execution stops when the selected task requests system service.

2. MMU SUPPORT FUNCTION

2.1 MEMORY MANAGEMENT SCHEME OF 80286

A memory management scheme interposes a mapping operation between logical addresses and physical addressing in memory. During its operation, a memory management scheme translates and checks access to memory. The ITRON/ MMU specification takes advantage of the 80286 on chip memory management. An explanation of the 80286's memory management scheme [5] follows. The mapping processes are illustrated in *Figure 2*.

There are several descriptor tables resident in memory recognized by the 80286. The 80286 contains two system address registers, GDTR (for the Global Descriptor Table) and LDTR (for the Local Descriptor Table) which correspond to the global or supervisor address space or the current local or user address space respectively. 'Current' meaning the LDT which identifies the address space of the current local task. Local tasks are switched under control of the task management mechanism of the 80286. These tables consist of descriptors which describe segment, physical base addresses, size, and access privileges for each segment type.

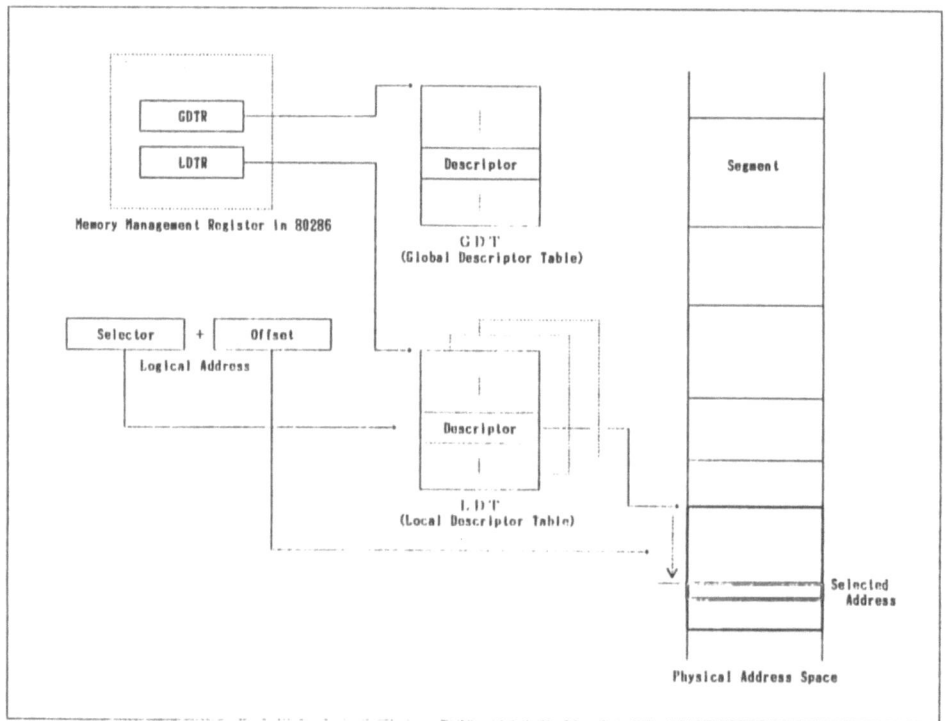

Figure 2. 80286 Memory Management Scheme

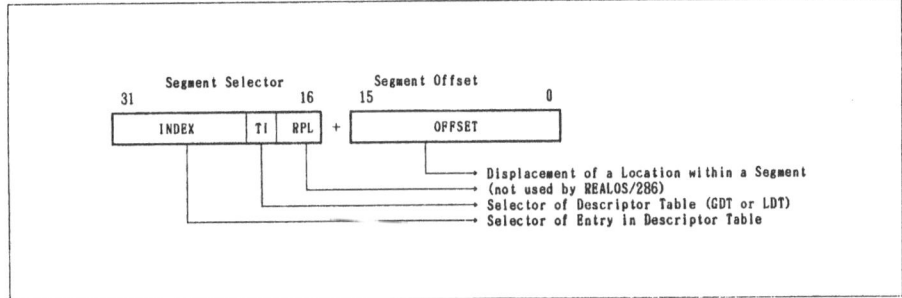

Figure 3. 32-Bit Logical Address

The logical address configuration is illustrated in *Figure 3* and consists of the Segment Selector and Segment Offset. The Segment Selector holds three types of information: 1) the TI-bit which indicates either GDT or LDT, 2) an Index which points to a descriptor, and 3) the RPL field not used by REALOS/286. The method of translation from logical to physical addresses is shown in *Figure 2*. The Segment Selector indicates the descriptor and the descriptor specifies the segment in physical memory. The Segment Offset then determines the displacement within the segment. This process is similar to the 8086 addressing mechanism where the selector is loaded into the segment register.

Associated with this memory management mechanism is a memory protection scheme. Memory access is performed according to information in the descriptors. The protection scheme is made up of three parts:

1) Separation of address space: The GDT and LDT determine the logical address space for each task. The LDT identifies a task's private address space. Generally, each task has an LDT and cannot reference descriptors in LDTs of other tasks. Each descriptor defines the private address space of physical memory associated with its task.

2) Privilege Level: The 80286 provides a four level increasingly- privileged protection mechanism. Software modules at a higher level are protected from lower level modules.

3) Segment Type: Each Descriptor identifies the segment type, such as code or data. The attributes of execute-only or readable for code segments, and read-only or writable for data segments ensure proper use of segments.

2.2 MMU SUPPORT FUNCTION

Figure 4 shows the logical address space structure of REALOS/286. REALOS/ 286 manages address spaces and allows tasks, which are usually under control of system tasks, to control the address space.

Memory Space was a concept added to the ITRON specification for management of logical address spaces. One Memory Space corresponds to one logical address space. Memory Space has two main attributes. One is Space ID, unique logical number representing Memory Space. The other is definition of memory mapping which determines the logical address space. The functions which control Memory Space are called MMU Support Functions. Using system calls of MMU Support Functions, a new Memory Space is created allowing use of another logical address space. In this way memory mappings are defined, changed, and deleted.

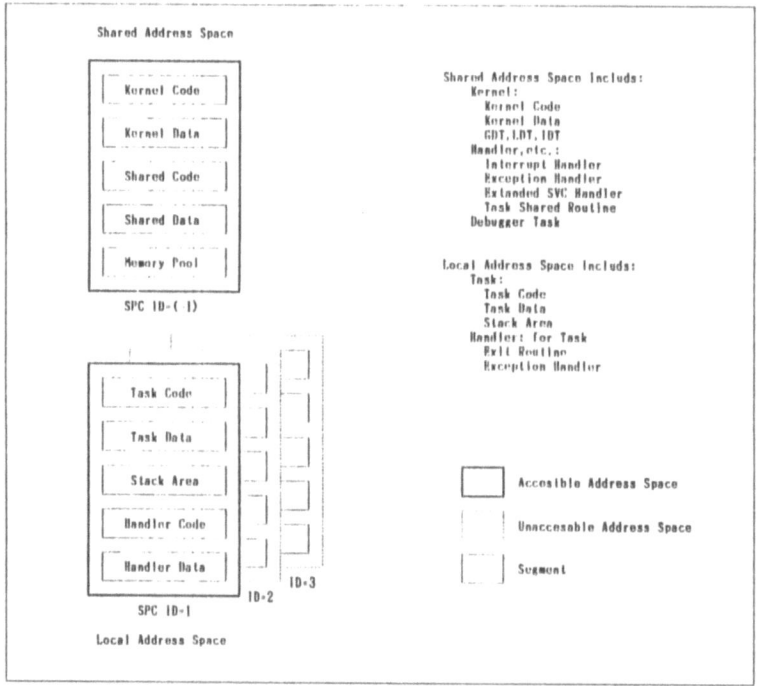

Figure 4. Logical Address Space Image of REALOS /286

SPC corresponds to Descriptor Table (GDT, LDT), MAP corresponds to Descriptor. permitting control of address spaces. MMU Support Functions have been specified at primitive level allowing great flexibility in their use. However, because the aim of REALOS/286 MMU is memory protection as opposed to dynamic memory management dynamic use of MMU Support Functions is difficult.

MMU Support Functions depend upon the architecture of hardware memory management, in this case 80286. Under REALOS/286, the essence of controlling logical address spaces lies in the manipulation of descriptor tables, GDT, and LDT. *Figure 5* shows the relationship between logical and physical address space. By way of the addition of Memory Space to ITRON, REALOS/286 provides the management of these tables.

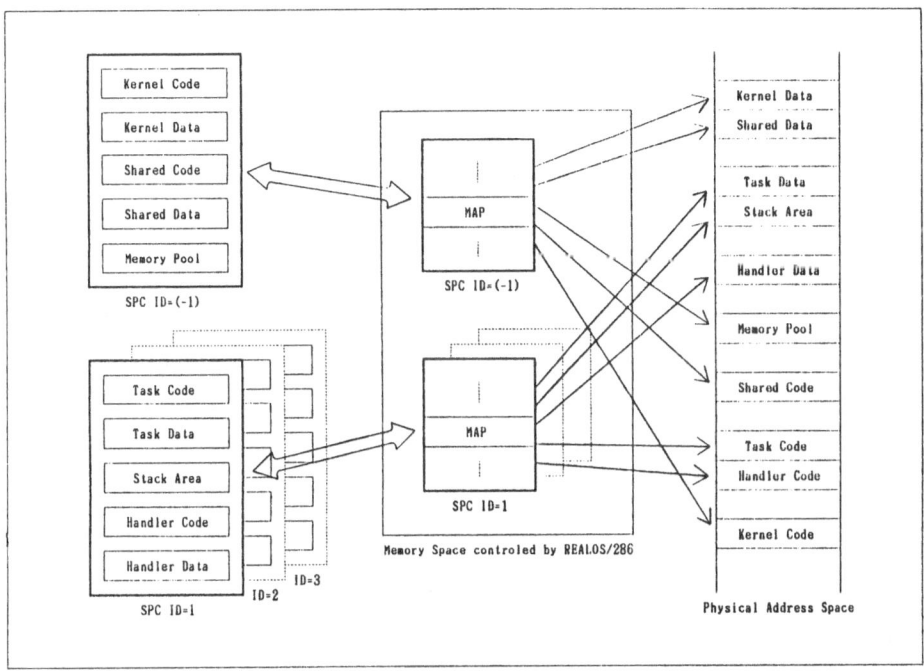

Figure 5. Concept of MMU Support

Initially, there may be some confusion in the use of memory mapping but an acceptable level of comfort is soon achieved because program errors are easily detected by exception interrupts.

3. DEVELOPMENT OF APPLICATION SYSTEM ON REALOS/286

The fundamentals of application development under REALOS/286 is similar to other realtime operating systems. The main difference is the use of MMU Support Functions for memory protection. Memory mapping must be defined before program execution.

Figure 6 shows how to set up the application and initialize memory space. An attractive feature of REALOS/286 during development is that programmers only have to deal with logical address space because in most cases, memory space is set statically and this can be done during initialization.

Source files created by text editors are translated or assembled into object modules via ASM286 or iC286. Object modules can then be linked via BND286. BLD286 produces the object modules and BLD File. The BLD File is a text file which contains configuration specifications. (i.e. memory definitions). The memory definition indicates physical addresses of memory allocated for the segments of input modules. BLD286 also creates

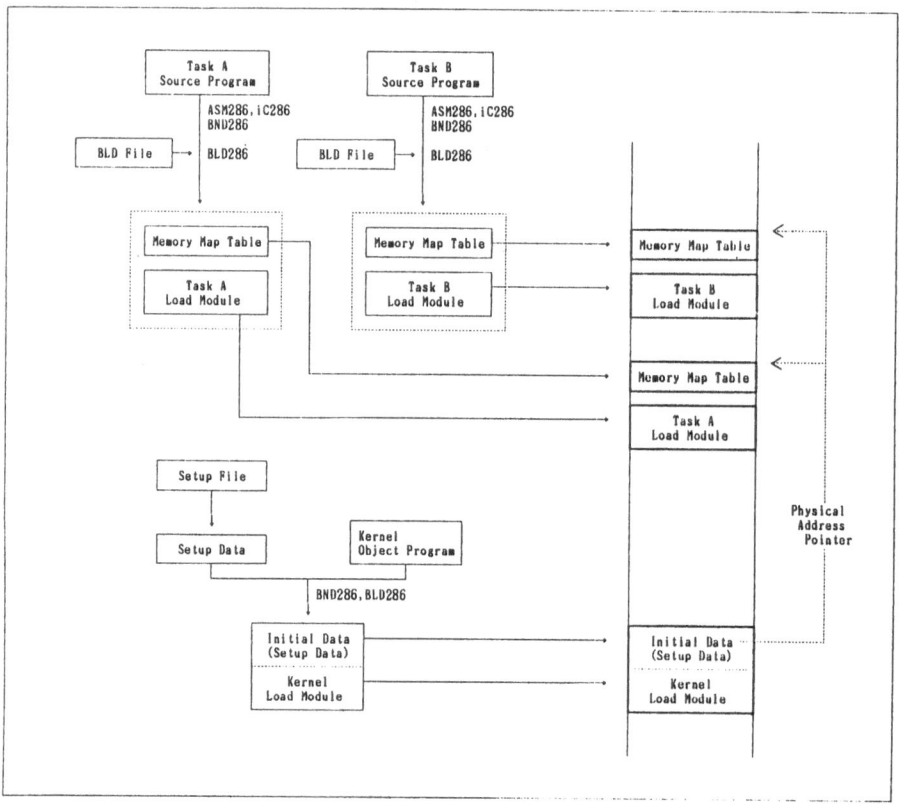

BLD File which is specified by BLD286 defines each program memory mapping. SetUp File which is specified by REALOS/286 defines system memory mapping.

Figure 6. Development of Application Program

executable modules and system information such as descriptor tables. Finally, the output is written in ROM based on the memory definition; this includes the executable module as well as system information.

Using Special System Calls cre_spc_ldt from REALOS/286, initial memory mapping can be included in the output of BLD286 leaving only the starting address of the descriptor table and the number of descriptors which have been initialized to be specified at runtime. These operations can be done during REALOS/286 initialization by using parameters of the Special System Calls to create a Set -Up File. See examples of List 1, part of a BLD File, and List 2, part of a Set -Up File corresponding to the BLD File of List 1.

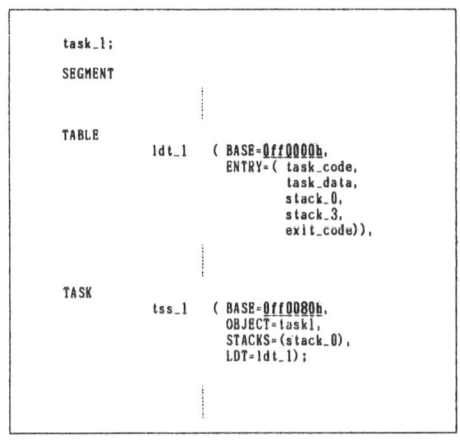

List 1. BLD File

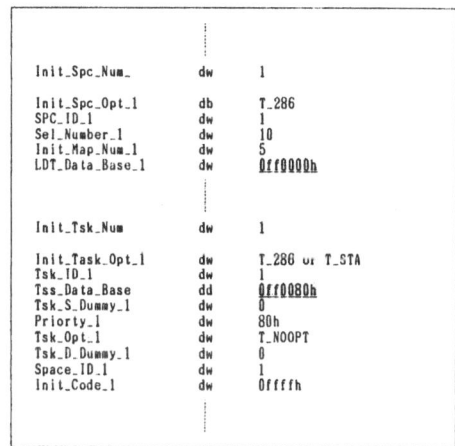

List 2. SetUp File

4. CONCLUSION

Through extending the original ITRON specification to ITRON/MMU, REALOS/ 286 provides a powerful development tools for realtime applications as well as an excellent runtime environment for embedded environments.

ACKNOWLEDGMENTS

I would like to thank Ken Sakamura, who helped us design and develop REALOS /286, and Rick Jensen, my colleague, who checked my paper and improved the quality of its representation.

REFERENCES

[1] K. Sakamura, "ITRON: An Overview," in this Proceedings.

[2] H. Monden, "Introduction to ITRON: The Industry-oriented Operating System," IEEE Micro, April 1987, pp. 45-52.

[3] K. Sakamura, "ITRON Real Time Operating System: Architecture and Future Perspective," Proc. Architecture Study Group, Information Processing Soc. Japan, 86-CA-61-1, 1986 (in Japanese)

[4] K. Kudo, A. Shimohara, H. Yasuda, A. Honda, "ITRON/MMU286," Proc. Architecture Study Group, Information Processing Soc. Japan, 86-CA- 61-4, 1986 (in Japanese)

[5] "iAPX286 Programmer's Reference Manual," Intel Corp. 1984.

Akira Shimohara is an engineer in Microcomputer Development Division, Semiconductor Group of FUJITSU LIMITED. He joined FUJITSU in 1984 after graduated from Tokyo University. He is a member of the Information Processing Society of Japan.

The HI Series of Operating Systems with the ITRON Architecture

Hiroshi Takeyama, Tsuyoshi Shimizu
Micro-computer System Engineering Department, Musashi Works, Hitachi Ltd.
1450 Josuihon-cho, Kodaira, Tokyo, 187 Japan

Ken-ichi Horikoshi
Electronic System Design Section, Hitachi Yonezawa Electronics Co., Ltd.
3-3274 Higashi Yagihashi, Hanazawa, Yonezawa, 992 Japan

ABSTRACT

Hitachi Ltd. has implemented on a 68000 microprocessor a realtime operating system conforming to the specifications of the ITRON (Industrial TRON) subproject of the realtime operating system nucleus (TRON) project. Intended for embedded applications, the operating system is named HI68K (Hitachi Industrial realtime operating system 68K). Shipments began in July 1987.

This paper starts by describing the features and functions of the HI68K implementation for the 68000, then covers its file management system, and concludes by sketching its growth paths toward the HI series of operating systems for the Hitachi H Series microprocessors: HI32 for the H32/200, HI16 for the H16, and HI8 for the H8. Plans also call for a series of file management systems supporting the HD68000, H32, and H16.

KEY WORDS

ITRON Specification, Realtime Operating System, Romable, Microprocessor, Multitask

1. HI68K

The ITRON subproject of the TRON project specifies the design of an industry-oriented realtime operating system. HI68K is a complete implementation of the industry-oriented operating system for a microprocessor of the 68000 type.

1.1 Features

While conforming fully to the ITRON specifications, the HI68K operating system offers some additional features:

(1) Romable
It can be placed in ROM for installing as a firmware component in machinery.

(2) Adaptions for extra speed
OS speed is a key factor in a computerized system that must keep pace with realtime events. For this reason, various adaptions were made in the HI68K design:

(a) High-speed system call processing
To speed up the processing of system calls made from application programs
to the operating system, parameter checking can be bypassed. Normally,
when a system call is made, the operating system checks for parameter
errors before executing the requested process. Such checks are essential
in the debugging stage, but when the bugs have been eliminated, parameter
checking needlessly slows down the response time. An HI68K feature
therefore permits the OS parameter checks to be bypassed, without requiring
any modifications to user programs.

(b) High-speed response to external interrupts

When the 68000
microprocessor receives
an asynchronous
interrupt signal from a
device controlled by the
system, OS processing is
stopped and control
passes directly to the
user program (interrupt
handler) with zero
system overhead. As a
result, the interval
during which external
interrupts to the 68000
are inhibited is
extremely short; the
interrupt handler begins
taking action within at
most 80 µs of the
occurrence of the
interrupt. (See Figure
1.)

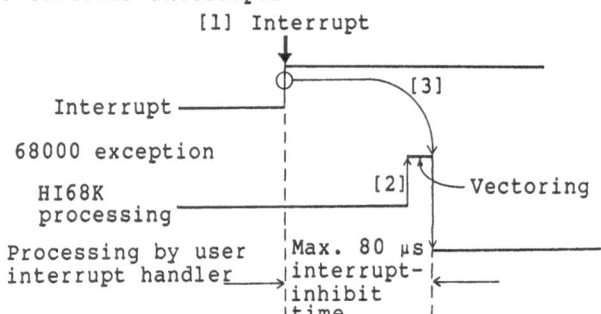

[1] An interrupt occurs.
[2] HI68K releases the interrupt
    inhibition within 80 µs.
[3] Control passes directly to the user
    interrupt handler with zero system
    overhead.

Figure 1

(3) Expanded use of system calls from non-task programs
Following the ITRON architecture, the HI68K operating system consists of a
chip kernel and chip kernel shell. The chip kernel is the nucleus of the
operating system and executes in the 68000 supervisor mode. It includes
user-coded interrupt handlers, exception handlers, and timer handlers,
which are referred to as non-task programs. A design target for HI68K was
to allow non-task programs to use the same number of system calls as
general user programs. The only system calls that cannot be used by non-
task programs are calls that reserve resources or involve waits, such as
wai_flg and cre_flg.

(4) Modular, building-block architecture
HI68K has a building-block structure. Unneeded functional blocks can be
eliminated to tailor the operating system to the application. Possible
configurations range from a 24K-byte minimum configuration consisting only
of the basic part of the chip kernel to a maximum 94K-byte configuration.
(See Table 1.)

Table 1   HI68K Module Configuration

Memory pool module	3.5K			
Mailbox module	1.7K		Help module	2.6K
Semaphore module	1.5K		Printer module	0.5K
Event flag module	1.5K		Trace module	4.8K
Debug module	6.8K	Printer driver 2.0K	Break module	2.8K
Basic module	24K	Console driver 1.5K	Basic debug module	40.3K
Nucleus	39K	Standard drivers 3.5K	Debugger	51K

(5) Portability
HI68K can run on any hardware system incorporating an HD68000 or HD68HC000 microprocessor and adequate memory in which the 68000 vector area (hex 008 - hex 3FF) must be located in RAM.

(6) On-line debugger
Application tasks can be debugged efficiently using the HI68K debugger, which permits an arbitrary task to be debugged in a multitask environment.

1.2 Functions

Of the HI68K functional blocks, those enclosed in the thick line in Figure 2 are supplied as standard components. Most of them are located in the chip kernel, the high-speed part of the system that supports realtime multitasking. The debugger is located in the chip kernel shell, which requires comparatively less speed. The chip kernel also includes interrupt and exception handlers created by the user to match the requirements of the application system.

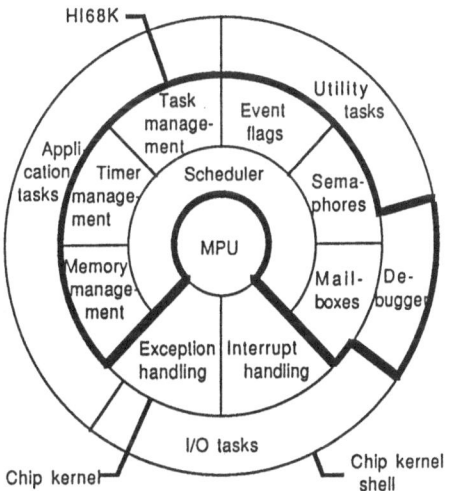

Figure 2 HI68K System Configuration

1.2.1 Task Management Functions

(1) Task
HI68K manages user application programs as tasks which run independently in parallel on the chip kernel. The user can divide an application program into tasks and register them through system calls. The chip kernel controls task execution according to the resources in the system, task status, and task priority. It can manage a maximum of 65,535 tasks.

(2) Task status
In HI68K there are seven types of task status, described below. Task status transitions can be caused by events in external equipment or system calls generated by other tasks, etc. (See Figure 3.)

(a) Nonexistent
The task is not present in the system (has not been created).

(b) Dormant
The task has been created but not started.

(c) Ready
Preparations for execution have been completed and the task is waiting to be dispatched.

(d) Run
The task has been dispatched and is executing.

(e) Wait
The task is waiting for an event to occur.

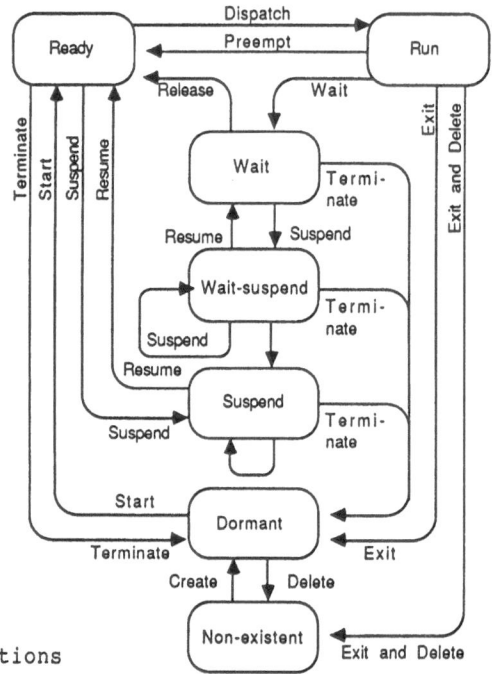

Figure 3
Task Status Transitions

(f) Suspend
Execution of the task was suspended by another task.

(g)Wait-suspend
The task is in the wait state and has also been suspended by another task.

1.2.2   Scheduler

The scheduler dispatches ready tasks in order of task priority, which is denoted by a number from 0 to 255. Priorities can be adjusted dynamically by the chg_pri system call. Tasks with equal priority are queued in a separate ready queue for each priority level. In standard scheduling the ready queue is a first-in-first-out (FIFO) queue. User-defined round-robin scheduling is also possible, in which the ready queue is rotated by a rot_rdq system call, enabling tasks on the same priority level to be scheduled on an equal basis.

1.2.3   Timer Management

HI68K employs a 48-bit timer implemented by counting interrupt signals generated at fixed intervals by hardware. The standard timer device for HI68K is the HD6840 programmable timer module, but by writing a timer handler the user can use a different timer module. The ITRON specifications do not stipulate what the timer interval should be (the minimum for HI68K is 1 ms).

1.2.4   Synchronization and Communication

According to the ITRON specifications, tasks synchronize and communicate with each other through event flags, semaphores, and mailboxes created by system calls. HI68K can accommodate a maximum of 65,535 event flags, 65,535 semaphores, and 65,535 mailboxes at once.

(1)   Event flags
Event flags provide the fastest means of synchronization between tasks. An event flag is composed of 32 bits, each indicating whether an individual event has or has not occurred. These bits can be set singly or in combinations by a system call. Another system call enables a task to wait for one or all of a specified subset of the 32 bits to become true. Indefinite waits can be avoided by a time-out option.

(2)   Semaphores
Semaphores are used for allocating resources to tasks. A semaphore is essentially a counter (0 - 65,535) indicating the number of units of a resource currently available. When a task needs the resource it performs a P operation: a system call stating the number of units required. If the required number of units are available, the semaphore is decremented by that number and the task proceeds. If they are not, or if another task is already waiting for the resource, the requesting task must queue up until the resource becomes available. The queue can be managed on either a task-priority or FIFO basis. If a task does not want to wait indefinitely it can specify a time-out option.

(3)   Mailboxes
Mailboxes are used for synchronization that involves an exchange of data between tasks. The sending task specifies a mailbox and sends a message to it. The receiving task specifies the same mailbox to receive the message. The mailboxes are managed by the system, which controls the associated message and task queues. The queues can be managed on either a priority or FIFO basis. A time-out option can prevent indefinite waits for message arrival.

1.2.5   Memory Management

HI68K allocates and deallocates blocks of memory requested by tasks from continuous memory extents called memory pools. Memory blocks can be allocated on either a task-priority or FIFO basis, with the usual time-out option. System calls can create up to 65,535 memory pools.

1.2.6   Interrupt Handlers

Interrupt handlers are non-task programs (in the chip kernel) that are activated by external interrupts. In the design and development of a realtime operating system, it is the interrupt handlers that require the highest performance, so the ITRON specifications regarding these handlers differ for each type of microprocessor. In HI68K the interrupt handlers are executed by direct vectoring in the 68000 microprocessor when an interrupt occurs, with zero system overhead. Registers must therefore be saved and restored by the handlers themselves. If a system call from an interrupt handler causes task switching, the task switching is performed at the ret_int system call that terminates the interrupt handler.

If a higher-level external interrupt occurs during execution of an interrupt handler, the handler currently executing is suspended and the higher-level interrupt handler is executed. When the higher-level

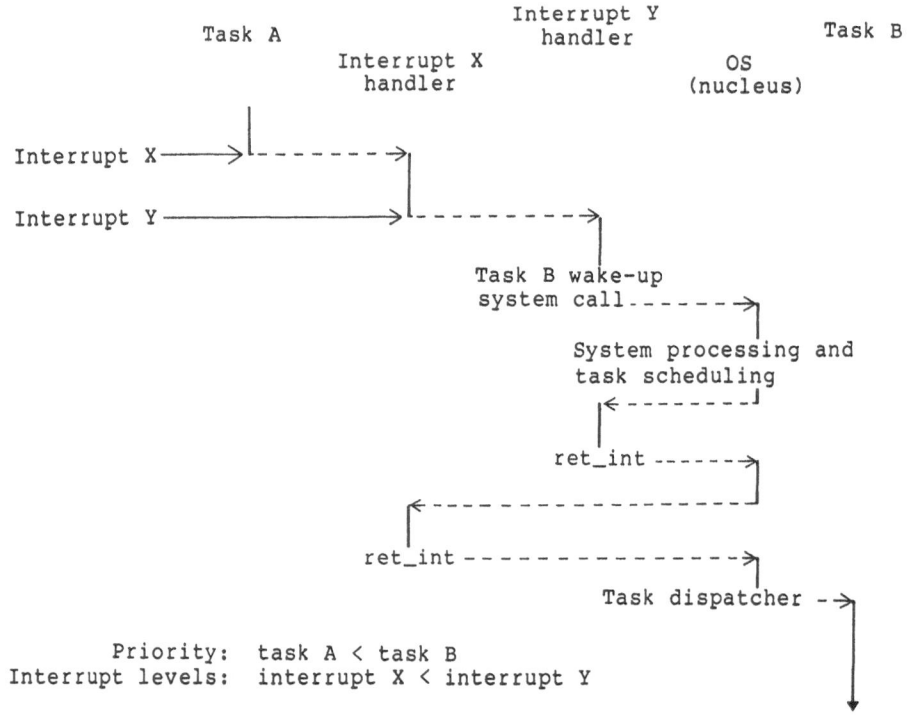

Figure 4   Flow of Interrupt Processing

interrupt handler terminates (by a ret_int system call), the suspended
interrupt handler can continue its processing.   (See Figure 4.)

1.2.7   Exceptions

In HI68K there are three types of exceptions:

o   CPU exceptions: Exception interrupts of the 68000, from Bus Error
    (vector No. 2) to Line 1111 (vector No. 11).
o   Trap exceptions: Exceptions generated by 68000 Trap instructions, from
    Trap #4 (vector No. 36) to Trap #15 (vector No. 47).
o   System call exceptions: Exceptions generated by HI68K when there is a
    parameter or other error in a system call.

Exceptions are handled by programs called exception handlers.   Exception
handlers can be installed for a particular task, for all tasks, and for
non-task programs (programs in the chip kernel).

1.2.8   Debugger

The HI68K debugger program executes as a task, enabling on-line debugging
of other tasks in the system through commands entered at the console. A
set of 27 commands is provided to control tasks, set breakpoints (at up to
32 points), trace system calls, and perform other debugging functions
efficiently in a multitasking environment. User-defined debug commands can
be added. (See Table 2.)

Table 2   Debugging Commands

Category	Command	Function
Task control	CRE_TSK STA_TSK SUS_TSK RSM_TSK TER_TSK DEL_TSK	Create task Start task Suspend task Resume suspended task Terminate task Delete task
Display and modification of memory contents	FB, FW DB MB, MBO MOV SCH	Initialize memory contents Display memory contents Modify memory contents Move memory contents Search memory contents
Breakpoint set/clear	BS B BC GO	Set breakpoint Display breakpoints Clear breakpoint Execute task from breakpoint
Task register modification	RM	Modify task register contents
Task status display	TSK STS	Display TCB information for specified task Display all tasks in specified status
System call trace	TSCST TSCED TSCDP TSCPT	Start system call trace End system call trace Display system call trace result Move trace display pointer
Printer assignment	PRA PRD	Attach printer Detach printer
Date/time setting	DT	Set/display date and time
Help messages	HLP	Display explanation of debugger commands
Exit from debugger	EXIT	Exit from debugger

1.3   System Calls

In HI68K there are 50 system calls, of which the first 49 are for realtime control. The 50th system call enables the user to define additional system calls. (See Table 3.) The system calls conform exactly to the ITRON/68K specifications, which define the system interface in assembly language and C language. A C-language interface library is also provided.

2.   File Management System

The BTRON specifications (for the business-oriented operating system of the TRON project) include a system for managing files in terms of real and virtual objects. Embedded applications do not require the full set of business-oriented file management functions, but they may require a subset. To be useful in both large and small embedded systems, the file management functions must be supplied on a series of levels, enabling the appropriate level to be selected. For HI68K, Hitachi has implemented the minimum functions required by embedded applications in a system named HI68KA. (See Figure 5.)

Table 3   HI68K System Calls

System call	Function	System call	Function
Task control		↑/↓del_mbx	Delete mailbox
↑cre_tsk	Create task	↑/↓snd_msg	Send message
↑/↓sta_tsk	Start task	↑rcv_msg	Receive message
↑/↓del_tsk	Delete task	↑/↓mbx_adr	Get mailbox access address
↑def_ext	Define exit routine		
↑ext_tsk	Exit self task	**Interrupt handling**	
↑exd_tsk	Exit and delete self task	↑/↓ def_int	Define interrupt handler
↑abo_tsk	Abort self task	↓ret_int	Return from interrupt handler
↑/↓ter_tsk	Terminate other task	↑/↓set_int	Set interrupt mask
↑/↓chg_pri	Change priority	↓iret_wup	Return from interrupt handler
↑/↓rot_rdq	Rotate ready queue		and wake up task
↑/↓tcb_adr	Get TCB (Task Control Block) address		
↑/↓tsk_sts	Get task status	**Exception handling**	
↑/↓sus_tsk	Suspend task	↑/↓def_exc	Define exception handler
↑/↓rsm_tsk	Resume suspended task	↑/↓ret_exc	Return from exception handler
↑slp_tsk	Sleep task		
↑wai_tsk	Wait for task to wake up	**Memory management**	
↑/↓wup_tsk	Wake up sleeping task	↑cre_mpl	Create memory pool
↑/↓can_wup	Cancel task wake-up requests	↑/↓del_mpl	Delete memory pool
↑/↓cyc_wup	Wake task up cyclically	↑get_blk	Get memory block
↑/↓can_cyc	Cancel cyclic task wake-up	↑/↓rel_blk	Release memory block
		↑/↓mpl_adr	Get memory pool access address
Synchronization and communication			
↑cre_flg	Create event flag	**Timer management**	
↑/↓del_flg	Delete event flag	↑/↓set_tim	Set time
↑/↓set_flg	Set event flag	↑/↓get_tim	Get time
↑wai_flg	Wait for event flag to be set		
↑/↓flg_adr	Get event flag access address	**Version management**	
↑cre_sem	Create semaphore	↑/↓get_ver	Get version identifier
↑/↓del_sem	Delete semaphore		
↑/↓sig_sem	Signal semaphore (V operation)	**System call expansion**	
↑wai_sem	Wait on semaphore (P operation)	↑/↓def_svc	Define additional system call handler
↑/↓sem_adr	Get semaphore access address		
↑cre_mbx	Create mailbox		

↑:   Can originate from task
↓:   Can originate from non-task program

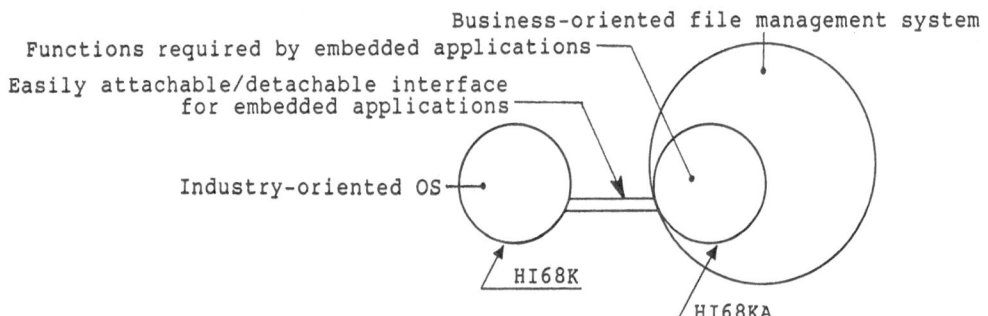

Figure 5   HI68KA File Management System

HI68KA is a subset of the business-oriented file management system. Compatibility was ensured by adherence to the following design requirements:

(1) Files created by HI68KA must be completely readable and writable by any system complying with the BTRON specifications.
(2) Files (objects) created by such a system subject to certain restrictions must be completely readable and writable by HI68KA.
(3) System call names and parameters must be the same, and the C-language system call interface must be the same.

2.1 HI68KA Functions

(1) File System Configuration

A file system is a way of organizing data on a single medium such as a floppy or hard disk. Figure 6 shows the file system configuration according to the BTRON specifications. The system is organized as a network with a single root file and pointers (called links) from one file to another. The files correspond to the real objects mentioned earlier; the links correspond to the virtual objects.

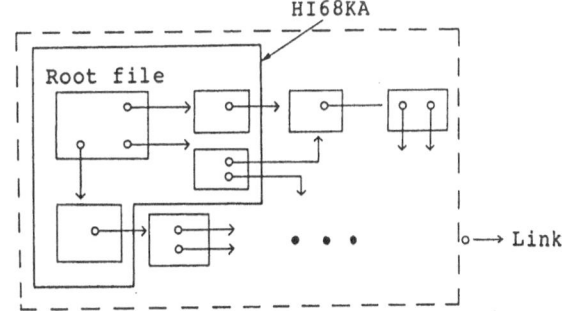

Figure 6   File System Configuration in BTRON and ITRON specifications

The business-oriented file network topology is practically unrestricted and links can be nested to any depth. In HI68KA, however, the file system is limited to the root file and the files linked directly to it.

(2) File structure
A file is structured as a record stream: a sequentially ordered set of variable-length records. Each record consists of four fields:

o   Record type: This field indicates the type of record; for example, 0 indicates a link record.
o   Record subtype: A record type can have various subtypes.
o   Record size: This 32-bit value indicates the byte length of the record data.
o   Record data: This is the record itself, consisting of the number of bytes of data indicated by the record size.

The record-stream structure and the structure of the records in the stream is the same in both HI68KA and the BTRON specifications.

(3) File access management
The BTRON specifications are targeted at an office environment in which access to files must be controlled by identifying the source of the access as the owner of the file, a member of a special group, or a general user. Industrial systems embedded in machinery do not require these user identification functions, so they have been removed from HI68KA. HI68KA supports only the write-protect and delete-protect attributes which prevent a file from being modified or deleted by mistake. (See Figure 7.)

(4) Record operations
The business-oriented BTRON specifications include the following operations on records:

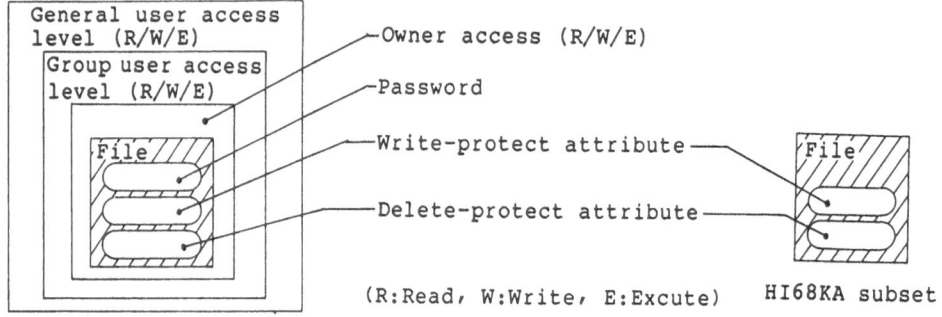

Full set

Figure 7 File Access Management

```
Read:      Read a record
Write:     Rewrite the data in a record
Append:    Append a record
Delete:    Delete a record
Insert:    Insert a record
Truncate: Reduce record size
Lock:      Inhibit record operations
Unlock:    Permit record operations
```

Embedded realtime systems require only some of these functions. In small
systems, such as a system that reads control data from disk and logs a
series of transactions, only the read and write functions are necessary.
As noted earlier, the solution is to provide the business-oriented
operations on a series of levels, allowing the user to select the level
appropriate for a given embedded application system. HI68KA implements the
minimum level indicated in Figure 8.

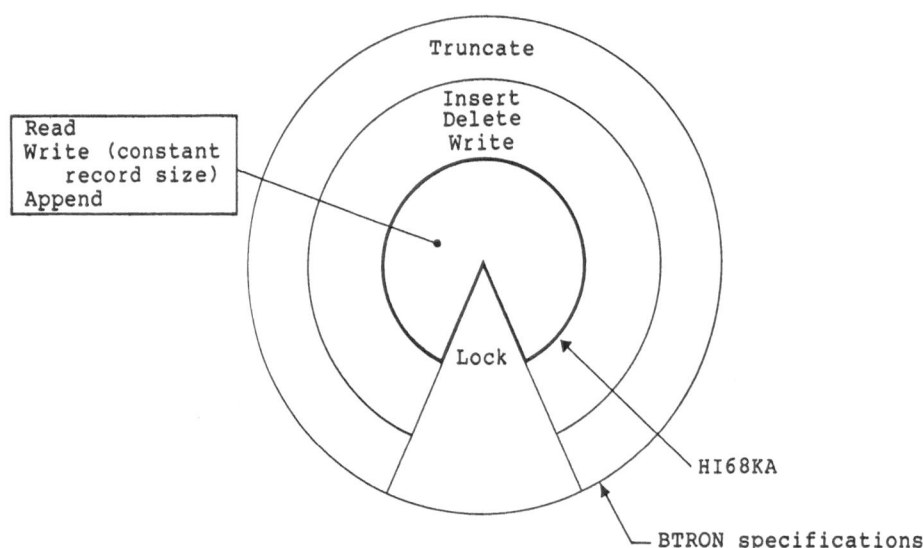

Figure 8 Record Operations

2.2   Implementation of File Management

The file management module is intermediate between the user task and the device driver task. It interfaces to the user task by file management system calls and to the device driver by a mailbox.

A file I/O system call from a user task starts a file manager which determines the necessary physical input/output and places a device I/O request in the device driver's mailbox. The device driver controls the device (disk drive) directly and performs the physical I/O. When the I/O process is finished, the device driver task places a termination message in the file manager's mailbox.

In I/O, data are transferred directly by DMA between the disk media and a buffer in the file manager or user task. Execution of the user task resumes when the file manager's processing is completed.

The file manager is a non-task program, but it is dispatched by the scheduler and behaves in the same way as the task that requested the I/O. (See Figure 9.)

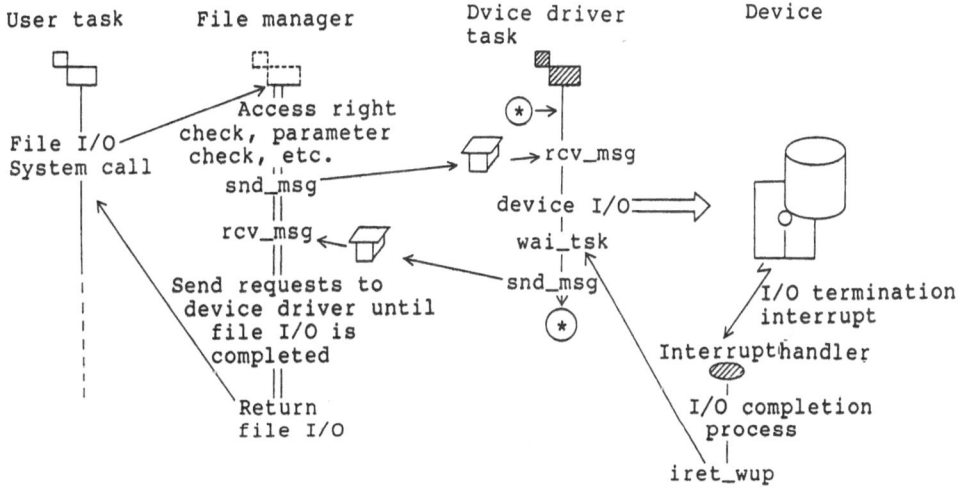

Figure 9   Processing by File Management System

3.   Growth Paths to the HI Series

HI68K was designed in such a way as to ease the porting of user systems to Hitachi's original H Series of microprocessors, comprising the H32/200, H16, and H8. The architecture of each microprocessor in the H Series is optimized for a particular application area. The 32-bit H32 microprocessor is a high-speed engine implementing the TRON architecture and designed for data processing applications requiring an advanced man-machine interface. The H16 is a 16-bit microprocessor with high-speed task switching and bit-field manipulation features, designed for control of large equipment systems requiring rapid transfer of large quantities of data. The H8 is an 8-bit microcomputer system-on-a-chip with non-volatile memory, designed for controlling medium-scale office, industrial, and consumer equipment. These

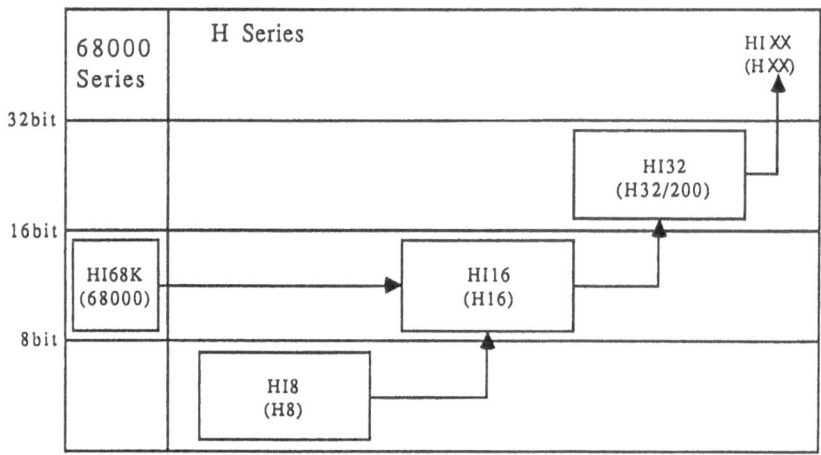

Figure 10   HI Series Growth Path

microprocessors will be supported by a family of operating systems
conforming to the ITRON specifications, designated HI32, HI16, and HI8.
(See Figure 10.)

3.1 HI32: Implementation on the H32

The H32, a 32-bit VLSI microprocessor based on the TRON architecture,
offers a high-speed engine for running systems designed to ITRON and BTRON
specifications.   (See Table 4.)   The nucleus (chip kernel) of HI32 will use
instructions provided by the H32 for context switching, queue manipulation,
and bit-field manipulation.

The context-switching instructions LDCTX (Load Context) and STCTX (Store
Context) enable the hardware context of a task, namely the contents of
control registers, to be saved to or restored from a task control area with
a single instruction, instead of requiring an interrupt-masking instruction

Table 4   High-Level Instructions Supporting ITRON-Specification OS
          (Instructions in parentheses use task gates)

	H32	MC68020	iAPX386	NS32032
Context switch	LDCTX	--	(CALL)	--
	STCTX	--	(JMP)	--
			(IRET)	
Queue manipulation	QINS	--	--	--
	QDEL			
	QSCH			
Bitmap manipulation	BVCPY	--	--	--
	BVMAP			
	BVPAT			
	BVSCH			

by software and several data transfer instructions as in conventional systems. This greatly shortens task switching time.

The queue manipulation instructions QINS (Insert into Queue), QDEL (Remove from Queue), and QSCH (Search for Queue Element) enable a single instruction to insert, delete, or find an element in a double-linked queue. These instructions speed up the chip kernel's processing of the ready queues, wait queues, and other queues used in the system.

The variable-length bit-field manipulation instructions BVMAP (One-Line Bit-Field Operation), BVCPY (Copy Variable-Length Bit-Field), and BVPAT (Cyclic Bit-Field Operation) permit efficient operations on a bit-mapped display, while the BVSCH (Search for 0 or 1 bit in variable-length bit-field) instruction shortens the search time when the ready queue and other system queues are managed in terms of individual bits, thereby speeding up the task scheduling process.

3.2 HI16: Implementation on the H16

The main feature of the H16 is its register banks. The 16 general registers (R0 to R15) are assigned to space in the H16's 1024-byte on-chip RAM. Since each register is 4 bytes long, the RAM can accommodate up to 16 separate banks of 16 registers each. The number of register banks used can be selected by a value in the bank mode register (BMR), and the current bank can be selected by setting a number in the global bank number register (GBNR). (See Figure 11.)

Bank switching can be performed by privileged instructions. If register banks are allocated to interrupt handlers and high-priority tasks, the saving and restoring of bank registers when tasks are switched or an interrupt handler is started can be performed very quickly just by switching banks, enabling fast response to external interrupts.

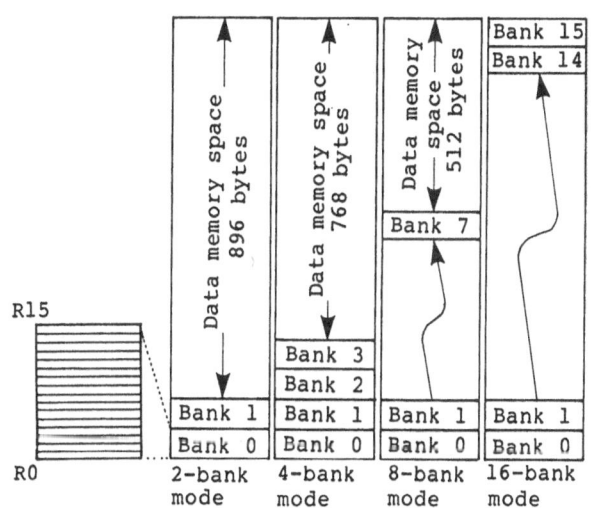

Figure 11   H16 Register Banks and Internal RAM

3.3   HI8:   Implementation on the H8

The H8 microcomputer has an 8-bit external data bus but its internal data width is 16 bits. Instruction execution time is shortened because internal memory can be accessed 16 bits at a time. Included on the H8 chip are peripheral functions such as EPROM, RAM, timers, a serial interface, an A/D converter, and controllers with 8 interrupt levels. The chip kernel of HI8 will reside in on-chip ROM, and a set of romable drivers will be provided for I/O, timers, etc. By writing the necessary modules into ROM, the user will be able to configure the desired system-on-a-chip.

References

[1] K. Sakamura, "Real-time Operating System ITRON," Operating System Study Group 24-10, Information Processing Soc. Japan, 1984 (In Japanese)
[2] K. Sakamura, "ITRON Real-time Operating System," J. Robotics Soc. Japan, 1985, pp. 41-48 (in Japanese)
[3] K. Sakamura, "ITRON Real-time Operating System; Architecture and Future Perspective," Proc. Architecture Study Group, Information Processing Soc. Japan, 86-CA-61-1, 1986 (in Japanese)
[4] K. Sakamura, "TRON Project," Proc. IMAC 84, pp. 203-208
[5] K. Sakamura, "TRON Total Architecture," Proc. Architecture Workshop in Japan, Information Processing Soc. Japan, 1984 (in Japanese)
[6] K. Sakamura, "Making of TRON," Bit, Kyoritsu Shuppan, Tokyo, 1986 and 1987 (in Japanese)
[7] K. Sakamura, New Concepts from the TRON Project, Iwanami-shoten, Tokyo, 1987 (in Japanese)
[8] K. Sakamura, "The TRON Project," IEEE Micro, Apr. 1987, pp. 8-14
[9] H. Monden, "Introduction to ITRON," IEEE Micro, Apr. 1987, pp. 45-52
[10] E. Yabe, "ITRON/68K," Proc. Architecture Study Group, Information Processing Soc. Japan, 86-CA-61-2, 1986 (in Japanese)
[11] HI68K User's Manual, HS68KITNS1SJ, Hitachi, Ltd., System LSI Engineering, Electronic Parts Marketing, 1-5-1, Marunouchi, Chiyoda-ku, Tokyo, Japan 100, 1986 (in Japanese)
[12] Hitachi, Ltd., Real-time Operating System HI68K, Personal Media Co., 1987 (in Japanese)

H. Takeyama joined Hitachi, Ltd. in 1969 and is now a senior engineer in the Microcomputer System Engineering Dept. at the Musashi Works of Hitachi's Semiconductor Division. Since 1983 he has participated in research and development of realtime operating systems for microcomputers and in-circuit emulation software, and in product planning for microcomputer support tools. He received his BA in electronic engineering from Fukuoka Institute of Technology in 1969.

T. Shimizu joined Hitachi, Ltd. in 1978 and is now an engineer in the Microcomputer System Engineering Dept. at the Musashi Works of Hitachi's Semiconductor Division. He is currently engaged in research and development of realtime operating systems for microcomputers. He received his BA in informatics from the University of Osaka in 1976 and his master's degree from the same school in 1978.

K. Horikoshi joined the Hitachi Yonezawa Electronics Co., Ltd. in 1975 and is now an engineer in the Electronic System Design Section. His current work is in research and development of realtime operating systems for microcomputers. He was graduated from Yonezawa Polytechnic Institute in 1975.

Chapter 3: BTRON

BTRON: An Overview

Ken Sakamura
Department of Information Science, Faculty of Science, University of Tokyo
Hongo,Tokyo,113 Japan

ABSTRACT

BTRON is an operating system architecture designed in the TRON project. BTRON specification aims at establishing operating systems for workstations in 1990's. BTRON workstations will offer ease of use and learning, efficient operation for experienced users, support for many languages of the world including the support for many character sets, data interchange across different BTRON machines, consistent data model, uniform man-machine interface, and a set of functions which will make it easy for application developers to build programs that use similar man-machine interface.

Keywords: Man-Machine Interface, Data Compatibility, Ease of Use, Data Model, Operating Systems

1. INTRODUCTION

BTRON is an operating system architecture designed to enable personal computers and workstations to handle in an integrated fashion all aspects of the man-machine interface or MMI. It is equipped with functions for data exchange between applications, management of objects (or files, in the conventional sense), and multilanguage processing. BTRON stands for business-oriented operating system for the TRON project.

Our primary objective in the design of BTRON was to make it easy to use. We assumed that it would be employed with hardware such as a bitmapped display and a pointing device, along with the necessary software.

The BTRON specification regards the real-time performance emphasized in the TRON project as a characteristic essential for human-oriented operation.

The next point given attention in the design of the BTRON specification was the trade-off between ease of operation for beginners and efficiency for practiced users. Users are required to make a certain effort to understand the system. In BTRON, what they learn will not be changed in the future due to different implementations, differences in the hardware environment handled by the BTRON operating system, or differences in the applications being run. This will not only ease learning but improve teaching, since teachers will not have the burden of teaching many different and inconsistent systems.

2. BTRON FUNCTIONAL OBJECTIVES

New applications designed to be run on computers based on the BTRON concept use computers as a medium for information exchange and presentation.

What functions are essential in a system that is to be used as a medium? It must process large numbers of different characters. It must support as many different languages as possible (if possible, all of the characters used in the world), that is, be equipped with a character code system for that purpose. It must have the ability to input and output a specific language at a level which satisfies the user.

The BTRON specification was designed from the start to accommodate a large numbers of characters, for which reason its internal code is a either 8 or 16-bits long. The 16-bit code makes it possible to use Japanese or Chinese character groups. Further, it makes it possible to select different character groups for each language. Depending on the language used, application programs can switch the language environments to handle various language specific input/output processing such as formatting.

The exchange of figures and drawings must be possible. A BTRON subproject defines a common format for graphical data, and the operating system based on the BTRON specification has utilities for editing and displaying such data. In addition to simulating the advantages possessed by a sheet of paper, the BTRON operating system has dynamic document (or hypertext) functions such as an outline processor and the ability to link documents in network fashion.

3. BTRON DESIGN GUIDELINES

3.1 REAL OBJECT/VIRTUAL OBJECT MODEL

In the design of the BTRON specification, we used the following principles as guidelines for realizing the functions discussed above:

Creation of a consistent data model was deemed essential so that the handling of data across applications would become standardized. We constructed a model for implementing the handling of integrated data (multimedia data) and dynamic documents. (see *Figure 1.*) This model replaces the file system model of conventional operating systems. We also constructed BTRON object (file) management functions on this model. This is called real/virtual object model. The BTRON specification proposes a new operational model—the real object/virtual object model—to model data storage, expression, and management in the integrated operational environment. The BTRON object (file) system is designed to efficiently implement this model.

Figure 1. Using the dynamic documents made possible by the real object /virtual object model

In this model, an accumulation of data is referred to as a "real object", which is referenced by a tag called a "virtual object". Just as the text and figures in a conventional document can, a virtual object can be embedded in a real object as standard unit of data: this is the basic idea of the real object/virtual object model. (The Japanese term used here translates literally as "body"—meaning the body of data—but its meaning is closer to "object" in English.) On a bitmapped display, virtual objects are shown as a collection of rectangles. By pointing to the rectangles with a pointing device, a user can perform actions on them. (see *Figure 2.*)

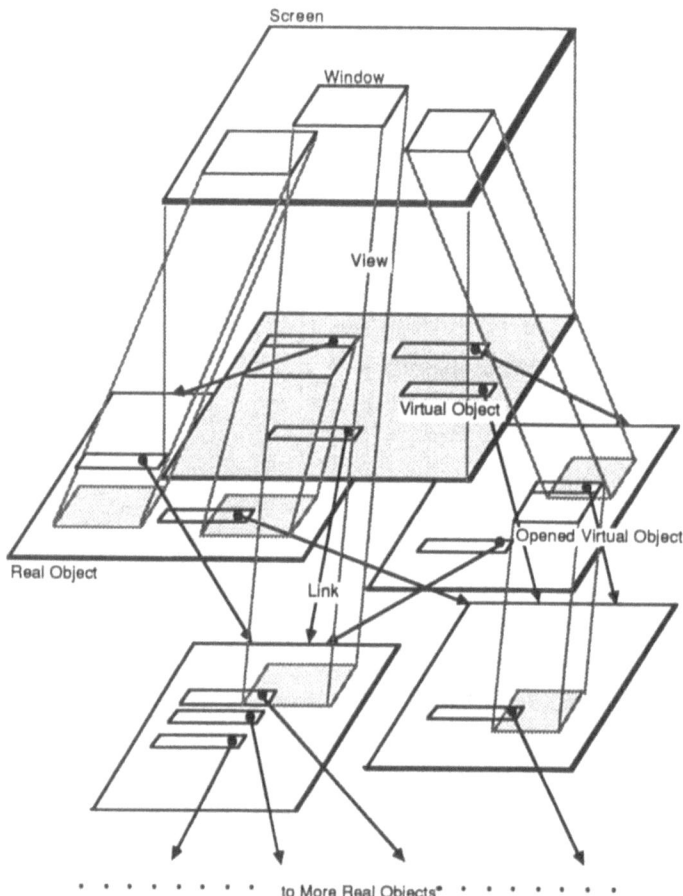

Figure 2. Real object/virtual object model of BTRON

3.2 SEPARATION OF DESIGN STANDARDS AND IMPLEMENTATION

Separation of design standards and implementation was essential. In order to separate design standards and implementation methods, and to admit implementations having different levels of performance, we deemed a hierarchical structure (with interfaces between different levels) to be essential. This hierarchical structure is the basic concept behind the TRON project, and hence separation of design standards and implementation was realized in the initial stage of the BTRON project.

3.3. UNIFORMITY OF MAN-MACHINE INTERFACE

An uniform man-machine interface must be supplied over various hardware systems. To ensure that applications running on operating systems based on the BTRON specification would all have similar operational methods, we developed the TRON Design Guideline to promote uniformity in the design of all software and hardware components.

4. DATA COMPATIBILITY THROUGH TAD

In conventional systems data compatibility requires specific conversion programs for different situations. For general data compatibility, then, the only approach is to restrict the file structures used. Such restriction, however, reduces the degree of freedom allowed in application specifications, and reduces efficiency. The real object/virtual object model offers a solution.

The basic concept is to divide data into an sharable part and an application-specific part, and to standardize the data description for the sharable part only. The sharable part is for objective data—data input and output by an application so it can communicate with human beings, data expressed as text and figures. This data should be exchangeable among all applications. It should never have to be retyped, even in the worst case. Hence, its description should be standardized. This has been done in the BTRON project.

Text and figures are used as the base of information exchange (or minimum assurance) in the BTRON project, then. Primitives required for the interpretation and display of text and figures exist at all times in systems based on the BTRON specification and can be utilized by all programs. In other words, the interpretation method for text and figures is designed to be generally applicable. For example, a graph generated from a table is a figure real object, one into which the user can easily write comments by employing the basic figure editor.

The application data on existing computers corresponds to "fusen", while applications on computers based on the BTRON architecture do not use an application-specific data structure but store data in text and figure real objects, and disperse and embed as fusen in the text and figure real objects auxiliary application-specific data that cannot be shared among applications. This approach means that even if a conversion program does not exist for interapplication data transfer, the text and figures can be extracted from the real objects themselves for assured transfer. This concept and standard in the BTRON project is referred to as TAD (the TRON application data bus).

5. AUTOMATIC OPERATION THROUGH TAC

The idea of automatic operation implemented in the BTRON the design standards for the application programs making it possible are called TAC (the TRON Application Control flow).

TAC command macros are created by combining fusen. In the framework of BTRON, data is composed of real objects, most of which have fusen attached. The real objects correspond to the normal programming language data, and the fusen correspond to the directives that determine processing. Real objects with fusen are networked together through their virtual objects. This structure implements data structure and scope in program data terms.

6. BTRON CONFIGURATION: HIERARCHICAL STRUCTURE

The BTRON architecture is hierarchical. The operating system based on the BTRON architecture is composed of a nucleus (called the BTRON nucleus) and a shell surrounding it. Applications are constructed on the shell. "Shell" does not mean a command language interpreter here. Structurally the BTRON nucleus provides functions found in conventional operating systems, such as device management, process management, resource management, and file management (in the form of real object/virtual object management). In addition, it also includes display primitives and bitmapped display drivers not found in conventional operating systems.

Many hardware layers can be concealed in the nucleus.

The external shell includes four modules, namely TAD (the TRON application data bus), MII (the machine-independent interface), TAC (the TRON application control flow), and MMI (the man-machine interface). (see *Figure 3*.) The MMI module is composed of nested-viewport system functions for the implementation of the BTRON real object/virtual object model, a Kana-Kanji conversion function for Japanese-language input (in Japan, that is), and basic editing functions. Input and editing functions are switchable to support different language and different character set.

Applications on computers based on the BTRON architecture are built upon the high-level functions found in the external shell. As a result, the applications themselves are compact, the number of MMI modules in application programs is vastly reduced, and uniformity across applications is enhanced. The uniformity of the MMI is an especially large advantage not found in other machines.

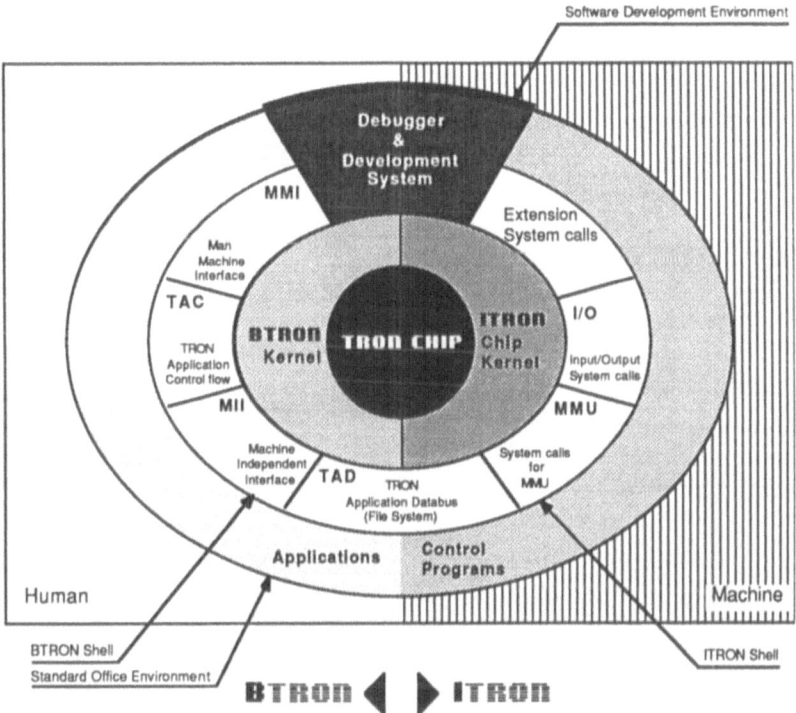

Figure 3. The hierarchical structure of BTRON (left side of diagram)

7. SYSTEM APPLICATIONS

The user operates directly at the application level. The BTRON specification does not include conventional operating-system interfaces such as a command line interpreter, and hence all operations are handled through the application. The TRON Design Guideline and the standard data model provide a common foundation for all application designs, thereby providing uniform operations for future applications.

8. CONCLUSION

The design of the new personal computer architecture in the BTRON subproject of the TRON project included as its objectives the implementation of high-level information presentation capabilities such as the dynamic document, the use of computer as a communication medium, data compatibility, support of the division of labor in the office, a uniform man-machine interface, and ease of use. To meet these objectives, new tools and concepts were created in the BTRON project, such as the TRON Design Guideline, the new data management model called the real object/virtual object model. Also created was automatic operation, which uses these concepts.

Operating system prototypes based on the BTRON architecture have already been implemented by a number of manufacturers. They have confirmed that the BTRON approach—the use of the TRON Design Guideline and the real object/virtual object model—is effective in the realization of the design objectives.

Ken Sakamura: see *"The Objectives of the TRON Project"* in this proceedings.

BTRON: Human-Machine Interface

Ken Sakamura

Department of Information Science, Faculty of Science, University of Tokyo
Hongo,Tokyo,113 Japan

ABSTRACT

There are several approaches in designing human interface of computer systems. Performance indices such as understandability and helpfulness are important in design considerations. However, considering such performance indices per se is not enough for good design. The popularity of a particular interface is very important from the users' viewpoint. For example, the more existing programming environments can be realized using a particular human interface, the more useful such a human interface becomes.

This paper discusses the design method of BTRON human interface, which aims at establishing uniformity among different implementations by separating specification and implementation clearly. BTRON human interface principle can be applied to wide variety of applications and is very useful for users

Keywords: Human Interface, Graphical Interface, Standardization, Metaphor, BTRON.

1. INTRODUCTION

Computer power has increased very much thanks to the advances in the hardware technology over the last several decades. The powerful capability of computers today can now be used for various tasks. Today computers are used more in interactive fashions than they were before. The computational power of personal computers is increasingly used to make computers easy to use.

As the power of computer increases and the price of computers decreases, more people have started using computers. It has become very important to design computers that are easily used by many users. The human-machine did not attract much attention in the early stage of computer history. But it has become a major design issue today.

The recent research of human interface on computers has brought multi-window systems, icons, menus, pointing devices and other methods and devices. The research of human interface has focused on the design of easy to use and learn human interfaces.

From the viewpoint of users, aside from the intrinsic goodness of a human interface, it is very important whether a given interface can fit well with the tools the users are using. The throughput of man-machine system depends heavily on how accustomed the operator is to a given human-interface.

Using unaccustomed systems is not only a pain for the operator but it degrades the performance very much. We can say that, in doing a given task on a computer, human operator who are accustomed to an old human-interface will outperform a human operator who is not accustomed to a new (possibly good) human interface.

From the view point of evaluating human-machine interface, it is very important that an interface is designed with a view to make it popular and fit with many tasks. The research of human-interface has paid attention to the intrinsic goodness of the human-interface systems but did not pay attention to how the systems can be made popular or be accepted by the user community. The researchers' attitude may be summarized as follows. Why bother? If the system is good, it will become popular.

In this paper, we discuss the design of human-interface from the view point of making the resulting system popular and making it work with many varied tasks. Some approaches studied in the BTRON subproject of the TRON project are discussed. [1], [2]

2. OBJECTIVES

When we say that human-machine interface is popular, we mean two things. One is that it is used with many applications on one system. The other is that it is adopted on many different computer systems. In order to achieve the former, the basic design of the human-machine interface must be adaptable to various applications. The latter requires some kind of framework that allows different implementors on various machines to develop a possibly slightly different but basically the same human-machine interface using different software and hardware resources.

Of course, the ease of learning is a necessary feature of a human-machine interface system, which is meant to be widely available.

In summary, we think the following three objectives must be satisfied for a human-machine interface to be widely used.

(1) The basic design must be adaptable or fit to various applications.

(2) There must be a conceptual framework within which independent implementors can produce basically similar human-machine interface on various hardware systems.

(3) The human-machine interface system must be easy to learn.

3. POSSIBLE APPROACHES

3.1 USE OF METAPHOR

One possible approach to designing human interface is a simulation of the real physical world on the computer. We call such approach as use of metaphor approach. Xerox Star was probably the first commercial system to use such metaphor. On the system, desktop which consists of icons is used to organize the operator's work just like the notebooks or books on a real desktop. [3]

Since the simulated real physical world is already familiar to users, the objective (2), namely the conceptual framework, described above is satisfiable. Also, since users are already familiar with the metaphor, the objective (3), namely ease of use, is also satisfiable.

However, the simulation of real world forces the computer to simulate the limits of the physical world as well. Such simulation can keep computers from offering powerful human-interface. For example, on real paper, if you change some words in the middle of a document, you may have to erase or move around some sentences with a pair of scissors, glue, and an eraser. Using word processors on computers, it is more likely that the programs automatically refill or justify the changed paragraph. People do not want to go through the simulation of real paper in this case. In a sense, the literal simulation of real world may be called Literalism in the use of metaphor. On the other hand, automatic justification and nice things done on the computers may be called Magic. [4] These two standpoints have merits and demerits.

In order to take advantage of computers, Magic has to be used. So approach using metaphor can meet the objectives (2) and (3), but cannot meet the objective (1) if standpoint of Literalism is strictly maintained.

In any case, the use of metaphor has influenced the design of human-machine interface on many personal computers and workstation including Star. Desktop consisting of icons, and menus handled with pointing devices are two major features of such systems. In some cases, Magic replaces the Literalism to some extent.

3.2 USE OF SYSTEM-SUPPLIED FUNCTIONS

From the view point of a system implementor, the use of built-in functions to support man-machine interactions is a very effective way to achieve standardized man-machine interface across applications running on one machine. The use of such library of system-supplied man-machine interface functions can be attractive if it reduces the cost of development and if it makes it easy for the application writers to follow system upgrade by insulating the application via the library from native system software. If all application programmers begin using one set of system man-machine interface library, the interfaces supported tend to be similar to each other, and the objective (2) will be realized.

However, if the functions supported in such a library are restrictive, it is not possible to use such interface in all applications. Thus, we cannot possibly meet the objective (1), namely the wide adaptability, in such cases. One way to solve this problem is to allow the application writers to register user-written routines as a part of the system-wide library. or to replace given functions with user-written functions. Such user-defined functions in system-wide library make it possible to write application-oriented human-interface using the (possibly modified) system-supplied library.

An example of efforts to standardize application interface with built-in functions is seen on Apple Macintosh. The library on Macintosh is called ToolBox. The approach has turned out to be very effective, and the use of ToolBox has contributed much to the standardization of human-interface of applications running on Macintosh.

XEROX Star has made its interface functions open under the name of ViewPoint System. IBM OS/2 will have Presentation Manager which provides functions for human-machine interaction. In this way, the use of system-supplied library to build human-interface has become rather standard on personal computers.

On what are called engineering workstation, the standardization of window system has been discussed much recently. However, the standardization of human-interface has been left out from the discussion. SunView on Sun Microsystem's SUN computers, Dialog on Apollo Domain computers, and X-ray on HP9000 series computers are some examples of system-supplied library interface for human-interface building.

3.3 BUNDLED SOFTWARE APPROACH

This is an approach that a vendor of new computer system may take. In this approach, software products for basic tasks such as document editing and graph drawing are bundled with the hardware. These bundled software are to be used widely among the users and will play the role of showing the de facto standard of human-interface on the particular hardware. The bundled software will set the minimum standard for subsequent products. It is quite likely that the third party software vendors may follow the human-interface of the bundled software as a model of human-interface when they develop similar, but more powerful programs. The similarity will make it easier for the users to learn the operation of new programs.

Since not many software products will be available on the new hardware for some time, the bundled software will fill the gap before more programs will become available. Aside from being a possible model of human interface, these bundled software can also have chance to define standard data format to store data in external storage . This is because many newer programs will have the function to convert to/from the bundled software's data format.

The bundled software approach can meet the objective (2), the conceptual framework, by using the specification of bundled software as a frame of reference. If the newly developed applications use the similar human-interface, which is likely to occur, the approach can meet the objective (3), ease of use, as well.

In order to make this approach successful, the bundled software must leave room for the succeeding generation of applications to offer new features. Also, the functions provided in the bundled software should cover wide range of human-machine interactions and should be usable in mixed ways.

Examples of bundled software applications are word processor, graphics editor, database, spreadsheet, and chart drawing.

Apple Macintosh is an example of a computer that has used the bundled software approach. It comes with MacWrite and MacPaint, which is word and bitmap graphics editor respectively.

4. OBJECTIVES IN BTRON

In BTRON, we try to offer unified and standardized human-machine interface on wide range of hardware systems. This is in contrast to the case of Apple Macintosh.

Apple Macintosh has adopted the use of metaphor, built-in functions, and bundled software products to offer standardized human-interfaces across various applications. And it has been successful. When users of Macintosh evaluate the new software, one of their criteria is "how well does the software conform to Mac interface?".

However, the Apple Macintosh computer has been a rather easy environment to achieve standardized human-interface. It is a computer from one manufacturer, and did not have add-on hardware boards for a long time, and the only available OS was one from Apple Computer Inc. In a word, it has a very closed architecture. We could always assume the same OS and the same hardware configuration. It was a big help in designing a standardized human-interface.

However, if we go after a human-machine interface that is widely used on different machines, as we do in the BTRON subproject, we must make sure that such human-machine interface be available on machines from many manufacturers.

Probably the easiest way to achieve such human-interface is to make the manufacturers use the same blueprint for hardware and system software. But this does not fit well with our wish to allow different manufacturers to produce competitive products. Forcing the making of identical products will preclude healthy competition in the market. The use of detailed blueprint at the hardware level as specification will tie a computer architecture unduly to the state of the hardware of a particular era. We must make sure that there is flexibility to absorb the advancement of hardware technology.

On the other hand, unrestricted extensions to make products attractive can possibly make it very difficult to build standardized human-interface. So in order to design the human-interface for BTRON, the following objective must be met.

(4) Separate clearly the specification and implementation-dependent features and make it possible for the implementors to produce "different" products that do not preclude standardized human-interface.

5. APPROACHES IN BTRON

Approaches described in section 3 all address the problem of meeting the objective (2). They also addressed the objective (3) to some extent. However, the objective (1) is not addressed very well and only paid a little attention during the design process. The objective (4) is usually left out. So during the design of the BTRON human-interface, on top of the known approaches, we have investigated other approaches to meet the objectives (1) and (4).

5.1 STRESS ON TRAINING

In using the metaphor of the real world to design human-interface, we still have to use "magical" actions on the computer to take full advantage of computer's power. Magical actions have no correspondences in the real world.

In order to meet the objective (2), conceptual framework, we do not have to rely on the simulation of real world as long as we can offer consistent model of human-machine interactions. The importance of objective (3), ease of use, can vary depending on how much we stress the importance of training.

Consistent model of human-machine interface can facilitate the training of users. Once users get accustomed to it, the users can guess the working of other applications that use

the same model of interface. When the users can predict the behavior of programs based on their understanding of human-interface model, the working of human-interface is no longer "magical".

Human operators who are part of man-machine systems have the ability to get accustomed to machines. When human operators get the hang of one human-interface, they will begin performing better than they do at first. So the value of training cannot be ignored in discussing the design of new human-interface. If we assume that we can train users adequately, then the design of the interface is such that the users can achieve good performance after initial training period passes. (It could be that untrained users cannot perform well on the system.)

It is important to train system developers and application developer about the standardization of human-interface. The objectives (1) and (4) require much freedom to be left in the specification standard. If restrictive specification cannot be used, the consensus among designers is necessary to achieve the objective (2). Training the designers to reach such consensus is necessary.

In our view, simple system that does not require initial training will not take advantage of the full potential of computer power in the long run. In the TRON project, we aim to build computers which may require training but which can offer good services to trained users. At the same time, we aim at making the training efforts small.

It was our primary goal to make the specification consistent and make the number of exceptional cases small. Aside from the designing of specification and guidelines, we are studying what to prepare for training users, system developers, and application programmers. These include textbook, programs, teaching methods, and core curriculum. Such prepared materials should make the training easier, and thus the objectives (1) and (4) can be paid due attention to.

5.2 THE TRON DESIGN GUIDELINE

The TRON Design Guideline is the norm to design consistent human-interface which is adaptable to many tasks. The TRON Design Guideline in current form can be divided into three levels; concept level, design method level, and specification level. The concept level is the most abstract level. The specification level guideline is derived from the design method level which, in turn, is derived from the concept level. [5]

The difference between design method level and specification level is that the former gives guidelines which do not depend on the nature of particular applications while the latter offers guidelines in various application fields.

For example, "Do not make users make decisions which can be made by the computer program." is a guideline at the concept level. "Show reasonable default values as much as possible when the parameters are set" is the derived guideline at the design method level. The corresponding specification level guideline will be derived for concrete applications such as setting parameters for timer operations, etc. Guidelines at design method level and specification level will be enriched as the number of application programs grow.

5.3 HARDWARE STANDARDIZATION

Minimum hardware standardization was deemed necessary to build similar human-interfaces on many computer systems. Although compatibility at electric or mechanical level will make it easy to build such human-interfaces, the objective (4) precludes such strict standardization. Our aim is to define a reasonable hardware interface and leave the implementation details to each implementor.

Keyboard, pointing device, and some switches have been standardized.

(a) TRON Keyboard Unit

Input of characters, hand-written symbols, or locating object must be done efficiently. Keyboard is the device of choice to input characters. Specifying location and input of hand-written symbols can be done well with an digitizer with pen-like stylus. We call it electronic pen.

The lack of standard in keyboard operation and standard way of locating object is the source of confusion in using computers today. Inputting and editing characters on different computers requires training.

In the TRON project, a keyboard unit which has keyboard and a built-in digitizer has been designed. This is to standardize the input operation and make it easy to train users. It was felt that the current keyboard shape and key layout has fatigue-related problems. So, based on the measurement of hand size, we design the keyboard which is efficient and causes less fatigue. (see *Figure 1*.) [6][7]

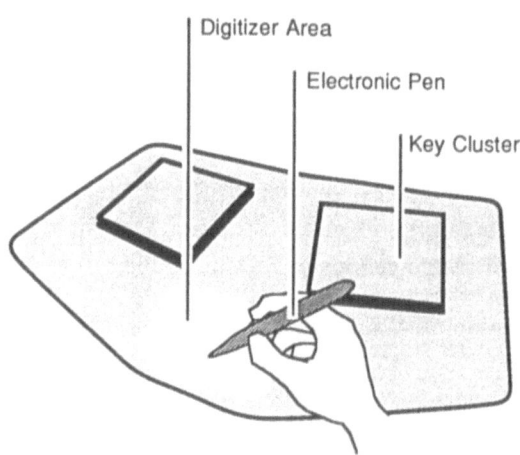

Digitizer Area

Electronic Pen

Key Cluster

Figure 1. The TRON Keyboard Unit

(b) Standardization of Hardware Operations

The users can get confused when the operation of similar hardware devices differs very much. How to change printer papers, how to change the brightness of display, and how to take out floppy disks are such operations. To lessen the confusion, we have provided a standard for such operations with enough freedom to incorporate future technological innovations. Also, we have standardized the menu display of hardware operation methods so that users can know at a glance how to operate hardware devices.

Handling of floppy disks and power switch has caused a of lot of grief for personal computer users. Many computers have floppy disk drives from which users can take out disk at any time. But disk can become broken if the computer is accessing the disk. It will become useless if the content of disk and the content of data in main memory do not match when the user takes it out from the disk drive. In order to avoid such accidents, the BTRON specification calls for an auto eject mechanism, which ejects disk under computer control.

Power switch must be handled carefully, too. Cut off of power in virtual memory environment or during I/O to external storage can be fatal. BTRON specification calls for a use of software power switch mechanism that processes the power-down procedure first before physically cutting off the power under computer control. In order to prepare for power black out, the specification calls for backup battery to keep the computer running until the power-down procedure is finished.

5.4 REAL OBJECT/VIRTUAL OBJECT MODEL.

A data model called Real object/Virtual object model has been designed to meet the objective (1) at the system level, and to achieve high data compatibility.

The data handled by applications are called real objects. Virtual objects are descriptors for real objects. In the real object/virtual object model of BTRON, virtual objects can be incorporated into document or figures together with characters or graphics data. Manipulation of these basic data including virtual objects are performed via system-supplied functions. These system-supplied functions are sometimes called system applications.

Virtual object is displayed as a rectangular figure by Basic Editor, which is a system application. Within this rectangle, pictogram to indicate the type of real object, the name of the real object to which the virtual object points, and other information are displayed. Virtual object is used as the title bar of the window which is opened through the virtual object. (see Figure 2.) Basic Editor, which is a system application, can manipulate virtual objects, characters, and graphical figures. Via Basic Editor, we can invoke various system functions in a uniform manner.

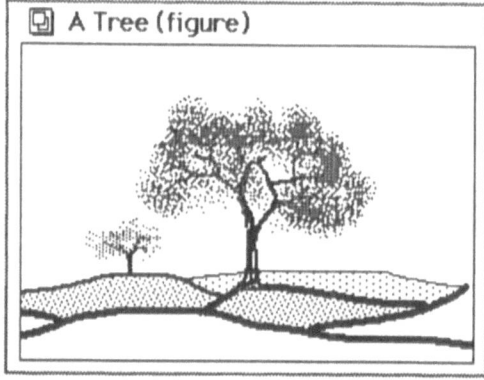

a) Virtual Object

b) Opened Virtual Object

Figure 2. A virtual object (a) and an opened virtual object (b)

The virtual object contained in a real object can point to another real object. Such nesting relation can be used to make directory-like information trees. Several virtual objects can point to the same real object. Hence it is possible to offer multiple viewpoints to look at the same data.

Many existing file systems permits only tree-like directory structure. Relations among real object/virtual objects can be arbitrary network. (see *Figure 3*.) Tree-directory can be mapped into a metaphorical representation of nested paper folders. In a sense, Literalism rendition is possible. However, arbitrary network structure cannot be represented using such metaphor.

Arbitrary network is clearly more flexible than tree-like network. It is easy to adapt to various applications. The human knowledge is likely to be represented using network. The use of such network model and the assumption that the proper training will get the users acquainted with the model adequately distinguishes BTRON from other approaches.

5.5 MMI UTILITIES

Software subsystems of BTRON are operating system nucleus, external shell, and system applications. Operating system nucleus means the conventional OS kernel and graphics

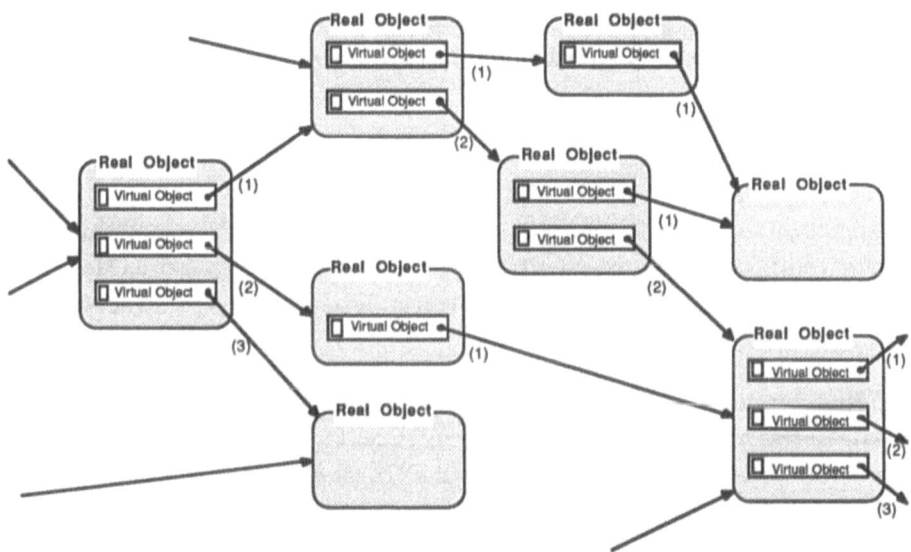

Figure 3. Real Object/Virtual Object Network

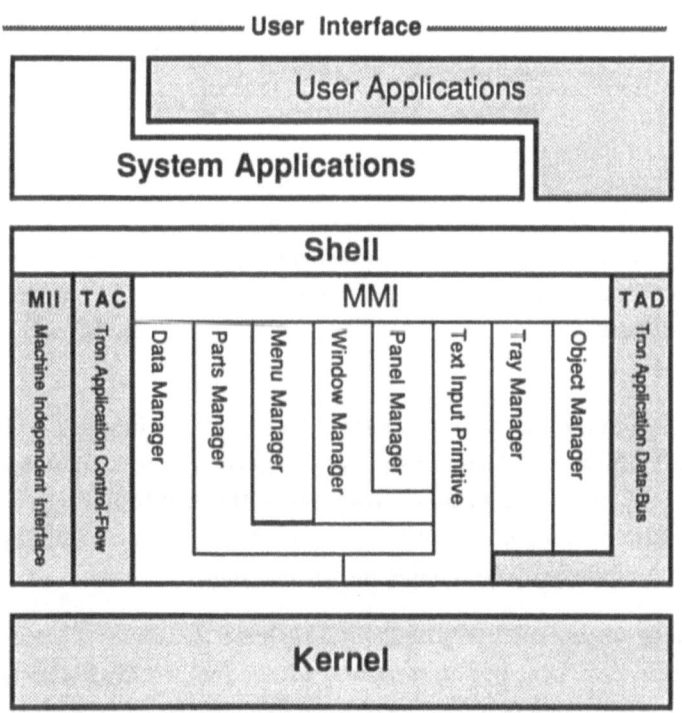

Figure 4. Software Configuration of BTRON-based Systems

primitives. External shell provides high-level utilities for man-machine interactions and other services. The built-in functions for human-interface interaction are provided as MMI utilities at the external shell layer of BTRON. (see *Figure 4.*)

MMI utilities can be divided into 8 groups according to their functions. It should be noted that there is object manager to handle real object/virtual objects in BTRON.

5.6 SYSTEM APPLICATIONS

System applications operate on data consisting of real object/virtual objects. These applications will behave as standard applications to which application designers can model their applications. Also, at the operator level, the system resources will be accessed through system applications.

Basic Editor handles objects and invocation of application programs. Basic Editor can move data across object boundaries. Searching, Printing, and Communication functions are made into standalone system applications. These functions can be applied to the network of real object/virtual objects.

Using only these system applications, BTRON machine can handle simple wordprocessing, drawing, database, and communication. These functions will be enough for individual usage. It is true that specialized application programs will be capable of offering higher functionality and be more efficient. However, the system applications will be available on any machine and will be more familiar to the users.

5.7 OPEN ARCHITECTURE

In the world of science, openness or free exchange of information is a key to the advancement of human knowledge. In engineering fields, too, there are cases that openness is important to quick development of new ideas. Computer technology is such a field.

It is very desirable that computer architecture to be used widely in the society is known to large audience. Unless the basic design philosophy of the computer architecture is known widely, it is impossible to take advantage of the real benefit of such architecture. For example, uniform human-interface across machines becomes fully appreciated only when such human-interface is available on various machines.

In order to bring about such environment, we have to have a standard (or a set of standards). But who will decide the standard? In the real world, de facto standards used by the most powerful company in the market are likely to become the standards of various standard organizations.

The problem of adopting such de facto standard owned by one company is the technology cannot be freely used by others unless the organization which has developed the de facto standard makes the technology open to other parties. So we face a dilemma. While the users would like to see the widely used de facto standard to become industry standard, the company which has developed the technology is not so readily inclined to make the technology open to public after it has spend time and money to develop it. We cannot blame the company for the action.

So it is a natural conclusion that someone should build a standard and make it public and readily accessible to others. The TRON project is doing just that. Openness of its specifications are major goal of the project.

In the TRON project, the government-run University of Tokyo has the initiative in the research and development to produce a set of standard specifications, and many computer companies are joining the research activities directly or indirectly. No claims are going to be made on the standard specifications by the companies. No computer architecture has been designed this way before the TRON project.

Again, it should be noted that the open specifications of the TRON project will be disseminated for nominal fees. By making it an open architecture, we hope that the human-interface of BTRON will be used very widely.

6. CONCLUDING REMARKS

The design of unified human-interface of BTRON has been described. The human-interface should unify the operation methods of devices, have effective initial training, be easy to use, and be uniform and similar across different machines in order to become widely used in the user community. Such human-interface can be used easily on different machines, and users will face less confusion than they do today.

The BTRON approach is to prepare a set of design guidelines and show them to designers to form a general consensus among them, and thus give the designers much freedom in implementation while standardizing the human-interface to an extent. This "lenient" standardization approach can incorporate the advances of technologies in the future into the human-interface and at the same time achieve the similarity to bring real benefits to computer user community.

The goal of the TRON project is to design a set of specifications and develop a number of applications which solve the current problems and to make them widely available in the world. The specifications will cover VLSI microcomputer, system software, human interface and applications running on them. What's more, training of users will be addressed from the beginning.

The approaches discussed in this paper are not pure computer-science approaches. Some of them are definitely business-oriented. This is natural. In order to design human-interface architecture that will be used in a computerized society of tomorrow, we must bear in mind that it must become widely used. The wide use of a human-interface system is its performance index. Only when the same human-interface is used on many machines, the advantage of having similar interface on different machines will be appreciated.

We believe the human-interface designed in the BTRON project will be used widely in the future.

REFERENCES

[1]   K. Sakamura, *"TRON Total Architecture"*, Architecture Workshop in Japan '84.

[2]   K. Sakamura, *"Proposal of a New Unified Model of Man-Machine Interaction in the BTRON Environment,"* Information Processing, Information Processing Soc. Japan, Vol. 26, No. 11, 1985, pp. 1321-1328 (in Japanese).

[3]   D. Smith et al., *"The Star User Interface: An Overview,"* AFIPS Proceedings of National Computer Conference, 51, 1982.

[4]   R. B. Smith, *"Experiences with The Alternate Reality Kit: An Example of the Tension Between Literalism and Magic."* Proceedings of the conference on Human Factors in Computing System and Graphics Interface. (Toronto, April 1987), pp. 61-67.

[5]   K. Sakamura *"BTRON MMI Standardization Project,"* Proceedings of the 34th National Conference of Information Processing Soc. Japan, 1987 pp. 951-952 (in Japanese).

[6]   K. Sakamura, *"Method to Input Japanese Characters in the BTRON Environment,"* paper, Japanese Input Study Group, Information Processing Soc. Japan, 86-JDP-07-2, 1986 pp. 1-8 (in Japanese).

[7]   K. Sakamura, *"The TRON Keyboard and the Data of the Physical Size of the Japanese,"* Proc. Second Symp. Human Interface, 1986, pp. 99-104 (in Japanese).

Ken Sakamura: see *"The Objectives of the TRON Project"* in this proceedings.

Multi-language Character Sets Handling in TAD

Ken Sakamura

Department of Information Science, Faculty of Science, University of Tokyo
Hongo,Tokyo,113 Japan

ABSTRACT

TAD (TRON Application Databus) is the standard to provide data compatibility among the computers designed according to the TRON architecture. This papers describes the multi-language character sets handling in TAD.

The handling of multi-language character sets in TAD features

1) handling multi-language characters sets in uniform manner, and

2) efficient character code system, and

3) independence of application programs from particular character code system, thus making programs easy to port to different countries.

In order to achieve these features, TAD incorporates

1) language specification code to explicitly switch among different languages, and

2) the use of one byte and two bytes code systems to achieve space efficiency, and

3) the use of language-specific environment, which contains the input methods, typesetting rules and parameters, and other language-specific features, and is switched each time the different language character set is specified.

Keywords: Multilingual, Script, BTRON, TAD, TRON Code.

1. INTRODUCTION

Desktop publishing has become very popular thanks to the advent of computing power, and high-resolution bitmap display and laser printers. It has become possible to obtain high-quality printed materials using these equipments. Optical typesetter turns out to be not absolutely necessary to obtain the quality of desktop publishing. The wide spread of desktop publishing has made it very desirable to handle many symbols and many character sets on computers. Some computers, most notably XEROX STAR or APPLE Macintosh II, have addressed the handling of many characters. However, there are still much to be desired. From the viewpoint of someone using Japanese, for example, the handling of Japanese characters on these machines are yet to be improved.

The BTRON (Business-TRON) subproject of the TRON project aims at establishing computer architecture for workstations. In the subproject, TAD (TRON Application Databus) standard is designed to provide data compatibility among computer applications based on the BTRON architecture. In the TAD standard, so called language-specific TAD environment is defined to handle many character sets of many languages. The language-specific TAD environment will support Japanese character set, for example.

The handling of multi-language characters in TAD aims primarily at the handling of documents that have characters from various languages. Simply assigning codes to various character sets of many languages is not enough. The way people write down characters differ from one language the other. For example, characters are written from left to right in English. However, Arabic characters are written from right to left. Line break can, in principle, occur anywhere in Japanese text. English writing does not permit such freedom. It must occur between words or in permitted positions within a word using a hyphen. In this way, each language has a set of rules to handle the characters in documents. The phrase, language-specific TAD environment, describes an environment that incorporates these rules on top of the particular character code system assigned to the character set.

The second objective of the multi-language character sets handling in TAD is the efficiency. If we count characters in many character sets of various languages in the world, the total will exceeds 100,000. Simple-minded coding will require three bytes assigned to each character. However, in view of the fact that majority of the document contain only one language, we need a better coding scheme. Many European language character sets require only 8-bit byte code to handle characters. Simple-minded three bytes code is a waste of space for these languages.

The third aim of the language-specific TAD environment is to offer application programs the portability over national boundaries. Many applications should become language-independent by taking advantage of the language-related services offered by the BTRON-based OS.

In this paper, we describe the current design of language-specific TAD environment.

2. HANDLING OF MULTI-LANGUAGE CHARACTER SETS.

2.1 CHARACTERS IN THE WORLD

It is said that the number of currently used languages in the world are between 3,000 and 4000. Primary among these are about 200 languages, and the most popular 100 languages can cover 95 percent of world population. [3] Characters used in languages which are in some sense important (for example, having newspapers written in it) can be classified into 29 character families summarized in *Table 1*. [4]

Characters used in English, French, and German belong to the Latin family. Their alphabets are very similar. Some languages use several character sets. For example, Japanese uses *Hiragana*, *Katakana* and Chinese characters. Korean uses *Hangul* and Chinese characters. Characters used in Esperanto, an artificial language, belong to the Latin family.

In practical applications such as used in business, support of these 29 character families (we call these families SCRIPTs) will suffice. However, for academic purposes, more SCRIPTs must be supported. In academic circles, foreign characters or characters used in ancient civilization are now handled in computer programs. But the way they are handled are different among researchers, and this causes much difficulty to in sharing database.

Multi-language character sets handling in TAD allows the uniform handling of such characters in one document.

One policy in the multi-language characters sets handling in TAD is to assign code to almost any conceivable character. This task takes time and needs much support from people in many fields and from all over the world. But this policy is the best method to handle characters of the world on computers.

Ad-hoc code assignment done by the user to many symbols on many applications systems uses "unused" codes for such purposes. But this makes the data less portable. Sending font data together with the document may alleviate some of the problems. But user-prepared fonts cannot be used on printers with different resolution or with different font encoding. Hence, we believe that assigning codes to special symbols in various application fields is one good way to solve the problems associated with handling these characters and symbols on computers.

2.2 LANGUAGE-SPECIFIC RULES

Each language has a set of rules that governs the way the characters are laid out when they are written. Character sets and these rules define the way a language is handled on computers. We describe some of these rules below.

(a) Direction

As we have stated, languages are written from left to right, from left to right, or from top to bottom. 9 such directional models are proposed to describe the way characters are written in modern languages as well as extinct languages.[4] Some languages use complex writing directions. For example, switching of direction takes place on alternate lines, or mirror image is used in some cases. The modern Japanese uses both horizontal and vertical directions. Left to right writing is standard for horizontal writing although right to left writing is sometimes accepted. (They often appear in the signs on the side bodies of vehicles.)

(b) Change of character shape in context

Arabic is known for the change of character shapes in context. There are independent, initial, medial and final forms which are used when the character is used alone, or preceded and/or followed by other characters. In German, the letter s changes its shape when it is at the end of a word.

(c) Usage of special symbols.

In French, ' « ' and ' » ' are called "guillemets" used for quoting. In German, the same set of symbols are used for quoting, but their order is reversed; ' » ' comes before ' « '. The usage of ' , ' to divide the large number for ease of reading and the usage of ' . ' to represent the decimal point of a number are totally reversed in some languages. These usage of special symbols must be recognized to treat numbers correctly or to handle linebreak and other formatting rules correctly.

(d) Combined Symbol (ligature)

For aesthetic reasons, some characters in tandem may be combined into one symbol called ligature. For example, ' f ' followed by ' f ', ' i ' or ' l ' are combined into one symbol in printed English text. The spelling of these symbols must be recognized as the tandem combination of separate characters although the outlook on display seems one symbol. Otherwise searching through database looking for these character combinations will become very difficult. At the same time, when these characters are capitalized or placed with much space in between, they must be displayed as separate characters.

(e) A Character That Looks Like Two.

In Spanish, CH is the fourth letter of the alphabet and is tread as one character. In Spanish dictionary, words that starts with CH comes not under C but under CH. We can assign code to CH, but still we have to show them as C and H when the character spacing is large.

(f) Formatting rules

Japanese language allows line breaking almost anywhere. English, on the other, does not allow line breaking within a word. Use of hyphen is necessary to break a line inside a word and only in restricted positions. Many formatting rules adopted on word processors on personal computers are subsets of the many formatting rules obeyed in print shops.

(g) Input method

Input of characters can pose problems when larger character sets must be handled. Japanese, Korean, and Chinese are such examples. Many methods have been proposed. Even small language character sets have posed problems. For example, ' ä ' has to be input using two key strokes on popular keyboards.

2.3 SIZE OF CHARACTER SET

Languages can be roughly separated into two groups; one that uses several hundred characters, the other that uses more than 5,000 characters. Many languages including English belong to the former group. The latter group consists of the languages that use Chinese characters and Korean that uses about 4,000 Hangul characters.

The size of the character set affects the size of character codes to be used on computers. In order to handle the former group, 1 byte character code is likely. For the latter, 2 byte character code is necessary.

The currently available largest Chinese-character to Japanese dictionary is *Daikanwa Jiten*. [5] This is a lexicon that gives Japanese meaning, pronunciation for easy *Kanji* entry. (Chinese character is called *Kanji* in Japanese).

This dictionary has about 50,000 Kanji entries. Of course, some of these are not used daily in modern Japan. However, there are characters that are used today and are not in the large dictionary. So, the number of *Kanji*s that must be handled exceeds 50,000.

3. MULTI-LANGUAGE CHARACTER SETS HANDLING IN TAD

3.1 BASIC POLICY

In the TAD data exchange standard, the following policies have been adopted in order to handle the problems outlined in the previous sections.

(a) Identification of language-specific algorithms

In order to make application program language-independent as much as possible, language-specific algorithms necessary to handle a particular language on computers must be identified and packaged so that these algorithms can be switched when a program moves from one language environment to the other.

Input algorithms are used to input character strings from input devices such as keyboard. Output algorithms are used to display characters strings in language dependent way. Output algorithms include algorithms to handle different fonts. For example, smooth connection of longhand characters should be handled.

Sorting is also an important operation on character strings. Sorting algorithm differs from one language to the other. In ASCII code system for English alphabet, we can use simple code order. In general, we need complex algorithms. In German, ' ö ' must comes after ' o '. But *König* must come before *Konzert*. Thus, ' ö ' and ' o ' must be handled very carefully.

In TAD, these algorithms are packaged into a language-specific operating environment. This operating environment is an insulation layer for application programs to deal with the idiosyncrasies of many languages. Language-specific environments will be switchable so that application programs does not have to pay much attention to the special characteristics of languages. Then most language-dependent parts of application programs will be the message data that must be prepared for target languages.

(b) **Language-Specifier Code**

In order to explicitly switch from one language environment to the other, language-specifier codes are used to indicate such transition.

(c) **Separation of** *display* **and** *storage*

Storage here refers to the way the text data is stored, and *display* refers to the way the text is represented on a paper or on a computer display. The way text is represented can differ depending on fonts, or other display parameters even when the underlying stored text is the same. For example, consecutive ' f ' and ' i ' can be displayed separately or as a combined one ligature. It is necessary to separate clearly the information about the text itself and the way text is displayed. In TAD, how the text is displayed is dynamically derived from the stored information.

(d) **Use of Character GROUP**

Each of the small character set languages, such as English or German, has less than 256 characters. However, if we consider the languages in the Latin SCRIPT, the number of different characters exceeds 256. Hence, simple-minded character code assignment requires two bytes code system for Latin SCRIPT characters. However, as we all know, that there are common characters used in the languages in Latin SCRIPT group.

In order to handle the problem, we introduce a subset of SCRIPT character set. Each subset is called GROUP. For European languages, GROUP can be small enough to use 1 byte code system within it. We define multiple GROUP's so that all the characters in one SCRIPT falls in GROUP(s) and each character set of French, English, etc. is subset of one GROUP. We define a mapping of GROUP code to SCRIPT code. The SCRIPT code is two bytes long.

In this way, the small character set languages can use one byte GROUP code system, and the characters of the languages in a SCRIPT has a consistent character code system. We extend the notion of SCRIPT a bit further by incorporating additional display symbols such as the ones to stand for ' fi ' and ' fl '. GROUP code is used to store text while SCRIPT code is used at the final stage of display.

(e) Hierarchy in Language Environment

LANGUAGE, GROUP, SCRIPT, and FONT layers comprise the TAD language-specific environment. (see *Figure 1.*)

LANGUAGE layer is where we deal with the normal notion of "different" languages such as German, English, Arabic, Chinese, and Japanese. This layer will have as its components, input algorithms, display algorithms, sorting algorithms, and the mapping function from character code to the GROUP code. The code system used in this layer is derived by means of mapping from a subset of GROUP code. Actually, the mapping function of language layer code to GROUP code is uniquely determined when the GROUP layer is fixed, But, because the language switching is explicitly done at the language layer level by the application program, the mapping function is attached to the language layer.

GROUP layer is used to store text as code. Language-specifier code determines both the LANGUAGE and the GROUP. This layer is used to handle languages that can have different SCRIPTs. For example, Uighur (spoken in Sinkiang Uighur autonomous region in China) can be written in both Latin SCRIPT and Russian SCRIPT.

Mapping function to GROUP is simple for small character set languages. We can build a table that has at most 256 entries to show the mapping. However, languages that uses large character set will build huge tables if such mapping table is built. So, for most of the characters, the mapping is identity, that is the language-layer code is equal to the GROUP code.

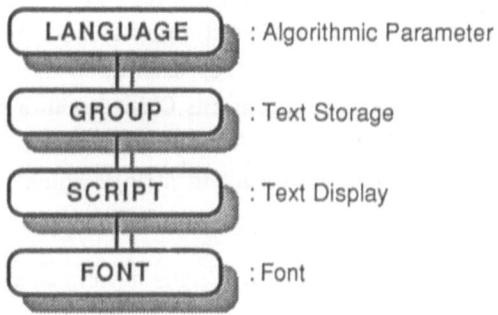

Figure 1. layers in the TAD language-specific environment

SCRIPT Layer defines the character code for all the characters in languages that belong to one SCRIPT group. This layer also handles the display function to some extent.

Let us take Latin SCRIPT for example. In the case of Latin SCRIPT, several Latin language character set codes are mapped to the Latin SCRIPT code. Each Latin language uses one byte character code. Each of them share some common characters such as A, B, and C. Latin SCRIPT code are two bytes long. There are only ONE entry for each of A, B, and C in Latin SCRIPT code. The one byte code for A, B, and C in each of the Latin language code system is mapped to the two bytes SCRIPT code for A, B, and C.

Because SCRIPT layer handles part of display functions, combined symbols which are necessary for display are included as characters in the SCRIPT character code system. The symbols which are assigned the SCRIPT character code are the ones which must be designed when new font is designed.

FONT layer defines a font code for each SCRIPT. FONT means a recognized characteristic shape of a particular drawing style of characters. Helvetica, Courier, Mincho (明朝 for Japanese) are some examples of fonts. When only the thickness of character stroke is different, it is regarded that the different font is used. Each font set assigns codes to all conceivable characters and symbols so that all these characters and symbols can be displayed. But implementors are allowed to prepare only the necessary images for often used characters.

3.2 INPUT ALGORITHM

Use of packages of language-specific algorithms is a way to achieve language independence of application programs. *Figure 2* shows the process how input data from input device is transformed into the GROUP code strings. When the user does certain input operations, the Character Input Device Driver (CIDD) transforms the data into the character code string.

Let us take Japanese input as an example. CIDD first transforms the key location code (the code assigned to easy keytop in the keyboard) into a *Kana* code. Then the input *Kana* character string is transformed into another representation used in the layer. That is, *Kana* string is transformed into one that contains Chinese characters. Input algorithms can be applied in tandem. So called *Roma-ji Kana-Kanji* transform method transforms a Roman alphabet strings from CIDD into a *Kana* string, which is subsequently transformed into one with Chinese characters.

CIDD's can be switched to handle input from various devices such as voice input device, character reader, or keyboard. (see *Figure 2*.)

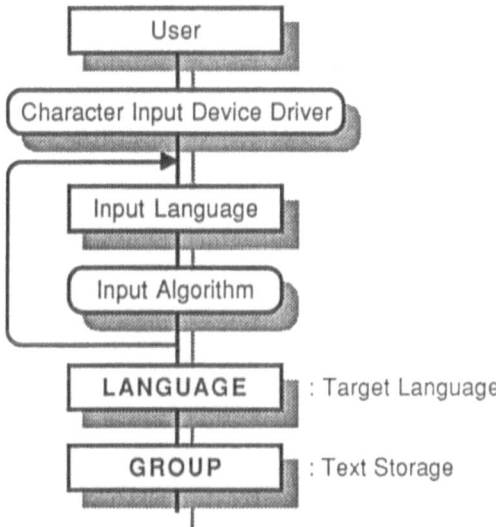

Figure 2. Input Process

4. TRON CODE

TRON character code system uses both one byte and two bytes codes. It uses language-specifier code to switch between from one language to the other thus making it possible for both one byte code and two bytes code to coexist.

4.1 TRON ONE BYTE CODE

TRON one byte code has control codes, character codes, language specifier codes, escape codes, and other special character codes. (See *Figure 3*.)

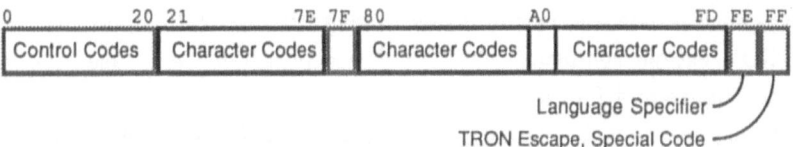

Figure 3. TRON One Byte Code

There are 34 control characters which are from hexadecimal (00) to (20), and (7E). They have basically similar meaning to the corresponding ones in the ASCII. Among these control characters, the following characters have special meaning as text separator.

(09)	Tab character.
(0A)	End paragraph and start new one.
(0D)	End line and start new one.
(20)	Separator.

Other control characters can be used for controlling communications. But they do not have special meaning as components of text.

Character (20) is a separator. Separator is different from (A0), blank. Separator is used to show the logical separation of words, or clauses. How the separator character is handled depends on the languages. In English, it is regarded as space character. It is used as the linebreak character or as a variable-length space character for proportional spacing display.

Character codes are from (21) to (7E), from (80) to (9F), (A0) to (FD). (A0) is a blank character and is treated as a space with fixed width. In English, this is called as required space, and is treated as a character that belongs to a word and linebreak cannot occur before or after the character.

Language-specifier code (FE) is used to specify language and GROUP when the following code is from (21) to (7E) or from (80) to (FD). Also, this sequence can be repeated to incorporate more language and GROUP combinations.

(FE) (FE)* (xx)   where (xx) is from (21) to (7E) or from (80) to (FD), (x)* stands for a null or repetition of character (x).

(FE) and one following character can specify up to 220 language and GROUP combinations. Another use of (FE) immediately following the previous (FE) can increase the number of specifiable combinations by 220.

When TRON special code (FF) is followed by a code from (21) to (7E), it is regarded as a special TRON code. These are used by TACL and will be embedded within text data.

When TRON special code (FF) is followed by a code from (80) top (FE), the code sequence is used as TRON escape sequence. The TRON escape sequence is used as separators between text, figure and *Fusen* segments. (*Fusen* means attached memo in Japanese.) This escape sequence can be extended using (FE) as in the case of language-specifier code.

(FF) (xx)   where (xx) is from (80) to (7E).

(FF) (FE) (FE)* (yy)   where (yy) is from (21) to (7E) or from (80) to (FD).

Two bytes escape sequence can represent 126 different separators. Each addition use of (FE) can increase the number of separators by 220.

4.2 TRON TWO BYTES CODE

The code map of TRON two bytes code has language has language-specifier zone, TRON escape code, TRON special character code, and four character code zone called **A, B, C,** and **D**. (See *Figure 4*.)

Control characters including tab, paragraph, newline, and other separators coexist as one byte character with other two bytes TRON codes.

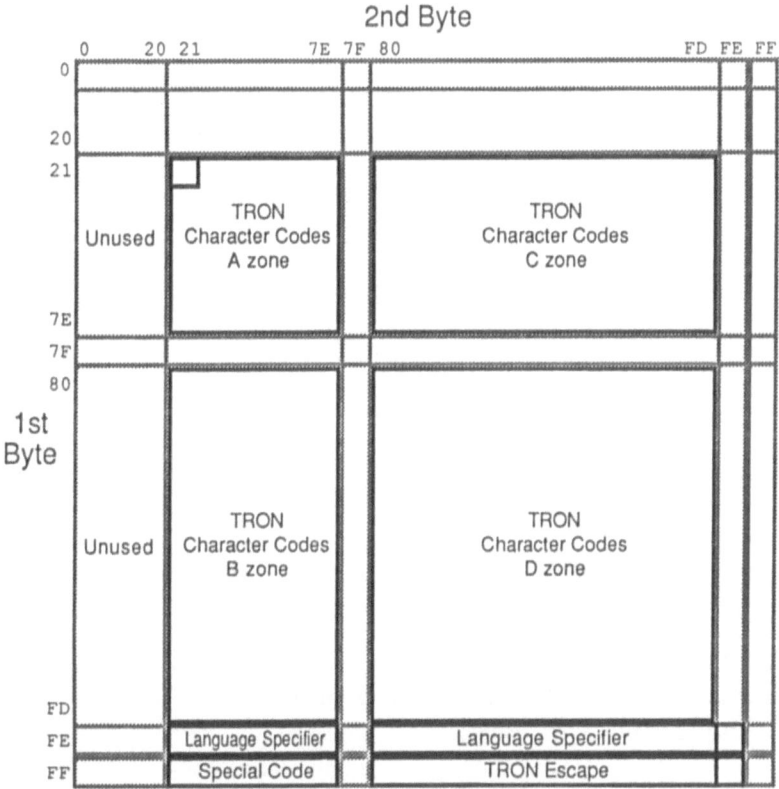

Figure 4. TRON Two Bytes Code

TRON character codes fall in the code area

  (21)(21)...(7E)(7E) called **A** zone that has 8,836 characters,
  (80)(21)...(FD)(7E) called **B** zone that has 11,844 characters,
  (21)(80)...(7E)(FD) called **C** zone that has 11,844 characters, and
  (80)(80)...(FD)(FD) called **D** zone that has 15,876 characters.
  In total, there are 48,400 codes.

(21)(21) is blank with fixed width. Other function codes such as language specifier, TRON special code, and TRON escape sequence are the same as in the case of TRON one byte code.

4.3 LANGUAGE-SPECIFIER CODE

Language-specifier code is used to pick up a combination of language and GROUP. The assignment of these specifying codes are now being done. Some examples are shown in *Table 2*.

Table 2

Two byte	Language	GROUP	Comment
	Japanese	Japanese	Common
	Japanese	Japanese-A	Rare Characters
	Korean	Korean	Hangul and Chinese
	Chinese	Chinese-A	Simplified Chinese
One byte	Language	GROUP	
	English	Latin-1	
	French	Latin-1	
	...	...	
	Swahili	Latin-1	
	Tagalog	Latin-1	
	...	...	
	Rumanian	Latin-2	
	Polish	Latin-2	
	Esperanto	Latin-2	
	...	...	
	Vietnamese	Latin-3	
	...	...	
	Greek	Greek	
	...	...	
	Arabic	Arabic-1	
	...	...	

In *Table 2*, the additional letter or number at the end of GROUP have special meaning. Number means that a GROUP covers several languages. Letter means that one language requires more than one GROUP code sets.

4.4 JAPANESE TRON CODE

TRON code for Japanese is two bytes long. GROUP of Japanese is for the ordinary characters which are defined in JIS X0208 code set and some additional characters and symbols.

GROUP of Japanese-A is for rarely used characters.

A zone in GROUP of Japanese code system are almost equal to the ones in JIS X0208 code except for Latin alphabets in JIS X0208. Since the alphabets in JIS X0208 are not enough for serious applications, **B** zone is used. The rest of **B** zone are used for some popular characters which are not covered by JIS X0208. **C** and **D** zone are used for less often used characters. Characters not found in GROUP of Japanese are covered by the GROUP code of Japanese-A.

The Latin alphabets covered by the GROUP code of Japanese are not regarded as the alphabets covered by the GROUP code of Latin-1. Hence these symbols are regarded as Japanese character symbols. Hence, if you really would like to mix English and Japanese text, for example, you must switch between English and Japanese and use GROUP code of Latin-1. However, since the many use of Roman alphabets in Japanese are for short titles or acronyms, the Roman alphabets exist in the GROUP code of Japanese so that users can use these symbols for short titles and acronyms without bothering to switch between languages.

4.5 GROUP OF LATIN-1

Figure 5 shows the GROUP code assignment for characters of the languages of Latin SCRIPT group. From (00) to (7F), it is the same with ASCII. Latin-1 GROUP code can support the languages in *Table 3* at the least.

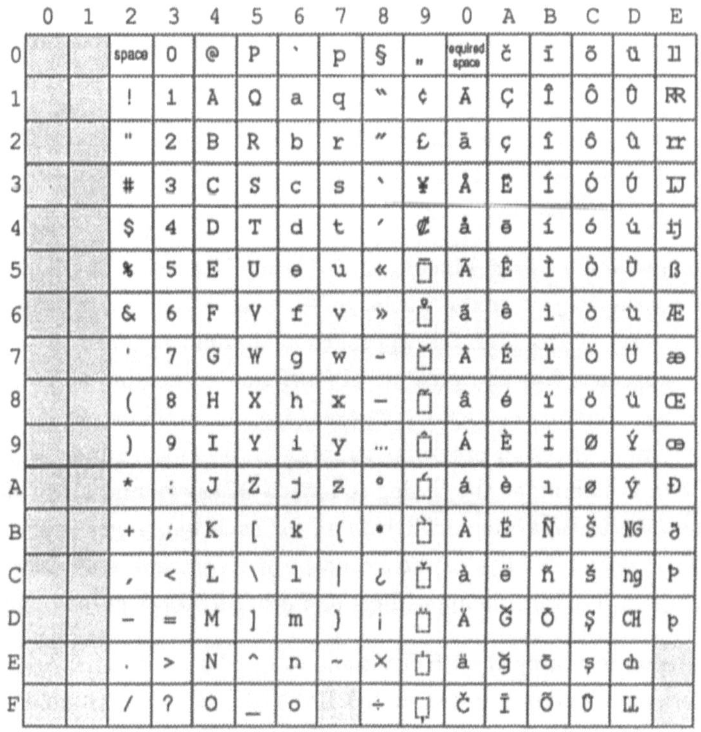

	0	1	2	3	4	5	6	7	8	9	0	A	B	C	D	E
0			space	0	@	P	`	p	§	„	required space	č	ī	õ	ŭ	Џ
1			!	1	A	Q	a	q	ʽ	¢	Ă	ç	î	ô	û	ŔŔ
2			"	2	B	R	b	r	"	£	ã	ç	ï	õ	ŭ	ɪɪ
3			#	3	C	S	c	s	`	¥	Ã	Ė	í	ó	ú	Ĳ
4			$	4	D	T	d	t	´	¢	å	ē	ī	ó	ú	ŧj
5			٭	5	E	U	e	u	«	Ő	Ą	Ê	ì	ò	Ů	ß
6			&	6	F	V	f	v	»	Ő	ã	ê	ī	ò	ù	Æ
7			'	7	G	W	g	w	-	Ő	Á	É	ĭ	ö	ŭ	æ
8			(	8	H	X	h	x	-	Ő	â	é	ĭ	ŏ	ŭ	Œ
9			)	9	I	Y	i	y	...	Ô	Á	È	ī	ø	Ý	œ
A			٭	:	J	Z	j	z	°	Ő	á	è	ı	ø	ý	Đ
B			+	;	K	[	k	{	•	Ő	À	Ë	Ñ	Š	NG	ð
C			,	<	L	\	l	|	¿	Ő	à	ë	ñ	š	ng	Þ
D			-	=	M	]	m	}	¡	Ő	Ä	Ğ	Ö	Ş	CH	þ
E			.	>	N	^	n	~	×	Ő	ä	ğ	õ	ş	ch	
F			/	?	O	_	o		÷	Ợ	č	ī	õ	ű	ĿĿ	

Figure 5. Latin-1 GROUP

Table 3

Afrikaans
Danish
Dutch
English
Fijian
Finnish
French
German
Ilocano
Indonesian
Italian
Japanese (Roma-ji, i.e. Roman writing)
Pilipino (Tagalog)
Portuguese
Sebuano
Spanish
Swahili
Swedish
Turkish

5. SUMMARY

Multi-language character sets handling in TAD aims at (1) handling documents with many characters from more than one language, (2) using efficient code system, and (3) making application programs language-independent as much as possible.

In order to achieve these objectives, TAD employs (1) language-specifier code to explicitly switch languages, (2) mixing one-byte and two bytes code to gain space efficiency, and (3) switchable language-specific environment which has typesetting rules, and other parameters for a particular language.

XEROX STAR [6] and APPLE Macintosh II [7] are examples of computer systems to handle many character sets of the world. STAR uses a code system for multi-national characters, and uses object-oriented approach to handle program independence from language. The approach has the problem of inefficient execution of programs based on object-oriented paradigm on current hardware. Also, the architecture is a closed one and is not accessible to application programs running on other machines. Macintosh II uses the timing of font switching as the timing to switch SCRIPTs and associated algorithms. It requires the user to separately switch fonts for each languages used in a document. The Macintosh II does not have explicit concept of "language" and may not be able to handle differences in typesetting algorithms and other features of languages.

In TAD, the system is equipped with functions to handle multi-language character sets, and these functions are offered in hierarchy; LANGUAGE layer, GROUP layer, SCRIPT layer, and FONT layer. It will become easier then to write application programs which are language independent than it is now. In this way, the TAD standard helps the dissemination and sharing of information.

Lastly we would like to thank the members of the BTRON subgroup of the TRON Association and volunteers who have contributed to the compilation of character sets and classification of languages in the world.

REFERENCES

[1] K. Sakamura, *"The TRON Project,"* IEEE MICRO, pp.8 - 14, Apr. 1987 Vol. 7, No. 2.

[2] K. Sakamura, *"BTRON: The Business-oriented Operating System,"* IEEE MICRO, pp. 53-65, Apr. 1987 Vol. 7, No. 2.

[3] K. Katzner, *"The Language of the World,"* Routlege & Kegan Paul, 1986.

[4] A. Nakanishi, *"Writing Systems of the World,"* Charles E. Tuttle Company, Inc., 1980.

[5] T. Morohashi, *"Daikanwa Jiten"*, Taisyukan, 1986 (in Japanese)

[6] D. Smith, et al., *"The Star User Interface: An Overview,"* AFIPS Proceedings of National Computer Conference, 51, 1982.

[7] G.Williams and T.Thompson, *"The Apple Macintosh II,"* BYTE,pp.85-106,Apr. 1987. Vol.12, No.4.

Ken Sakamura: see *"The Objectives of the TRON Project"* in this proceedings.

An Implementation Based upon the BTRON Specification

Yoshiaki Kushiki, Makoto Ando, Masaaki Kobayashi, Yoshihiko Imai
Central Research Laboratories, Matsushita Electric Industrial Co., Ltd.
Yagumo-nakamachi, Moriguchi, Osaka, 570 Japan

Ken Sakamura
Department of Information Science, Faculty of Science, University of Tokyo
Hongo,Tokyo,113 Japan

ABSTRACT

BTRON stands for Business-oriented operating system (OS) specification in the TRON (The Realtime Operating system Nucleus) project and is a computer architecture for office workstation. The major objective is to offer unified man-machine interface (MMI) and handling multi-media data. Special features of the BTRON specification are (1) unified MMI method, (2) data transportability, (3) handling multi-media data. In order to archive these objectives, the BTRON specification proposes a data model called the real object/virtual object model. To evaluate the BTRON specification, the nucleus and extended nucleus were developed on the experimental 80286 based system, and evaluated. In this paper, the software architecture of the BTRON specification, functional features, and implementation of our experimental system are discussed.

KEY WORDS

BTRON, 80286, Nucleus, Extended Nucleus, the real object/virtual object model

1. INTRODUCTION [1],[2],[3],[4],[5],[6],[7]

The most important objective of the BTRON design is to offer unified and easy-to-use man-machine interface and to assure data compatibility among systems built according to the BTRON specification. The second is to establish a method to pass control and data among application programs so that computers can simulate the division of labor found in society. The third is to realize a documentation management system which has the expressive power of ordinary paper, such as the capability to mix text and figures, and which can reflect the logical structure of documents. The forth is to treat many different character sets including Japanese in a uniform manner.

We have proposed a new data model called the real object/virtual object model in order to achieve the third objective, namely the implementation of a documentation management system with rich expressive power and structure.

In this paper, the software architecture, the real object/virtual object model and other features are described. Also, we discuss the implementation and evaluation of the experimental system.

2. OUR APPROACH TO THE IMPLEMENTATION OF THE BTRON CONCEPT

Features of the BTRON architecture are described below, including:

(1) Unified man-machine interface (MMI),
(2) The real object/virtual object model,
(3) Accommodation of multiple-languages,
(4) Realization of real time performance, and
(5) Accommodation of multi-media.

(1) Unified Man-Machine Interface

In solving the problem of existing computer systems having "different man-machine interfaces even for operating similar jobs",the BTRON specifications are designed so that "the user can operate systems using BTRON consistently in all aspects". In other words, it is designed so as to unify an operational environment for computer systems, which includes operation models and operation methods.

To realize the BTRON specification-based OS, software parts for a unified man-machine interface (MMI) are developed. By using these parts, unification of operational methods can be achieved even in different applications. As to an object handling method, data handling in the desktop environment is standardized based on the real object/virtual object model. On the other hand the OS nucleus supports the following three features:

1) At the start-up of the system, each software part can be installed into the system by inputting the parts' names;

2) At any time when an application program requires some software parts, each part can be installed into the system; and

3) At any time the part can be removed from the system.

(2) Real Object/Virtual Object Model

In the BTRON specification-based OS , the accumulation of data is referred to as a real object , and this is referenced by a tag called a virtual object. On a bitmapped display , virtual objects are shown as a collection of rectangles (Figure 1). The displayed data as the virtual objects are independent of what the real objects will be. Operators can manage the document structure to handle the multiple virtual objects on paper. For example, when the operator moves the virtual object of image data, the position of image data corresponding to the virtual object will be moved on the print out as indicated. By pointing to the rectangles with a pointing device, the viewport displayed on the bitmapped display becomes an "opened" virtual object. Opened virtual objects display the contents of the real objects. Specific applications can handle the displayed contents of opened virtual objects.

In order to realize the real object/virtual object model in existing computer systems at a high efficiency, the operating system interface should be designed to accommodate to the real object/virtual object model. Therefore, the file management system for BTRON has the following features:

1) File configuration in the order of variable-length records(record stream);

2) Reference to network formed by links between virtual objects in files;

3) File access controlled by a user level for protecting the file contents.

In the real object/virtual object model, a file corresponds to the real object and a link corresponds to the virtual object one to one. The virtual object is directly managed by the BTRON file management system. The contents of the virtual object are kept by the same function of the BTRON file management system. The features of the BTRON real object/virtual object model can be summarized as follows:

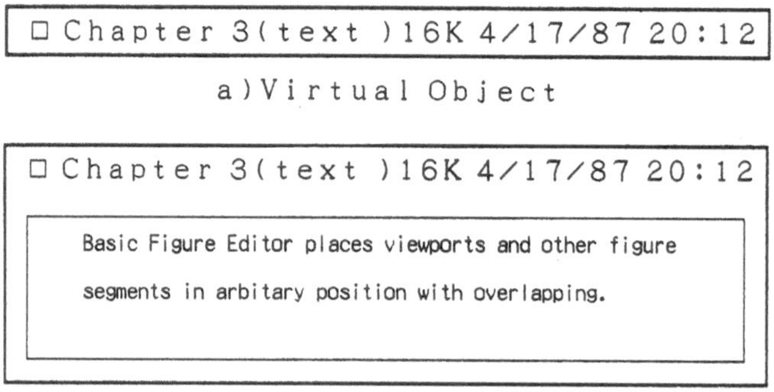

```
┌─────────────────────────────────────────────────┐
│ □ Chapter 3( text )16K 4/17/87 20:12 │
└─────────────────────────────────────────────────┘
```

a)Virtual Object

```
┌─────────────────────────────────────────────────┐
│ □ Chapter 3( text )16K 4/17/87 20:12 │
│  ┌────────────────────────────────────────────┐ │
│  │ Basic Figure Editor places viewports and other figure │ │
│  │ segments in arbitary position with overlapping. │ │
│  └────────────────────────────────────────────┘ │
└─────────────────────────────────────────────────┘
```

b)Opened Virtual Object

Figure 1. Virtual object

1) Relationships between real objects are expressed as linked network configurations;

2) Links in real objects are expressed by virtual object and/or "opened" virtual objects;

3) Data in real objects can be arrayed in one and/or two dimensions;

4) Links can co-exist with data and can be handled in the same way as data;

5) "Opened" virtual objects operate as viewports which describe the contents of a real object;

6) Therefore "opened" virtual objects may be nested; and

7) Since viewports are "opened" virtual objects and also data in real objects, these are expressed as sequentially arranged rectangles which have a certain order, of two-dimensionally arranged rectangles which may overlap each other.

If annotations or memorandums are embedded as virtual objects in sentences, this model is applicable to such a document management that the details can be referred by opening the virtual objects if needed. Also it is possible to apply to an outline processor where sentence structure data including volumes, chapters and paragraphs are to be expressed as an inserted slave relation to the real object.

(3) Multiple-Language Capability

The purposes to realize multiple-language capability in the BTRON are as follows:

1) Data Exchange: "multiple-language data on a computer shall be processed one at a time."

For example, it is expected that the data representing documents written in different native languages, such as Japanese, English, ...etc., will be transmitted through international computer networks onto one computer. In this circumstance, the computer is required to, for instance, display the document data on the monitor screen and edit them as needed.

The BTRON specification-based OS is designed to implement either "simultaneous multiple-language inter-mixed process" when a plurality of native languages exist in one document, or "multiple language switched process" where each of the native languages is required to be used in one document. The TRON code is specified as an efficient character code system to handle such multiple-language data.

2) Software compatibility: "Each software package shall handle a plurality of native languages."

For example, if software developed in the U.S.A. can be used in Japan without any modification, worldwide program distribution will be easily and naturally expanded due to program compatibility. "Object code compatibility" and "source code compatibility" are used properly as a compatibility level. To assure this software compatibility, it is necessary to separate a program into a language dependent part and a language independent part.

(4) Realization of Real Time Operation

"Assuring that the system has real time end-user performance" is one of the unique features of the BTRON specifications. In the BTRON specification-based OS, input data from a keyboard/pointing device are put together into "events". An application program is described as a corresponding process based on the input events. This event driven programming is one of the important factors for an interactive operation program in which MMI is a key issue. To realize the event driven programming, the system has an event management function, which enables the event driven programming under a multi-processing environment.

(5) Multi-Media Capability

"It is generally required for current computer systems to have a multi-media capability which enables the system to handle audio and visual data as well as document and graphic data." "In the personal computer environment, data which is handled by the computer is expanded from numerical to character data, and further to graphic data. In the future, even in a personal computer area, it will be required to handle large scale information, such as motion video information and audio information, which requires real time operation. Therefore, a future computer should have a capability to handle various media information efficiently so as to be a multi-media machine."

To realize those requirements, the BTRON system has a file management function to secure continual recorded areas on a physical disk so as to handle a large capacity file, such as image data, at a high speed.

3. ARCHITECTURE OF BTRON 286 SYSTEM [8],[9]

To evaluate the BTRON specification which is an operating system specification based on the TRON concept, we have built an experimental system. This system has an 80286 for CPU, a 3.5-inch floppy disk drive and 20 MB hard disk , with 2 MB of main memory , a 1024 X 1024 bitmapped VRAM , an ergonomically designed keyboard and tablet with electric pen built to the TRON specifications. The 2HD floppy disk drive is an auto eject type that is standard in the BTRON specification.

The BTRON specification consists of nucleus, extended nucleus and system application of the BTRON specification. The software configuration is given in Figure 2.

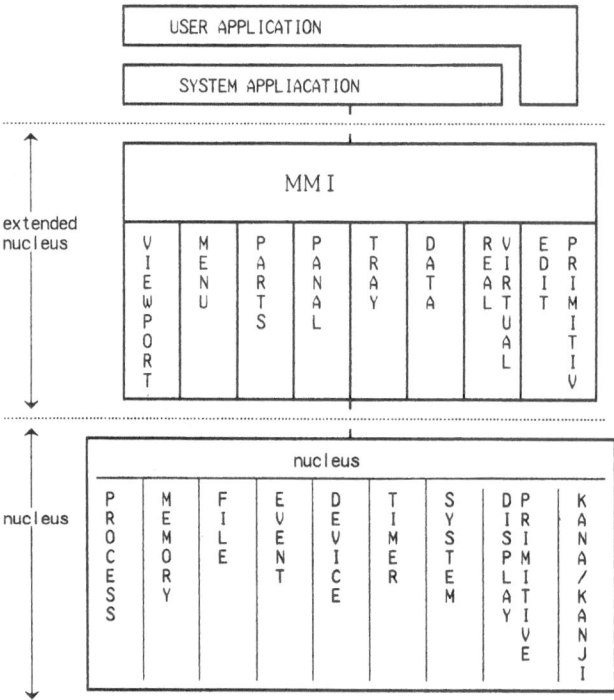

Figure 2. Software structure of the BTRON specification

4. IMPLEMENTATION OF REAL/VIRTUAL OBJECT MODEL [10]

The real object/virtual object model is realized by the functions of the file management system in the BTRON nucleus, and the real object/virtual object manager, in the extended nucleus, which expresses the data structure visually and manages the execution of application programs.

Application programs can be operated as the virtual objects and become executable in the BTRON system by means of registering to the real object/virtual object manager. On the other hand, application programs request the file management system to take out the link pointer(See 5.(9)) and access to the files. Further, application programs request the MMI manager and the display primitive to operate viewports and display menus, characters and figures.

The relationship of the above-mentioned softwar are shown in Figure 3.

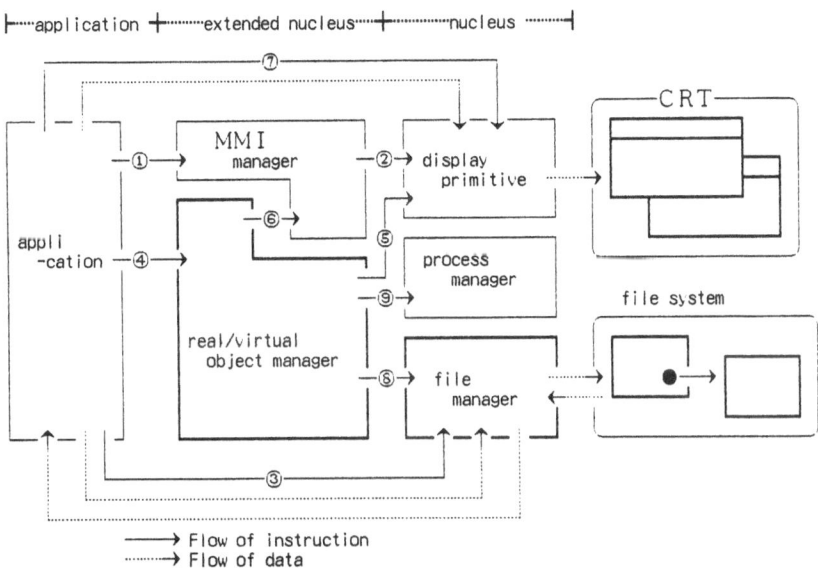

① Request of operating viewports/menus
② Request of indicating viewports/menus
③ Request of operating files
④ Request of operating virtual objects
⑤ Request of indicating virtual objects
⑥ Request of operating viewports/menus
⑦ Request of displaying characters/figures
⑧ Request of obtaining informations of files
⑨ Request of creating processes

Figure 3 . Relationship of software in order to implement the real object/virtual object model

Thereal object/virtual object manager is one of the external nucleus and offers several functions of supporting the real object/virtual object model. Application programs can visually operate the real objects and virtual objects by means of calling extended system calls. Thereal object/virtual object manager offers the functions of registering/deleting programs, so usually all application programs are controlled by that manager.

The followings are picked up as the functions of the Real/Virtual object manager.

1) Indicating/operating virtual object,
2) Indicating/operating Fusen(Fusen is Japanese word meaning "tag" or "label"),
3) Management of application program(for example registration and deletion of an application),
4) Setting up menus,
5) Management of attaching file systems.

5. IMPLEMENTATION OF BTRON NUCLEUS [11]

In order to take out features of the BTRON specification, the following functions of Operating System Nucleus which are necessary for realizing extended nucleus and system applications are prepared. These basic functions of the OS nucleus based on the BTRON specification are divided into the following 9 functions.

(1) Process management

Process management consists of single user/multiprocess management, message passing among processes, synchronization/mutual exclusion by semaphore and shared memory among processes. One process has an

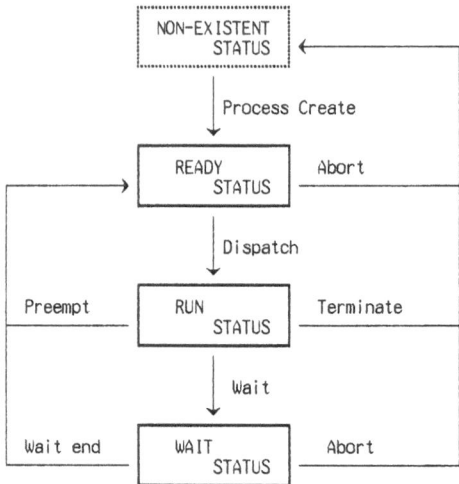

Figure 4. Process Status and Status Transition

independent address space and is executed in it. The address space of a process consists of local address space (code region, data region, local memory (heap) region and stack region) and global address space (global memory).

A process has the following 4 fundamental statuses

Non-Existent --- the status which a process is not created
Ready   --- the status which a process is executable and waits dispatcher
Run   --- the status which a process is executing
Wait   --- the status which a process waits message, timer, I/O etc.

Each status moves to a different status according to Figure 4, when supervisor calls or scheduling (dispatcher, preempt) has been occurred.

(2) Message passing

The fundamental form of the message passing is the transmission of message. A message which has message type is sent by specifying receiver process and is received by specifying range of message types. Usually the received message is stored in the message queue and is taken out according to the request of receiving message. The receiver process can process non-synchronously when it receives a message with the specified type by means of defining the message handler, which is a kind of interrupt processing.

The semaphore function is offered to the exclusive processing of the resource owned jointly among processes and synchronization among processes. This semaphore is a counting semaphore which is owned jointly among processes.

(3) Memory management

Memory management consists of management of local memory of a process, management of global memory of all processes. The memory region which each process can use is the following 2 kinds of region and is mutually offered the functions of acquisition/releasing of the memory blocks.

Local memory region :
  This is a memory region which a process can use and other processes can not access this memory region. When a process exits, this region is released similarly to the process environment.

Global memory region :
  This is a memory region which all processes can use and consists of several memory pools dynamically created/deleted. Once a memory pool is created, it exists until it is deleted, and has no relationship with the existence of the process which creates it. The global memory region is used as the datawhich is used jointly among several processes and which the extended nucleus uses.

(4)Event management

Keyboard/pointing device management for input interaction. An event is not only caused by hardware but by software. Event data include its occurring time information which is used for getting an order of events and an interval there between.

(5)Device management

Handling of I/O devices through uniform interface. Device drivers are under the supervision of device management. A device driver interfaces the nucleus with a device and it is developed depending on hardware. When a computer system is booted, device drivers are loaded and registered into the system.

(6)Timer management

Real time clock management. The system keeps date and time using this management. Timer management has functions to set and get this data.

(7)System management

Exception handling, shared library, extended system call support.

Exception handling support enables users to define interrupt processing for exceptions.

Shared library support manages dynamic loading/unloading of executable programs, for example device drivers, extended programs, shared programs and so on. These programs are shared by multi processes. Extended system call support is the method to define various system calls added to nucleus basic system calls. Its primary use is for registering the extended nucleus system calls.

(8)Display primitive, Japanese processing

Display of basic figure and text. Kana-kanji transform to process Japanese.

(9)File management

Variable-length record stream, network-like directory and access control file system to support the real object/virtual object model. In the real object/virtual object model, the accumulation of data is referred to as a "file", and this is referenced by a pointer called a "link"(Figure 5). So the file corresponds to Real object and the link corresponds to Virtual objects. The file consists of an ordered sequence of variable-length records (record stream) and the link is a sort of records. Therefore the file(Real object) includes plural links(Virtual object). Then the file is pointed to by plural links. Consequently the real object/virtual object model implements network-like relations.

For supporting this data structure, it is necessary to control multiple relationship between one file and multiple links, to treat networks without depending on devices and manage files which consist of a stream of variable-length records, efficiently.

Then file management controls the reference relationship by plural links, using a reference counter. A reference relationship independent on devices is implemented, using an indirect link.

The file doesn't consist of a stream of bytes but a stream of records and it is possible to read, write, insert, delete and truncate each record. To implement these operations efficiently, the file management system provide the following features.

1) As data can be inserted and deleted for not only each file but each record, the system manages space of disks, not for each block, but more minutely.

2) In insertion or deletion of a record, the system updates a record index efficiently.

3) Even though records are deleted or inserted while a file to which these records belong is being accessed, the system function is to continue to access a present record in this file.

4) The system has a function to access massive data such as image and voic, speedly.

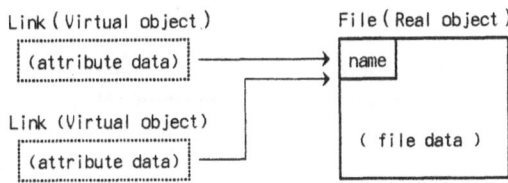

Figure 5. File and Link

6. IMPLEMENTATION OF VIEW PORT SYSTEM [12],[13]

In the BTRON concept, the object handling method is based on the real object/virtual object model. Special features of the viewport system ,which supports the object handling method, are discussed below:
(1) Nested viewport.

In the BTRON concept, document structure and document management are handled through parent-child relations. The environment capable of displaying and operating this document structure and document management uses a multi-viewport system that fulfills the requirements of such parent-child relationships. Thus viewports may be nested.
(2) All viewports can be displayed simultaneously.

All viewports which a running process possess can be displayed simultaneously under the multi-tasking OS.

There are technical difficulties to implement the viewport system in order to satisfy the features :

1) Implementation of graphic systems for viewport system. For example, the graphic environment should control the complicated clipping relation generated from the real object/virtual object model.

2) Arrangement of the process's role for viewport management under the multi-tasking OS .

3) Implementation of viewport's software structure that has quick response to user.

In order to overcome these technical difficulties, we developed the implementation methods of viewport manager below. Especially, we discuss the graphic environment of viewport, relationship between process and viewport, and implementation of real-time performance software.

6.1 Graphic environment of the viewport

In the BTRON concept, the viewport supports object operation method based on the real object/virtual object model. To implement the viewport, the graphic environment requires following functions:

1) Fixing of the viewport's graphic coordinate when the coordinate moves, because of viewport movement. The viewport's graphic coordinate must be fixed while the viewport's coordinate moves, when the viewport moves or scrolls.

2) Handling of complicated clipping relation generated for Real object/virtual object model.

a: Viewport manager must adjust clipping relation automatically when clipping relation is changed because of change of viewport's overlapping relation or viewport's movement.

b: In the BTRON concept, nested viewport is clipped by parent-viewport which includes child-viewport. Viewport manager must adjust this clipping relation automatically.

3) All viewports can be displayed simultaneously.

All viewports , which a process possess, must be displayed simultaneously.

To achieve these functions, the graphic system which is called "the display primitive" are prepared. This graphic system can quickly draw figures and write characters on the bitmapped display. It also provides for the overlapping viewport's function, MMI functions and business graphics .

The implementation of viewport manager together with a graphic environment is discussed below:
(1) The viewport manager adjusts the graphic coordinate system to fix the origin of view port's coordinate when the coordinate moves, because of viewport movement or viewport scroll (See Figure 6).

This graphic system can set up the starting point at any place on the bitmapped area. Viewport manager adjusts the origin of coordinate when the coordinate moves because of viewport movement or viewport scroll, so that the viewport origin is fixed at the left corner of viewport.

(2) Handling of complicated clipping relation generated for Real object/virtual object model.

This graphic system has multi-clipping function which consists of 3 clipping areas (rectangle), namely port rectangle (***PortRect***),view rectangle (***ViewRect***) and a list of foreground rectangles (***fgRect***) (See Figure 7).

The multi-clipping function can view the area which satisfies the following conditions.

a: area which is contained in PortRect.

b: area which is contained in ViewRect.

c: area which is NOT contained in fgRects.

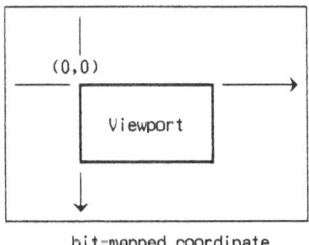

Figure 6. Coordinate

Viewport manager implements clipping caused by overlapping relations by using fgRect.

Viewport manager utilizes this multi-clipping function to set the viewport graphic environment.

PortRect : This area is the same as the maximum size of the viewport, and is controlled by the viewport manager. Viewport manager controls this rectangle.

ViewRect: This is controlled by application programs.

fgRect : This is controlled by the viewport manager. The area which indicates the maximum area of viewports in front of a current viewport. The viewport manager utilizes fgRects to implement clipping caused by an overlapping function. In Figure 7, parts of fgRect 1 and fgRect 2 become blind areas. and clipping of viewport A and B is done by the viewport manager.

The viewport manager impelments clipping of nested viewport by using PortRect.

In Figure 8, the viewport manager sets PortRect to the Parent-viewport area size. The visible area becomes the area that is common to both PortRect and ViewRect. Clipping of a nested viewport is realized this way.

(3) Viewport manager provides a different parameter setting graphic environment to each viewport. Every viewport has the independent graphical environment, which can be used to draw figures simultaneously. So The viewport manager can assure that all viewports can display simultaneously.

6.2. Arrangement of the process's role for viewport management

The relationships of process and viewport under the multi-task OS requires the following features:

1) Management of dialog-status which is exclusive status to get user input information from the keyboard or a pointing device.

2) Clarification of the viewport management role of processes which possess the viewport.

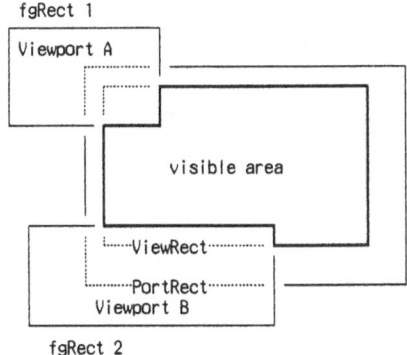

Figure 7. Clipping Area

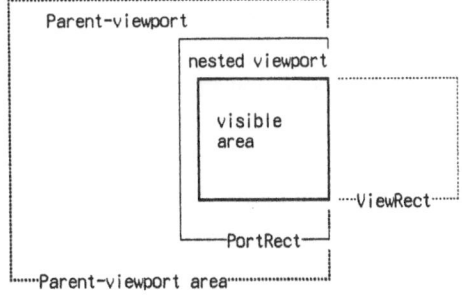

Figure 8. Clipping of Nested Viewport

To achieve these features, the viewport manager has adopted the following methods:

(1) Process, which possesses viewport, should manage its own viewport.

For example, when process receives the viewport's repair message , process which must repair the view of the viewport.

(2) Process, which possesses' dialog-status, should manage the total viewport system .

For example, when it becomes necessary to transfer the dialog-status and to repair the display of viewports, process which possesses dialog-status, must transfer the dialog-status to another process and send the viewport repair message.

(3) Transferring the dialog-status or sending viewport repair messages, is done in the extended nucleus, not application. So application programs do not need to program these operations.

For example, Figure 9 shows how to transfer the dialog-status from process 1 (viewport1) to process 2 (viewport2). In the BTRON specification, viewport, which possess the dialog-status, moves to the top of viewport overlap relation. So in Figure 9, viewport2 moves to the top in the viewports.

Transferring the dialog-status from viewport1 to viewport2 is done as follows:

Step 1: The viewport manager of process 1 moves viewport2 to the top position in the viewport overlap relation.

Step 2: The viewport manager of process 1 sends message to process 2. Message content is to request transfer of dialog-status from process 1 to process 2.

Step 3: When process 2 receives this message, dialog-status is sent from process 1 to process 2. After that, process 2, which possess dialog-status, is able to get user information.

6.3 Implementation of real-time performance

In the BTRON concept, the assurance of real-time qualities in the system was given priority in design. In order to achieve this concept the following methods are adopted :

1) Event-driven system. Input events from the keyboard and a pointing device wake up the responsible application in real-time.

2) Well-balanced coordination of MMI system and application programs.

To support the quick response system further, following implementation methods are used.

(1) The MMI system are resident in memory, and available as OS extended system call. This enables the high-speed call of these functions.

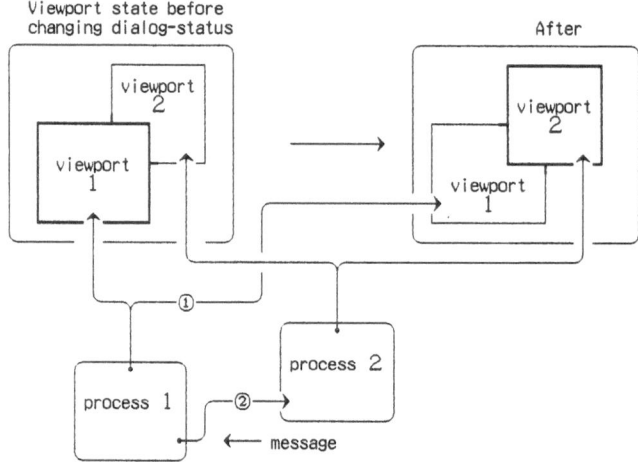

Figure 9. Delivering of Dialog-Status

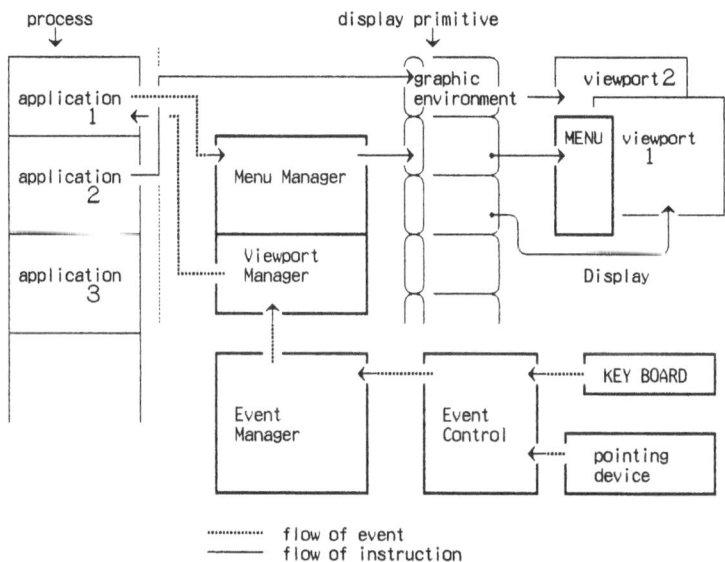

Figure 10. Flow of Input event and Instruction

(2) Application program template, which assures quick response using the event-driven programming is provided for application developers.

Figure 10 shows the flow of input event and instruction in the system. Application 1 is the process which possess the dialog-status.

Step 1: Inputs from keyboard or pointing device are grouped as events, and events are supplied to event manager through event control subsystem, and then supplied to application from viewport manager.

Step 2: Application 1, which is woken up by the input event, checks the input event, and operates according to the input event content.

Step 3: Simultaneously, Application 2 is displaying on the viewport2.

7. DISCUSSION ON IMPLEMENTATION OF MULTILINGUAL-PROCESSING [14],[15]

Figure 11 depicts the concept of Multilingual Information Processing (MLIP) on the BTRON specification OS from the view point of implementation. MLIP on BTRON specification OS consists of the language-independent, the language-dependent, and the common portions, shown in Figure 11. The language-dependent portion has three layered MLIP structure; the language-dependent, script, font layers. The language-dependent modules controlling input, output,and character conversion enable the multilingual data processing and the software compatibility via switching those modules to adapt them to proper language.

MLIP manager in Figure 11 is an interface to mask the language-dependent portion to operators. The common dictionary in Figure 11 consists of the direct translation of terminologies in manuals, messages of BTRON specification OS, and so forth among different languages.

In input and output of Japanese-data, the multilingual-data processing manager switches to the Japanese-data processing module. The data input via KANA-KANJI character conversion software in the Japanese-data processing module goes through the language-independent software and the common module, and comes out on a display.

On editing text in which the Japanese-, English- and Arabic-data coexist, the multilingual-data processing module selects the Japanese-, English-, or Arabic-data processing module at switching demands.

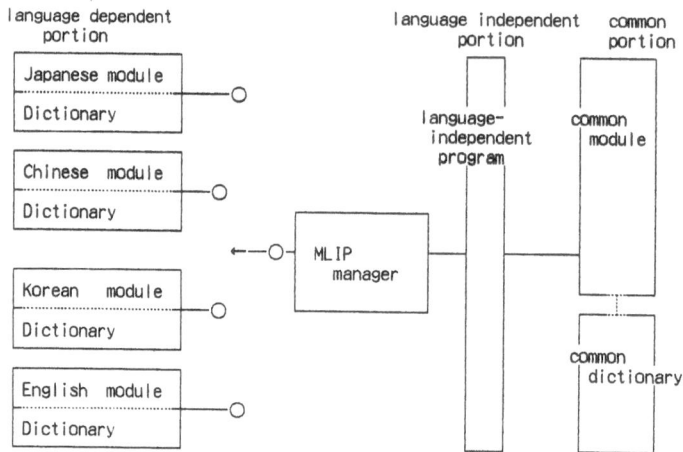

Figure 11. An Example of Multilingual Information Processing System

Each module works for the language-dependent editing operation in each language: Kinsoku-shori peculiar to Japanese-character strings, hyphenation and punctuation for English-character strings, character-expression modification based on location in words for Arabic-character string, and so forth. The language-independent module works for the language-independent editing operation, such as draw line and underline. The text edited in these editing modules goes through the common module and comes out on a display.

8. PERFORMANCE EVALUATION

The implementation nucleus except for the display primitive and Kana-Kanji Transform , supports 116 system calls , and the program size occupies a code volume of about 180 KB , with a data volume of about 140 KB.

In performance evaluation from using event driven application software , we confirm comfortable response time in real time operation , trying to set a suitable value for the time slice of scheduler or priority of process of the kernel.

We can implement to ensure the functions , necessary to management for multi-media data , to support high-speed access and transform of massive continuous data volume with device management and file management.

The implementation extended nucleus consists of about 150 functions , with a program code of 215 KB and data of 126 KB. The system menu display time (the time from the user instruction to the menu display) is approximately 0.2 seconds (80286 at 6 MHz , for a 10-item display menu) .

9. CONCLUSION

We implemented the nucleus and extended nucleus based on the BTRON specification, and evaluated function and capacity. Performance evaluation is yet to be required along with performance measurements such as speed , response time and ease of use. The tune up of the nucleus and extended nucleus and the addition to system call are under investigation. Moreover we plan to investigate to support extended functions like network environment , and to transport to other CPU's.

Finally, we would like to acknowledge the support and cooperation from the member of TRON project of the Japan Electronic Industry Development Association and the project members of our company.

REFERENCES

[1] K. Sakamura, "The TRON Project," IEEE MICRO, Vol.7, No.2, April 1987, pp.8-14.

[2] K. Sakamura, "BTRON: The Business-oriented Operating System," IEEE MICRO, Vol.7, No.2, April 1987, pp.53-65.

[3] K. Sakamura, "A Proposal of New Unified Model of Man-machine Interaction in the BTRON Environment," Information Processing, Information Processing Soc. Japan, Vol.26, No.11, 1985 (In Japanese).

[4] K. Sakamura, "BTRON Super Personal Computer," Computer Architecture Study Group 57-4, Information Processing Soc. Japan, 1985 (In Japanese).

[5] K. Sakamura, New Concepts from the TRON project, Iwanami-Shoten, Tokyo, 1987 (In Japanese).

[6] K. Sakamura, "Making of TRON," bit, Kyoritsu-Syuppan, Tokyo, 1986 and 1987 (In Japanese).

[7] K. Sakamura, "File Management System in BTRON," The 1st technical meeting on TRON real-time architecture, Institute of Electronics Information and Communication Engineers of Japan, April 1987 (In Japanese).

[8] Y. Kushiki, Y. Imai, M. Kobayashi, M. Ando, "Implementation example," IEEE MICRO, Vol.7, No.2, April 1987, pp.62-63.

[9] Y. Kushiki, K. Sakamura, "The operating system based upon BTRON specification on an 80286," Micro computer Study Group 45-4, Information Processing Soc. Japan, 1987 (In Japanese).

[10] Y. Iwamura, T. Ishida, Y. Imai, Y. Kushiki, "An Implementation of the Real/Virtual object model," The 1st technical meeting on TRON real-time architecture, Institute of Electronics Information and Communication Engineers of Japan, October 1987 (In Japanese).

[11] M. Ando, Y. Imai, Y. Kushiki, "An Implementation of nucleus based upon BTRON specification on an 80286," The 1st technical meeting on TRON real-time architecture, Institute of Electronics Information and Communication Engineers of Japan, April 1987 (In Japanese).

[12] M. Kobayashi, S. Takenouchi, Y. Kushiki, K. Sakamura, "THE SOFTWARE STRUCTURE OF EXTENDED NUCLEUS BASED ON BTRON SPECIFICATION," T2B(TRON and Logic Programming Architecture) Session, Proceedings of the FJCC, October 1987.

[13] M. Kobayashi, S. Takenouchi, Y. Kushiki, "The Software structure of extended nucleus based on BTRON specification," The 1st technical meeting on TRON real-time architecture, Institute of Electronics Information and Communication Engineers of Japan, April 1987 (In Japanese).

[14] Y. Kushiki, "A study on implementation of multilingual-processing," The 1st technical meeting on TRON real-time architecture, Institute of Electronics Information and Communication Engineers of Japan, October 1987 (In Japanese).

[15] Y. Kushiki, T. Kabasawa, J. Kubota, K. Sakamura, "Multilingual Information Processing on BTRON Specification Operating System," position paper of Panel Session F-3W (Recent Advances in Asian Multilingual DP and Computing) of COMPSAC, October 1987.

Yoshiaki Kushiki was born in Tokushima Prefecture, Japan, on January 17, 1946. He received the B.E. degree in electronic engieering from Kyoto University, Kyoto, Japan, in 1968. He joined Matsushita Electric In dustrial Co., Ltd.(MEI) in 1968. He has been engaged in the research and development of office system architecture, such as OS, DB, MMI and AI. He is currently with MEI Central Research Laboratory, Moriguchi, Osaka, Japan. Mr. Kushiki is a member of IEEE, ACM, IECEJ and IPSJ.

Makoto Ando was born in Hyogo Prefecture, Japan, on October 18, 1957. He received the B.E. and M.E. degrees in information engineering from Osaka University, Toyonaka, Osaka, Japan, in 1980 and 1982, respectively. He joined Matsushita Electric Industrial Co., Ltd.(MEI) in 1982. He has been engaged in the research and development of operating system and compiler. He is currently With MEI Central Research Laboratory, Moriguchi, Osaka, Japan. Mr. Ando is a member of the IPSJ.

Masaaki Kobayashi was born in Hyogo Prefecture, Japan, on September 6, 1954. He received the B.E. and M.E. degrees in system engineering from Kobe University, Kobe, Hyogo, Japan, in 1978 and 1980, respectively. He joined Matsushita Electric Industrial Co., Ltd.(MEI) in 1980. He has been engaged in the research and development of man-machine interface system. He is currently With MEI Central Research Laboratory, Moriguchi, Osaka, Japan. Mr. Kobayashi is a member of the IPSJ.

Yoshihiko imai was born in Shiga Prefecture, Japan, on April 1, 1952. He received the B.E. degree in information science from Kyoto University, Kyoto, Japan, in 1974. He joined Matsushita Electoric Industorial Co., Ltd.(MEI) in 1974. He has been engaged in the research and development of operating system and data bese system, such as the MMDB. He is currently with MEI Central Reseach Laboratory, Moriguchi, Osaka, Japan. Mr. Imai is a member of the IPSJ and the ASJ.

Ken Sakamura is an associate professor in the Department of Information Science at the University of Tokyo. H e initiated the TRON project in 1984. Under his leadership, several universities and over 50 manufacturers are now participating in the project in order to build the computers for the 1990's. In addition to his involvement with TRON, Sakamura chairs several committees of the Japan Electronics Industry Development Association and the Information Processing Society of Japan. He has written numerous technical papers and books. He received the BS, ME, and PhD degrees in electrical engineering from Keio University at Yokohama in 1974, 1976, and 1979, respectively.

μBTRON Bus: Design and Evaluation of Musical Data Transfer

Ken Sakamura

Department of Information Science, Faculty of Science, University of Tokyo
Hongo,Tokyo,113 Japan

Kanehisa Tsurumi, Hiro Kato

Center for Musical Instrument and Software Development, Yamaha Corporation
10-1 Nakazawa-cho, Hamamatsu, 430 Japan

ABSTRACT

μBTRON bus is designed to connect electronic stationery goods to BTRON-based workstations. The design objectives of μBTRON bus are described and then the performance of musical data transfer on the bus is discussed according to simulation results. The results show that the μBTRON bus offers satisfactory performance for this application.

Keywords: μBTRON bus, electronic stationery goods, MIDI, token ring LAN

1. LAN FOR ELECTRONIC STATIONERY GOODS

BTRON workstations are personal workstations meant to be used in an environment where one workstation is available for every man and woman. The workstation will help each individual in creative activities. Hence varied input and output devices will be connected to BTRON workstations to augment the processing capabilities of the workstations. These input and output devices include image scanners, cameras, printers, scales, measurement instruments, and electronic musical instruments. These are called electronic stationery goods.

BTRON specification calls for several LAN's each suited for particular application field. One of the LAN's is called μBTRON bus and is used to connect electronic stationery goods to BTRON workstations. One BTRON workstation will be connected to many electronic stationery goods. μBTRON bus can be used to support certain shared resources such as laser printer for several BTRON workstations. However, it should be noted that a full-fledged LAN is employed to connect multiple BTRON workstations. And such LAN's are being designed. μBTRON bus is primarily meant to connect electronic stationery goods to one BTRON workstation.

Requirements on μBTRON Bus

The requirements for μBTRON bus are summarized below.

(1) The bus should be capable of controlling several devices simultaneously. In a typical application, one μBTRON workstation controls many electronic stationery goods.

2) Bandwidth should be several megabits per second (Mbps).

3) The physical cable must be thin and flexible to be used in office environment.

4) The system operation should not be disturbed severely even if device is connected or disconnected, or if the power supply to devices is turned on/off.

5) The cable, connector, and controller should be inexpensive.

6) It should be capable of interfacing with HOME BUS (see the explanation about HOME BUS below).

7) Realtime transfer of voice or musical data should be possible.

8) LAN cable should be extensible to a few hundred meters long.

9) It should support one hundred nodes at the maximum.

The background of these requirements are as follows.

It is desirable to print bitmap image data at the rate of 10 to 20 pages per minute on a laser printer. Assuming the A4 size paper, the transfer rate of several Mbps is necessary.

The cable should be thin and flexible since we would like to connect rather small stationery goods. Also, the handling of cable should be fool-proof because ordinary users will have to connect and disconnect the devices. The system should not stop every time user modifies the device configuration.

In Japan, HOME BUS standard to facilitate home automation has been established since the beginning of 1987. Some electronic appliances which conform to HOME BUS have already stated to appear in the market. In order to control these devices from BTRON workstations, the μBTRON bus should be capable of interfacing with HOME BUS via gateway.

It will become very important to handle human voice as part of human-machine interface. Electronic stationery goods are certain to handle human voice. In order to handle realtime voice communication, we have to pay attention to both the bandwidth and the delay time of transmission. In order to handle such realtime data as voice or musical data, μBTRON bus must support realtime response for these applications.

The length and the number of nodes are determined according to the typical applications the designers had in mind.

In the TRON project, the μBTRON bus to satisfy the above requirements are being designed.

In order to attain the realtime response, CSMA/CD protocol was deemed inappropriate. Instead, token ring protocol was tentatively adopted for μBTRON bus. The current interim specification uses twisted pair cable, uses 4 Mbps transmission rate. Delay time can be predictable. However, the token ring protocol as standardized in IEEE802.5 is for full-fledged LAN and was considered too large for supporting electronic stationery goods. Hence μBTRON bus standard being designed is simpler than IEEE802.5.

In the following, how μBTRON bus can handle realtime transmission of musical data is discussed according to simulation results. It is shown that the simplified token ring protocol tentatively adopted in μBTRON bus can satisfy the design requirements and can be used for high speed realtime transmission.

2. MUSIC LAN AS A REAL TIME LAN

Since its release in 1983 (IMA, 1983), MIDI , Musical Instrument Digital Interface, has become one of the most widely used computer related technologies in the musical application fields. However, when various MIDI devices (such as computer, sequencer, sound modules, and so forth) are connected into an integrated MIDI network, MIDI is not necessarily an ideal interface for complex musical system.

Some drawbacks have been pointed out as following;
1) MIDI is one-way serial line per cable and "one to many" broadcast technique without hardware handshaking function from the receiver. Large scale MIDI network requires too many cables to be connected, making cable routing too complex and too confusing.
2) Baud rate is fixed to 31.25 Kbps. The speed is not fast enough when multiple channeled information is transferred, or bulk data transfer is required.
3) MIDI is "one to many" broadcast technique without hardware handshaking function from the receiver. This simple structure makes the mixture of different data types (e.g., real time data and file data) to be sent simultaneously on the network very difficult.

The requirements of musical applications in the 1990's have much in common with the requirements of μBTRON bus. We list them in the following.
1) Network must be truly real time.
   - accomplish 10 times as much of actual data transfer rate of MIDI
   - allow no longer than 2 msec delay between consecutive event messages

2) Different data types (bulk data such as voice patches, PCM wave forms, graphic images and etc.) must simultaneously co-exist with musical events on the network.

3) Cables must be light-weighted and flexible.

4) Total length of the network must be long enough to cover performers movement on stage.

5) Connectors must be small, easy to handle, and inexpensive.

6) Nodes must be able to join or leave the network without disturbing the operation of other devices on the network, or at least without causing serious delay to recover from error condition of the network.

According to our experience in music network application, an typical network traffic would be described as; —while large bulk data such as voice patches or sequence data are transferred on the back ground of the network, relatively small packets of event information such as "note on's" and "modulation wheel" are frequently exchanged on the foreground of the network. When each event information is to be sent, it should not be delayed longer than 2 msec.—

We consider this network usage to be pretty demanding compared to most non-musical real time network application. Therefore, examining how a musical application run on the network can be regarded as a good evaluation of real time performance of the μBTRON bus.

Among many LAN's currently being used, Ethernet (IEEE802.3) and other CSMA/CD buses seem to be a mainstream of the LAN technology. CSMA/CD has a strong advantage on the ability to easily connect or disconnect the node. However it is not best suited for the real time bus application because of its inherent data collision occurrences under high data traffic condition and consequently its inability to control accurate delay time.

To obtain predictable and controllable delay time, ring type network is desired.

Token Ring (IEEE802.5) is such a network which has its priority control scheme for the real time requirement.

μBTRON bus is similar to Token Ring network with the following modifications for compactness of the specification and more responsiveness for real time applications.

1) Smaller frame with shorter address and FCS length.

2) Limited maximum frame length.

3) Ability to send consecutive frames from the same node.

3. SUMMARY OF μBTRON BUS SPECIFICATION FOR SIMULATION

The following lists important parameters of the μBTRON bus specifications that are needed for the simulation.

Data transfer speed	4 Mbps
Node delay [1]	3 bits
Number of nodes	32
Number of consecutive frames allowed [2]	2
Token length	24 bits
Frame length [3]	88 bits + data
(maximum length	1024 bits)

Token and Frame formats are depicted as following;

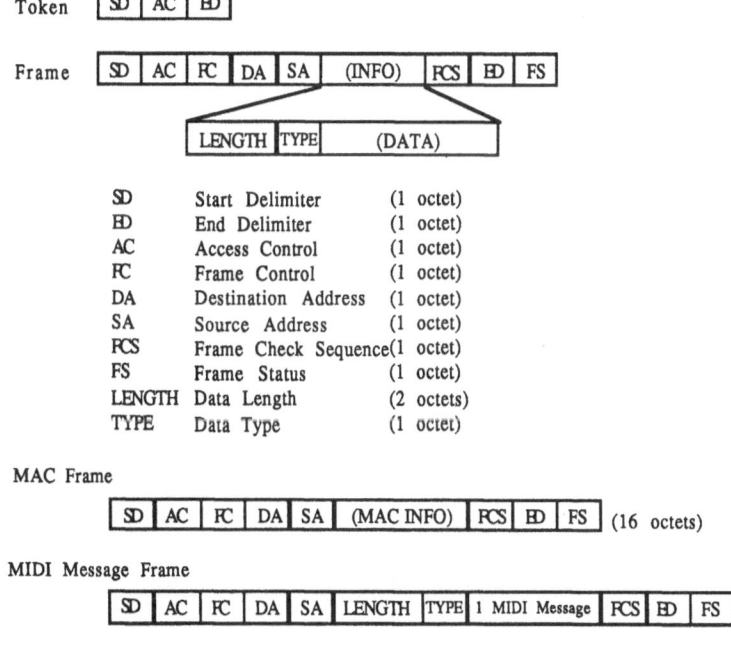

SD	Start Delimiter	(1 octet)
ED	End Delimiter	(1 octet)
AC	Access Control	(1 octet)
FC	Frame Control	(1 octet)
DA	Destination Address	(1 octet)
SA	Source Address	(1 octet)
FCS	Frame Check Sequence	(1 octet)
FS	Frame Status	(1 octet)
LENGTH	Data Length	(2 octets)
TYPE	Data Type	(1 octet)

Fig.1   Format of Token or Frame

[1]Node delay includes the delay on the cable between nodes.

[2]Number of consecutive frames allowed. If necessary, each node can own the loop and send multiple number of frames consecutively. If this number is too high, the node tends to monopolize the loop too long. In this simulation, this number is limited to 2.

[3]Frame length. There exists either a token or a frame on the loop, and both never simultaneously exist.

Note:

1) MAC frame.

   MAC, Media Access Control, frame is assumed to be 16 octets in length and to be dispatched into the loop every 5 msec.

2) MIDI message frame.

   Data packed into the frame is based upon the MIDI data format. No running status (see MIDI specification 1.0) is used.

   Typical data length;

Message	MIDI message length	Frame length
MIDI clock	1 byte	96 bits
Note on	3 bytes	112 bits
Note off	3 bytes	112 bits
Pitch bend	3 bytes	112 bits
Modulation wheel	2 bytes	104 bits

4. MUSICAL PERFORMANCE SIMULATION

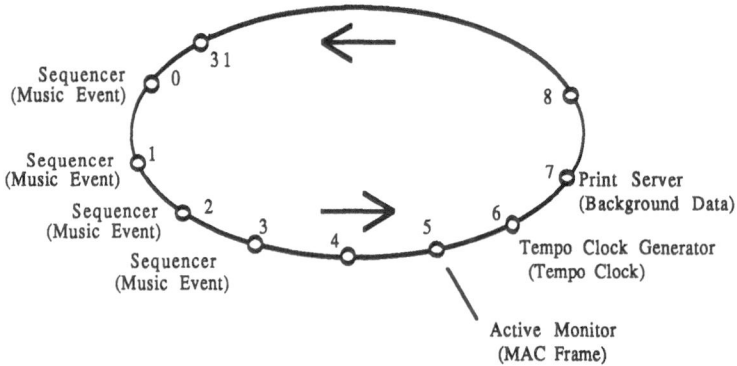

Fig.2   Node Configuration on Simulation

Fig.2 depicts node usage of the simulated loop.

There are 32 active nodes numbered from 0 to 31. Four sequencers are connected to nodes from 0 to 3. Just like an orchestra, each sequencer played its assigned tracks of entire music. Thus entire performance is accomplished by simultaneous playback of 4 sequencers. Musical performance frames sent from node 0 - 3 travels along the loop and are received by sound boxes connected to the nodes between 8 and 31.

All four sequencers are driven by an external clock that is connected to node 6.

That is, node 6 keeps dispatching tempo click information at the clock rate of 1/96 note duration. During the simulation, the tempo is kept at 160 QPM (Quarternotes Per Minute), which is typical for the type of the performance data used in the simulation. Clock rate of 1/96 note duration at 160 QPM is translated to the interval of 15.625 msec.

Node 6 therefore dispatches clock frame every 15.625 msec. Node 6 is a master of total performance, and tempo of each sequencer is thus controlled by the reception of tempo click information from the master (i.e., node 0-3 are slave devices).

Original form of MIDI tempo clock (f8h in terms of MIDI message) and performance data are packed into the frame as illustrated in Fig.1.

In the loop, node 5 is assigned as a monitoring device of the loop. It kept dispatching MAC frames every 5 msec. Also node 7 is assigned as a hypothetical printer server that kept dispatching 1024 bit data frame whenever the loop is available (when no performance data is on the loop). Node 5 and 7 were treated as lower priority devices, and their network usage was withheld until the network became completely free.

During the simulation, "delay" is kept track of by every MIDI tempo clock. Delay indicates the interval between the timing of MIDI tempo clock (start of events) and the completion timing of all events on the network associated with that start.

Two different type of performance data were played on the nodes 0 - 3.

Sample A:

4 tracks (each track played by each node)

44 measures long

Total number of events   5361

(This sample is recorded from human performance, and contains heavy usage of modulation wheel and pitch bender information. This is typical professional contemporary keyboard performance.)

Sample B:

16 tracks (4 tracks by each node)

152 measures long

Total number of events   25526

(This sample was generated by a score writing program, and contains large number of note on/off events. Since performance is deadly accurate, events tend to get concentrated at each beat clock timing. In addition to a large number of events to handle, a severe timing requirement tends to overwhelm the MIDI capacity.)

5. SIMULATION RESULTS

5.1 STATISTICS OF ENTIRE PLAYBACK

Sample A:

	μBTRON bus		MIDI
Printer server	on	off	—
Total events counted	5361	5361	5361
Total clocks counted	4224	4224	4224
MAC frame ratio (%)	0.64	0.64	—
Data frames ratio (%)	95.47	1.02	9.8
Delay statistics			
max delay (msec)	1.452	1.236	31.040
average delay (msec)	0.356	0.085	1.515
number of 1 msec delay	2	1	581
number of 2 msec delay	0	0	390
number of 3 msec delay	0	0	593
number of 4 msec/more delay	0	0	408

Sample B:

	μBTRON bus		MIDI
Printer server	on	off	—
Total events counted	25526	25526	25526
Total clocks counted	14592	14592	14592
MAC frame ratio (%)	0.64	0.64	—
Data frames ratio (%)	95.49	1.11	12.8
Delay statistics			
max delay (msec)	3.247	3.231	102.400
average delay (msec)	0.359	0.097	2.062
number of 1 msec delay	51	0	746
number of 2 msec delay	0	0	1012
number of 3 msec delay	1	1	363
number of 4 msec/more delay	0	0	2930

5.2 VARYING PARAMETERS

The following results show the effect of network performance on the variations of network parameters or sample performance data. The simulation was done on the first 10 measures of sample B data. Back ground printer server was kept enabled.

(a) Adding more data into each event frame

Event frame (note on/off) size in bits	112	112+96	112+216
Total events	2289	2289	2289
Total clocks	960	960	960
Delay statistics			
max delay (msec)	3.247	5.800	8.990
average delay (msec)	0.377	0.424	0.491
number of 1 msec delay	7	43	73
number of 2 msec delay	0	0	19
number of 3 msec delay	1	0	0
number of 4 msec/more delay	0	1	1

(b) Increasing event frames (same event is repeated after each event)

Additional number of events after each event	0	4	9
Total events	2289	11445	22890
Total clocks	960	960	960
Delay statistics			
max delay (msec)	3.247	16.059	32.072
average delay (msec)	0.377	0.679	1.088
number of 1 msec delay	7	142	160
number of 2 msec delay	0	25	45
number of 3 msec delay	1	22	52
number of 4 msec/more delay	0	4	44

(c) Changing node delay (speed=4 Mbps)

Node delay (bit)	3	6	9
Total events	2289	2289	2289
Total clocks	960	960	960
Delay statistics			
max delay (msec)	3.247	5.791	8.741
average delay (msec)	0.377	0.441	0.515
number of 1 msec delay	7	41	75
number of 2 msec delay	0	0	18
number of 3 msec delay	1	0	0
number of 4 msec/more delay	0	1	1

(d) Changing transfer speed (node delay=3 bits)

Transfer speed (Mbps)	4	2	1
Total events	2289	2289	2289
Total clocks	960	960	960
Delay statistics			
max delay (msec)	3.247	7.125	14.850
average delay (msec)	0.377	0.712	1.534
number of 1 msec delay	7	197	509
number of 2 msec delay	0	7	169
number of 3 msec delay	1	0	33
number of 4 msec/more delay	0	1	12

(e) Changing number of nodes (speed =4 Mbps)

number of nodes	32	64	128
Total events	2289	2289	2289
Total clocks	960	960	960
Delay statistics			
max delay (msec)	3.247	5.773	11.615
average delay (msec)	0.377	0.452	0.640
number of 1 msec delay	7	50	116
number of 2 msec delay	0	0	22
number of 3 msec delay	1	0	4
number of 4 msec/more delay	0	1	1

5.3 SUMMARY OF SIMULATION RESULTS

1) Simulation -1 shows that, in both sample A and B performances, actual time used by any performance frames on the network is only 1% of total available time.

   This means that μBTRON bus should be capable of playing wide variety of fast music while simultaneously maintaining ordinary LAN operation on the back ground.

2) Simulation-1 shows a substantial difference between the absolute speed of message transfer of MIDI and μBTRON bus. When delay statistics of μBTRON bus and MIDI is compared, it is safe to say that μBTRON bus is about 10 times faster than MIDI.

3) Also simulation-1 shows that, average delay of each event induced by the back ground data is about 250 - 300μsec (difference between average delays of printer server on and off). And average delay of each clock is within 1 or 2 msec. This is even under the interval of 1/5 of MIDI clock running at 160QPM.

4) In the music LAN of the 1990's, it may be required to send more information attached to currently simple "note on" MIDI message.

   This means we may have to send either larger data frame or more data frames. Simulation 2-a) shows that enlarging the size of each data frame will not so seriously increase the network delay as will the increased number of frames (simulation 2-b) to carry the same amount of information.

In simulation 2-b), when number of data frames are increased (with hypothetical data attached to each event), maximum delay becomes larger than MIDI clock interval (15.625 msec), and thus performance tempo could become no longer consistent.

5) Simulation 2-c) shows the effect of slowing down the node delay.

When it exceeds 6 bits or more, the network delay seems to become rapidly unacceptable.

6) Simulation 2-d) shows the effect of slower transfer speed. 2 Mbps may be barely acceptable, and 1 Mbps is certainly unacceptable.

7) Simulation 2-e) was a result from different number of nodes in the network.

It seems 64 active nodes (at 4 Mbps) in the network is still acceptable for most of music applications.

We also tried to change the relative location (node number) of nodes in the loop. However it did not show a significant difference of the performance by the change of node location.

6. CONCLUSION

The simulation results have shown that token ring μBTRON bus can support the musical application in which realtime musical data transfer takes place in the foreground and bulk data transfer can happen in the background. μBTRON bus is an important LAN technology to connect electronic stationery goods to high-performance workstations. These electronic devices will become increasingly important as computers are introduced to education, homes, and for entertainment. Realtime data transmission will be important, too. μBTRON bus is important in the sense that it enhances the workstation with devices for creative tasks. In a sense, μBTRON bus will be used as nerve network for BTRON workstation and electronic stationery goods. Its specification is being designed and will be made public in the future.

REFERENCE

[1] Buxton, W. (1987), "Masters and Slaves versus Democracy: MIDI and Local Area Network", IMA 1987

[2] IMA (1983), "Musical Instrument Digital Interface Specification 1.0"

Kanehisa Tsurumi
1979   Nagoya University, BS
1981   Nagoya University, MS
Currently   Software engineer/researcher of Center for Musical Instrument and Software Development, Yamaha Corporation.

Hiro Kato
1966   Ibaraki University, BS
1972   Columbia University, MS
Currently   Manager of Center for Musical Instrument and Software Development, Yamaha Corporation

Ken Sakamura is an associate professor in the Department of Information Science at the University of Tokyo. He initiated the TRON project in 1984. Under his leadership, several universities and over 50 manufacturers are now participating in the project in order to build the computers for the 1990's. In addition to his involvement with TRON, Sakamura chairs several committees of the Japan Electronics Industry Development Association and the Information Processing Society of Japan. He has written numerous technical papers and books. He received the BS, ME, and PhD degrees in electrical engineering from Keio University at Yokohama in 1974, 1976, and 1979, respectively.

An Implementation of the TRON Keyboard

Sadao Tachibana
Physical Design Department, Engineering Division, Data Processing Group
Oki Electric Industry Co., Ltd., 3-1 Futaba-cho, Takasaki, 370 Japan

Ken Sakamura
Department of Information Science, Faculty of Science, University of Tokyo
Hongo,Tokyo,113 Japan

ABSTRACT

Two important objectives of keyboard input method are to gain speed and to lessen the fatigue of operators. The TRON keyboard layout is based on the data of the physical size of hands of Japanese. Firstly, physical placement of keytops which are easy to strike and causes less fatigue was determined using the data. Secondly, character frequencies in real documents was used to decide the final location of each character in the keyboard. In addition, an electronic pen is proposed for figure input.

Oki Electric Industry Co., Ltd. has built a TRON keyboard prototype on the basis of the TRON keyboard specifications. This paper discusses the design of the keyboard that reflects the TRON specifications for its implementation as a product.

Keywords: Input Device, Keyboard, Finger's Reach, Electronic Pen

1. TRON KEYBOARD DESIGN PHILOSOPHY

The paper [1] describes the design philosophy on the TRON keyboard in detail. This chapter describes its fundamental philosophy.

1.1 KEY LAYOUT

The TRON keyboard has a key layout based on measured data of the extent in which typical Japanese people can move their fingers, i.e., the "finger's reach." The data were collected from about 150 Japanese men and women 20 to 60 of age.

Each of the people tested had each of his/her fingers rested in the center of a key on a keyboard in its home position indicated on a jig, with the thumb and wrist fixed. The extent of each finger's reach was traced. Then the trace of the finger was digitized and extents of finger's reach grouped by percentage of the people tested were defined using contour lines. The 64 keys, beside a cursor key, required by the TRON keyboard were laid out to ensure that all of them should be accommodated toward the center of the trace. The key layout thus determined is shown in *Fig. 1*. The traces drawn in contour lines indicate extents of finger's reach by percentage of the samples: from the inner side, 80%, 60%, 40%, and 20%.

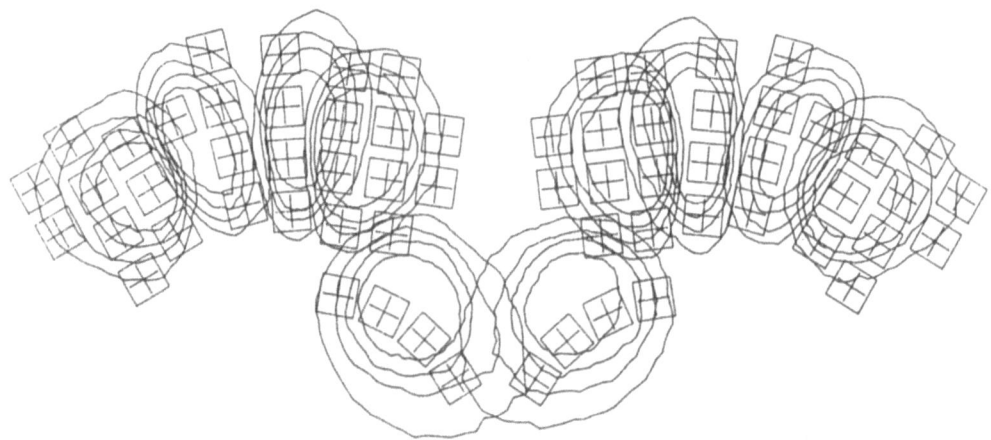

Fig. 1 Layout of TRON Keyboard

Table 1 shows measured data of the distance from the wrist to the tip of the middle finger (hand length). The difference in hand length between maximum and minimum is 51.5 mm; one size alone cannot offer a keyboard which matches all human hands. The TRON keyboard comes in three different sizes, S, M and L, to choose from according to the size of hands.

Table 1 Hand Length Data (in mm)

	Men	Women	Both
Average	194.2	178.9	189.5
Standard deviation	10.6	8.2	12.2
Maximum	218.0	200.0	218.0
Minimum	171.5	166.5	166.5

Consider the spacing between the forefinger and the middle finger in their home position as an example of analyzing the three different sizes. According to the measured data, the width of the distal knuckles joint (the joint nearest to the fingertip) of the middle finger is 16.3 mm on the average, 1.3 mm in standard deviation, 19 mm maximum and 13 mm minimum. From these results, a value of about 16 mm (calculated value: 16.07 mm) is selected as the home-position spacing between the forefinger and the middle finger on the size-M TRON keyboard. The value 16 mm is increased by 2 for size L (18 mm) and decreased by 2 for size S (14 mm).

1.2 THREE-DIMENSIONAL KEYBOARD LAYOUT

Again, the TRON keyboard should give the operator as little fatigue as possible, in addition to achieving enhanced input efficiency. In light of this, the aforementioned considerations to the two-dimensional keyboard layout alone were not satisfactory for the TRON keyboard and further analytical efforts were directed to its three-dimensional layout.

The basic concept is that the keyboard design should allow the operator to hit keys in a natural position where his/her muscles are free to develop the highest force. To this end, the keyboard is split into two clusters: the right-handed block and the left-handed block, arranged in a fan-shaped pattern with a certain spacing between them. The keyboard is angled at the front and on both sides. The front is extended to form a wrist support. What angles should be made along the three edges is detailed in the paper [2]. A keyboard layout based on these parameters is shown in *Fig. 2*. Also, the dimensions of the TRON keyboard (size M) defined from *Figs. 1* and *2* are given in *Fig. 3*.

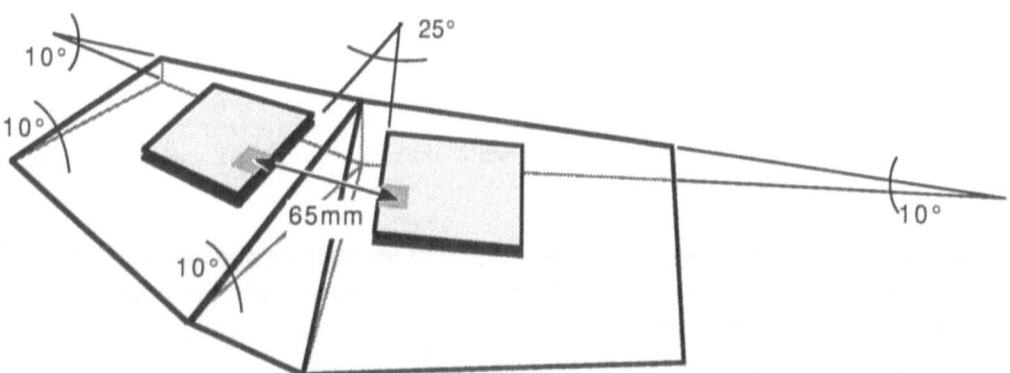

Fig. 2 Three-dimensional Layout of TRON Keyboard Unit

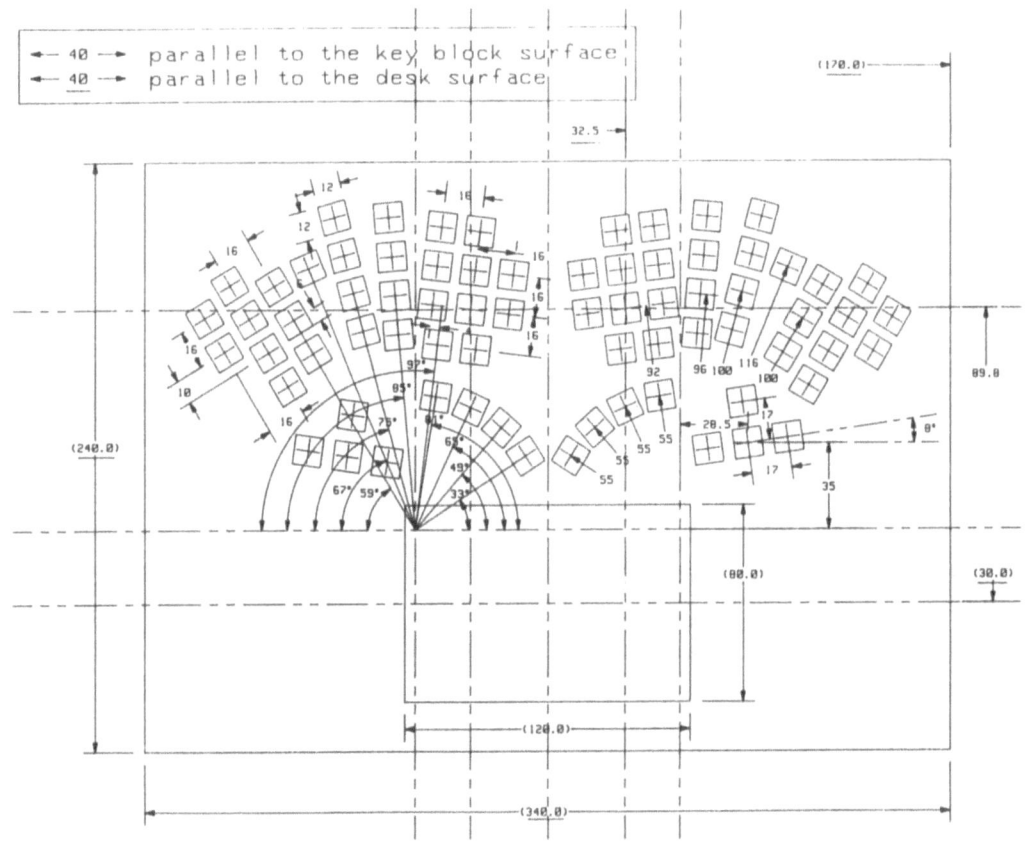

Fig. 3 Dimensions of TRON Keyboard (Size M)

1.3 LOGICAL KEYBOARD LAYOUT

The term "logical keyboard layout" means what character should be assigned to what key.

With a view to selecting an optimum logical keyboard layout, a lot of Japanese sentences were analyzed to know the frequency of individual characters being used and that of a combination of two consecutive characters appearing. From the data thus obtained, the following four major design rules were derived for key assignment:

1) The middle row of the keyboard is most frequently used, followed by the upper row and the lower row in that order.

2) Two consecutive characters can be hit alternately from right to left and from left to right.

3) Chances of using the same finger repeatedly are reduced.

4) The frequency of the forefinger and the middle finger is increased, while that of the ring finger and the little finger is decreased.

The alphabetic characters are arranged in accordance with the Dvorak system. *Figs. 4* and *5* show layouts of the Japanese character keys and the alphabetic characters, respectively.

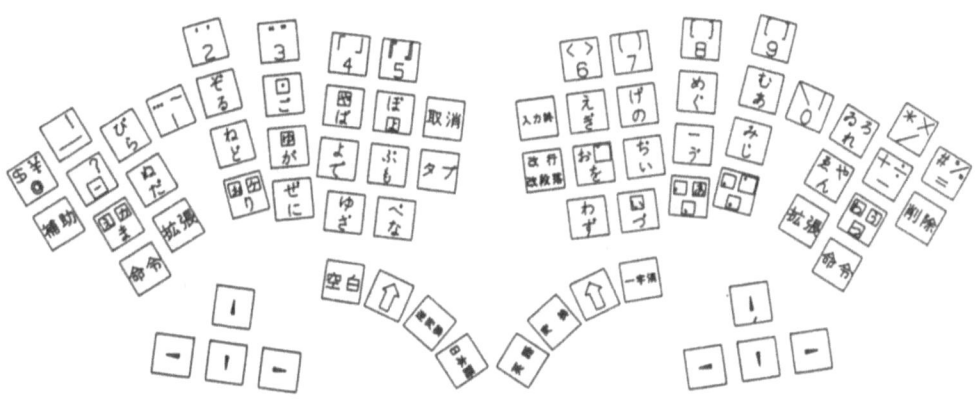

Fig. 4 Logical Layout of TRON Keyboard (in Japanese)

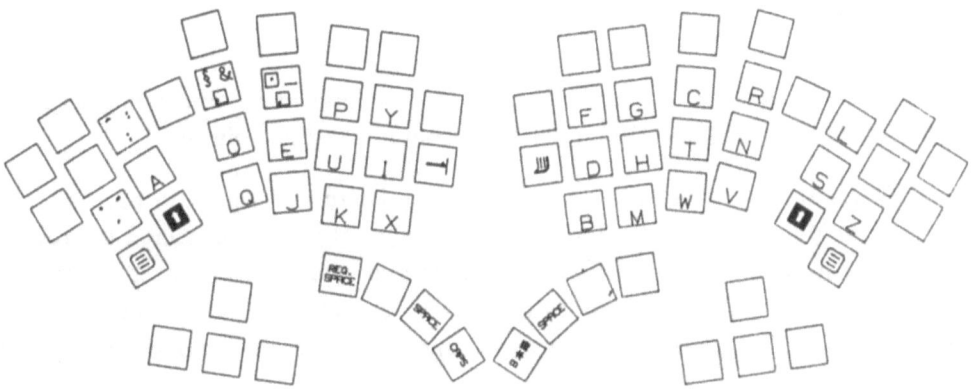

Fig. 5 Logical Layout of TRON Keyboard (in alphabetic)

1.4 TABLET

(a) Pointing Means

The term "pointing means" is defined as a means of pointing to a particular place on the computer CRT screen.

Today, pointing means such as a cursor key, tablet, mouse, track ball, and joystick are individually used according to applications. Of them, the cursor key is not a proper means in the bit map display environment. The mouse requires a certain area of space for its manipulation on the screen. It is difficult especially for a hand-held computer to work with the mouse. As a result of trade-off studies on all of such performance penalties, a small tablet with a pen has been selected as the pointing means of the TRON keyboard.

(b) Input Means for Handwritten Graphics

One may wish to insert figures, pictures and other graphics into a document being edited on the computer CRT screen for use in an office. This cannot be implemented without using a handwritten graphics input means. It may be a tool of the same type as the pointing means. A tablet with a pen has also been chosen with the TRON keyboard as it is considered most suitable for handwriting purposes.

(c) Electronic Pen

For purposes of this paper, the small tablet with a pen used for pointing or entering handwritten graphics is called an electronic pen. The electronic pen has a short-stroke switch at its top so that the operator may use it with the same feeing of manipulation as if it were an ordinary writing means. For the BTRON keyboard, the electronic pen has another switch — a modifier switch — on its body to get th menu frame on the CRT screen.

The tablet should have an appropriate size; if it is too large, it requires a larger space to move in or greater travelling distance of the operator's hand for pointing.

Where should the tablet be located? The TRON keyboard is designed to have its tablet placed in the front center of the board because the front is not considered to provide a useful space for any other purposes. Other important reasons are that, if the tablet is located there, it gives no handicap in the way of manipulation to the operator, right-handed or left-handed and its both sides can support the operator's wrists during keying operation.

2. DESIGN FOR THE TRON KEYBOARD IMPLEMENTATION

The following two basic guidelines underlay the actual designing of a TRON keyboard in accordance with the proposal (see Section 1):

- The dimensions (for size M) given in *Fig. 3* are critical and should not be significantly deviated.

- The resulting product should be compatible with the typical build and sensitivity of Japanese people.

2.1 DESIGN CONCEPT

Most conventional computers and keyboards give an impression of coolness. By contrast, the TRON keyboard should have something warm and a new aspect of value in its interface with human beings. In order to develop a futuristic image, the TRON keyboard basically should be thinner and smaller with curved or angled portions taken in its surface construction from both ergonomic and aesthetic points of view.

2.2 CONSIDERATIONS TO OUTLINE DIMENSIONS

The significant factors governing the final outline dimensions of the TRON keyboard unit are the outline dimensions and thickness of the key switch and tablet.

A key switch 14-16 square-mm, found popularly on most traditional keyboards, is too large for the key switch configuration with the keytop size specified in *Fig. 3*. This is especially true with the two central keys in the lowermost row. Since these two keys are tilted 10 degrees outwards, they come closer to each other as they approach the printed circuit board. Installing the two keys without mutual interference requires a special design strategy. In the present sample of design, the above problem was solved by using two face-to-face key switches each having a deviation of the center to that of the keytop. Further efforts are needed to develop appropriate key switches that can be commonly used with all sizes (S, M, and L) of the TRON keyboard.

The tablet should be designed to have as small outline dimensions as possible with a minimum thickness, while maintaining the effective area shown in *Fig. 3*. The surface of the keyboard cover has such a shape that the two curved areas — tilted 10 degrees to the right and left, and 10 degrees to the front — are partially scraped by the plane of the tablet tilted 10 degrees to the front. The ridge that is formed by the tablet plane should give no feeling of hostility to the operator when resting his/her wrists or hands on that plane during keying or pen-writing. This problem was analyzed by moving the tablet in both longitudinal and vertical directions, thereby determining its optimum position.

Fig. 6 shows an outside view of the TRON keyboard (size M) developed this time, with its rough dimensions included. It maintains nearly the same dimensions as proposed in Fig. 3; only the significant difference is that its depth is about 30 mm greater toward the operator side. This change would not decrease the operability of the TRON keyboard, one of the primary targets in its development. Thus it may safely be concluded that the proposed three-dimensional keyboard configuration has successfully been achieved.

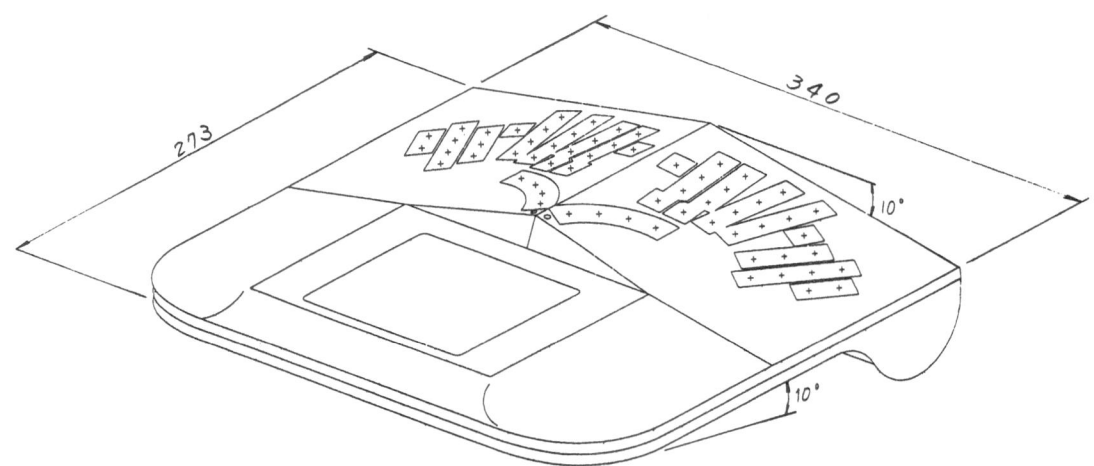

Fig. 6 Outside View of TRON Keyboard (Size M)

2.3 SIZE AND SHAPE OF KEYTOP

(a) Keytop size

The keys on the TRON keyboard (size M) shown in *Fig. 3* has a basic pitch of 16 mm. However, since the keys are laid out in a fan-shaped pattern in the right-handed and left-handed key blocks, there should be differences from keytop to keytop in the vertical and horizontal lengths that can be implemented depending on the position each key takes. With the character layout taken into account, a keytop size of 15 mm (vertical) by 12.5 mm (horizontal) has been selected, which is the largest possible and which can be installed in any position within the two key blocks.

The keytops in the lowermost row differ in both shape and size from any other key as shown in *Fig. 7*. They are trapezoid as viewed from the top and have a major width of 16.5 mm, about 4 mm greater than other keytops. The reasons for such keytop design are that they substantially are positioned in the lowermost row in the fan-shaped layout pattern and that they are manipulated by the thumb which is the thickest of the five fingers.

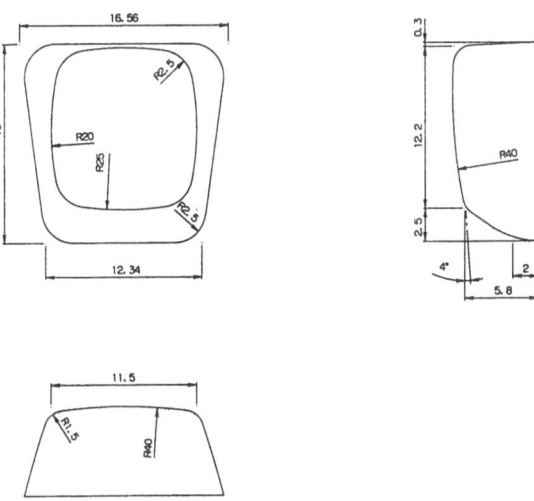

Fig. 7 Shape of Keytop Operated by the Thumb

The wide keytop design provides the operator with good reliance when he/she is using the thumb to operate them.

(b) Keytop shape

Three keytop mock-ups were prepared: one cone-cape type and two cylindrical types as shown in *Fig. 8*.

These were analyzed from various points of view. The result has shown that the cone-cape type keytop with a larger radius of curvature (*Fig. 8(c)*) is the best in both affinity for the finger and operability.

The front side of the keytop is designed to have a length enough to accommodate for character printing requirements and to be angled so that the characters printed on it may be reasonably visible by the operator. The top side of the keytop has as large a

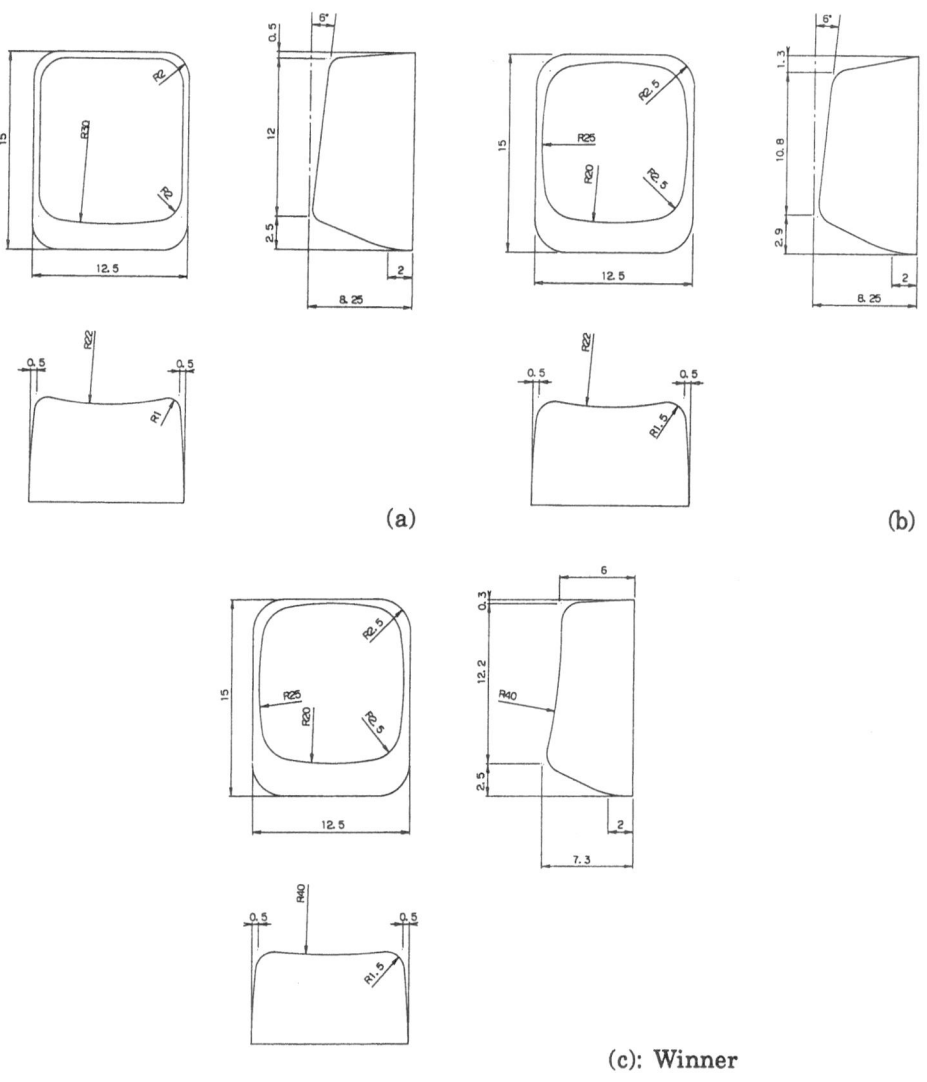

(a)

(b)

(c): Winner

Fig. 8 Shape of Keytop

character printed area as possible (23 mm by 11.5 mm) with its surrounding ridges configured with a maximum radius of curvature. This assures the finger of soft touch when it hits the keytop from any direction. With these features, the resulting keytop fully satisfies the two functional requirements — affinity for the finger and character indication — despite its considerably small size compared with conventional keytops.

3. CONCLUSION

We believe that a TRON keyboard (size M) having high operability and breakthrough in keytop shape and dimensions has successfully been developed. The Keyboard virtually follows the dimensions shown in *Figs. 2* and *3* with respect to the mechanical layout of keys and the three- dimensional configuration of the unit. We hope that many people will have chances of using the TRON keyboard and verifying its operability through their experience.

REFERENCES

[1]   KEN SAKAMURA, "Method to Input Japanese Characters in BTRON Environment — Design of TRON Keyboard", Information Processing Society of Japan, Japanese Documentation Processing Study Group, 7-2 (1986)

[2]   MASARU NAKASEKO, "Ergonomic Design of Keyboard", Human Engineering, Vol. 22, No. 2 (1986)

Sadao Tachibana: Engineer of Physical Design Department, Engineering Division, Data Processing Group, Oki Electric Industry Co., Ltd. Graduated from Iwate University, Faculty of Engineering, Department of Mechanical Engineering and joined Oki in 1974. Since then, he has been engaged in the development and engineering of input devices in the data processing world.

Ken Sakamura is an associate professor in the Department of Information Science at the University of Tokyo. He initiated the TRON project in 1984. Under his leadership, several universities and over 50 manufacturers are now participating in the project in order to build the computers for the 1990's. In addition to his involvement with TRON, Sakamura chairs several committees of the Japan Electronics Industry Development Association and the Information Processing Society of Japan. He has written numerous technical papers and books. He received the BS, ME, and PhD degrees in electrical engineering from Keio University at Yokohama in 1974, 1976, and 1979, respectively.

Chapter 4: CTRON

CTRON: An Overview

Ken Sakamura
Department of Information Science, Faculty of Science, University of Tokyo
Hongo,Tokyo,113 Japan

ABSTRACT

CTRON is a specification of OS for servers in a network of TRON-based computers. It is meant to support file servers, database servers, network gateways, and other specialized servers. Portability and other design issues are addressed in the design of CTRON specification.

Keywords: Operating System, File Server, Portability, Multi-user System

1. CTRON

CTRON is a subproject of the TRON project. [1] It is to produce a specification for computer systems that function as file servers or database servers in a computer network. The implementation target machine is not necessarily a computer that uses TRON VLSI CPU chip but possibly existing mainframe computers. Hence portability of CTRON-based OS is an important design topic considered in the design of CTRON specification. [2, 3, 4]

2. CTRON DESIGN OBJECTIVE

The design of CTRON specification calls for technical solutions to the following problems.

1) How do we design a CPU-independent interface to achieve high portability across different CPU's?

2) How do we design application-independent interface to achieve high portability across various application fields?

Assuring sufficient functions and high performance so that high level of parallel processing can be done in the CTRON-based OS is very important.

A preliminary research has proposed various methodologies to solve the questions and meet the requirements. [2] These include two-level design, black model of operating system functions, configuration management functions for many implementations on different computers.

3. DIFFERENCE BETWEEN CTRON, ITRON AND BTRON

CTRON is different from ITRON and BTRON in the following respects. [5, 6] ITRON is meant for embedded applications and there is no notion of user in ITRON specification. BTRON is meant for a workstation used by an individual so there is a concept of a user although existence of multiple users are visible only when network access is involved. On the other hand, the existence and management of multiple users is the major design issue of CTRON specification. Access authentication and resource allocation among users are just two examples of functions necessary in CTRON specification in order to deal with the existence of multiple users.

CTRON specification assumes that no direct man-machine interaction takes place on the CTRON-based computer systems. Rather such man-machine interactions take place on BTRON machines connected to CTRON-based systems. By eliminating the need for very complex man-machine interface, the designers of CTRON specification can concentrate on improving the overall system performance of CTRON-based computer systems.

4. CTRON: COMMON CHARACTERISTICS WITH ITRON

CTRON and ITRON have much in common; CTRON does not directly handle human interactions, and CTRON needs realtime response in order to communicate with ITRON and BTRON machines. Hence the initial design of CTRON was based on ITRON specification. If similar concepts, similar system calls, and similar system functions are required in both systems, we have tried to name them identically.

However, the lack of multiuser environment on ITRON-based systems makes it impossible to extend ITRON to CTRON smoothly. So we have analyzed what will become problems if we tried to build multi-user systems using ITRON-based OS. By analyzing the problems and deciding what new features are necessary to build such multi-user systems, we have determined the new features to be added to the CTRON specification.

5. CTRON: ADDED FEATURES

Let us summarize some added features. CTRON scheduling policy includes round-robin scheduling mechanism. This is vital for TSS (time sharing system). On the other hand, ITRON scheduling policy does not have such mechanism. In ITRON, one high-priority task can preempt all lower-priority tasks and can monopolize the CPU.

The design approach of ITRON intentionally avoids the approach of virtual machine to enhance the portability. This was because the overhead incurred by such approach was deemed to be too large for microprocessors. However, because CTRON is expected to run on powerful mainframe computers, the designers of CTRON use the virtual machine approach more casually.

6. INTEGRITY IN MULTIACCESS ENVIRONMENT

CTRON design calls for more secure system operation. For example, ITRON specification does not call for automatic release of system resources held by a task when the task ceases to exist. On the other hand, CTRON specification calls for such automatic releases. This is because the ITRON specification assumes that all the tasks in ITRON-based systems are designed and developed as cooperating processes and that such releasing of resources can be done by application programmers. CTRON specification assumes that users of CTRON systems are unrelated and compete for resources and that the OS is the only reliable allocator of such resources. Hence CTRON-based system must release resources held by a dying task.

7. CTRON: CENTER MACHINE FOR BTRON, ITRON COMPUTERS

CTRON does not have much in common with BTRON in the sense that BTRON has rich MMI functions and that CTRON does not deal with human operators directly. CTRON specification is tailored to mainframe computers so that their computing powers can be used fully.

8. IMPORTANCE OF CTRON

Why is CTRON important? Large-scale realtime systems have become popular; electronic funds transfer, automatic tellers at the banks, nation or world-wide ticketing service for airlines or railways are such examples. Many systems are now built using general purpose machines using the operating systems for these machines. Realtime response of these systems are very important. However, the general-purpose OS on the mainframe computers often lacked sufficient realtime response. Hence a great deal of efforts are made to offer realtime response by writing software for front end processor, etc. Clearly there is a gap between the mainframe OS designed long time ago and the requirements created by today's applications.

9. DISTRIBUTED PROCESSING WITH PC

Distributed computing using PC's or other specialized computers is clearly the way to go. Again, such distribution of computing tasks requires the careful design of central server systems so that a part of computing task can be done locally on the PC's and then the result be merged back on the mainframe computer and then be disseminated to other users on the same host. It is easier said than done. Retrofitting such distributed processing capability to existing OS is a major problem today.

10. OS FOR MULTIMEDIA SUPPORT

Mainframe computer OS was not designed to handle so called multimedia data such as figures, drawings, images, or voice in a clean way. These data must be dealt with each application in an ad-hoc way. However, the use of such data will become popular and there will be a need for OS services for handling such data.

CTRON will satisfy these needs very well. Realtime responsiveness is carried over from ITRON specification. Distributed processing will be done in conjunction with BTRON machines where man-machine interaction takes place and with ITRON machines from where machines communicate with CTRON servers. CTRON file system will support portable data format in the BTRON specification (TAD).

11. CONCLUDING REMARKS

In today's computing environment, a simple thing like operating a mainframe computer system through an advanced man-machine interface on a bitmapped display using window system has not been available commercially. CTRON, BTRON, and ITRON combination will make it possible.

CTRON specification is being designed and will be made public when it is finalized.

REFERENCE

[1]   Ken Sakamura. The TRON Project, IEEE MICRO, April 1987, p.8-14.

[2]   Toshikazu Ohkubo et al. Configuration of the CTRON Kernel, IEEE MICRO, April 1987, p.33-44.

[3]   Ken Sakamura. Making of TRON: part-11, bit, Kyoritsu, March 1987. (in Japanese)

[4]   Ken Sakamura. Architecture of the TRON VLSI CPU, IEEE MICRO, April 1987, p. 17-31.

[5]   Ken Sakamura. BTRON: The Business-Oriented Operating System Architecture, IEEE MICRO, April 1987, p.53-65.

[6]   Hiroshi Monden. Introduction to ITRON: the Industry-Oriented Operating System, IEEE MICRO, April 1987, p.45-52.

Ken Sakamura: see *"The Objectives of the TRON Project"* in this proceedings.

Design of CTRON

Tetsuo Wasano
NTT Network System Development Center
2-1, Uchisaiwai-cho 1-chome, Chiyoda-ku, Tokyo, 100 Japan

Masato Ohminami, Yoshizumi Kobayashi, Toshikazu Ohkubo
NTT Electrical Communication Laboratories
P.O. Box 8, Yokosuka Post Office, Kanagawa, 238 Japan

Ken Sakamura
Department of Information Science, Faculty of Science, University of Tokyo
Hongo,Tokyo,113 Japan

Abstract

Information communication networks are being developed which provide a variety of services integrating information processing and communications. A high realtime processing capability and high reliability are required in switching and other nodes making up such networks. Multi–user processing and large–scale data processing functions are also required, especially in information processing nodes. In addition, as the network develops, in order to realize a diversity of services reliably and efficiently it should be possible to incorporate similar functions in a number of nodes, and to change the distribution of functions among nodes. Software portability across nodes is thus an important factor. This paper will outline the design principles and configuration of CTRON, which is a set of operating system interfaces designed to meet these requirements in information communication networks.

Key Words

CTRON,Information communication networks, realtime processing, software portability

1. Introduction

Computer networks are configured hierarchically, for example, as wide area, metropolitan area, and local area networks. These networks contain different nodes for switching, communication processing, information processing, and workstations.Various information processing and communication services are provided by assigning functions appropriately to these nodes. Accordingly, these networks can be called information communication networks.

In the nodes of such information communication networks (hereinafter simply "networks"), especially in switching nodes, a high level of realtime processing capability and high reliability are required. At the same time, there are requirements characteristic of information processing, such as efficient assignment of resources to many network users, and processing data on a large scale. In addition, as the network develops, in order to realize a diversity of services reliably and efficiently it should be possible to incorporate similar functions in a number of nodes, and to change the distribution of functions among nodes. Software portability across nodes is thus an important factor (Figure 1–1). Operating systems in use up to now, however, even when providing the same functions, have provided different kinds of interfaces for different hardware or for different services, such as information processing and communication processing.,Thus, software portability could not be assured.

The emphasis in operating system research has conventionally been placed on achieving more effective use of computer resources, providing more advanced functions, and enhancing performance and reliability. More recent studies accent the standardization of operating system interfaces with a view to greater software portability. Some of these efforts concentrate on software portability among microprocessors [1,2], while others attempt to design standard interfaces based on existing conversational–mode operating systems [3,4].

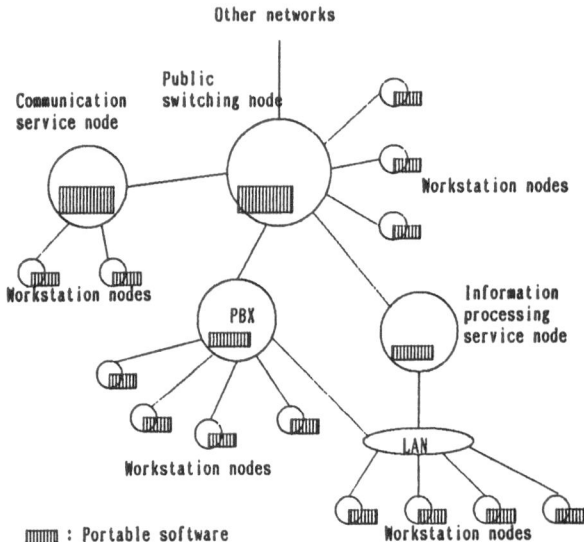

Figure 1-1. Software portability in networks

The TRON project [5] is studying operating system interfaces suitable for realtime processing. This project consists of several subprojects, including ITRON for industrial embedded systems [6], BTRON for business workstations [7,8], TRON CHIP for a microprocessor used in ITRON and BTRON, etc. [9], CTRON* for use in network nodes [10,11,12], and MTRON for managing the overall network containing these TRON nodes .

CTRON is a set of common operating system interfaces applicable to each of the information communication network nodes including ITRON and BTRON nodes. CTRON interfaces are applied to various processors from microprocessors to mainframe processors in networks,whereas ITRON and BTRON interfaces are used on microprocessors such as TRON chips.Although ITRON interfaces have no idea of a user and BTRON interfaces have a concept only of a single user,CTRON interfaces can manage multiple users existing in networks.

This paper discusses the concept and configuration of CTRON operating system interfaces, which can be used for realizing the functions and performance required in network nodes, and for achieving software portability across different kinds of nodes.

Sections 2 and 3 describe the CTRON interface design principles and outline its configuration, while section 4 discusses the actual interface design based on the design principles.

2. Design Principles

A. Function and performance requirements

The network nodes to which the CTRON interfaces are applied can be classified broadly into four types, based on forms of services:

(a) switching nodes (for circuit switching, packet switching, etc.), which exchange ınformation transparently without treating its form or content;

(b) communication processing nodes (for voice storage service, facsimile communication processing, etc.), which convert information formats and protocols without treating the information content;

(c) information processing nodes (for files and databases, banking processing, etc.), which store and process the information itself;

(d) workstation nodes, which are responsible for man—machine interface.

---

* This name was derived as follows: TRON is an acronym for "The Realtime Operating system Nucleus," while C stands for "Communication" and "Central."

These nodes each have different features (see Table 2–1), and their requirements of the operating system likewise differ from one type of node to another.

Switching nodes are required to exchange a multiplicity of information sets among many network nodes at the same time. Accordingly they must have an extremely high degree of multiple processing capability, and must meet severe realtime processing demands. Moreover, inasmuch as any fault in a switching node can have a large effect on the network as a whole, they must be fault tolerant.

Information processing nodes must process information on a massive scale, extending to as many as several gigabytes in database services. In addition they are required to meet the diverse processing needs of different users. Therefore they must be able to effectively control the demand load on processor and memory resources.

Workstation nodes must be able to control various I/O devices, for example bit–map displays or pointing devices, in order to provide a user–friendly man–machine interface. This requires among other things flexible interrupt control functions. In addition, rapid response and realtime capability are required for assuring ease of use at the level of man–machine interface.

Communication processing nodes have requirements similar to those of switching nodes, in that they must simultaneously control multiple communication circuits. Thus they must be capable of an extremely high degree of multiple processing in realtime, and must also have fault tolerance. In addition they have requirements like those of information processing and workstation nodes, since they must control various media–conversion devices and store information temporarily.

Since CTRON is a subproject in the overall TRON project, the terms used to describe concepts, and the forms of expression used for the interface, must match those of other TRON subprojects like ITRON and BTRON. When a workstation using BTRON interfaces, for example, is hooked up to a network, for the sake of load sharing between it and nodes containing CTRON interfaces, the CTRON nodes must be able to handle the BTRON files.

The above requirements can be summed up in the following set of design principles.

Principle 1: An interface able to realize multiple processing on an extremely high order, as well as realtime functions.

Principle 2: An interface with adequate functions to assure fault tolerance.

Principle 3: An interface able to realize multi–user and large–scale processing.

Principle 4: An interface conform to the TRON total architecture [4].

B. Software portability

To assure software portability across each of the nodes in the network, the following conditions must be satisfied.

(a) The operating system interfaces must be commonly applicable to each of the nodes.

(b) The software should be written in standard high–level languages.

Each type of network node has a different set of conditions that it requires of an operating system. If interfaces are specified differently in accord with each set of conditions, software portability across

Table 2-1. Characteristics of network nodes

Item / Node	Realtime performance	Number of tasks handled simultaneously	Amount of data per service unit	Device variation
Switching control	Up to several msec	5,000 to 10,000	Up to several K bytes	Switching devices
Communication service	Up to several msec	5,000 to 10,000	Up to several 10K bytes	Media–conversion devices
Information processing service	10 msec to 100 msec	100 to 1,000	Up to several G bytes	Peripheral devices
Workstation	10 msec to 100 msec	Up to 50	Up to several M bytes	Man–machine interface devices

nodes cannot be achieved. Rather, interfaces must be specified which are common to each type of node, that is, which are not dependent on the application fields.

Furthermore, within a network there are many kinds of hardware with different architectures. Only by providing virtual hardware interfaces which mask these differences in architecture can common–use interfaces be achieved, applicable to different hardware. Common–use operating system interfaces are then those which do not depend on the application fields or the hardware architecture.

An operating system can be defined as that which provides the access interface to physical and logical resources. Accordingly, if interfaces are to be applicable in common to different nodes, virtual interfaces must be provided for physical resources, and common–use interfaces for logical resources. Physical resources include those such as processors and memory, which provide the running environment for software (processor architecture), and also those such as magnetic disks and printers, which are the objects of software processing (device architecture).

Each of nodes in a network has its own physical and logical resources. If software in one node is to be moved efficiently to another, interfaces should be provided that enable resources to be obtained, accessed or released without dependence on the resource distribution.

Interfaces must be specified using standard high–level languages (language binding), thus permitting software to be written in such languages. This requires that the operating system interfaces be specified in a form that is not dependent on language specifications.

Principle 5: An interface independent of application fields.

Principle 6: An interface independent of hardware architecture.

Principle 7: An interface which does not require consciousness of how resources are distributed in the network.

Principle 8: Specification of the operating system interface in language–independent form and in standard high–level languages (language binding).

C. Subset specifications

In CTRON, interfaces are being specified which are applicable to various kinds of architectures and nodes. A specific node, however, is not likely to require all of the interface functions at one time. Rather the interface functions required by a node should be made available selectively. Accordingly, the CTRON interfaces consist of different interface units, which can be selected and combined as needed to provide the required functions.

Simply allowing interface units to be selected and combined freely, however, would endanger software portability. To avoid such a situation, subset specifications are prescribed, which indicate the allowable combinations of interface units; and subset series are further prescribed which guarantee upward compatibility of software.

These measures not only achieve portability, but at the same time make possible construction of an operating system that is matched to the requirements of different nodes.

Principle 9: An interface consisting of separable interface units that can be combined as needed.

Principle 10: Prescription of interface unit combinations (subset specifications), and of subset series that guarantee upward compatibility of software.

D. Openness and harmonization with international standards

The CTRON interface specifications are being prescribed originally, exclusive of any licensed information. They are not the property of any specific companies or individuals. Any who bears his share of the expenses for their delivery can get and use them, although he must not modify them so that software portability may not be assured. This policy has been adopted in order to provide a broad basis for software portability.

Functions for which international standards have already been decided are being based on those standards, to avoid unnecessary duplication of investment and to prevent needless confusion. On the other hand, where such standards do not yet exist, new proposals will be put forward actively.

Principle 11: Offering interface specifications to the public free of charge.
Principle 12: To follow international standards, or in the case of functions where standards have not yet been firmly established, to propose new international standards based on the CTRON interfaces.

3. CTRON Interface Configuration

In order to satisfy the design principles for assuring software portability, the CTRON interfaces are configured in two layers. One layer has virtual interfaces for physical resources (basic operating system interfaces), while the other layer has common-use interfaces for logical resources (extended operating system interfaces) (Figure 3–1). Moreover, the CTRON interfaces include those which do not require consciousness of how resources are distributed in the network. Thus an extended operating system and its upper software can be configured without dependence on differences in architecture or on distribution of physical and logical resources, promoting greater software portability.

The basic operating system interfaces consist of a kernel interface which fulfills the role of hiding processor architecture, and an I/O management interface for hiding device architecture. The extended operating system interfaces include separate interfaces for management or control of different logical resources, for example file management and communication control interfaces. Dividing the interfaces into separate elements allows parallel consideration of different aspects of the interface specifications. Another advantage of this approach is that it enables minimizing the relationship among interfaces so that they may be added or removed as needed.

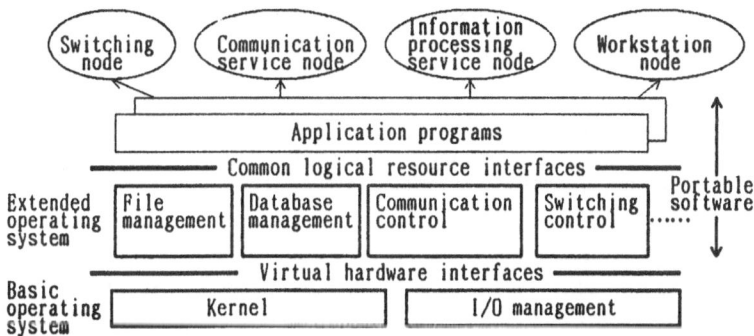

Figure 3-1. Overall CTRON interfaces

4. Design of the CTRON Interfaces

A. Kernel interface

A.1 Kernel model

In design of the kernel interface, a kernel model is proposed for the sake of hiding processor and memory architecture (Figure 4–1). The kernel consists of a mechanism for control of tasks assigned to processors, a memory mechanism enabling programs and data to be accessed, a mechanism for synchronization and communication among tasks, a timer mechanism for time management, and mechanisms for notification of asynchronous events originating in hardware or software.

A.2 Kernel interface design

(1) Enhancement of realtime functions
In order to realize ultra-multiple and realtime processing (Principle 1), the following functions have been provided in the interface specifications for task control.

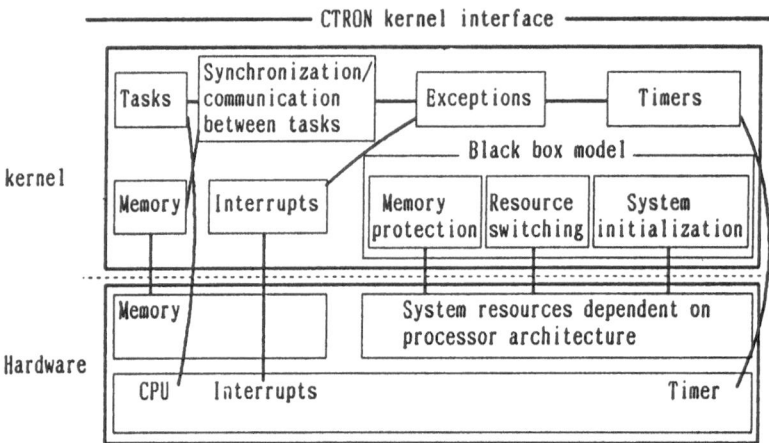

Figure 4-1. CTRON kernel interface and interrelationship
of hardware resources

a) Preemptive scheduling is specified, whereby tasks that must be processed in realtime are scheduled at the same time as an event occurs. This is to assure prompt handling of the sudden sporadic events that occur in switching and communication processing nodes, for example.

b) To avoid memory overload, some tasks must compulsorily be taken off the dispatch queue (suspended state). These cannot be tasks requiring realtime processing, however, since there would then be no guarantee of processing performance. Accordingly tasks are divided into two types, those which may be put in suspended state and those which may not.

c) To speed up the starting of tasks which perform periodic processing, a cyclic scheduling function is specified.

(2) Virtualization of processor architecture

To ensure software portability, an interface independent of processor architecture is provided in the kernel (Principle 6). Indiscriminately specifying the kernel interface independent of hardware architecture, however, runs the risk of lowering performance and preventing its application to realtime processing. The interface is thus specified as outlined below, within a range that does not run this danger of lowered performance.

a. Memory architecture

A distinction can be made between real memory and virtual memory architecture. The memory functions, such as those for obtaining and releasing memory space, and for defining and deleting memory pools for specific use, are required in both architectures, and are accordingly specified in common in the interface. In addition, virtual memory architecture interface specifications include functions for reserving virtual memory space and allocating real memory space for this reserved space, thus ensuring efficient use of the virtual memory mechanism. In the case of memory protection functions, which differ greatly from one architecture to another, only the names of such functions are specified, in what is called a "black box model." Clues are then given for determining the parts of programs to be modified when software is transported.

b. Asynchronous events

Asynchronous events are classified as those transferred to tasks (called exceptions), and those transferred to processors (called interrupts). Exceptions are divided into internal exceptions, originating in task execution, and external exceptions, resulting from other causes. These exceptions are specified without dependence on architecture . Since interrupts strongly depend on processor architecture, no specification is made of interrupt causes.

(3) Kernel subset specifications

The CTRON interfaces, as we have noted, are made up of different interface units. These are of two kinds. One is a common interface unit, which must always be implemented when the CTRON interfaces are applied to different processors and network nodes. The other kind is a selectable interface unit which is implemented only for certain processors and nodes. The specification of each CTRON operating system instance is a particular subset combining these interface units.

The kernel interface consists of four interface units (Principle 9). One of these is a common interface unit, while the other three are selectable (realtime model, composite model and virtual memory model). These can be combined into six subsets and two subset series (one series for switching and communication processing nodes, the other for information processing and workstation nodes). In each of the subset series, upward portability of software is guaranteed (Principle 10) (Figure 4-2).

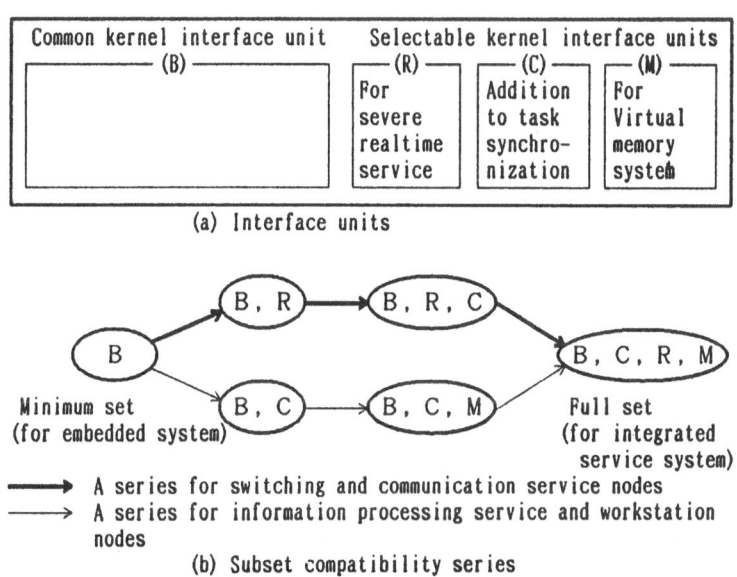

(a) Interface units

(b) Subset compatibility series

Figure 4-2. Interface units and subset compatibility series
in CTRON kernel interface

B. I/O management interface

B.1 I/O management model

I/O devices (or more precisely, device controllers) themselves have functions for transferring data back and forth between memory and devices based on instructions from the processor, and for informing the processor of the results. For system administration, functions are necessary that can register I/O devices with the system, or cancel that registration. I/O management primitives can accordingly be listed as below.

a) Connection and disconnection functions for enabling or disenabling recognition of devices by the system.

b) Activation and deactivation functions, for enabling or disenabling access to devices.

c) Input/output functions.

d) Control functions for other than input/output.

e) Functions for informing the processor of input/output completion, hardware faults and the like.

I/O devices are far more diverse than processors, and are subject to remarkable advances in functions. Moreover, it is sometimes necessary for flexible and high-speed control to be carried out by

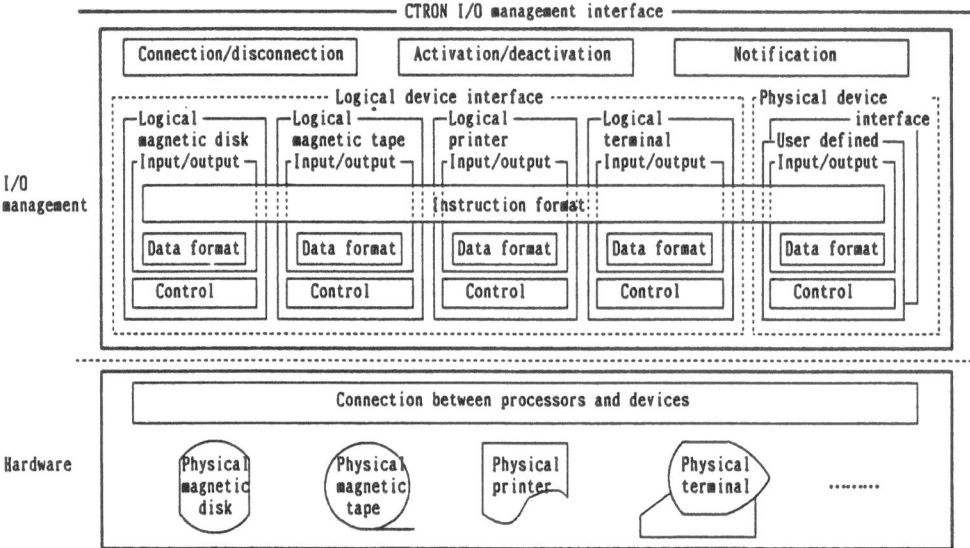

Figure 4-3. CTRON I/O management interface

software in accord with the device characteristics. For these reasons, the three types of interfaces below are provided (Figure 4-3).

(1) Functions such as connection/disconnection, activation/deactivation, and notification, which have little to do with the specific features of different devices, are specified as an interface common to all devices.

(2) The following two types of interface are provided for input/output and control.

a) Logical device interface: The architectures of devices like magnetic disks or magnetic tapes show relatively little variation, and such devices can be classified into a few types, called logical devices. For the sake of user convenience, input/output and control interfaces are specified for each logical device. The architecture differences within each device type are thus hidden.

b) Open-ended interface: An interface is specified enabling direct control of physical characteristics of devices. This interface is for the sake of efficient control of a variety of devices, including those devices for which a logical device interface is specified.

B.2 Subset specifications for I/O management

The types of devices that are connected to a network node depend on which functions are assigned to that node in the network. Accordingly, no subset series is specified, but a subset is specified for each logical or physical device.

C. File management interface

C.1 File management model

File management functions, as will be described below, consist of those for managing location of files and those for accessing files (Figure 4-4).

(1) Management of file location

It should be possible to manage files in groups, for ease of managing the correspondence between files and detachable physical devices (strictly speaking, media), and also to facilitate logical management of

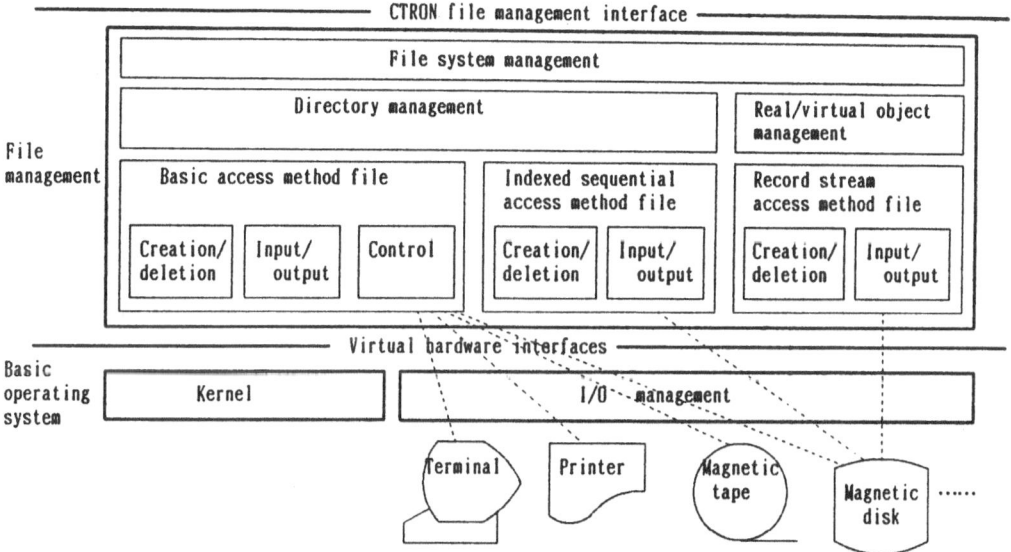

Figure 4-4. CTRON file management interface

files. Ease such file group, considered as a management unit, is called a file system. Management of file location can accordingly be classified as that for individual files and that for file systems.

Two methods are specified for managing location of individual files. One is a tree–structured directory management, for keeping efficient track of files of large numbers of users. The other is real/virtual object management [7], in which the relations among files are expressed as a network, thereby efficiently realizing superior man–machine interface at workstations. Management of file system location includes that of directory–shaped file systems and that of network–shaped file systems. BTRON file systems can thus be handled in CTRON as well (Principle 4).

(2) File access management
    The basic file access management functions are those for creation and deletion of files, and the input/output functions for reading from and writing to files.
    Files are logical resources; but among the devices corresponding to them there are some, such as printers, whose physical characteristics are directly visible to users. There are times when it is desired to create file contents that make use of these device characteristics. In order to deal with such instances, another function is specified for indirect control of devices through files.
    Three different file types are specified, as follows.
 a) The basic access method file, permitting input and output in various units, including high–speed input/output in multiple blocks (Principle 1).
 b) The indexed sequential access method file, in which records are easily retrieved, inserted, deleted, etc. according to keys.
 c) The record stream access method file [7], for ease of creating and editing document and other files at workstations (Principle 4).

C.2 Subset specifications for file management interface

The file management interface consists of four interface units, and of a subset series made up of four subsets, for switching, communication processing, workstation, and information processing nodes .

D. Database management interface

D.1 Database management model

Database can be classified technically into the following two types, based on such factors as their logical structure and the nature of data operations.
a) Network databases
Databases patterned after a data model based on a network structure (a tree structure is a special type of network structure).
b) Relational databases
Databases patterned after a data model based on a table structure. The type of databases specified in CTRON are relational databases. This choice is based on the operational superiority of such databases, as well as on the state of progress being made in standardization. Specifically, the ISO standard SQL interface has been adopted (Principle 12).

D.2 Subset specifications for database management interface

Database management interface subsets may be created in line with the followng six levels of standards permitted by the ISO, depending on the purpose and scale of the application system.
a) Conformity with all level 1 SQL standards
b) Conformity with all level 2 SQL standards
c) Conformity with all level 1 SQL–DDL standards
d) Conformity with all level 2 SQL–DDL standards
e) Conformity with all level 1 SQL–DML standards
f) Conformity with all level 2 SQL–DML standards

E. Communication control interface

E.1 Communication control model

The communication control interface for which prescription is made in CTRON is based on the international standard OSI (Principle 12). A communications control reference model is shown in Figure 4–5.

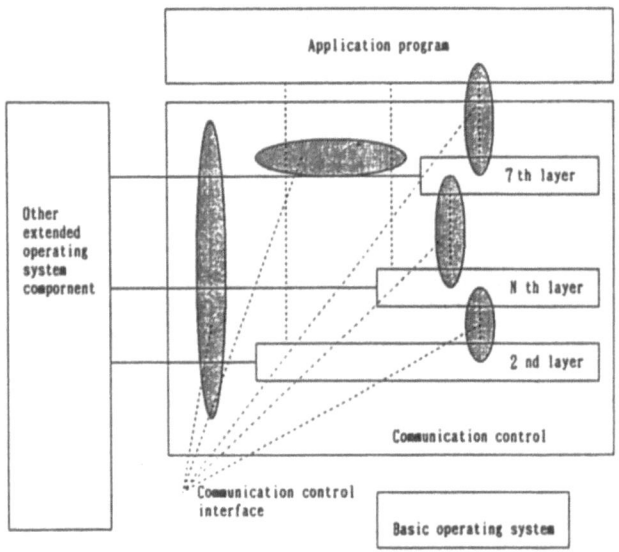

Figure 4-5.   Communication control interfaces

E.2 Communications control interface design

Design conditions for the communications control interface are as follows.
a) The protocol to be followed is that of OSI.
b) The protocol layers are those from layer 2 through 7.
c) The following profile is assumed:

Layer 2: LAPB, LAPX, CL–LLC
Layer 3: X.25, T.70CSDN,CLMP
Layer 4: Class 0, 2, 4
Layer 5: Kernel functional unit, half–duplex functional unit, duplex functional unit, typed data functional unit, minor synchronize functional unit, major synchronize functional unit, re–synchronize functional unit, exceptions functional unit, activity management functional unit
Layer 6: Under study
Layer 7: Under study

d) Communications control interface specifications are to be determined for each layer, based on the OSI reference model. The interface is to be prescribed so as to be as little dependent as possible on the profile of each layer.

In communications control, each layer will likely consist of the following functions.
(1) CCL (Communications Controller)
A functional module for realizing connection and disconnecion, data transfer and other OSI–based services involved in communications, as well as the management services necessary for their realization, such as activation and deactivation of OSI resources, supervision and testing of those resources, etc.

(2) OAM (Operation Administration and Maintenance)
A functional module which provides actual management of OSI resources, making use of (1) above.
CCL–CCL interfaces are prescribed between layers, and CCL–OAM interface within layers. No communications control interface is prescribed within OAM, however, so as to allow a greater degree of freedom in network management structuring (Figure 4–6).

E.3 Subset conditions for communications control interface

As noted in E.2, communications control specifications are made for each layer based on the OSI reference model. Subsets are defined within each layer specification.

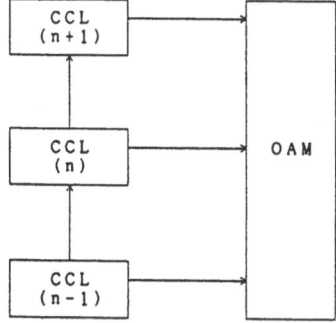

CCL······ Communication controler
OAM······ Operation administration and maintenance

Figure 4-6. Communication control interface classfication

F. Execution control

CTRON is required to have functions enabling use of computer resources in all sorts of ways, in order to meet service needs in all the different application fields. These functions are offered as execution control functions.

Execution control interfaces consist of two main groups of functions.

a) Basic environment and service primitives
   Process control
   program execution control
b) Service control functions for realizing the various service forms
   Transaction control
   Interaction control
   Batch control

The execution control interface reference model is shown in Figure 4–7.

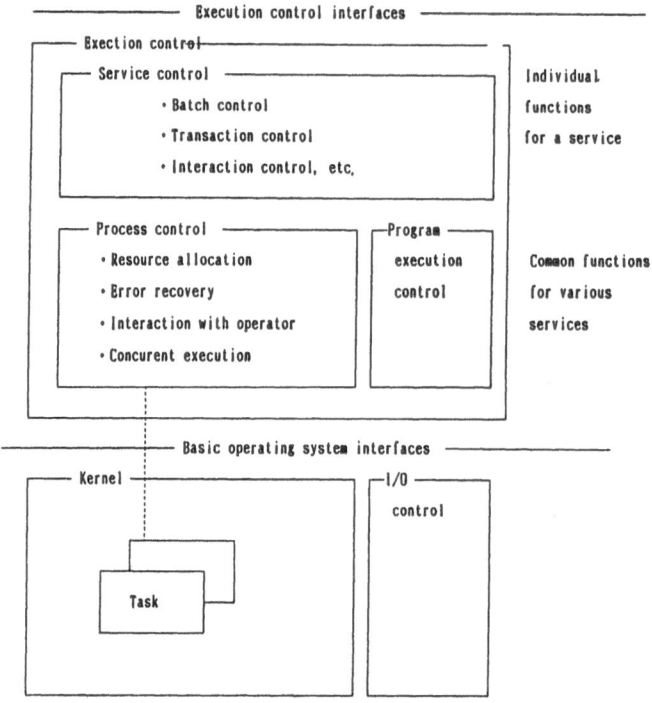

Figure 4-7. Execution control interfaces

F.1 Process management interface

In CTRON, the nature of user awareness of computer resources differs at each level. The higher the level, the more comprehensive is the awareness possible of different resources. Examples are tasks and processes. The processing units in the kernel are tasks. In CTRON execution control, one or more tasks are taken as a process and become a processing unit. For each form of processing, and optional configuration can be made of the tasks within a process. This makes it readily possible, for example, to effect a sharing of memory and file resources among tasks in the same process. Typical configurations of processes for transaction control and interaction control are shown in Figure 4–8. These processing units are always visible from application programs running on the extended operating

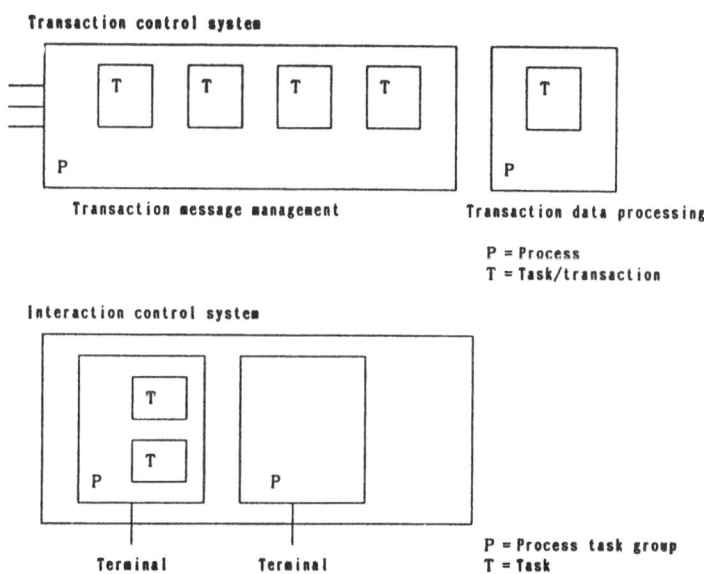

Figure 4-8. Process configuration example

system interface. Environment and resources are allocated to these processes and managed. (In the case of application programs that themselves perform multiple tasks, it is possible for processing to take place with awareness of the several tasks.)

F.2 Program execution control interfaces

(1) Program execution control model
CTRON program execution control functions include a search function for locating programs stored in files, a search function for loading programs from files to memory and a function for starting up program execution (Figure 4–9)
(2) Program execution control interface design
Realtime functions— Here the approach taken to achieving rapid startup of programs will be discussed, since this is an essential realtime function (Principle 1). Before a program can be started, the file in which it is stored must be specified and the file content loaded into memory. In order to achieve faster program starting, the series of preprocesses up to program load have been separated from the transrfer of control to the program, and separate system calls have been prescribed for each of these two aspects. This allows the user to control program residency, enabling speeding up of the start of programs to be controlled from the user's side. In addition, for the sake of users of interactive systems, a complex function has been prescribed for performing the series of preprocesses through program start with a single system call.

F.3 Subset conditions for execution control interface

In creating execution control interface subsets, the common interface unit consists of a process management and program execution control interface common to all environments and services. The selectable interface units dependent on the service form are subsets for transaction control, interaction control, and batch control.

170

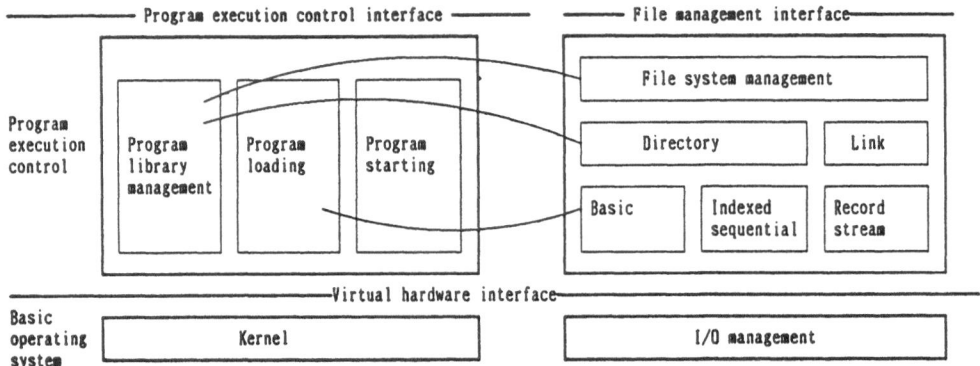

Figure 4-9. Program execution control and interrelationship of file management

5. Conclusion

This discussion has focused on the design principles of the CTRON interfaces, and the design methods based on these principles. The CTRON interfaces are applicable to each of the nodes in information communication networks and ensure software portability across different nodes. Up to now operating systems have been constructed separately for different applications, specific to the various kinds of hardware used in a network. The CTRON interfaces are being designed systematically for use in information communication networks. Their features include the following.

(1) To provide the functions and performance required at network nodes, the CTRON interfaces are given the total capabilities for realizing the very high order of multiple processing and realtime functions, demanded in the communications field, along with the multi–user and large–scale processing demanded in the information processing field.

(2) To assure software portability across network nodes, two–layer interfaces are specified, with one layer for virtualization of physical resources and the other for common use of logical resources. The virtual hardware interfaces consist of a kernel interface in which processor architecture is hidden, and an I/O management interface in which device architecture is hidden. The common logical resource interfaces are specified according to the different logical resources, and are made up of separable interface units which can easily be added or removed as needed.

(3) To allow operating systems to be constructed in accord with the particular characteristics of different nodes while still retaining software portability, interface subset specifications are specified, along with subset series in which compatibility among subsets is guaranteed.

(4) The CTRON interface specifications are to be offered to the public nearly free of charge, and are being designed based on international standards.

Operating system interfaces must have frameworks for incorporating new functions in the future. The CTRON interfaces, for example, will eventually include the specifications required for artificial intelligence applications. These will be added to network nodes, thereby enhancing network services. The design approach with regard to artificial intelligence, fault tolerance and distributed processing interfaces will be reported on at another occasion.

Acknowledgements

The authors wish to express their deep appreciation for the valuable advice given by Dr. Fukuya Ishino, and for the guidance and cooperation provided by those involved in the CTRON project at Fujitsu Ltd., Hitachi Ltd., Mitsubishi Electric Corporation, NEC Corporation, Oki Electric Industry Co. Ltd., and Toshiba Corporation.

References

[1] D.L.Jackson and J.Cowan, "The Proposed IEEE 855 Microprocessor Operating Systems Interface Standard," IEEE Micro, Aug. 1984, pp. 63–71.

[2] D.L.Jackson (chm.), IEEE Trial–Use Standard Specification for Microprocessor Operating Systems Interfaces, Institute of Electrical and Electronics Engineers, Inc., New York, 1985.

[3] J.Isaak (chm.), IEEE Trial–Use Standard Portable Operating System Environment P1003/D6, Computer Society of the IEEE, Washington, D.C., 1985.

[4] D.W.Cragum, "Portable Operating System Environment," Proc. 5th Annual Phoenix Conf. on Computers and Communications, IEEE, New York, 1986.

[5] K.Sakamura, "The TRON Project," IEEE Micro, April 1987, pp. 8–14.

[6] H.Monden, "Introduction to ITRON, the Industry–oriented Operating System," IEEE Micro, April 1987, pp. 45–52.

[7] K.Sakamura, "BTRON: The Business–oriented Operating System," IEEE Micro, April 1987, pp. 53–65.

[8] M.Kobayashi, S.Takenouchi, Y.Kushiki and K.Sakamura, "The Software Structure of Extended Nucleus Bases on BTRON Specification," Proc. FJCC '87, Dallas, 1987.

[9] K.Sakamura, "Architecture of the TRON VLSI CPU," IEEE Micro, April 1987, pp. 17–31.

[10] I.Kogiku, T.Ohrui, T.Ohkubo and Y.Hamada, "A Real–time Portable Operating System Common to Switching and Information Processing Applications," Proc. ISS 87, Phoenix, 1987.

[11] T.Ohkubo, T.Wasano and I.Kogiku, "Configuration of the CTRON Kernel," IEEE Micro, April 1987, pp. 33–44.

[12]T.Wasano, M.Ohminami, Y.Kobayashi, T.Ohkubo and K.Sakamura, "Design Principles and Configuration of CTRON," Proc. FJCC '87, Dallas, 1987.

 Tetsuo Wasano is a executive engineer at NTT Network Systems Development Center. He is presently engaged in computer architecture strategy planning. Since joining the laboratory in 1970, he has been engaged in developmental research on DIPS operating systems and in research into artificial intelligence. He graduated from Tokyo University in 1970 with a BE degree. He is a member of the Institute of Electronics, Information and Communication Engineers of Japan(IEICE) and of the Information Processing Society of Japan(IPS).

 Masato Ohminami is a senior reserach engineer, supervisor at NTT Communications and Information Processing Laboratories, where he conducts research into operating system architectures. Since joining the company in 1972, he has been engaged in developmental research on DIPS operating Systems. He received the BE degree in 1970 and the ME degree in 1972 at Tohoku University in Sendai. He is a member of the IPS.

 Yoshizumi Kobayashi is a senior research engineer at NTT Communications and Information Processing Laboratories. Since joining the company in 1973, he has been engaged in the research and development of compilers and operating systems. He has played role in construction of principles required for the CTRON design and in the design of program management interface within CTRON. He received the BE degree in 1971 and the MS degree in 1973 at Osaka University. He is a member of the IEICE and the IPS.

 Toshikazu Ohkubo is a senior research engineer, supervisor at NTT Telecommunication Networks Laboratories, where he conducts research into operating system architectures. Since joining the company in 1971, he has been engaged in developmental research on DIPS operating systems and communication control systems. He received the BE degree in 1969 and the ME degree in 1971 at Waseda University in Tokyo. He is a member of the IEICE, the IPS and the Computer Society of the IEEE.

 Ken Sakamura is an associate professor in the Department of Information Science at the University of Tokyo. He initiated the TRON project in 1984. Under his leadership, several universities and over 50 manufactures are now participating in the project. In addition to his involvement with TRON, Sakamura chairs several commitees of the Japan Electronics Industry Development Association and the IPS. He has written numerous technical papers and books. He received the BS, ME, and PhD degrees in electrical enginerring from Keio University at Yokohama in 1974, 1976, and 1979, respectively.

Design of the CTRON File Management

Kimihito Kumazaki
Software Works, Hitachi Ltd.
Totsuka, Yokohama, 244 Japan

Abstract

The CTRON file management is a functional block of the extended operating system layer in CTRON. It prescribes interfaces used in common in various application fields and assures the portability of the upper-layer software. It provides two kinds of files: an ordinary file and a device file. It provides two kinds of file organization; a basic organization and an indexed sequential organization. It controls file location by means of a tree-structured directory. This paper describes these features of the CTRON file management.

Key Words

CTRON, File Management, Common Interfaces, File Organization, Tree-Structured Directory

1. Introduction

CTRON [1,2] is the name of a specification designed by the TRON project [3] . It defines functions of the operating system for network nodes that provide services for network users. It prescribes interfaces independent of service configuration and the type of processors of the system. CTRON aims at improving portability of operating system software as well as application software. It is divided into two functional layers. One layer consists of functions that hide the processor architecture and is called the basic operating system layer. The other layer consists of functions independent of the processor architecture and is called the extended operating system layer.
In this paper I introduce the design of the CTRON file management that is a functional block of the extended operating system and provides the unified access means for files and data.

2. Design policy of the CTRON file management

The design policy of the CTRON file management is the following.

(1) Providing common interfaces and assuring software portability

It is not easy for file users to have to attend to the physical attributes of various file devices. The file management prescribes logical interfaces so that users do not have to attend to the physical attributes.

It provides common interfaces and assures the portability of upper software. In addition, the file management prescribes the interfaces to other functional blocks of the extended operating system so that the latter may be made portable.

(2) Interfaces used in common in various application fields

CTRON may be placed in the network nodes for information processing, communication processing, switching, or workstations. So various design prerequisites are set for the file management. In the on-line and real-time processing environment, functions to efficiently process a great amount of files and data are required. In the software development environment, where files are created, registered and deleted frequently, functions for easy-handling of files are required. The file management program should be fit to be used by programs in the operating system, such as language processors and programed-file management programs. So the file management needs to provide the functions of file-access and the file-organizations to satisfy above conditions.

(3) Considering the standardization efforts

The CTRON file management prescribes the functions and the interfaces, taking into consideration the file management interfaces prescribed by the operating system standard such as MOSI [4] , and the file management specifications prescribed by the language specification of COBOL [5] , FORTRAN [6] , and the like.

3. Kind of file

There are two kinds of files. One is called device file, and the other is called ordinary file. The device file is such that a whole device is treated as one accessible file. The device files are peripheral logical devices; the specifications of logical devices are prescribed by the input-output control [7]. To be concrete they are a magnetic disk device, a flexible disk device, a write-once type optical disk devide, a magnetic tape device, a printer, and a dispiay device. The ordinary file is such that whole space on the logical device (medium) is divided into several subspace and each subspace is treated as an accessible file. To be concrete they are a magnetic disk device, a flexible disk device, a write-once type optical disk device, and a magnetic tape device.(Table 1)

Table 1. Relationship between devices and kinds of file

Logical device	Device file	Ordinary file
Magnetic disk	O	O
Flexible disk	O	O
Optical disk	O	O
Magnetic tape	O	O
Printer	O	X
Display	O	X

4. File organization and the function

4.1 File organization

There are two file organizations. One is called a basic organization, and the other is caiied an indexed sequential organization. A basic organization is the file organization where data are placed sequentially in a file. It can be placed on all logical devices handled by the file management.   Providing the same access interfaces for all logical devices gives the following merits:
① For sequential input or output, user can handle a printer and a display device as easily as a magnetic disk device.
② User can code his application program independent of the device. For example, user can dump data to a magnetic disk device temporarily instead of printing on a printer using the same program.

An indexed sequential organization is the file organization to which user can access by keys. It consists of a group of records; where each record is distinguished by one key or multiple keys, and of the index for searching for the position of the record. This file organization applies only to an ordinary file on the magnetic disk device and the flexible disk device. For an ordinary file, the physical structure of these file organizations is not prescribed in the CTRON file management, and any structure is allowed so long as the access interfaces to these file organizations are provided. The structure is defined by the implementor of the CTRON file management program. Accordingly if the file management program on one processor is different from that on the other processor, the physical structure is also different in general; and it may be inconvenient because a file conversion program for the file transportation between these processors are needed. But prescribing no physical structure enables the implementor of a particular application for the optimal structure.

4.2 Function on a basic organization file

The file management provides the following functions on a basic organization file.

(1) File creation
This is a function to register a file to the file management and ensure the file space.
(2) File deletion
This is a function to cancel a file from the registry of the file management and return the file space.
(3) Dynamic file space extension
This is a function to extend file space dynamically when there is not enough file space where the data are to be stored.
(4) File truncation
This is a function to release the unused part of the file space and to enable users to use the released space when file space is needed.
(5) File access (read and write)
This is a function to read data from a file and write data to a file. It enables to access multiple data as well. The location pointer of the file is set automatically at the subsequent data after each access; or it is possible to access the data by the specified location in case of a disk device group, which are good for direct access. It is possible to specify either mode at each access.
As for the completion synchronization of input-output of a file access, there are two methods of synchronization: by the file management and by the user program. The former is called synchronous access, and the latter is called asynchronous access. As for the asynchronous access, the file management provides two waiting options: one is waiting for the completion of the specified data, and the other is sending the completion to user's

message box so that multi-waiting by a user program is made possible.
(6) Change of access location pointer
This is a function to change the access location pointer.
(7) Set of the end-of-file
The file management manages the end of the effective data in a file
(end-of-file) and treats reading the end-of-file as a type of error. In
the language specification like FORTRAN it is possible to set the end-of-
file, so the file management provides this function for the ease of
realizing this specification.
(8) Opening of file access
This is a function that a user program notifies the opening of a file
access to the file mamagement.The file management obtains necessary
resources so that access operations may be handled efficiently.
(9) Closing of file access
This is a function that a user program notifies the closing of a file
access to the file management.

4.3 Function on an indexed sequential organization file

The file management provides the following functions on an indexed
sequential organization file.

(1) File creation
(2) File deletion
(3) Secondary key creation
The indexed sequential organization includes the key in a record and it is
possible to include multiple keys in a record. The file management
recognizes the key by the relative position in a record and the size. The
position and the size of a primary key are specified at file creation, but
those of the secondary keys are specified at the secondary key creation.
The function of the file management for secondary key creation is to
return the position and the size of the secondary key and to generate the
necessary index for the secondary key.
(4) Secondary key deletion
(5) File access (read and write)
In the function of reading it is possible to read the record either with
the key specified value or with the subsequent key value of the record
accessed preceedingly. In the function of writing it is possible to update
the record, or to add the record with the key value not existing in a file.
(6) Record deletion
This is a function to delete the record with the specified key value.
(7) Change of access location
(8) Key selection
This is a function to notify to the file management which key is used in
the access of a record. The file management accesses using the key
specified by the key selection till the next key selection. At the first
time the primary key is selected.
(9) Opening of file access
(10) Closing of file access
(11) Loading the index part
This is a function to load the index part to memory space. Thereby it
becomes unnecessary to read the index part from a medium and the access
becomes high-spead.
(12) Unloading the index part
This is a function to release the memory space which has been ensured for
the loading of the index part.

4.4 Support of file connection

In handling a file the operating system begins by searching the location of
the file information and, after finding it, loading it to memory space.
When a task carries out several functions for the same file, the searching

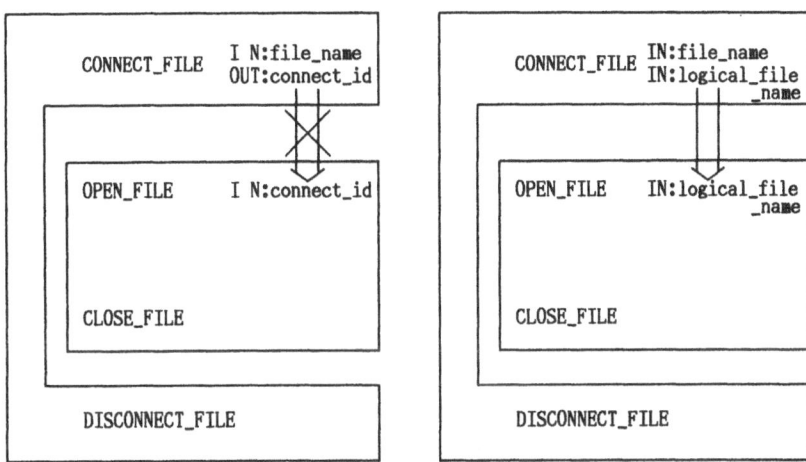

Figure 1. File Connection Interface

and loading of the file information is repeated, and this operation becomes overhead. The CTRON file management provides the function of file connection with a task.
MOSI has adopted the concept of file connection as well where a connect-id is returned by the file connection system call, and is used as an argument by the subsequent file system calls. This interface dose not come into question in the environment like MOSI where a file connection and the opening of the file access are called together in simple sequence by the application program. But in the environment where many user programs are executed, a batch control that uniformly manages the connection between the user job task and a file is required. Then the question arises that a connect-id cannot be passed from this batch control to the application program. The CTRON file management adopts the user defined logical file name instead of a connect-id for the parameter of the file system call and solves this question in the way that this logical file name is connected to a real file name by the system call of file connection.(Figure 1)

5. Exclusive control for a file

In case that several tasks operate on the same file or the same data, collision may arise between reading from the file and writing to it , and the operation may not be executed properly unless users establish contact with each other and control so that inconsistency among tasks may not arise. The CTRON file management provides the exclusive control for a file at the following three levels so as to improve user's operability.

(1) Exclusive control during the entire interval using a file
The occupation of a file by a task guarantees the continuous and consistent file operation for the same file. This indicator is specified in the parameter of the system call of file connection. It is expected that this function is used by batch control, as batch control usually starts a user program after occupation of file resources.
(2) Exclusive control during the entire interval of file access.
This is an exclusive control of file operations between opening and closing of file access, and prevents the inconsistency in data processing of a file.
(3) Exclusive control in every access

This prevents the inconsistency in data access processing (e.g. updating one data). For this type of exclusive control, it is made possible to lock not only data but also the file from reading to writing.(Figure 2) In addition to the function of exclusive control, the CTRON file management provides the function of file security by the access right control which can restrict the file access from other user's.

6. Management of file location

6.1 Directory

The CTRON file management manages file location by means of a tree-structured directory. This directory consists of a root node that is the starting point, file nodes, and directory nodes joining a root node and file nodes.(Figure 3)   But the physical structure of the directory depends on the implement action of the file management as well as the file, organization.   There is a name for each node, and in order to distinguish each node in the directory, the user uses a name called path name made by joining the node names.

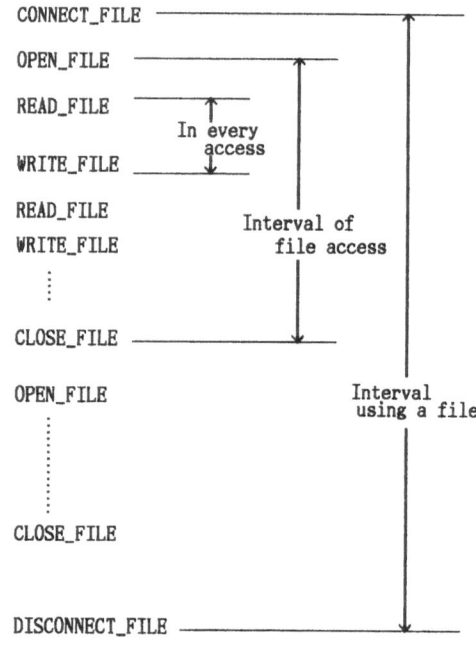

Figure 2. Exclusive Control Levels

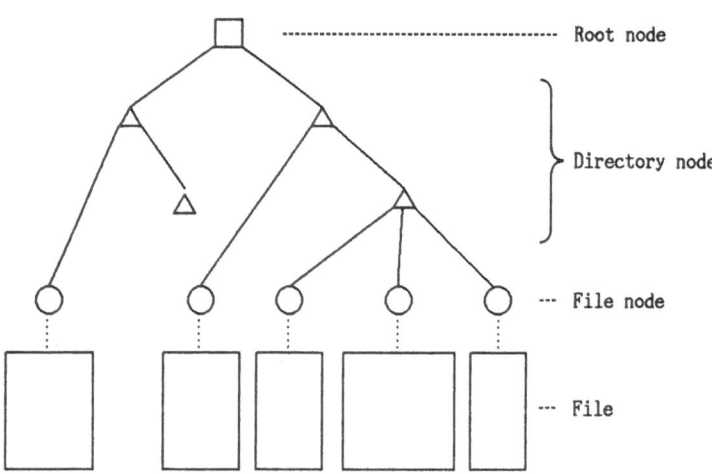

Figure 3. Directory structure

6.2 Logical path name

In accessing a group of files under the same directory node, it is troublesome to specify the path name every time and it takes much loading time for the file management to trace from the root node to the node. In order to solve this problem the file management provides the function to define the path name to a specified directory node as a logical path name and thus enables the user to specify the logical path name and the file node name for the file. Other operating systems with a directory provide the similar function named " Working Directory ", but they can define only one node at one time that becomes the starting point. The CTRON file management enables the user to define multiple nodes by the adoption of a logical path name. Thereby efficiency of file processes is improved when a user uses several groups of files; for example, compilers process a group of source files and a group of object files. Moreover the CTRON enables users to use null string as a logical path name and to use such notation of a path name as by working directory.

7. Subset specifications

The CTRON file management includes a number of functions used in various application systems; but in a specific system all these functions are not needed. For this problem the file management functions are classified into four function groups, each is called a subset unit. They are subset unit B, which consists of basic functions necessary to control a basic organization file, subset unit E, which consists of functions concerning a basic organization file exclusive of subset unit B, subset unit I, which consists of functions concerning an indexed sequential organization, and subset unit R, which consists of functions concerning a distributed file (under study at present). The file management prescribed five subsets as significant combination of these subset units and a subset

Subset unit	Functions
B	Control of a basic organization file (basic functions)
E	Control of a basic organization file (additional functions)
I	Control of an indexed sequential organization file
R	Control of a distributed file

(a) Subset units

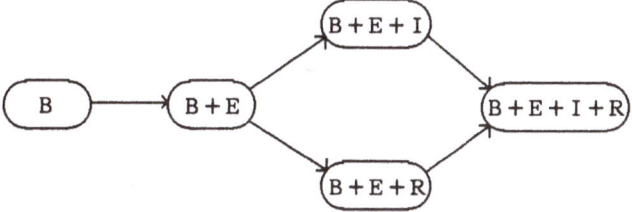

(b) Subset and its compatibility series

Figure 4. Subset specification

compatibility series.(Figure 4)   Subset B is the smallest functional subset of these subsets and is applied to a high-speed real-time environment such as communication service. Other subsets may be applied to information processing service, conversation service, and so on; and it is possible to select the most suitabe subset according to the application requirement.

8. Relation to BTRON file [8,9]

In the TRON project, it is BTRON that subscribes the operating system for super personal computer and man-machine interfaces.   The BTRON provides the unique file system with a network-structure that integrate a directory and a universal file so that it can support directly real-object/virtual-object model.   On the other hand, the CTRON is used as the operating system for the center machine of the computer network which consists of ITRON [10].and BTRON; therefore it needs to have the function of the file server for the BTRON.   The compatibility between the CTRON file and the BTRON file is required.   However, the CTRON need to be applied in the application filed with a large-scale database that is supported on a large-sized computer, so it is not reasonable to make use of te BTRON file specification that is optimized for real-object model.
The CTRON treats the functions of the file management with compatibility to the BTRON as the high-level file management like a database management. (Figure 5)   That is, by constructing the BTRON file system using the CTRON system calls on the basic organization file of CTRON, the functins that warrant the compatibility to the BTRON file and of the file server for the BTRON can be provided.(Figure 6)

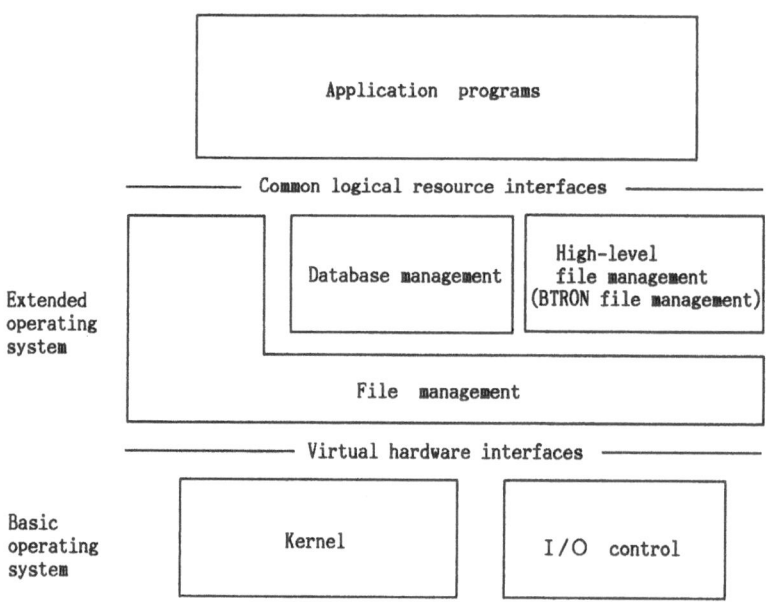

Figure 5. Position of high-level file management in CTRON
(BTRON file management)

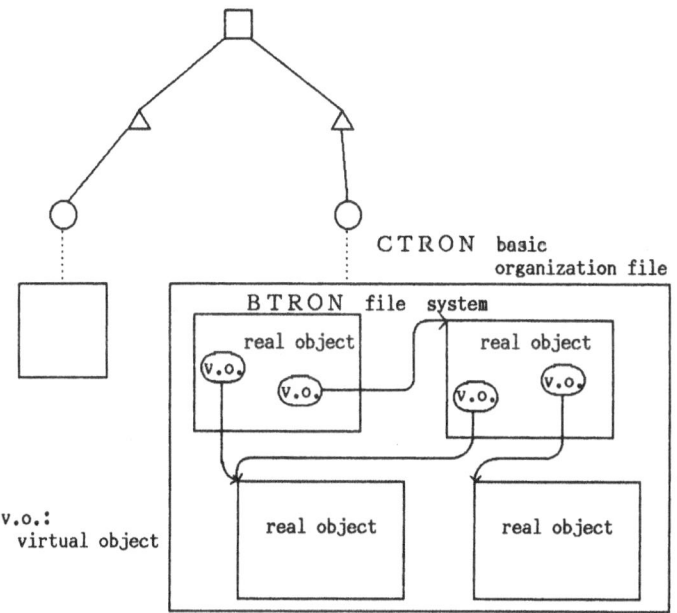

Figure 6. BTRON file system in CTRON

9. Conclusion

The present status of the CTRON file managemet is that the interface
specification (without the prescription concerning the distributed file
control) is completed. It is scheduled to be made open to the public
shortly. This paper has explained the outline of the CTRON file
management functions. In near future we expect that the file management
program with good performance based on this specification will be developed
and utilized by many application programs.

Acknowledgements

I express my special gratitude to Prof. Ken Sakamura, Dr. Fukuya Ishino
and the members of CTRON technical committee for their helpful advice in
the study of the CTRON file management.

References

[1] T.Wasano, M.Ohminami, Y.Kobayashi, T.Ohkubo and K.Sakamura,
"Design Principles and Configuration of CTRON", FJCC'87, October 1987
[2] T.Ohkubo, T.Wasano and I.Kogiku, "Configuration of the CTRON
Kernel", IEEE Micro, April 1987, pp.33-44.
[3] K.Sakamura, "The TRON Project", IEEE Micro, April 1987, pp.8-14.
[4] D.L.Jackson(chm.), IEEE Trial-use Standard Specification for
Microprocessor Operating Systems Interfaces, Institute of Electronics
Engineers, Inc.,New York, 1985
[5] Japanese Standards Association, "JIS C 6205(1980) Programming Language
COBOL", JIS Handbook Information Processing

[6] Japanese Standards Association, "JIS C 6201(1982) Programming Language
FORTRAN", JIS Handbook Information Processing
[7] S.Narimatsu, "Design of CTRON Input-Output Control Interface",
this issue
[8] K.Sakamura, " BTRON:The Business-oriented Operating System",
IEEE Micro, April 1987, pp.53-65.
[9] K.Sakamura, "File Management system in TRON", paper, Real-time
Operating System-TRON study Group, Institute of Electronic, Information and
Communication Engineers of Japan, 1, April 1987, pp.2-21.
[10] H.Monden, "Introduction to ITRON, the Industry-oriented Operating
System", IEEE Micro, April 1987, pp.45-52.

Kimihito Kumazaki is a senior engineer of DIPS
Department in Software Works, Hitachi, Ltd.
He joined the company in 1971 after graduating
from University of Tokyo with a B E degree. He
is a member of the Information Processing Society
of Japan.

Design of CTRON Input-Output Control Interface

Shinichiro Narimatsu

Software Development Department, System Engineering Division-IV, FUJITSU LIMITED
Kitasaiwai, Nishi-ku, Yokohama, 220 Japan

ABSTRACT

The function of the CTRON input-output control is to enable to port the operating system components, such as file management, using the access interfaces which conceal hardware architecture differences. However, performance and specification expandability should not be sacrificed to ensure this portability.

This paper discusses CTRON input-output control interfaces which were investigated based on these design issues. The results of this investigation are documented in " CTRON INPUT-OUTPUT CONTROL INTERFACE SPECIFICATION Version 1 ".

KEY WORDS

CTRON,input-output control,software portability

1. INTRODUCTION

In the CTRON reference model, the operating system is divided into two layers. One layer, called the Basic OS, serves to conceal differences in hardware architecture from the other layer, called the Extended OS, and enables the components which make up the Extended OS to be portable [1] . The Basic OS is further divided into two components. One is the kernel, which hides the difference in the processor architecture [2] . The other is the input-output control, which is main topic of this paper.

The CTRON input-output control essentially the same role as in ordinary operating systems. This means that the input-output control offers a primitive access interface to higher level software, such as programs for file managment and program management. The difference between the CTRON input-ouput control and that of ordinary operating systems is that the former is located on the Basic OS and serves to ensure portability of the higher level software that make up the Expanded OS. Therefore the primary consideration of CTRON input-output control design has been what kind of access interfaces to provide to enable portability to access users.

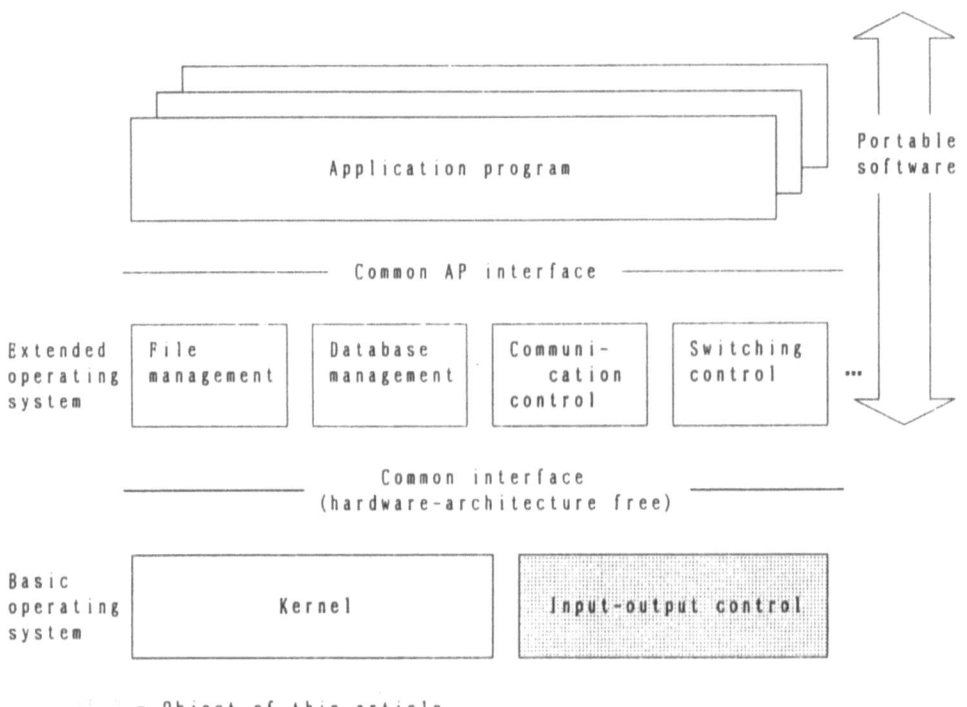

= Object of this article

Figure 1-1 Overall CTRON structure

However, portability should not be guaranteed at the sacrifice of expandability and performance. Therefore, the second consideration is how to maintain the expandability and performance. As a member of TRON families, the CTRON input-output control should have affinity with ITRON and BTRON. It should also be applicable to a wide service field. These are also items which must be considered in designing the CTRON input-output control.

The following chapters elaborate on these design considerations and describe the outline of the resulting CTRON's input-output control and its specifications.

2. DESIGN CONSIDERATIONS

The following description deals with design considerations of the CTRON input-output control and with what measures are being taken.

2.1 Enabling Software Portability

For access users such as apprication programs, operating system should absorb the following hardware variations, and conceal them from access users if portability, regardless of hardware type, is desired

(1) Differences in specifications for device startup instructions and for completion notice of input-output operations
There are many detail variations, but they can be roughly divided into three types:

① program control mode - in which instructions are given to transfer byte or word units between the processor registors or between the memory and the device.
Low speed printers and memory-mapped displays directly connected to the memories can be classified in this type.

② direct memory access mode - in which the device transfers multiple byte or word data as a single unit between memories, independent of the processor. An example is a high-speed file device connected to a bus.

③ channel control mode - in which a dedicated I/O processor, which is called a channel or IOP, sequentially executes at a series of I/O operations with another device when a startup instruction is given.

(2) Connection interface to devices
This is generally called an I/O interface. In addition to standard interface such as RS-232-C, RS-422, SCSI, and GPIB, there are many unique supplier interfaces and many variations.

(3) Specification difference among the same device type
For example, some magnetic disk units have media with a fixed-length record format, while others have media with a variable-length record format. Also, some have movable heads, while others have fixed heads. These hardware differences cause a command set of operation instructions to be seen differently by the software. However, the ultimate purpose of input-output requests is to read and write a certain length of data, and it is necessary for operating system to absorb insignificant differences. The same thing can be said about magnetic tape units and other devices.

In ordinary operating systems, the specification differences mentioned in (1) and (2) above are absorbed by the input-output control, and those mentioned in (3) are absorbed by the file management. However the CTRON file management is a component of the Extended OS, and an object for portability. Therefore in the CTRON, the input-output control should absorb all specification differences mentioned in (1) ～ (3) above. Just as the file management of ordinary operating systems conceal hardware specifications by using the abstract concept called a file, the CTRON input-output control introduces the abstract concept called a logical device, which has enabled

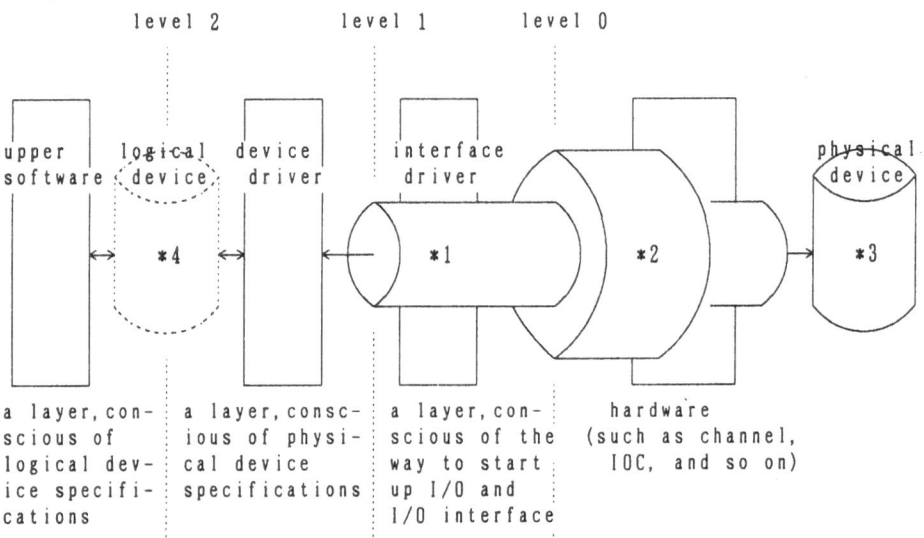

level 2   level 1   level 0

upper	logical device	device driver	interface driver		physical device
software	device				
	*4		*1	*2	*3

a layer, con-   a layer, consc-   a layer, con-   hardware
scious of   ious of physi-   scious of the   (such as channel,
logical dev-   cal device   way to start   IOC, and so on)
ice specifi-   specifications   up I/O and
cations   I/O interface

*1 ; path that the hardware shows (I/O interface)
*2 ; path to the physical device that the interface driver provides
*3 ; input-output device that actually exists
*4 ; abstracted device image that the device driver provides for the up
     per software

Figure 2-1   Layer Construction in the Input-Output Control

the Basic OS to hide the hardware specifications including (1) ~ (3) above.
Figure 2-1 illustrates the idea of layer in the CTRON input-output control.
The ineterface driver in the figure is a layer which is equivalent to the
input-output control of ordinary operating systems.   It provides a logical
channel for the device driver and for physical devices as it controls the
interface presented by the hardware.   The device driver also drives physical
devices and transforms an access request to logical devices to commands to
physical devices. Generally, only one interface driver is generated according
to the specifications in (1) and (2), but multiple device drivers are required
to accommodate the specification variations in (3).

To ensure higher level software portability, concrete specifications for
the logical devices must be specified as CTRON specifications. If hardware
differences are to be completely covered up, then the logical device
specifications must be uniquely determined.   However, this does not mean that
one would try to conceal the differences between a magnetic tape unit and a
magnetic disk unit using the input-output control. These devices have
primarily been designed for different purposes, and even if separate
interfaces are provided, it will not become a factor in obstructing software
portability. Therefore, in CTRON, commercially available devices are
classified into seven types according to their purposes. The common functions
of each device type have been extracted and are described in Chapter 4,
"Standard Logical Device Specifications".

2.2 Coping with Technical Development

As described in the preceding sections, the specifications for the standard logical device in the CTRON were set up to enable software portability . However, the technical progress in the field of peripheral devices has been remarkable, and it can be easily anticipated that the completely new devices, such as data base machines, will appear in the near future. It can also be anticipated that there will come a time when devices which can currently deal with standard logical device specifications will not be able to perform satisfactorily by using the same standards as the trend in high performance continues.

To cope with future technical progress, CTRON permits implementers to freely define specifications for logical devices. The interface to access these non-standard logical devices is called GIO(General IO), and is distinct from another interface called BIO(Basic IO). The BIO classifies the system calls according to access class (READ/WRITE/CONTROL), and stipulates the detailed parameter specifications. In contrast, there is only one type of GIO system call and no parameter specifications are setup in the CTRON specifications. For devices that are not included in the standard categorizations, loose specifications are temporarily applied in order to reduce the impact of the higher level software for which logical device specifications will be standardized in the future.

2.3 Performance Consideration

When the standardization attempts are made in the software industry, decrease in performance due to overhead becomes a serious problem. Consideration of this matter is especially crucial for input-output control because of its nuclear function in the operating system.

(1) Standardization at a high level

Interface standardization was carried out at a relatively high level among the input-output control levels. This has enabled the interface design to focus only on the essential functions without being affected by function details of I/O interfaces and devices. As a result, the interface with the higher level software has become concise, and has enabled reduce overhead for interface matching such as creation and check of channel commands.

(2) Insuring implmentation flexibility

Only the interface with the higher level software has been specified. No limitations have been established for devising input-output controls. Therefore, the device driver and interface driver can, if necessary, be produced as one body. Like this way, the implementor can make the most appropriate setup considering the system characteristics and performance requirements.

(3) Others

In addition to (1) and (2) above, an interface has been established which enables the reading and writing of multiple blocks with one system call with special emphasis on the file device performance.

2.4 Affinity with ITRON and BTRON

The relationship between CTRON input-output control and ITRON or BTRON input-output control is important because CTRON is a member of the TRON family [3].

CTRON and ITRON are similar in that both lack a man-machine interface [4]. BTRON is different because it has such an interface [5]. Therefore when deciding the CTRON input-output specifications, importance was placed on matching ITRON input-output control with regards to input-output layer and system call names. However, the two systems are not entirey same, for ITRON deals with build-in systems that have various input-output devices and CTRON deals with general purpose systems using mainly magnetic disk units. The comparison between the two systems are described in Table 2-1.

In contrast to the other two systems, the BTRON OS assumes that operations take place using the bit map display attached to the devices and does not incorporate the concept of "terminal", in the usual meaning of the word, nor does it require any terminal connections. The interface with the user does not involve input-output functions, but operates using higher level

Table 2-1   Input-Output Control Comparison between ITRON and CTRON

| | Agreed | Disagreed | |
		ITRON	CTRON
Aim	· providing easy-to-use standard interface · providing expansible interface	· lays a stress on the applicability for a individual system	· lays a stress on the portability and the generality
Logical Device	· specifying a logical device aimed for the expandability as GIO	· specifying CIO intends only for character devices	· specifying BIO intends for both character devices and block devices
Intended User	· program that controls devices such as display device and printer	· program that controls devices such as sensor	· file management, data base monitor, program management, and so on

programs like display primitive and event control. In addition, printing mainly involves image transmission and has little use for character-based control codes. In other words, when BTRON is compared with CTRON or ITRON, the difference is in input-output levels. Yet both CTRON and BTRON have similar system call names, and for both systems consideration is given to easy understanding of the operating system by the user.

2.5 Application to Diverse Service Field

CTRON may be applied to a variety of service fields such as information processing and work station processing. The peripheral device configuration differs according to the service field. For example, magnetic tape units are usually not used for work stations, so when implementing CTRON as the operating system of the work station, the access interface for magnetic tape units is not needed. Therefore, there is a need to define subsetting of the interfaces indicated by the input-output control depending on the device configuration. However, because conscious interface subsetting obstruct the portability of the higher level software, it was decided to stipulate the rules for subsetting.

3. INTERFACE SPECIFICATIONS

The CTRON input-output control interfaces include interfaces related to system call, which is utilized by users, and an interface that reports from the input-output control such as logical device notice information. The former handles "device control block operation", "process request by a system call", and "completion notice of a system call", and the latter handles "asynchronous event notice", "recovery process for hardware error", and "input-output error log notice".

3.1 Device Control Block Operation

A management table is generally used to define or control devices. The CTRON input-output control has also set up a management table, called a device control block, as management information logical devices. Creating the device control block means that a logical device and its device driver have been registered, and clearing it means that such data has been deleted. The device identifier that specifies a logical device when the device control block is created, comes out from the input-output control, and is used as a parameter when requesting input-output until the device control block is deleted. The device control block is classified into the following three parts, each being different in their specified level and purpose:

① Common section

This is the section in which the common information is defined regardless of the type of the logical device and proper system processing. Fundamental information is stipulated for control of the logical devices.

② Device specific section

This is the section where information is defined for each logical device mainly the information necessary for requesting input-output to the logical device.

③ System specific section

This is the section in which the information is defined for each system mainly the information required to implement the CTRON input-output control, such as physical device information. This part is not specified the contents by the CTRON input-output control interface specification.

3.2 Process Request by System Call

The system of the CTRON input-output system calls is broadly classified into the following two types. Individual system call names and the functions are listed in Table 3-1.

① System calls that control logical devices

These are system calls that register or delete logical devices and perform status control. Ordinary users are programs which perform management of the entire system, and are not programs which executes input-output process such as file management.

② System calls that demand input-output requests

These are system calls which demand or cancel input-output requests to logical devices. It is supporsed that users of these system calls are programs which execute input-output processes such as file management.

3.3 Completion Notice of System Call

For system calls which request input-output, there are two ways of notifying completion of the call. One is an internal synchronous completion notice that accesses a logical device when an input-output request is received, and returns the control after the completion. The other is an external synchronous completion notice that merely receives the system call or demands an access to a logical device when an input-output request is received, temporalily ends the system call before the completion of the access, and notifies completion of the call separately from completion of the access. In this case, the method of notification is message communication provided by Kernel, which is carried out by specifying parameters, such as message box ID, upon receiveing a system call.

Which completion notice is used depends on user's operating conditions, and does not concern input-output control.

Table 3-1 System Call List

Classification		System Call Name	Function
Logical Device Control	Logical Device Register/ Remove	CREATE-DEVICE	Registers a logical device in the system and creates its device control block.
		DELETE-DEVICE	Removes a logical device from the system and deletes its device control block.
	Logical Device Start/ Stop	INITIATE-DEVICE	Enables access to logical device.
		TERMINATE -DEVICE	Disables access to logical device.
	Device Control Information Get/Change	GET-DEVICE -CONTROL -INFORMATION	Gets the contents of a device control information.
		CHANGE-DEVICE -CONTROL -INFORMATION	Changes the contents of a device control information.
I/O Request	Demand for I/O Request	READ-BIO WRITE-BIO CONTROL-BIO REQUEST-GIO	Demands for I/O request to a logical device. Retries if fault occurs, and notifies the occurrence if not recovered.
	Cancel of I/O Request	CANCEL-IO -REQUEST	Cancels the demanded I/O request.

3.4 Asynchronous Event Notice

An asynchronous event is a notification from a logical device which is not directly concerned with input-output request. The events are set for each logical device. For example, in the case of a logical DK device, there are two types; a not-ready release notice and a reserve state release notice for shared device in the system. The asynchronous event is notified through message communication to a message box ID, which is the destination entered in the device control block .

3.5 Recovery process for hardware error

The recovery process for hardware error in a logical device is devided into three phases, each of which has a predetermined interface.

(1) Retry

This is a closed process in the input-output control that functions to retrieve intermittent errors. Therefore, there is no specific interface for the retry process. However, some input-output requests do not require the retry process. Therefore each system call for input-output request includes a parameter that specifies if the retry process is necessary or not.

(2) Error notice

If the retry has completed unsuccessfully, error information concerning the failure occurrence is sent to the party that issued the system call for input-output request. Occurence of the failure must also be notified to the management section, which is responsible for failure measures such restricting input-output requests. Notification is carried out by message communication to an message box ID, which is the destination entered in the device control block .

(3) Reconfiguration

After receiving the error notice, the device managing section begins reconfiguration of devices and restart operations. Since the concepts and conditions are different for each system, the process cannot always be stipulated for every system. Therefore, only system calls that provide merey means for the recovery process are stipulated.

3.6 Notice of Input-Output Error Log

If the hardware failure occurs as a result of I/O request execution, it is necessary to record information for carrying out hardware and system maintenance. This information is called an input-output error log. The input-output control notifies the managing section which collects and controls the logs, of the input-output error log output. This notice is transfered through message communication to a message box ID, which is the I/O log destination entered in the device descripter.

4. STANDARD LOGICAL DEVICE SPECIFICATIONS

In the CTRON input-output control, seven standard specifications of logical device are stipulated. These are listed below.

(1) Logical DK for magnetic disk unit
(2) Logical ODK for optical disk unit
        (SPECIFICATION Version 1 deals with write-once-type only)
(3) Logical FDD for flexible disk unit
(4) Logical MT for magnetic tape unit

Table 4-1 List of Logical Devices - Control Functions

Control Function	DK	ODK	FDD	MT	PR	DSP	CU
Reset	O	O	O	O	O	O	O
Diagnostic	O	O	O	O	O	O	O
Hard Log Collection	O	O	O	O	O	O	O
Shared Device Reserve between Systems	O	O		O	O		
Shared Device Release between Systems	O	O		O	O		
Forced Reserve	O	O		O	O		
Reserve State Read	O	O		O	O		
Medium Unload	O		O	O			
Faulty I/O Block Entry	O		O				
Backup I/O Block Entry	O						
Erase Block		O					
Mount		O					
Demount		O					
Change		O					
Eject		O					
Rewind				O			
Forward Space Block				O			
Forward Space File				O			
Back Space Block				O			
Back Space File				O			
Erase Gap				O			
Write Tape Mark				O			
Set Density				O			
Character Pattern Load					O	O	
Suspend							O
Resume							O

(5) Logical PR for printer

       (SPECIFICATION Version 1 deals with character-type only)

(6) Logical DSP for disply device

       (SPECIFICATION Version 1 deals with character-type only)

(7) Logical CU for communication unit

    These logical devices are defined to have control functions as well as read-write functions. These control functions for each logical device are summarized in Table 4-1. Especialy, control characters for Logical PR and Logical DSP are listed in Table 4-2 and Table 4-3.

Table 4-2 Control Character List for Printer

Control Character	Function
New Line	On completion of a line printing, advances the next character position to the beginning of the next line.
Form Feed	On completion of a line printing, advances the next character position to the predetermined line of the next form.
Horizontal Tabulation	Advances the character position to the predetermined position on the same line (tabulation position).
Character Tabulation Set	Sets a character tabulation stop in the printing direction.
Character Tabulation Reset	Resets a character tabulation stop in the printing direction.
Vertical Tabulation	On the completion of a line printing, advances the character position to the beginning of predetermined next line.
Line Tabulation Set	Sets a line tabulation stop on the printing line.
Line Tabulation Reset	Resets a line tabulation stop on the printing line.
Line Pitch	Changes a line pitch on the printing line. The value to be changed depends on each logical device.
Character Pitch	Changes a pitch between characters. The value to be changed depends on each logical device.

Table 4-3 Control Character List for Display Devices
(Output Data stream)

Control Character	Function
Tabulation Control	Sets /releases the tabulation and moves the cursor to the tabulation stop.
Scroll Control	Changes a scroll area and moves the display contents forward or backward within a specified scroll range.
Display Clear	Clears characters in the whole or part of the screen.
Clear within a Line	Clears characters in the whole or part of a line.
Active Position Movement	Moves the active position.
Active Position Movement Read	Requests for the report of the active position.
Active Position Display Control	Displays or not display the active position with a cursor.
Display Attribute	Specifies several display attributes on the screen (the details are omitted).
Insert/Replace Mode	Specifies the way to display new characters.
Character Edit	Inserts/deletes characters.
Line Edit	Inserts/deletes lines.
Bell	Sounds a bell.
Rule Line Draw/Clear	Draws/clears rule lines.

5. CONCLUSION

This paper describes details regarding the design themes for CTRON input-output control and the outline of the resulting interface specifications. In the final result, we have been able to establish access interface which enables software portability without sacrificing its expandability and performance. This investigation result has been documented as "CTRON INPUT-OUTPUT CONTROL INTERFACE SPECIFICATION Version 1". We plan to expand and revise these specifications on coping with technical development of peripheral equipments.

I would like to thank the following people:
Dr. K. Sakamura, who provided many useful suggestions.
Members of the "CTRON Technical Committee", who are continuously discussing
these subjects with great enthusiasm.

REFERENCES

〔 1 〕 T.Wasano,M.Ohminami,Y.Kobayashi,T.Ohkubo and K.Sakamura,"Design
Principles and Configuration of CTRON", Proc. FDJCC '87,Dallas,1987.
〔 2 〕 T.Ohkubo,T.Wasano and I.Kogiku,"Configuration of the CTRON Kernel",IEEE
MICRO,April 1987,pp.33-44.
〔 3 〕 K.Sakamura,"The TRON Project",IEEE MICRO,April 1987,pp.8-14.
〔 4 〕 H.Monden,"Introduction to ITRON,the Industry-oriented Operating System",
IEEE MICRO,April 1987,pp.45-52.
〔 5 〕 K.Sakamura,"BTRON:The Business-oriented Operating System",IEEE MICRO,
April 1987,pp.53-65.

Shinichiro Narimatsu is manager of 1st
Software Section in Software Development
Department,System Engineering Division- Ⅳ at
Fujitsu Limited. Narimatsu received his B.Sc.
degree in phisics at Kyoto University in 1970. He
is a member of IPS.

Chapter 5: TRON CPU

TRON VLSI CPU: Concepts and Architecture

Ken Sakamura

Department of Information Science, Faculty of Science, University of Tokyo
Hongo,Tokyo,113 Japan

ABSTRACT

The VLSI CPU designed in the TRON project is a new 32 bit microprocessor based on 1990's high VLSI technology. The TRON VLSI CPU is a high-performance microprocessor for computer applications in the 1990's. The architecture of TRON VLSI CPU has the following powerful features that do not exist in the conventional architecture of microprocessors:

1) Total architecture, under which the microprocessors and operating systems ITRON and BTRON have integrated design,

2) Expandability from 32-bit-series to 64-bit-series processors,

3) Compiler-oriented architecture and high execution speed,

4) Open architecture.

Recent microprocessors are so high-functional that it costs much man-power and long time to prepare development systems for them. Therefore it is a good approach to apply a single processor architecture to various kinds of applications, with some modification if necessary. The architecture of TRON VLSI CPU is designed to take such an approach.

The TRON VLSI CPU is a general purpose microprocessor with well-balanced functions which can be used for many applications in the 1990's, including super personal computers with BTRON-OS and intelligent objects with ITRON-OS.

In this paper, the features of TRON VLSI CPU are surveyed and are described with some examples such as instruction formats that how the architecture of TRON VLSI CPU is designed in order to increase its generality.

Keywords: Microprocessor, CISC, RISC, TRON VLSI CPU.

1. DESIGN PHILOSOPHY OF TRON VLSI CPU

The TRON project aims at establishing a new computer architecture that covers microprocessor, OS, MMI (Man-Machine Interface) and networking. The project consists of the following subprojects. ITRON for developing realtime OS for embedded computer systems, BTRON for developing OS and MMI on high-performance workstations, CTRON for developing OS on servers, MTRON for developing OS to control distributed computer systems, and TRON VLSI CPU subproject to design new VLSI CPU to support the OS developed in other subprojects. The project will take full advantage of the semi-conductor technology in 1990's.

TRON VLSI CPU is a generic name given to the 32 bit microprocessor developed according to the specification designed in the TRON project.

Primary manufacturers such as Intel and Motorola have already announced or started marketing 32-bit microprocessors. But is adding a new microprocessor system to the existing diversity a meaningful addition? The answer is Yes. The need for micro-processors with conceptually new architecture is greater than ever before. Why?

The first motivation for designing a new architecture was the history of constantly evolving microprocessor applications; we have judged that microprocessors applications in the 1990's would require a new architecture.

Many of the currently marketed 32-bit microprocessors, such as Intel's iAPX386, have an architecture constrained by the need for compatibility with prior 4-bit, 8-bit, and 16-bit microprocessors. Architectural downward compatibility with the past is important from the perspective of marketing strategy. It cannot be ignored when a new microprocessor is developed. However, the technical level of hardware and software development differs from era to era, from generation to generation, as do the demands made on them in application. Consequently, the optimum architecture must also evolve. If pursuit of compatibility encourages adherence to the same architecture for too long, that architecture becomes obsolete and unsuitable for applications in a later era.

Initially, microprocessors were designed to be used as controllers and sequencers; they were not designed for such new applications as bitmap display of workstations. The microprocessors of the 1990's, therefore, require a new architecture that take into account the applications and technical level of that period.

The second reason for designing a new architecture was the microprocessors in the 1990's will require an architecture that makes best use of the advantages of the von-Neumann-type computer. At present, architectures such as parallel processing and data-flow machines are being enthusiastically investigated. However, because of their general purpose capabilities and extreme technical refinement, the von-Neumann-machine will undoubtedly be the primary computer used in 1990's.

The von-Neumann-type computer must satisfy two important features: its ability to allocate broad linear addressable space and its high basic performance. Needs for these features are very widespread. Nevertheless, few microprocessors completely satisfy these needs. Some microprocessors have small segmented addressable space and it is not easy to write a program on them. Some microprocessors have low down its execution speed, because their instructions are too complicated.

These drawbacks may be unavoidable because existing microprocessor architecture was derived shortly after the advent of the first microprocessor. However 15 years have elapsed and the causes of these architectural problems have gradually become clear. The microprocessors needed now are perfected von-Neumann-type computers that will solve these problems.

The third reason was that a standard instruction set will be required for microprocessors. From the perspective of market share, de facto standard architectures such as Intel's and Motorola's already exist in the world of microprocessors. However, these standards depend on specific manufacturers; others cannot freely implement them. The instruction set of a processor is the kernel of the huge, complicated computer software system the processor supports today. The situation of instruction sets being manufacturer-dependent is undesirable. Moreover, the existence of a standard instruction set is also useful for textbook explanation of the assembler and compilers, as well the explanation of machine language algorithms.

Some computer languages such as ADA and PASCAL were standardized by academic or governmental institutes and can be used without restriction in order to explain algorithm in the text of computer science. Their compilers and interpreters can also freely implemented. However, there is no instruction set standardized by an academic or public institution. Besides, the Patent or Copyright Act strictly prohibits others from implementing an instruction set designed by an another manufacturer. For continued progress and dissemination of microcomputers, an open architecture permitting public use is needed. This architecture must be designed by a party without vested interest, an academic institution for example.

TRON VLSI CPUs are designed in order to satisfy the above-mentioned requirements. To solve the problems stated above, TRON VLSI CPUs has the following features.

(a) High-speed Execution

The TRON project analyzed expected applications of microprocessors in the 1990's. It then created a real-time system-resident OS called ITRON and a workstation-oriented OS called BTRON as operating systems best suited for TRON VLSI CPUs. The architecture of TRON VLSI CPUs was designed so that these OS' be executed extremely efficiently. That is, there is an integrated, total architecture under which TRON VLSI CPUs, ITRON, and BTRON were all designed together. As a result, high-speed execution of the Operating Systems and application programs was achieved.

(b) Large Address Space

TRON VLSI CPUs have the ability to allocate a large address space — an important feature of von-Neumann-type computers. At present, only the CHIP32 with 32-bit addressing capability is available. However, extending this to 48-bit then to 64-bit addressing using the same architecture is under consideration. That is, TRON VLSI CPU microprocessors will eventually be grouped into 32-bit CHIP32, 48-bit CHIP48, 64-bit CHIP64 series having upward compatibility. Instructions in TRON VLSI CPU were so designed as not to reduce the execution speed of basic instructions, while keeping reinforcement and symmetry of their instructions. Therefore, an short format for high-speed execution was prepared for frequently used basic instructions.

(c) Standard Instruction Set

The instruction set for TRON VLSI CPU was designed by the Sakamura Laboratory of Tokyo University, but TRON VLSI CPU implementing the instruction set are being developed by a number of semiconductor manufacturers. It is the world's first revolutionary event in which one party determines an instruction set, while a number of others develop the hardware implementation. In this sense, the instruction set for TRON VLSI CPU forms an open architecture and thus may become a standard instruction set in the computer industry and computer science. To be consistent with the open-architecture policy, we discreetly avoided those that might conflict with any patents concerning existing processors when determining the specifications of the instruction set.

In the following, RISC (Reduced Instruction Set Computers) architecture and TRON VLSI CPU architecture are compared. Then, the features of the TRON VLSI CPU architecture are explained.

2. TRON VLSI CPU AND RISC

RISC is a kind of architecture design philosophy to make the instruction cycle time as fast as possible by reducing the functions supported by the hardware. It has become popular to adopt RISC architecture for high-end workstations. However, the general-purpose processors such as iAPX386 or MC68020 are still popular and used on many workstations. One of the reason why RISC has not replaced these processors is that RISC requires high memory band-width, large cache, and good optimizing compiler to take advantage of its architecture. RISC will be used for some applications, but will not be used on low-cost personal computers, or in embedded computer applications.

The application of microprocessor will be very wide. In the TRON project, two application fields are focus of attention, namely high-performance personal computers and intelligent objects. It is assumed that one personal computer will be used for each operators task, and will be used for business, and home applications. BTRON or micro-BTRON OS will be used on such personal computers. The personal computer will be the tool to generate documents, manage schedule, handle personal databases, communicate with others via their personal computers, and control intelligent objects.

Intelligent objects are devices or equipment that have computers in them in order to respond to external environmental changes and act accordingly. These include air conditioner, illumination devices, and audio-visual equipments. They communicate with each other to obtain the best environment for the users. ITRON will be used to control these intelligent objects. MTRON will control the network of computer systems including intelligent objects.

It is ideal to use just one family of general-purpose microprocessors to build personal computers, intelligent objects, and other future computer systems. This is because the manufacturers can cut down the cost of VLSI fabrication by sharing the basic design among the different members of the family, and software development system including compiler can be shared. The users will find it convenient to deal with only one architecture.

The TRON VLSI CPU has been designed with this generality in mind. In order to achieve high generality, the TRON VLSI CPU subproject has investigated various applications, and considered how software and hardware will offer services in these applications. The specification of TRON VLSI CPU has been devised to offer a balanced CPU in terms of performance, functions, and object size after these considerations. These design steps have made the TRON VLSI CPU a very balanced general-purpose processor.

RISC architecture, on the other hand, cannot meet the needs of applications in 1990's. First of all, the object size of RISC tends to be large. Hence, low-cost systems using single-chip CPU is not likely to be implemented using RISC architecture. RISC's merit of simplified CPU design does not fit well for mass production of embedded computer systems if the size of necessary ROM and RAM is large. Also, the merit of RISC's performance cannot be fully utilized on battery-powered computers with low clock frequency, which will become popular in the 1990's,

So, in our view, RISC will be used for high-end workstations and minicomputers and will not replace the general-purpose microprocessors. Then again, it is not necessary to use RISC to have high-performance CPU, and general-purpose CPU like iAPX386 and MC68020 can compete with RISC for high-end performance as well. If the runtime performance of RISC and these general-purpose processors are close, then other benefits of general-purpose processors such as the wide availability of development tools will place general-purpose processors in favorable light.

3. FAST EXECUTION AND ORTHOGONALITY OF INSTRUCTION SET

Two objectives in designing the instruction format of TRON VLSI CPU were the shortening the instruction length and achieving the high orthogonality. In general, these two do not stand together very well. In designing the TRON VLSI CPU, we have tried to satisfy the two criteria.

Shortening the length, and thus making the object size small is important to make it possible to use TRON VLSI CPU in embedded computers. Also, the short instructions will make the instruction decoding unit to operator fast, and make the cache memory hit rate high. Hence, the short instructions are beneficial for workstations with large memory as well.

Orthogonality of instruction set here means that there are few constraints on the combination of function, addressing mode, and operand size. If, for example, an instruction can use register R0 to R7 as operand, but cannot use R8 to R15, or can use 16 bit operand, but cannot use 32 bit operand, the orthogonality is lost.

Recently, software productivity is regarded as increasingly important. An instruction set on which we can gain high software productivity is necessary for the advent of a new processor.

When writing programs in a high-level language, programmers cannot directly see the architecture of the processor. Therefore, some of them may be indifferent to the architecture if good compiler is provided. However, a high-quality compiler can hardly be produced with processors having an architecture designed regardless of software. Many years may be required to develop a compiler for such architectures. Anything that facilitates the creation of compilers is an important factor in the wide acceptance of chips.

The orthogonality of instruction set makes it easy to build good compilers. When the instruction set lacks the orthogonality, the compiler has to do a lot of case analysis to produce workable code sequence. Also, picking up optimal sequence will become very difficult when the orthogonality is lost. When, for example, we are to allocate two variables to four registers, and if the four registers function equivalently because of the orthogonality, we can use any two registers to hold the variable. However, if the four registers function differently, we can have 12 (4 x 3) ways of assigning variables to these registers, and the compiler has to evaluate these ways in terms of performance to generate good code.

On the other hand, when the orthogonality of register usage is broken, it is possible to allocate variables to registers according to the data types of the variables. For example, if the CPU has separate data registers and address registers, the pointer data will be assigned to address registers. However, when the number of available registers become small during the course of compiler execution, very complex cases arise. For example, if there is only one free address register, and two data registers, and we have to decide where to place two pointer variables, we must evaluate whether assigning one pointer variable in memory is better than assigning it to data register. If the register usage is orthogonal, such analysis will become unnecessary.

One possible drawback of obtaining high orthogonality is that it tends to make instruction length longer.

For example, some processors use 8-bit (just 1 byte) field to specify an addressing mode for each operand. Such an instruction format is very orthogonal because each byte data in the instruction stream represents the op-code or the operand independently. But using the instruction format, a 2-operand register-to-register arithmetic operation occupies as long as 3 bytes, while the operation is encoded into 2-byte instruction in most processors.Longer instruction often means less performance.

Hence, TRON VLSI CPU has two classes of instruction formats from the view point of instruction decoding. One is the "general" format that is general and orthogonal. The other is "short" format used for providing limited operations but with short length. Adopting these formats and use them mixingly achieves our objectives of obtaining the orthogonality and at the same time shorten the length of instructions.

There are several short formats which are prepared to handle various popular instructions such as MOV (transfer) and CMP (comparison). *Figure-1* shows the comparison of "general" and "short" formats of MOV instruction. Register orthogonality is maintained even in the case of short formats. Short formats only restrict the addressing mode, operand immediate value range, and size of the operands.

Some existing microprocessors have short formats for special operand or addressing mode. For example, MC68020 has MOVEQ instruction, which is two byte special instruction to offer the same functionality of MOVE instruction when its source operand is between -128 and 127 and the destination is a data register.

The position of "short" format in TRON VLSI CPU is more full fledged in the sense that many operations have short formats when special addressing mode, and operand size are used. The functions of the general format instruction and corresponding short format instruction, if it exists, are the same including the change of flags and exceptions.

Clearing a destination, which is often called CLR operation on many CPU, is a short format MOV instruction, written MOV:Z on TRON VLSI CPU. The function of MOV:Z, and the function of general format MOV:G with its source being 0 is completely the same.

POP instruction that pops data from stack is not a variation of MOV instruction on TRON VLSI CPU. It is possible to use MOV with stack addressing mode (@SP+) to achieve

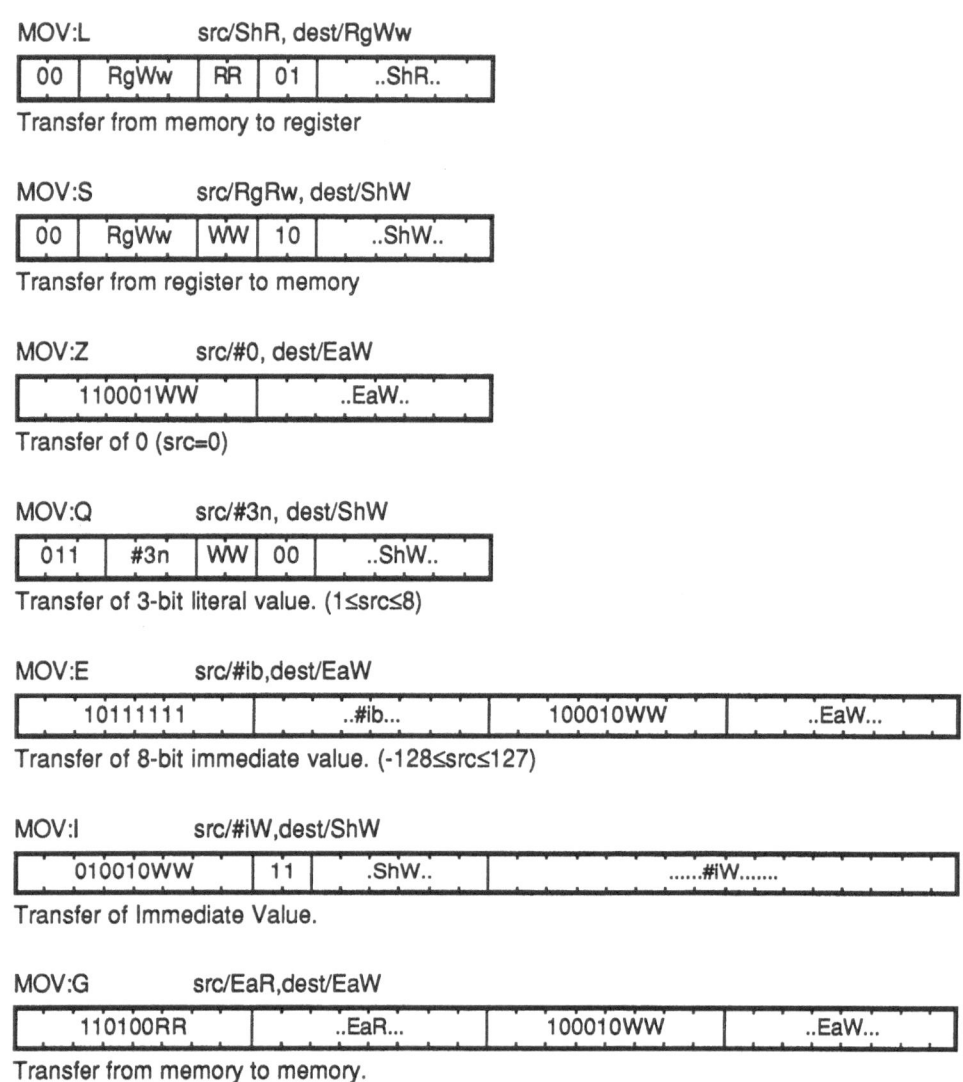

MOV:L   src/ShR, dest/RgWw

| 00 | RgWw | RR | 01 | ..ShR.. |

Transfer from memory to register

MOV:S   src/RgRw, dest/ShW

| 00 | RgWw | WW | 10 | ..ShW.. |

Transfer from register to memory

MOV:Z   src/#0, dest/EaW

| 110001WW | ..EaW.. |

Transfer of 0 (src=0)

MOV:Q   src/#3n, dest/ShW

| 011 | #3n | WW | 00 | ..ShW.. |

Transfer of 3-bit literal value. (1≤src≤8)

MOV:E   src/#ib,dest/EaW

| 10111111 | ..#ib... | 100010WW | ..EaW... |

Transfer of 8-bit immediate value. (-128≤src≤127)

MOV:I   src/#iW,dest/ShW

| 010010WW | 11 | .ShW.. | ....#iW........ |

Transfer of Immediate Value.

MOV:G   src/EaR,dest/EaW

| 110100RR | ..EaR... | 100010WW | ..EaW... |

Transfer from memory to memory.

EaR, EaW, ShR, and ShW are fields to specify addressing mode, RgWw, and RgRw are to specify registers, #3n, #ib, and #iW are to specify the literal or immediate value. RR, and WW to specify the operand size.

Figure-1 Instruction Formats of MOV Instruction

similar effect as POP. However, POP does not set flags while MOV sets them. When the destination address calculation involves the value of SP, MOV uses the incremented value of SP and POP uses the original value of SP. Hence the use of POP and MOV cannot be the same in all cases. This is one reason POP is not handled as a special case of MOV. (see *Table-1*.)

Table-1 Differences of MOV and POP

operation	action	SP afterward
POP @(d,SP)	mem[initSP] ==> mem[d+initSP]	initSP+4
MOV @SP+,@(d,SP)	mem[initSP] ==> mem[d+4+initSP]	initSP+4

@SP+:   addressing mode to pop data from stack.
@(d,SP):   addressing mode to access data at (SP+d).
mem[EA]: content of memory cell at effective address EA.
initSP: initial value of stack pointer SP.

The systematic introduction of "short" and "general" formats should help the learning of the instruction set. Users can learn, initially, the meaning or the purpose of each instruction, the processing that takes place, and the change of flags. At this stage, the user should not concern him/herself with the difference in short and general formats. Next, the user should learn the short formats prepared for each instructions, and learn the limitations of each short formats. The TRON VLSI CPU has many instructions with rich addressing modes. But it is not terribly difficult to learn its architecture because the systematic learning can be done.

The standard assembly mnemonic of TRON VLSI CPU should help the learning outlined above. Each instruction is given a unique name irrespective of short or general formats. The name is called generic mnemonic. This name corresponds to the first stage of learning, namely the specification of operation. If the user needs to specify the different format, format-dependent mnemonics are available.

There can be several format-dependent mnemonics for each generic mnemonic. The name corresponds to the second stage of learning, namely the knowledge of special format applicable when the special operands are used. For example, MOV is an example of generic mnemonic, MOV:Z, and MOV:G are format-dependent mnemonics.

From the standpoint of developing a compiler, the instruction set for TRON VLSI CPUs can be viewed as follows. An instruction with the general format has functional orthogonality, that is, it can specify any addressing mode, and can perform an arithmetic or logical operation on the operands of different sizes. A compiler can be greatly simplified if it needs to generate only object codes of mnemonics in the general format. The short format is indispensable for obtaining compact object codes that can be executed at high speed. Generic mnemonics are converted to format-dependent mnemonics one bye one. The general format may also be converted to the short format one by one. This optimization is made separately within each instruction, so relatively simple optimization algorithm is required. Therefore, compilers for TRON VLSI CPUs can generate high-quality object codes using the short format.

In order to increase the orthogonality of instruction set, the TRON VLSI CPU has "additional addressing mode" and "operations on data with different size".

Additional addressing mode is generalized indirect addressing mechanism. Generally speaking, an addressing operation can be decomposed into addition, indirect reference, and scaling operation. The additional addressing mode of the TRON VLSI CPU allows the multiple combination of these three primitive operations. *Figure-2* shows the processing of additional addressing, and *Figure-3* shows the bit assignment of the addressing mode. This addressing mode can be used for modular-programming.

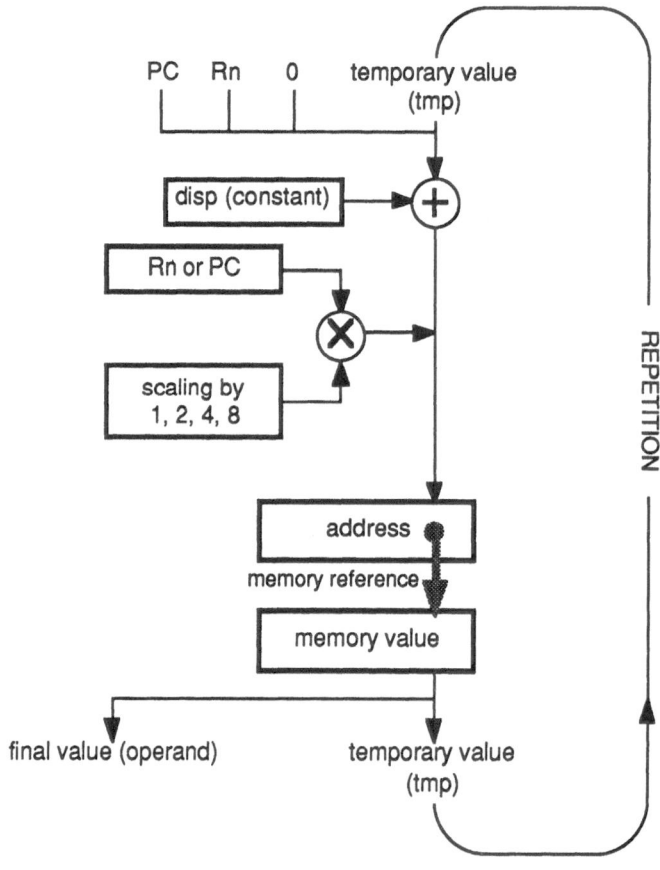

• It is possible to generate any addressing mode with combination of addition, scaling, and memory reference.

Figure 2. Additional Addressing mode of the TRON VLSI CPU

```
| EI |  Rx  | MS | PXXD |  d4  |        dispx        |
```

EI=00	No indirect reference, continue tmp + disp + Rx * Scale ==> tmp
EI=01	Indirect reference, continue mem[tmp + disp + Rx * Scale] ==> tmp
EI=10	Operand reference, finish tmp + disp + Rx * Scale ==> address_of_operand mem[address_of_operand] ==> operand
EI=11	Operand reference after indirect reference, finish mem[tmp + disp + Rx * Scale] ==> address_of_operand mem[address_of_operand] ==> operand

The number of '1' bits in all the EI fields in all the steps of additional addressing equal to the number of indirect and operand references.

M=0	Rx is used as index register.
M=1	
	Rx=0 Index register is not added.(Rx = 0) Rx=1 PC is used as index register.(Rx = PC)
D=0	d4 is multiplied by 4 and added as disp.
D=1	dispx(16/32/64 bit field) is added as disp The size of dispx is specified by d4. d4=0001 dispx is 16 bit. d4=0010 dispx is 32 bit.
XX	Scaling factor= 1/2/4/8
S	Size of index register. S=0 <Rx> is used as 32 bit signed quantity.
P	P bit to extend address space. Rx: Index register. disp: Displacement. tmp: Interim value during additional addressing calculation. mem[EA]: The content of memory cell at EA.

Figure-3 Bit pattern in Additinal Addressing Mode

Some existing processors have indirect addressing mode. But they have limitations such as the addition of index register is allowed only after the indirect reference, or only one index register can be used in producing the final address. There were few cases when compiler can take advantage of these limited addressing mode.

Operation on data with different size is to perform arithmetic or transfer operations with differently sized integer data.

For example, one instruction can add 8-bit signed data to 64-bit data or multiply 32-bit data by 8-bit data. The operations between different data size was developed as a result of making operand data symmetrical in size.

It is usually the case that the operations on the registers, or the address calculation are performed in the natural size (or register size) of the CPU. However, when data is stored into memory, only the necessary width is used. Hence, when operation involves memory data, it often becomes necessary to convert between different sizes. The operations on data of different size available on the TRON VLSI CPU can perform the size conversion and the operation at the same time, and can produce efficient code sequences. *Figure-4* shows such an example.

Example: Addition of 8 bits integer to 32 bits integer.

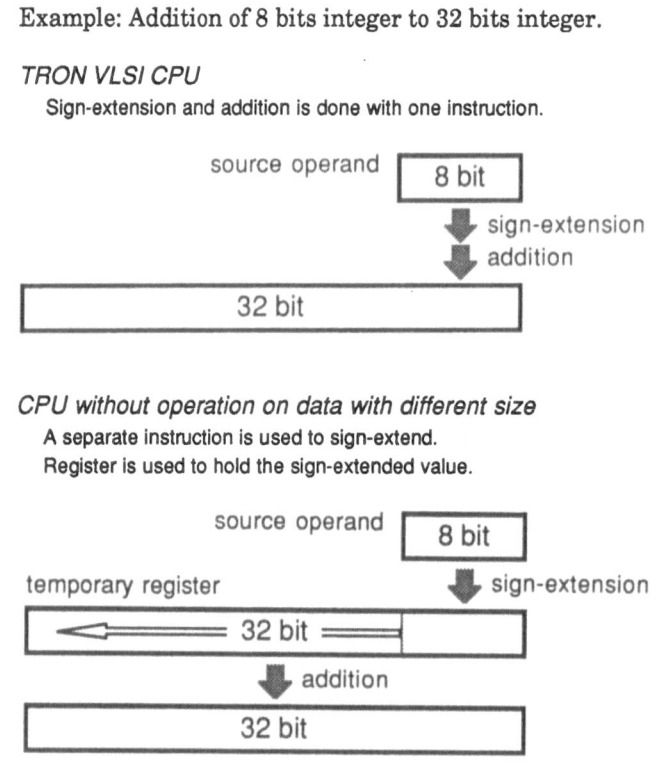

Figure-4 Operation on data with different size

A processor without this function has to expand smaller data to the size of larger data. As a result, the number of necessary instructions increases and more registers are required for storing temporary values. If temporary data registers are required, register allocation is affected and compiler logic has to be more complicated.

The instruction set of the TRON VLSI CPU is shown in *Table-2*. The register set is shown in *Figure-5*. *Table-3* shows the instruction bit-pattern for both the general and short formats. *Table-4* shows the addressing modes available on the TRON VLSI CPU.

Table-2 Instruction Set of TRON VLSI CPU -1

Data Transfer

MOV	src,dest	Data transfer with possible sign-extension
MOVU	src,dest	Data transfer with possible zero-extension
PUSH	src	Pushing to stack
POP	dest	Popping from stack
STM	reglist,dest	Store of multiple registers
LDM	src,reglist	Load of multiple registers
MOVA	srcaddr,dest	Obtaining effective address
PUSHA	srcaddr	Pushing effective address to stack

Comparison, Test

CMP	src1,src2	Comparison with possible sign-extension
CMPU	src1,src2	Comparison with possible zero-extension
CHK	bound,index,xreg	Range-check of array index.

Arithmetic

	ADD	src,dest	Addition with possible sign-extension
	ADDU	src,dest	Addition with possible zero-extension
	ADDX	src,dest	Addition with carry.
	SUB	src,dest	Subtraction with possible sign-extension
	SUBU	src,dest	Subtraction with possible zero-extension
	SUBX	src,dest	Subtraction with borrow
	MUL	src,dest	Multiplication
	MULU	src,dest	Unsigned multiplication
	MULX	src,dest,ext	Extended multiplication for bignum
	DIV	src,dest	Division
	DIVU	src,dest	Unsigned division
	DIVX	src,dest,ext	Extended division for bignum
	REM	src,dest	Remainder
	REMU	src,dest	Unsigned remainder
	NEG	dest	Negation
«L2»	INDEX	indexsize,subscript,xreg	Address calculation for array access

Logical

AND	src,dest	And
OR	src,dest	Or
XOR	src,dest	Exclusive or
NOT	dest	Invert all bits

Table-2 Instruction Set of TRON VLSI CPU -2

Shift

	SHL	count,dest	Logical shift
	SHA	count,dest	Arithmetic shift
	ROT	count,dest	Rotate
	SHXL	dest	Extended logical shift left
	SHXR	dest	Extended logical shift right
	RVBY	src,dest	Reversal of byte order
«L2»	RVBI	src,dest	Reversal of bit order

Bit Manipulation

BTST	offset,base	Test a bit
BSET	offset,base	Set a bit
BCLR	offset,base	Clear a bit
BNOT	offset,base	Negation of a bit
BSCH	data,offset	Search for 0 or 1 in one word

Fixed-length Bit Field

BFEXT	offset,width,base,dest	Extract a bit field	(signed)
BFEXTU	offset,width,base,dest	Extract a bit field	(unsigned)
BFINS	src,offset,width,base	Inserting a bit field	(signed)
BFINSU	src,offset,width,base	Inserting a bit field	(unsigned)
BFCMP	src,offset,width,base	Comparison of a bit field	(signed)
BFCMPU	src,offset,width,base	Comparison of a bit field	(unsigned)

Variable-length Bit Field

BVSCH	Search for 0 or 1 in a bit field
BVMAP	Bitmap operation
BVCPY	Bitmap transfer
BVPAT	Fill bitmap with a pattern

BCD Arithmetic

«L1»	ADDDX	src,dest	BCD addition
«L1»	SUBDX	src,dest	BCD subtraction
«L1»	PACKss	src,dest	Packing to BCD
«L1»	UNPKss	src,dest,adj	Unpacking from BCD

Table-2 Instruction Set of TRON VLSI CPU -3

String Manipulation

SMOV	Copy a string
SCMP	Compare strings
SSCH	Search within a string
SSTR	Fill a string with given data

Queue Manipulation

QINS	entry,queue	Insertion to a doubly linked queue
QDEL	queue,dest	Deletion from a doubly linked queue
QSCH		Search in a queue

Control Transfer

BRA	newpc	Jump	(PC-relative)
Bcc	newpc	Conditional jump	(PC-relative)
BSR	newpc	Call a subroutine	(PC-relative)
JMP	newpc	Jump	
JSR	newpc	Call a subroutine	
ACB	step,xreg,limit,newpc	Looping with incrementing an index	
SCB	step,xreg,limit,newpc	Looping with decrementing an index	
ENTER	local,reglist	Creating stack frame	
EXITD	reglist,adjsp	Freeing stack fame and return	
RTS		Return from a subroutine	
NOP		No operation	
PIB		Purge Instruction Buffer	(See Text)

Multiprocessor Support

BSETI	offset,base	Set a bit with bus lock
BCLRI	offset,base	Clear a bit with bus lock
CSI	comp,update,dest	Compare and store with bus lock

Table-2 Instruction Set of TRON VLSI CPU -4

Control Space, Address Space

LDC	src,dest	Load to control space	[Privileged]
STC	src,dest	Store to control space	[Privileged]
LDPSB	src	Load to PSB	
LDPSM	src	Load to PSM	
STPSB	dest	Store from PSB	
STPSM	dest	Store from PSM	
LDP	src,dest	Load to a physical address	[Privileged]
STP	src,dest	Store from a physical address	[Privileged]

OS-Support

«L1»	JRNG	vector	Inter-ring call	
«L1»	RRNG		Inter-ring return	
	TRAPA	vector	Trap	(Software-driven EIT)
	TRAP		Conditional trap	(Software-driven conditional EIT)
	REIT		Return from EIT handler	[Privileged]
	WAIT	imask	Wait for interrupt	[Privileged]
	LDCTX	ctxaddr	Loading a context	[Privileged]
	STCTX		Storing a context	[Privileged]

MMU Support

	ACS	chkaddr	Check of access right	
«LA»	MOVPA	srcaddr,dest	Obtaining physical address	[Privileged]
«LA»	LDATE	src,destaddr	Load to ATE(PTE,STE)	[Privileged]
«LA»	STATE	srcaddr,dest	Store from ATE(PTE,STE)	[Privileged]
«LA»	PTLB		Invalidating TLB	[Privileged]
«LA»	PSTLB	prgaddr	Invalidating TLB for a given address	
				[Privileged]

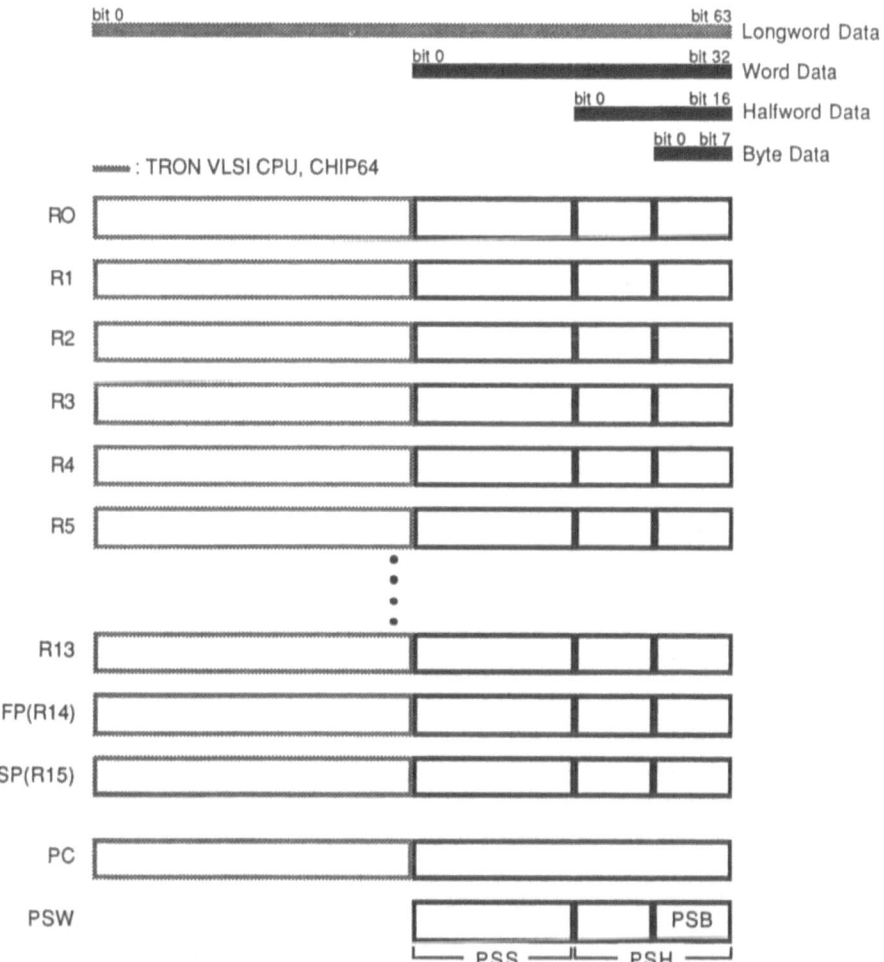

Processor status word (PSW) is 4 bytes long.
　　The lowest byte is to store processor status (Processor Status Byte -
　　PSB), the second lowest byte is to store user mode status (called
　　Processor Status Halfword in conjunction with PSB, - PSH), the
　　higher two bytes store the system status (PSS).

TRON VLSI CPU has memory protection scheme using 4 level rings.
　　SP is prepared for each rings (0 to 3) and for interrupt processing
　　and switched automatically.
　　PSW indicates in what ring the CPU is executing, and what stack it
　　uses.

Figure-5 Register Set of TRON VLSI CPU

Table-3 Instruction Bit Patterns of TRON VLSI CPU -1

[00??????]

CMP:L	00RgRwRR	00.ShR..
MOV:L	00RgWwRR	01.ShR..
MOV:S	00RgRwWW	10.ShW..
AND:R	00RgMw00	1100RgRw
OR:R	00RgMw01	1100RgRw
XOR:R	00RgMw10	1100RgRw
MOVA:R	00RgWP11	1100RgRP ......#d16......
MUL:R	00RgMw00	1101RgRw
DIV:R	00RgMw01	1101RgRw
5)Misc	00????1?	1101????
6)Misc	00??????	111?????

[01??????]

CMP:Q	010#3nRR	00.ShR!I
MOV:Q	011#3nWW	00.ShW..
ADD:Q	010#3nMM	01.ShM..
SUB:Q	011#3nMM	01.ShM..
SHL:Q	01#4s.MM	10.ShM..
SHA:Q	011#3cMM	11.ShM..
CMP:I	010000RR	11.ShR!I ......#iR........
ADD:I	010001MM	11.ShM.. ......#iM........
MOV:I	010010WW	11.ShW.. ......#iW........
SUB:I	010011MM	11.ShM.. ......#iM........
AND:I	010100MM	11.ShM.. ......#iM........
OR:I	010101MM	11.ShM.. ......#iM........
XOR:I	010110MM	11.ShM.. ......#iM........
{RIE}	010111MM	11.ShM.. ......#iM........

[10??????]

Bcc:D	10cccc00	..#d8...
ADD:L	10RgMw01	00.ShRw.
SUB:L	10RgMw01	01.ShRw.
BSET:Q	100#3z01	10.ShMfq
BCLR:Q	101#3z01	10.ShMfq
BSETI:Q	100#3z01	11ShMfqi
BTST:Q	101#3z01	11.ShRfq

Table-3 Instruction Bit Patterns of TRON VLSI CPU -2

```
JMP          10000010   ..EaA...
ACS          10000011   ..EaA...
POP          1001001W   ..EaWL..
PUSHA        1010001S   ..EaA...
PUSH         1011001R   ..EaRL..

LDCTX        10xx0110   ..EaA!A.
{RIE}        10**0111   ..EaA!A.

STM          1000101W   ..EaWmL. .......LsWL......
LDM          1001101R   ..EaRmL. .......L1RL......
JSR          1010101P   ..EaA...
JRNG:G       1011101P   ..EaRh!M

ENTER:E      1000111X   ..#ib... .......LnXL......
EXITD:E      1001111X   ..#ib... .......LxXL......
BRA:D        10101110   ..#d8...
BSR:D        10101111   ..#d8...
JRNG:E       10111110   ..#ib...
1)General#   10111111   ..#ib... ???????? ..Ea?...
```

[11??????]

```
CMP:Z        110000SS   ..EaR!I.
MOV:Z        110001WW   ..EaW...
NEG          110010MM   ..EaM...
NOT          110011MM   ..EaM...

2)General-A    110100RR   ..EaR... ???????? ..Ea?...
3)General-B    110101RR   ..EaR... ???????? ..Ea?...

4)General-Spec. 11011000  ..EaA... ???????? ..Ea?...
{RIE}          11011001   ********
{RIE}          1101101*   ********

LDPSB         11011100   ..EaRh..
LDPSM         11011101   ..EaRh..
STPSB         11011110   ..EaWh..
STPSM         11011111   ..EaWh..

coproc1       1110**??   ..Ea?.... ******** ********
coproc2       1111****   ********
```

Table-3 Instruction Bit Patterns of TRON VLSI CPU -3

1) General# / 2) General-A

2)General-A	110100RR	..EaR...	????????	..Ea?...
1)General#	10111111	..#ib...	????????	..Ea?...
ADD:G	110100RR	..EaR...	000000MM	..EaM...
ADD:E	10111111	..#ib...	000000MM	..EaM...
ADDU:G	110100RR	..EaR...	000001MM	..EaM...
ADDU:E	10111111	..#ib...	000001MM	..EaM...
SUB:G	110100RR	..EaR...	000010MM	..EaM...
SUB:E	10111111	..#ib...	000010MM	..EaM...
SUBU:G	110100RR	..EaR...	000011MM	..EaM...
SUBU:E	10111111	..#ib...	000011MM	..EaM...
ADDX:G	110100RR	..EaR...	000100MM	..EaM...
ADDX:E	10111111	..#ib...	000100MM	..EaM...
ADDDX:G	110100RR	..EaR...	000101MM	..EaM...
ADDDX:E	10111111	..#ib...	000101MM	..EaM...
SUBX:G	110100RR	..EaR...	000110MM	..EaM...
SUBX:E	10111111	..#ib...	000110MM	..EaM...
SUBDX:G	110100RR	..EaR...	000111MM	..EaM...
SUBDX:E	10111111	..#ib...	000111MM	..EaM...
AND:G	110100RR	..EaR...	001000MM	..EaM...
AND:E	10111111	..#ib...	001000MM	..EaM...
OR:G	110100RR	..EaR...	001001MM	..EaM...
OR:E	10111111	..#ib...	001001MM	..EaM...
XOR:G	110100RR	..EaR...	001010MM	..EaM...
XOR:E	10111111	..#ib...	001010MM	..EaM...
{RIE}	110100RR	..EaR...	001011MM	..EaM...
{RIE}	10111111	..#ib...	001011MM	..EaM...
SHL:G	110100RR	..EaR...	001100MM	..EaM...
SHL:E	10111111	..#ib...	001100MM	..EaM...
SHA:G	110100RR	..EaR...	001101MM	..EaM...
SHA:E	10111111	..#ib...	001101MM	..EaM...
ROT:G	110100RR	..EaR...	001110MM	..EaM...
ROT:E	10111111	..#ib...	001110MM	..EaM...
{RIE}	110100RR	..EaR...	001111MM	..EaM...
{RIE}	10111111	..#ib...	001111MM	..EaM...
MUL:G	110100RR	..EaR...	010000MM	..EaM...
MUL:E	10111111	..#ib...	010000MM	..EaM...

Table-3 Instruction Bit Patterns of TRON VLSI CPU -4

MULU:G	110100RR	..EaR...	010001MM	..EaM...
MULU:E	10111111	..#ib...	010001MM	..EaM...
DIV:G	110100RR	..EaR...	010010MM	..EaM...
DIV:E	10111111	..#ib...	010010MM	..EaM...
DIVU:G	110100RR	..EaR...	010011MM	..EaM...
DIVU:E	10111111	..#ib...	010011MM	..EaM...
{RIE}	110100RR	..EaR...	01010*MM	..EaM...
{RIE}	10111111	..#ib...	01010*MM	..EaM...
REM:G	110100RR	..EaR...	010110MM	..EaM...
REM:E	10111111	..#ib...	010110MM	..EaM...
REMU:G	110100RR	..EaR...	010111MM	..EaM...
REMU:E	10111111	..#ib...	010111MM	..EaM...
{RIE}	110100RR	..EaR...	011***MM	..Ea?...
{RIE}	10111111	..#ib...	011***MM	..Ea?...
CMP:G	110100RR	..EaR...	100000SS	..EaR!I.
CMP:E	10111111	..#ib...	100000SS	..EaR!I.
CMPU:G	110100RR	..EaR...	100001SS	..EaR!I.
CMPU:E	10111111	..#ib...	100001SS	..EaR!I.
MOV:G	110100RR	..EaR...	100010WW	..EaW...
MOV:E	10111111	..#ib...	100010WW	..EaW...
MOVU:G	110100RR	..EaR...	100011WW	..EaW...
MOVU:E	10111111	..#ib...	100011WW	..EaW...
{RIE}	110100RR	..EaR...	10010*SS	..Ea?...
{RIE}	10111111	..#ib...	10010*SS	..Ea?...
LDC:G	110100RR	..EaR...	100110WW	..EaW%..
LDC:E	10111111	..#ib...	100110WW	..EaW%..
LDP:G	110100RR	..EaR...	100111WW	..EaW%..
LDP:E	10111111	..#ib...	100111WW	..EaW%..
BSETI:G	110100RR	..EaR...	101000BB	..EaMfi.
BSETI:E	10111111	..#ib...	101000BB	..EaMfi.
BCLRI:G	110100RR	..EaR...	101001BB	..EaMfi.
BCLRI:E	10111111	..#ib...	101001BB	..EaMfi.
{RIE}	110100RR	..EaR...	10101*??	..Ea?...
{RIE}	10111111	..#ib...	10101*??	..Ea?...
BSET:G	110100RR	..EaR...	101100BB	..EaMf..
BSET:E	10111111	..#ib...	101100BB	..EaMf..

Table-3 Instruction Bit Patterns of TRON VLSI CPU -5

BCLR:G	110100RR	..EaR...	101101BB	..EaMf..	
BCLR:E	10111111	..#ib...	101101BB	..EaMf..	
BNOT:G	110100RR	..EaR...	101110BB	..EaMf..	
BNOT:E	10111111	..#ib...	101110BB	..EaMf..	
BTST:G	110100RR	..EaR...	101111BB	..EaRf..	
BTST:E	10111111	..#ib...	101111BB	..EaRf..	
BFCMP:G:R	110100RR	..EaR...	110000+X	..EaRbf.	==RRXw==	====RRXs
BFCMP:E:R	10111111	..#ib...	110000+X	..EaRbf.	.#6n..==	====RRXs
BFCMPU:G:R	110100RR	..EaR...	110001+X	..EaRbf.	==RRXw==	====RRXs
BFCMPU:E:R	10111111	..#ib...	110001+X	..EaRbf.	.#6n..==	====RRXs
BFINS:G:R	110100RR	..EaR...	110010+X	..EaMbf.	==RRXw==	====RRXs
BFINS:E:R	10111111	..#ib...	110010+X	..EaMbf.	.#6n..==	====RRXs
BFINSU:G:R	110100RR	..EaR...	110011+X	..EaMbf.	==RRXw==	====RRXs
BFINSU:E:R	10111111	..#ib...	110011+X	..EaMbf.	.#6n..==	====RRXs
BFCMP:G:I	110100RR	..EaR...	110100+X	..EaRbf.	==RRXwSS	..#iS8..
BFCMP:E:I	10111111	..#ib...	110100+X	..EaRbf.	.#6n..SS	..#iS8..
BFCMPU:G:I	110100RR	..EaR...	110101+X	..EaRbf.	==RRXwSS	..#iS8..
BFCMPU:E:I	10111111	..#ib...	110101+X	..EaRbf.	.#6n..SS	..#iS8..
BFINS:G:I	110100RR	..EaR...	110110+X	..EaMbf.	==RRXwSS	..#iS8..
BFINS:E:I	10111111	..#ib...	110110+X	..EaMbf.	.#6n..SS	..#iS8..
BFINSU:G:I	110100RR	..EaR...	110111+X	..EaMbf.	==RRXwSS	..#iS8..
BFINSU:E:I	10111111	..#ib...	110111+X	..EaMbf.	.#6n..SS	..#iS8..
{RIE}	110100RR	..EaR...	11100*+X	..Ea?bf.	********	********
{RIE}	10111111	..#ib...	11100*+X	..Ea?bf.	********	********
BFEXT:G	110100RR	..EaR...	111010+X	..EaRbf.	==RRXw==	====RWXd
BFEXT:E	10111111	..#ib...	111010+X	..EaRbf.	.#6n..==	====RWXd
BFEXTU:G	110100RR	..EaR...	111011+X	..EaRbf.	==RRXw==	====RWXd
BFEXTU:E	10111111	..#ib...	111011+X	..EaRbf.	.#6n..==	====RWXd
ACB:G	110100RR	..EaR...	11110PXX	..EaRX..	==RgMXSS	.#dS8..
ACB:E	10111111	..#ib...	11110PXX	..EaRX..	==RgMXSS	.#dS8..
SCB:G	110100RR	..EaR...	11111PXX	..EaRX..	==RgMXSS	.#dS8..
SCB:E	10111111	..#ib...	11111PXX	..EaRX..	==RgMXSS	.#dS8..

Table-3 Instruction Bit Patterns of TRON VLSI CPU -6

3) General-B

3) General-B	110101RR	..EaR...	????????	..Ea?...
CSI	110101RR	..EaR...	00RMC.00	..EaMiR.
{RIE}	110101RR	..EaR...	00****01	..Ea?...
CHK	110101RR	..EaR...	00RgWR1c	..EaRdR.
RVBY	110101RR	..EaR...	010000WW	..EaW...
RVBI	110101RR	..EaR...	010001WW	..EaW...
PACKss	110101RR	..EaR...	010010WW	..EaW...
UNPKss	110101RR	..EaR...	010011WW	..EaW... ......#iW.......
BSCH	110101RR	..EaR...	0101bdMM	..EaM...
{RIE}	110101RR	..EaR...	011***??	..Ea?...
LDATE	110101!R	..EaR...	10pttt00	..EaA...
{RIE}	110101!R	..EaR...	10****01	..Ea?...
MULX	110101!R	..EaR...	10RgWR10	..EaMR..
DIVX	110101!R	..EaR...	10RgMR11	..EaMR..
INDEX	110101!R	..EaR...	11RgMRSS	..EaR2..

4) General-Spec.

4) General-Spec.	11011000	..EaA...	????????	..Ea?...
{RIE}	11011000	..EaA...	0*****??	..Ea?...
STATE	11011000	..EaA...	100ttt+W	..EaW!S..
{RIE}	11011000	..EaA...	101000??	..Ea?...
MOVPA	11011000	..EaA...	101001+W	..EaW!S.
STC	11011000	..EaR%..	101010WW	..EaW...
STP	11011000	..EaR%..	101011WW	..EaW...
QDEL	11011000	..EaRgP.	101100+W	..EaW!S.
MOVA:G	11011000	..EaA...	101101+W	..EaW...
QINS	11011000	..EaMgP.	101110+-	..EaMgP2
{RIE}	11011000	..Ea?...	101111??	..Ea?...
{RIE}	11011000	..EaA...	11****??	..Ea?...

Table-3 Instruction Bit Patterns of TRON VLSI CPU -7

5) Misc.

5)Misc.	00????1?	1101????	
{RIE}	00****10	1101****	
ACB:R	00RgMw11	1101P000	--RgRwSS ..#dS8..
ACB:Q	00RgMw11	1101P001	.#6n..SS ..#dS8..
SCB:R	00RgMw11	1101P010	--RgRwSS ..#dS8..
SCB:Q	00RgMw11	1101P011	.#6z..SS ..#dS8..
TRAP	00cccc11	1101P100	
TRAPA	00#4z.11	1101P101	
LV-Instruction	00**0011	1101*110	
STCTX	00xx0111	1101P110	
PIB	00001011	1101P110	
NOP	00011011	1101-110	
RTS	00101011	1101P110	
RRNG	00111011	1101P110	
WAIT	00001111	1101-110	.......#ih........
REIT	00101111	1101P110	
PTLB	00p11111	1101P110	
{RIE}	00****11	1101P111	

Table-3 Instruction Bit Patterns of TRON VLSI CPU -8

6) Misc.

6)Misc.	00??????	111?????			
SCMP	00eeeeSS	1110P0Qb			
SMOV	00eeeeSS	1110P1Qb			
QSCH	00eeeeSS	1111P0mb			
SSCH	00eeeeSS	1111P10r			
Bcc:G	00ccccSS	1111P110	......#dS.......		
PSTLB	000000+-	1111P111	0-pttt--	..EaA...	
{RIE}	000000+X	1111P111	1***0*??	..Ea?...	
SHXL	000000+X	1111-111	1--010+-	..EaMX..	
SHXR	000000+X	1111-111	1--110+-	..EaMX..	
ENTER:G	000000+X	1111P111	1--011SS	..EaR!M.	......LnXL......
EXITD:G	000000+X	1111P111	1--111SS	..EaR!M.	......LxXL......
BVPAT	000001+X	1111P111			
{RIE}	00001*+X	1111P111			
BVSCH	0001bd+X	1111P111			
BRA:G	001000SS	1111P111	......#dS.......		
SSTR	001001SS	1111P111			
BSR:G	00101QSS	1111P111	......#dS.......		
BVMAP	0011bQ0X	1111P111			
BVCPY	0011bQ1X	1111P111			

Table-3 Instruction Bit Patterns of TRON VLSI CPU -9

Note

- (RIE) is an unused bit pattern, and will generate RIE (Reserved Instruction Exception) if CPU executes this bit pattern.
- -, = are reserved and set to '0'. +, ! are reserved and set to '1'.
- * can be either '0' or '1'.
- Ea field (Ea followed by some letters) is 8 bit addressing mode specifier. Sh field (Sh followed by some letters) is 6 bit addressing mode specifier.
- R or Rg field (R or Rg followed by some letters) is to specify registers.
- # field (# followed by some letters) is to store literal value, immediate constant, or constant displacement.
- L field (L followed by some letters) is to store register list.
- RR, WW, MM, XX, SS, W, M, X, S are bit(s) field to specify operand size.
- cccc is condition field for Bcc and TRAP instructions.
- eeee is to specify escape conditions such as search criteria for string instructions.
- P, Q are P-bit for extending address to 64 bits. They are reserved and set to '0' on CHIP32.
- b, r, c, d, m, p, ttt, xx are to specify certain variations of operations.
- Ea and Sh fields can have extended parts. These parts come immediately after Ea or Sh fields. Hence, the extended parts of the first operand can come before the second operand.
- The length of instructions are always even on TRON VLSI CPU. PC always contains even value. Short formats for PC-relative branch instructions (BRA:D, Bcc:D, and BSR:D) multiplies the value of #d8 field by two before adding it to PC, thus expanding the range of branch.
- PSB and PSM are 8 bits wide. However, LDPSB and LDPSM which load source data to PSB and PSM have 16 bit source operand. The reason for this is that the upper 8 bits of the source operand are used as mask bits so that LDPSB and LDPSM can update only part of the PSB and PSM.

225

Table-4 Addressing Modes of TRON VLSI CPU

8 bit (Ea)	6 bit (Sh)	Name	Action
P000 0000	00 0000	{RIE}	
P000 0001	00 0001	{RIE}	
P000 0010	00 0010	{RIE}	
P000 0011	00 0011	{RIE}	
P000 0100	00 0100	@SP+	mem[SP] ==> operand; Increment SP
P000 0101	00 0101	@-SP	Decrement SP; mem[SP] ==> operand
P000 0110	00 0110	{RIE}	
P000 0111	00 0111	{RIE}	
P000 1000	00 1000	{RIE}	
P000 1001	00 1001	@abs:16	mem[abs] ==> operand
P000 1010	00 1010	@abs:32	mem[abs] ==> operand
P000 1011	00 1011	Absolute ExA	0 ==> TMP of ExA; Process ExA
P000 1100	00 1100	#imm_data	imm_data ==> operand
P000 1101	00 1101	@(disp:16,PC)	mem[disp + PC] ==> operand
P000 1110	00 1110	@(disp:32,PC)	mem[disp + PC] ==> operand
P000 1111	00 1111	PC-relative ExA	PC ==> TMP of ExA; Process ExA
0001 <Rn>	01 <Rn>	Rn	Rn ==> operand
1001 ****	01 ****	{RIE}	
P010 <Rn>	10 <Rn>	@(disp:16,Rn)	mem[disp + Rn] ==> operand
P011 <Rn>	11 <Rn>	@Rn	mem[Rn] ==> operand
P100 <Rn>	-	@(disp:32,Rn)	mem[disp + Rn] ==> operand
P101 ****	-	{RIE}	
P110 <Rn>	-	register ExA	Rn ==> TMP of ExA; Process ExA
P111 ****	-	{RIE}	

Rn: Register Number.
disp: Displacement.
mem[EA]: Value of memory cell at effective address EA.
{RIE}: Unused bit pattern, generates RIE (Reserved Instruction Exception) if executed.
P: P-bit (Extension to 64 bit).
ExA: Additinal Addressing.
TMP: Initial value for additional addressing processing.

There are two addressing mode specifiers Ea(8 bit) and Sh(6 bit) which are used by different instruction formats. Sh is a subset of Ea in terms of bit pattern usage.

4. EXTENSIBILITY OF THE TRON VLSI CPU

An important advantage of the von-Neumann-type computer is its direct and free access to a large address space.

Application associated with Artificial Intelligence (AI) processing will vogue more rapidly from now. Many of these applications will require larger address space, especially when portions of the addresses is used for tags. If limited addressable space results in troublesome programming work, adverse effects will be generated in software migration and execution speed. Availability of a large address space is thus indispensable for improving the productivity of software not only in AI applications.

Because of the recent progress in device technology and reduction in storage costs, more real storage than can be addressed 32 bit (4G bytes) will be soon installed in some systems. Provided that the capacity of memory devices increases twofold every two years, a 1M-bit memory chip of current technology will be developed into 32M-bit memory chip in 10 years, 1997, and then 4G byte addressable space can be realized with only 1024 memory chips. This is a rather conservative guess. Moreover the upper limit of the addressable space be reached sooner since large logical space will be available if virtual memory system is used.

What is obvious from the above discussion of demand for larger addressable space and from the large-scale integration of storage is that present 32-bit addressing capability will soon be obsolete. Thus we designed the series of CHIP32, CHIP48, and CHIP64 together under the same architecture. From the perspective of addressable space size and usable data size, they are upwardly compatible from CHIP32 through CHIP48 and CHIP64. Therefore, when designing CHIP32, we devised instruction codes for 64-bit data manipulation and addressing, while reserving the 64-bit addressing mode bit (P bit) in the addressing mode specification field. And in all bit manipulation instructions, we also prepared 6-bit operands for specifying up to 64 bits. (see *Table-5*.)

Table-5 TRON VLSI CPU Family

	TRON CHIP32	TRON CHIP48	TRON CHIP64
Address Bus	32 bit	48 bit	64 bit
Data Bus	32 bit	64 bit	64 bit
Register	32 bit	64 bit	64 bit
Chip Scale	VLSI		ULSI
# of Devices (million)	0.5 - 1.0		Several
Available Date	End of 1987		1990's

The size specification of the TRON VLSI CPU is usually done with two bits field. 8, 16, 32 or 64 bits can be chosen as the operand size. However, if 64 bits is chosen as operand size on CHIP32, an RIE (Reserved Instruction Exception) occurs. Certain instructions such as PUSH or MULX do not allow 8 or 16 bits as operand size. In these cases, one bit field is still reserved to select either 32 or 64 as operand size.

Address extension bit (called P-bit) can be specified for each memory addressing. This bit is not used on CHIP32, but CHIP64 will use this bit to handle 64 bits address space. P-bit can be specified for each memory reference. For example, string transfer instruction (SMOV) have two P-bits for the source and the destination address. (They are shown as P and Q in Table-3.) Existing microprocessors have unused bit-patterns. But TRON VLSI CPU has explicitly reserved portions of currently used bit patterns to extend memory accessing methods. When P-bit is set on CHIP32, an RIE occurs.

Furthermore, in operation codes and addressing mode bit patterns of instructions for TRON VLSI CPUs, we have reserved many unused bit patterns for functional extensions in the future. These unused bit could be reserved only by making the TRON VLSI CPU architecture incompatible with the old 4-, 8-, and 16-bit microprocessors. Retaining compatibility with old processors results in wasted instruction codes and chip areas and in lessened expandability. We chose expandability for TRON VLSI CPUs, trading off compatibility with the old processors, because we were pursuing an architecture that will be long used into the future.

TRON VLSI CPU has paid attention to extending address to 64 bits in another respect. That is the continuation of SR (shared region) and UR (unshared region) when logical address space is extended from 32 bits to 64 bits. (see Figure-6.)

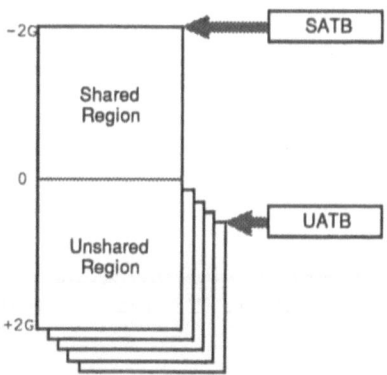

- Unshared Region/Shared Region are distinguished by MSB.
- Unshared Region used UATB register for address translation.
- Shared Region used SATB register for address translation.
- UATB register is changed whenever context switch task place, and multiple logical space are provided for each of context.

Figure-6. Multiple Logical Spaces of the TRON VLSI CPU

228

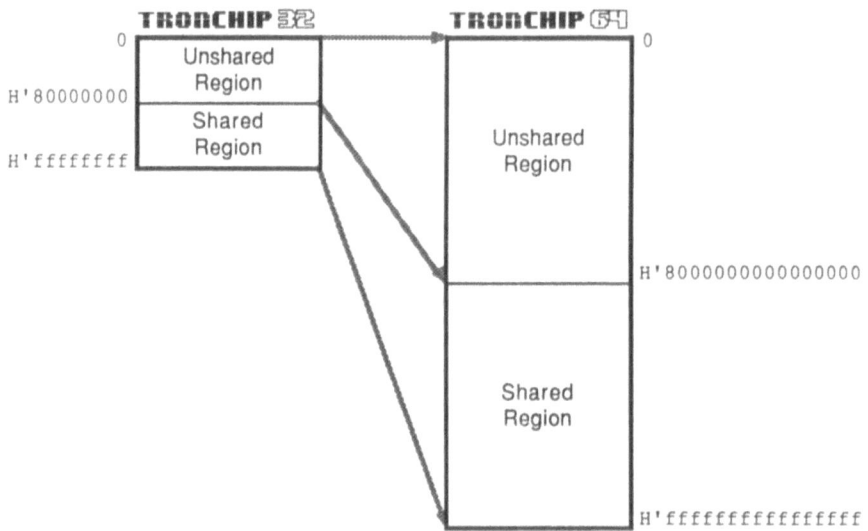

(a) If MSB of logical address is used to distinguish UR and SR, SR's position will change when we move from 32 bits to 64 bits address space.

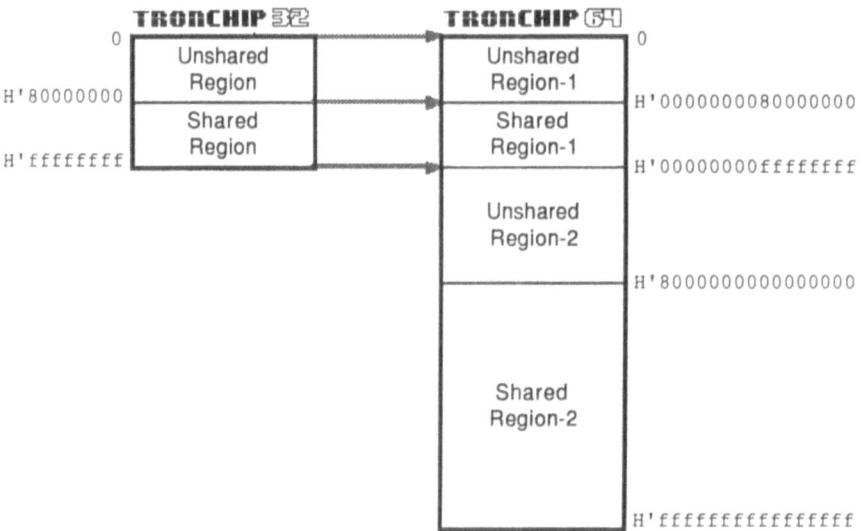

(b) If, in 64 bits address space, we use UR and SR at where they are in 32 bits address space, UR and SR will have divided regions.

Figure-7 Problem of Extending UR and SR in 64 Bits Address Space

The standard MMU (memory management unit) of the TRON VLSI CPU treats address range H'00000000-H'7FFFFFFF as UR and H'80000000-H'FFFFFFFF as SR. (H'xxx shows hexadecimal number.) MMU of the TRON VLSI CPU supports multiple logical spaces for each context such as task or process, but only UR is mapped separately for each context, and SR is shared by all the contexts. UR is mainly used by user programs and SR is used by OS.

The division of logical spaces of CHIP64 into UR and SR could be done in several ways. *Figure-7(a)* shows that use of MSB of address to divide the UR and SR. *Figure-7(b)* shows that the division in CHIP32 is reserved while new area is again divided into UR and SR. The method in (a) has this problem; the H'80000000-H'FFFFFFFF is SR on CHIP32, but UR on CHIP64. Method in (b) is a little clumsy since now we have two SR's and two UR's. In the TRON VLSI CPU,it was decided to regard logical address as signed number and then assign SR to negative address area, and UR to positive address area. *Figure-8* shows that now the continual extension of SR and UR from 32 bits address space to 64 bits address space is possible. In harmony with the notion that the logical address is regarded as signed number, short data is sign-extended during the address calculation. For example, in 16-bit absolute addressing (@abs:16), the 16 bit number is sign-extended to 32 bit logical address.

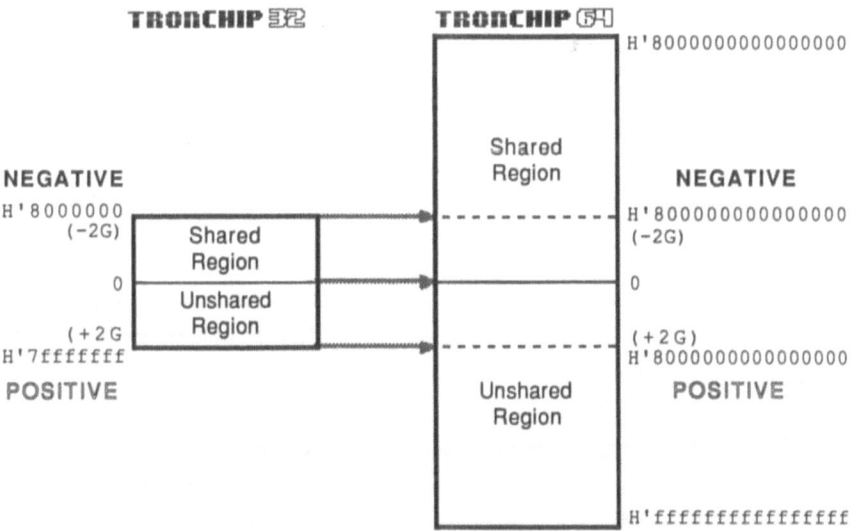

- If we regard address as singed number, we can extend SR and UR smoothly.

Figure-8 Extension of SR and UR on the TRON VLSI CPU

5. TOTAL ARCHITECTURE

It was usually the case that the hardware and OS was independently designed. In the case of TRON VLSI CPU, it has been designed in conjunction with ITRON OS for embedded computers, and BTRON for high-performance workstations. Hence, the TRON VLSI CPU has specialized instructions to support ITRON or BTRON. So it becomes possible to boost the performance of OS using these instructions. TRON VLSI CPU has instructions for context switching (LDCTX, and STCTX), for handling queues (QSCH, QINS, and QDEL). For supporting applications on BTRON, it has bitmap manipulation instructions (BVPAT, BVMAP and BVCPY), and string instructions (SSCH, SMOV, SCMP, and SSTR).

Introducing high-level instructions and increasing the execution speed of basic, frequently used instructions are both important but in different ways. Increasing the execution speed of basic instructions improves average performance, but not improve the performance in critical situations so much. For example, it is very important for ITRON to shorten the response time between when an interrupt is occurred and when the task processing the interrupt is activated. If this task activation is performed by hardware with a high-level instruction and its execution speed doubled, the response speed also doubles; thus improvement by introducing the high-level instruction is remarkable. On the other hand, if you want the response speed to be doubled using a combination of basic instructions, the execution speed of all instructions involved in processing during the response period must also be doubled. This approach is awkward.

Since even in real-time applications the above-mentioned task activations does not so frequently occur, doubling the response time does little to improve average performance such as MIPS value. For real-time applications, however, response speed is far more important than average performance. To improve specific features such as response time, high-level instructions must be introduced.

QSCH instruction of the TRON VLSI CPU finds a queue entry that satisfy a set of search criteria in a queue represented as linked list. Search criteria can be equality of a field in queue entry to a given value, or inequality (larger, etc.). QSCH instruction can be used to locate a desired position when ITRON inserts new task into task ready queue. Ready queue has TCB (Task Control Block) of ready task as its entry. There is a field called task priority in TCB. In ITRON, higher-priority tasks have smaller priority number and will run first. Hence, the ready queue is sorted according to the task priority. When a new task becomes ready, TCB of the task must be inserted immediately after the task which has the lowest task priority that is higher than the priority of new task, namely, after the task which has the largest priority number that is smaller than the priority number of new task. QSCH can be used to look for the TCB entry in the ready queue by comparing the task priority. Such usage is shown in *Figure-9*.

Example: A task with priority 8 becomes ready.
So it is going to be inserted into task ready queue.
↓
Where to insert the task in the queue is located by using QSCH instruction.
QSCH looks for the TCB of which priority is larger than 8.

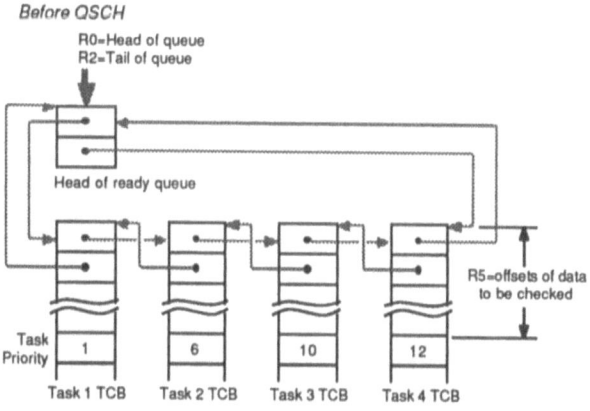

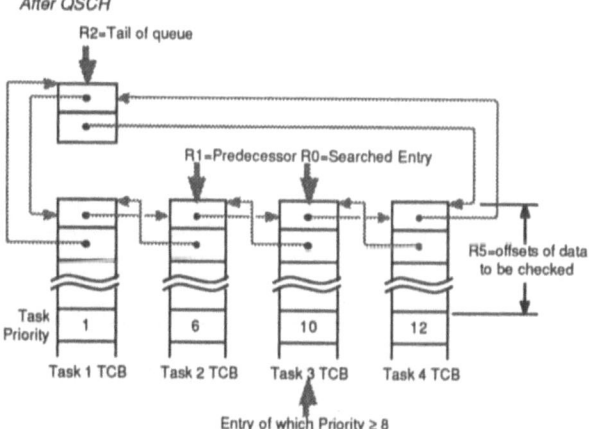

Figure-9 Ready Queue Manipulation Using QSCH of TRON VLSI CPU

- During the execution of QSCH, R0 points at the successive queue entry.
- End of queue is found by comparing R0 to queue end address in R2. If search failed when R0 and R2 are the same, then the instruction terminates.
- QSCH can support both doubly-linked and singly-linked queue. When the search stops, R0 points at the desired entry, and R1 points at the immediate predecessor. Even in a singly-linked queue, the data left in R1 is valuable in deleting the found element.
- R0 and R2 are set to the address of queue header.

Figure-9 Ready Queue Manipulation Using QSCH of TRON VLSI CPU

BVMAP, BVCPY, and BVPAT instructions of the TRON VLSI CPU are used to handle graphics data necessary for window manipulation in BTRON. BVMAP performs logical operations on variable-length bit fields in memory. It can perform transfer as well as performing the logical operation. BVCPY performs the transfer of bitmap data, which is also done by BVMAP, but BVCPY does it faster. BVPAT fills in variable length bit fields with repetition of bit pattern. BVMAP and BVPAT use registers to specify the logical operation. *Table-6* shows the correspondence of the logical operation and register value.

Table-6 Operations of BVMAP and BVPAT

Register	Value	Mnemonic	Operation
0000	F	False	0 ==> dest
0001	NAN	NotAndNot	~dest .and. ~src ==> dest
0010	AN	AndNot	dest .and. ~src ==> dest
0011	NS	NotSrc	~src ==> dest
0100	NA	NotAnd	~dest .and. src ==> dest
0101	ND	NotDest	~dest ==> dest
0110	X	Xor	dest .xor. src ==> dest
0111	NON	NotOrNot	~dest .or. ~src ==> dest
1000	A	And	dest .and. src ==> dest
1001	NX	NotXor	~dest .xor. src ==> dest
1010	D	Dest	dest ==> dest
1011	ON	OrNot	dest .or. ~src ==> dest
1100	S	Src	src ==> dest
1101	NO	NotOr	~dest .or. src ==> dest
1110	O	Or	dest .or. src ==> dest
1111	T	True	1 ==> dest

.and. stands for logical and, .or. for logical or, '~' for bit reversal.

A separate chip could be used such as a graphic processor for bitmap processing. However, the overhead of communication between the graphic processor and main processor is a big problem; because the bitmap manipulation is very important for the BTRON-controlled man-machine interface and the datapath between both processors must be very wide. Therefore, bitmap processing by the main processor is better choice for improving overall performance than processing by a separate chip.

6. OTHER ARCHITECTURAL FEATURES

TRON VLSI CPU has other interesting architectural features aside from the ones covered in the previous sections.

6.1 PIB INSTRUCTION

In principle, it is possible to modify the instructions which will be later executed on a stored-program computer. However, instruction pipelining or the use of instruction cache makes it very difficult for the CPU to execute the correct instructions if the instructions are modified on the fly. Existing microprocessors do not define the operations in these cases or guarantee the correct operations only if instruction cache is purged. Some processors used on superminicomputer use additional hardware to check instruction cache for these rare cases, and make sure that CPU always execute the intended instructions. This has been necessitated to support existing programs which ran on the non-pipelined or non-cache version of the computer. Additional hardware on these computers cost much.

Instruction-cache on the TRON VLSI CPU is implementation dependent. There must be a way to support instruction-rewriting programs in an implementation-independent way even when instruction cache or pipelining exist. PIB instruction is used for this purpose. PIB declares that the instruction has been rewritten. Programs that change instructions on the fly must execute PIB after the rewriting. In actual implementations, PIB is likely to purge the instruction cache and clear the instruction pipeline. If no such mechanisms exist, or additional hardware takes care of the correct execution, then PIB acts as if it were a NOP (no operation) instruction. PIB assures the processor-independent correct execution of on the fly rewriting of instructions. Rewriting of instructions during execution is necessary for OS's program loading and for some sophisticated applications such as AI applications. (see *Figure-10*.)

6.2 EIT PROCESSING.

EIT processing on the TRON VLSI CPU takes place asynchronously with the normal execution of program code. EIT stands for Exception which takes place when error is recognized, Interrupt which is generated by external hardware signal, and Trap which is generated intentionally by software.

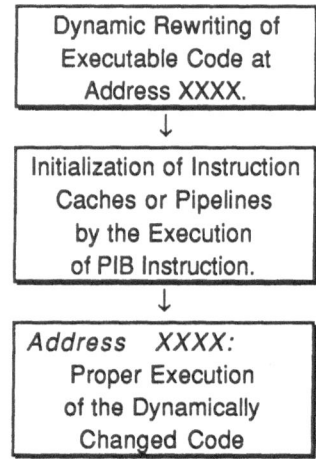

Figure-10 Usage of PIB Instruction

When an EIT occurs, the processor fetches the from EIT vector table (EITVT) an entry (EITVTE), and then set the part of PSW and PC according to EITVTE. The program flow then transfers to the EIT processing handler, which takes care of the causes of EIT and returns the control after processing it. The PC and PSW at the time of EIT occurrence, and EIT-related information are stored on stack. EIT processing handler can execute REIT (Return from EIT) instruction to restore PC and PSW and then to return to the original program flow which was interrupted at the time of EIT occurrence.

It should be noted that, on the TRON VLSI CPU, not only PC but also part of PSW can be changed according to the entry in EITVT. Interrupt mask (IMASK), address translation specification field (AT), and debug mode bit (DB) can be set at the time of EIT occurrence. This feature to change PSW makes it possible to automatically mask off uninteresting interrupts, to enter critical section automatically, or to disable address translation temporarily.

PSW of TRON VLSI CPU is shown in *Figure-11*. The format of EITVTE and the change of PSW at the time of EIT occurrence are shown in *Figure-12*.

SM	RNG	XA	– –	AT	– – –	DB	IMASK	–	PRNG	– – – – –	– –	F	X	V	L	M	Z

'–'	Reserved and set to '0'.
SM, RNG = 000	CPU handles interrupt in in Ring 0.
SM, RNG = 100	CPU executes in Ring 0.
SM, RNG = 101	CPU executes in Ring 1.
SM, RNG = 110	CPU executes in Ring 2.
SM, RNG = 111	CPU executes in Ring 3.
XA = 0	32 bit address context.
AT = 00	No address translation, no protection.
AT = 01	Address Translation, and ring protection. (Standard MMU of the TRON VLSI CPU)
AT = 10	No address translation, but simple protection.
DB = 0	Context is not in debugging mode.
DB = 1	Context is in debugging mode
IMASK	Interrupt mask.
PRNG	Ring number of the calling context.
F	F_flag: Functional (General) Flag Used, for example, to check for the escape condition.
X	X_flag: Extension Flag Used, for example, for carry in multiple-word arithmetic
V	V_flag: Overflow Flag
L	L_flag: Lower (Less than) Flag Set if the first operand is smaller in comparison.
M	M_flag: MSB Flag Set if the operation result has 1 in MSB position.
Z	Z_flag: Zero Flag Set if the operation result is 0.

Figure-11 PSW of TRON VLSI CPU

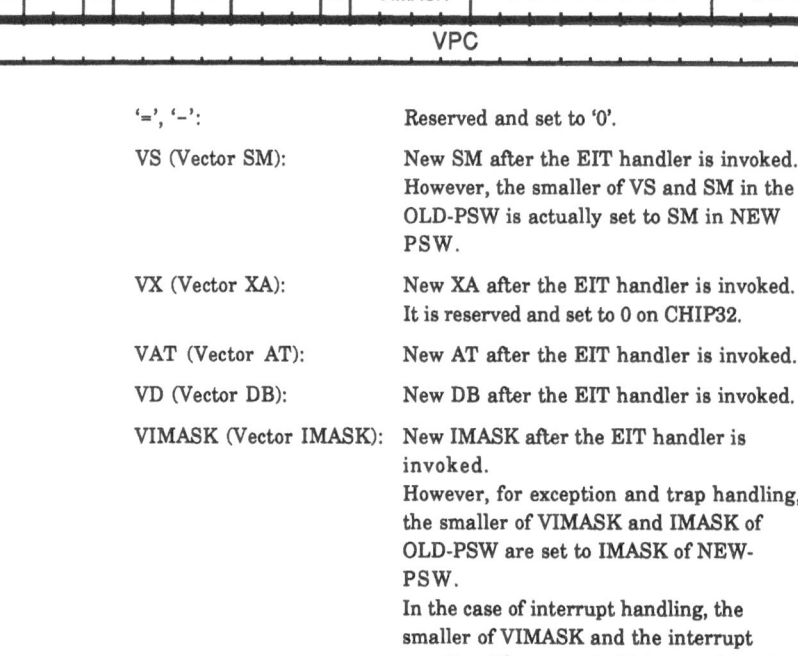

| '=', '-': | Reserved and set to '0'. |

VS (Vector SM):   New SM after the EIT handler is invoked. However, the smaller of VS and SM in the OLD-PSW is actually set to SM in NEW PSW.

VX (Vector XA):   New XA after the EIT handler is invoked. It is reserved and set to 0 on CHIP32.

VAT (Vector AT):   New AT after the EIT handler is invoked.

VD (Vector DB):   New DB after the EIT handler is invoked.

VIMASK (Vector IMASK):   New IMASK after the EIT handler is invoked.
However, for exception and trap handling, the smaller of VIMASK and IMASK of OLD-PSW are set to IMASK of NEW-PSW.
In the case of interrupt handling, the smaller of VIMASK and the interrupt priority of the generated interrupt is set to IMASK of NEW-PSW.

Figure-12 Format of EITVTE and Change of PSW at EIT Handler Invocation

7. COMPATIBILITY OF TRON VLSI CPU

In the design of the TRON VLSI CPU, the fundamental architecture has been created. It is the designer's intention to adapt the CPU by subsetting of the specification or by the extension of specification. The use of only one fundamental architecture is to take advantage of the common development systems and training materials.

However, it naturally follows that we lose compatibility if subsetting or extension of specification is done. Moreover, the implementors are free to extend specifications individually in several functions. For example, cache-related operations or support for in-circuit emulators are such features.

In order to limit the chaotic proliferation of subset or extended specifications, major subsetting and extension of the specification has been already done. *Table-7* shows the various levels of the specification. Application program that runs on TRON VLSI CPU can indicate how much portability it has by showing the CPU level it has assumed.

Table-7 Classes of Specifications of the TRON VLSI CPU

Specification Level

«L0» (Level 0)	The minimum specification that TRON VLSI CPU must satisfy; basic instructions, bit patterns, etc. This is «L1» minus some high-level instructions
«L1R» (Level 1 - Real)	Specification for CPU without MMU. «L1» minus MMU support instructions.
«L1» (Level 1)	This is the preferred current specification.
«L2» (Level 2)	This includes some extensions, and planned features. For example, INDEX.
«LX» (eXtension)	Planned specification of CHIP64. 64 bit operations.
«LA» (Alternative)	Alternative implementation can be different from the one suggested in the TRON VLSI CPU specification. For example, handling of control registers.
«LV» (Variable)	Implementation is up to implementors. For example, instructions to interface with In-circuit emulator.

On the other hand, TRON VLSI CPU specifications do not stipulate whether an MMU, a TLB, or a cache memory ought to exist or to be contained within a same package as CPU. Matters like this are at manufacturer discretion, as are the types and positions of chip pins. However, a standard bus must be determined for a peripheral chip to be shared by the TRON VLSI CPUs of different manufacturers. We have designed such a bus and named it TOBUS.

TOBUS is a 32-bit general-purpose system bus performing asynchronous transfer and using distributed bus arbitration method. Its features are expandability to the 64-bit environment and fault-tolerance. The latter feature consists of twofold and threefold bus functions and a self-diagnostic function. Use of TOBUS enhances the reliability of a computer system.

8. CONCLUSION

The architecture of TRON VLSI CPUs excels the architectures of conventional processors in that:

1) It has taken into account expandability to TRON VLSI CHIP64.

2) It places importance on creation of software such as compilers.

3) It reflects demands by Operating Systems designed in conjunction with TRON VLSI CPUs.

TRON VLSI CPU specifications are designed by an academic institute and multiple manufacturers have been invited to implement TRON VLSI CPU specifications. Thus the architecture is said to be an open architecture. The attempt to build such an architecture made by us was the first attempt in the world. Such a maker-independent architecture may become a standard architecture.

The development of the TRON VLSI CPU has come near to the completion thanks to the cooperation of several manufacturers. It is expected that the first sample will be available by the end of 1987. The development system such as compiler, ITRON, and BTRON for the CPU are now being done. The designers would like to see that many people will start using the TRON VLSI CPU and that the wide user group will pressure the manufacturers to providing better development systems, and useful variations of the TRON VLSI CPU's. Since several manufacturers have already started their work to provide TRON VLSI CPU's to the market, the designers' wish is likely to be answered. It is believed that the general-purposeness and open architecture of the TRON VLSI CPU have been accepted very favorably.

We hope that the TRON VLSI CPU will benefit the human kind as basic components of computer systems.

ACKNOWLEDGEMENTS

We would like to express our hearty thanks to the manufacturers who concurred with the purpose of the TRON project and helped its realization.

REFERENCES

[1] Ken Sakamura: "Development of TRON Chip: A single chip VLSI computer architecture in the 1990's", Proceedings of International Conference on Very Large Scale Integration, Tokyo (VLSI 85), Aug. 1985, pp.115-124.

[2] Ken Sakamura: "The TRON Project", IEEE Micro, Vol. 7, No. 2 (Apr. 1987), pp.8-14.

[3] Ken Sakamura: "Architecture of the TRON VLSI CPU", IEEE Micro, Vol. 7, No. 2 (Apr. 1987), pp.17-31.

[4] William A. Wulf: "Compilers and Computer Architecture", IEEE Computer, Vol. 14, No. 7 (July, 1981), pp. 41-47

Ken Sakamura: see *"The Objectives of the TRON Project"* in this proceedings.

Design Considerations
for TRON Cache Memories

Alan Jay Smith
Computer Science Division, EECS Department, University of California
Berkeley, CA 94270, U.S.A.

Abstract

CPU cache memories are small, high performance associatively accessed memories used to hold currently active portions of the main memory contents. The high ratio of CPU speed to main memory speed makes effective cache design crucial to machine performance.

In this paper, we discuss the components of cache performance, including miss ratio and access time, describe a typical cache design, and then provide a brief overview of the various design choices for cache memories including cache size and location, line (block) size, fetch algorithm, organization, main memory update policy, split vs. unified cache, multi-cache consistency and input/output, virtual vs. real addressing, replacement algorithm, TLB design, error detection and correction, pipelining and arbitration. We then review some factors of particular applicability to the TRON design.

Keywords: Microprocessors, Cache, TLB, TRON CPU.

1. Introduction

CPUs are typically built from a logic technology considerably faster than that used for most main memories, with the result that machine performance would suffer greatly if main memory were used directly. The solution to this speed mismatch is the *cache memory*, which is a high speed associatively addressed buffer memory placed between the functional units of the CPU (the I-unit and E-unit) and main memory. The cache and its associated components (TLB, translator, etc.) comprise the S-unit, or storage unit of the CPU. The cache memory receives main memory addresses from the I-unit (instruction fetch and decode unit) or the E-unit (execution unit) and responds if it contains the contents of the referenced memory location; if the cache does not have the information, the cache is loaded from main memory.

Caches have been consistently observed to yield good performance, in that their *hit ratio* (the probability of finding the referenced data in the cache) is always much higher than the ratio of the size of the cache to that of main memory. A cache will usually be less than 0.5% of the size of the main memory, and all but the smallest and most primitive caches will have hit ratios of 80% to 99%. This high hit ratio is explained by an empirical observation known as the *principle of locality* [1], which can be stated as follows: **Information in use in the near future is likely to consist of that information in current use** *(locality by time)* **and that information logically adjacent to that in current use** *(locality by space)*. The principle of locality is widely applicable, and also explains the success of main memory paging, disk caching, and file migration.

Although cache hit ratios are typically "high", machine performance is still extremely sensitive to the cache design for two reasons. First, the large ratio of access time between the cache memory and main memory makes performance vary sharply with the value of the *miss ratio* (= 1-hit ratio). Second, even though the cache memory is much faster than main memory, it is typically still somewhat slower than the CPU, and in most machines the cache contains or is on the critical path; the critical path is the one preventing further reductions in the cycle time.

From the discussion above, we see that there are two primary factors by which to evaluate a cache design:

(1) (Mean) Access time to the cache on a hit.

(2) Probability of a hit.

More generally, we would like to minimize the mean memory access time T. If we let Tm be the memory access time on a cache miss, Th be the access time on a cache hit, m be the miss ratio, and E be a term to account for the other factors discussed below, then $T = m*Tm + Th + E$.

There are a number of other factors which affect memory access time: (3) the time (Tm) to satisfy a read miss, (4) any extra time for a write to the cache, (5) delays to update main memory after data is modified, (6) queueing delays at main memory in a multiprocessor system or when I/O occurs, and (7) cache cycles taken by consistency operations and prefetch operations. These factors all have relatively small effects on performance, except for Tm, which is difficult to change significantly.

In the remainder of this paper, we will consider how cache performance is affected by various design choices. First, we will provide a short description of the operation of a typical cache memory. We will then provide very brief comments on a number of aspects of cache design, including the cache size and location, line size, fetch algorithm (demand / prefetch), organization (set associative, direct mapped, fully associative, sector), main memory update policy (write through, copy back), unified vs. split (instruction / data), multi-cache consistency mechanism, the effect of input/output, virtual vs. real addressing, the replacement algorithm, TLB design, pipelining, arbitration, and error detection and correction. In almost all cases, our discussions will be brief. We refer the reader to [5,6] for a much more detailed overview of the subject of cache memories; see also [10] for a brief but more recent treatment. An extensive bibliography is provided in [9].

2. Typical Cache Operation

In this section, we provide a brief summary of the operation of a standard cache memory. The cache we describe is typical of that in many mainframes such as the Amdahl 470 or the IBM 3033. This description is somewhat simplified; some of the possible complications and design alternatives will be described in the next section.

A virtual main memory address is generated by the I- or E-units of the CPU. That address can be partitioned into the higher order bits (the page number), which must be translated, and the lower order bits (the byte within page, or byte address) which are the same in both virtual and real forms. The page number is sent to the TLB (translation lookaside buffer) to be translated into a real address. The TLB is often a set associative memory, in which case, a set is selected using some of the bits of the page number. (In some machines, the set is selected by hashing some of the page number bits with a process identifier. In others, the set is directed directly, as a binary decode of some of the address bits.) The page number is then compared with the appropriate virtual tag portion of the TLB entries; if a match is found, the corresponding real address is read out and forwarded to the comparators described below. If no match is found, a hardware mechanism uses the page number as an index into the segment and page tables, translates the virtual page number into a real one, and loads the {virtual,real} pair into the TLB; the machine then resumes processing. (If the translation is not possible, due to a missing page table entry, a page fault takes place.)

In parallel with the TLB access, the high order bits of the byte address are used to select a set in a set associative cache memory. The tags for the entries in that set are read into a set of comparators. The real address received from the TLB is compared with each of the real addresses obtained from the cache address tags. If a match is found, the corresponding line is read out into a multiplexor. If there is no match, a cache miss occurs and the missing line is loaded from main memory into the cache; the real address from the TLB plus the byte address from the virtual address are used to reference main memory. After the missing line is loaded, the cache is again accessed and the line read into the mux. The lower order bits of the byte address are used to select the appropriate bytes from the line, and the resulting data is sent forward to the CPU; the bytes are shifted and aligned if necessary.

The above summary of cache operation is simplified in two ways. First, it describes a specific cache design, whereas a wide variety of designs are possible. Second, it omits some of the special cases and considerations, such as line crossers or input/output, that must be accounted for. In the following section, we survey the design alternatives, and indicate some of the special cases.

3. Design Choices and Considerations

A number of cache designs are possible, depending on cost / performance tradeoffs, technology used, instruction set compatibility issues, machine architecture features, and tolerance for complexity. A brief description of most of those appears in this section.

3.1. Cache Size(s) and Location(s)

Given equal levels of performance, a cache should always be as large as possible, so as to maximize the hit ratio. Larger caches, however, are often slower, costlier, and consume more power, and the cache size may face a physical limit of board space or chip area. Miss ratios as a function of cache and line size may be estimated using the *design target miss ratios* found in [11].

Typically, the ratio in access time between main memory and cache is in the range of 5 - 10. That range is too small to justify the use of a multi-level cache. The increase in VLSI density now suggests a role for two level caches, with a small on-chip cache and a larger board level cache.

3.2. Line Size

The line (or block) is the unit of transfer between cache and main memory. One wishes to select a line size that minimizes the value of [(miss ratio)*(delay for a miss)], where with increasing line size the miss ratio usually drops and the delay increases. Data in [11] provide a basis for selecting the line size. Line sizes in the range of 16-64 bytes seem to be satisfactory for a large range of cache and memory performance parameters. Other considerations are the frequency of line and page crossers, which decrease with larger lines, and the possibility of I/O overruns, which increase with line size. Very small lines are costly in terms of the large number of address tag bits required.

3.3. Fetch Algorithm

The fetch algorithm determines when to bring information into the cache. Most machines use *demand fetch*, by which lines are fetched only when referenced. Some machines use a *prefetch algorithm*, by which lines are brought into cache in anticipation of use. As shown in [4], [5], and [7], prefetching cuts the miss ratio significantly, especially for instructions. Experience, however, has shown that very careful implementation is required if the decrease in miss ratio is to be accompanied by a performance improvement. The principal problem is that additional cache cycles may be required (depending on the design) to examine cache tags, and fetch and load prefetched lines.

3.4. Cache Organization

Caches must be associative; addresses refer to main memory and not cache. Small caches may be made *fully associative*, and in VLSI, fully associative memories of 32 or 64 entries are quite possible. Fully associative memories tend to have disadvantages when made large however; depending on the design, they become slow and/or expensive, and in VLSI, associative cells are significantly larger than RAM cells. The alternative is a *set associative* cache. In such designs, a subset of the address bits select a set, and then the associative search is confined to that set. If the set size is one, the organization is referred to as *direct mapped*.

Miss ratios tend to increase with decreases in the set size, but small sets, and in particular direct mapped caches, can often be faster. Results in [3] suggest that for larger caches, direct mapped designs are optimal, and for smaller caches, set associative designs (with 2 - 4 elements/set) seem to be best.

It is also possible to use a *sector cache*, by which sectors are divided into subsectors. Address tags are associated with sectors, and validity bits with subsectors. Sector caches have high miss ratios, but can have lower bus traffic [2].

3.5. Main Memory Update

Writes by the processor must eventually be reflected in main memory. This can be done using *write through* (store through), by which every write is sent directly to main memory, or with *copy-back*, by which writes are made to cache, and then a modified line is copied back to main memory when the line is replaced. Write through tends to be simpler, make cache consistency easier to maintain, and enhance reliability, but memory traffic is higher and performance is often lower.

3.6. Data / Instruction Cache

The essence of the Von Neumann architecture is that both instructions and data are just bit patterns in a common memory. This view is reflected in the standard cache design, in which there is a single cache containing both instructions and data. Splitting the cache into instruction and data portions has the advantages that access time can be decreased, bandwidth increased and arbitration and access simplified. For new architectures, in which the correct execution of self modifying code is not required, split data/instruction caches have become popular.

3.7. Multi-Cache Consistency

Systems with multiple CPUs, each with caches, sharing a common main memory, have the problem of maintaining a consistent view of the main memory contents. A number of approaches to this problem have been proposed including centralized directories, distributed directories, shared caches, software control, and broadcast writes. (See [5], [8] and [12] for a discussion of these possibilities.) Most popular currently are the bus based methods, which work by requiring all transactions which threaten consistency to be broadcast on a common bus, and require that all cache controllers watch and act on all transactions on that bus. Sweazey and Smith describe a class of consistency protocols which are supported in the

IEEE Futurebus [12]. Multi-cache consistency is a particularly important issue (and hot research topic) due to the excellent cost/performance achieved by high performance microprocessors.

3.8. Input / Output

Input/output is a problem in two ways for caches. First, consistency must be maintained between the cache contents and main memory, while I/O usually references main memory directly. The same mechanisms can be used for this purpose as for multi-cache consistency, as mentioned above. The second effect of I/O is to use cache cycles and (depending on the machine architecture) possibly increase the cache miss ratio. Since the amount of I/O traffic is usually low, performance effects are usually minor.

3.9. Virtual vs. Real Addressing

Most caches are referenced using real addresses, as was described in section 2. Real address caches require at least some delay for address translation, although much of it may be overlapped. If the cache is large, the limited number of untranslated bits may require a large set size and a wide associative search. If the set size is too large, the translation and cache access may have to be made sequential.

Virtual address caches are those caches accessed using the virtual address. They are potentially significantly faster than real address caches, but require a resolution of the *synonym problem*. The problem is that more than one virtual address (*synonyms*) may map to the same physical address. Some mechanism must be included to deal with this problem, and also with the problem of I/O, which uses real addresses. The two solutions generally considered are a *reverse translation buffer (RTB)*, which translates real to virtual addresses to check for synonyms, and the imposition of a global virtual address space; the latter solution is only feasible for completely new architectures and new software.

3.10. Replacement Algorithm

When there is a cache miss and corresponding fetch, some line must be replaced. Such a replacement must always be within the same set as the fetch. Typically LRU or some approximation to LRU are used (see [5] for details). Performance tends to not be very sensitive to the replacement algorithm. One experiment [5] showed that FIFO had about a 10% higher miss ratio than LRU. For very small caches (e.g. instruction buffers), the loop behavior of programs sometimes makes random replacement preferable to LRU.

3.11. TLB Design

The TLB (*translation lookaside buffer*, translation buffer (TB), or directory lookaside table (DLAT)) is a small cache memory used to translate virtual to real addresses. Some of the same factors described above also apply to TLBs, including: size, organization (set or fully associative), and replacement algorithm. There are some issues that are peculiar to TLBs, including mapping (hashed or bit select) and the use of a process identifier. Some recent designs, based on the RISC approach to computer design, have placed the TLB control in software rather than hardware.

3.12. Pipelining and/or Multi-cycle Cache

Because the cache is usually the limiting factor for the machine cycle time, cache access time can be made to stretch over 2 or more cycles, so as to improve overall machine performance. In pipelined machines, this multi-cycle access has been used to pipeline the cache, so that more than one access can be in progress at any one time. This is particularly useful in machines with unified (instructions and data) caches, for which cache bandwidth may be a problem.

3.13. Arbitration

There are usually two or more sources of reference to a cache: instruction unit, execution unit, TLB, main memory or bus, TLB, prefetch logic, etc. These sources of requests must be arbitrated, so as to produce correct and deadlock free operation, and also to maximize performance.

3.14. Error Detection and Correction

The tight timing requirements for cache memories make it infeasible to do error detection and correction as part of a cache access. There are two alternate approaches. One is to do the ECC in parallel, and provide a delayed trap to the CPU in the case that an error is found. The other is to omit ECC on the cache entirely, after noting that the mean time between transient failures is typically more than a year.

4. Factors of Particular Importance to TRON

Almost all of the factors noted above apply to the design of a cache for a TRON machine, and almost all factors that affect TRON are listed above. In this section, however, we make some additional mention of factors of particular importance.

The TRON specification includes a sophisticated ring-structured protection scheme similar to that used in Multics. Protection is typically specified in the page or segment tables and is typically enforced via fields in the TLB. Encodings for the protection fields must be selected, and checking mechanisms devised, that don't impose significant delays on cache access time.

Most (or all) initial TRON implementations are microprocessors. Microprocessor based systems are typically constructed around a common memory bus, such as the TRON bus. It is important that the bus design and operation algorithms be selected so as to permit cache consistency in multiprocessor systems, and to permit bus units (cards) from different vendors to operate together.

Current levels of technology permit useful on-chip cache memories, but those caches may not be large enough to take the role of a large board level cache. TRON machines should be designed with the possibility that they will operate either with or without an outboard cache. The necessary signals to and from the chip should be provided to permit cache consistency to be maintained.

Because TRON is a new architecture, for which completely new software is being written, it should be possible to produce software which facilitates the implementation of virtual address caches.

5. Conclusions

Memory access time is the critical factor in modern CPU performance, and cache memories are the most effective way to optimize this factor. Despite the simplicity of the concept of caching, the variety of possible cache designs and the subtlety of some of the issues make cache design a difficult and tricky problem. In this paper, we have briefly reviewed the issues in cache design and in some cases have outlined the preferred solutions. We have also mentioned some factors of particular importance to the TRON design.

Acknowledgement

The material presented here is based on research supported in part by the National Science Foundation under grant MIP-8713274, and by the State of California MICRO Program.

Bibliography

[1] Peter J. Denning, "On Modeling Program Behavior", Proc. SJCC, 1972, pp. 937-944

[2] Mark Hill and Alan Jay Smith, "Experimental Evaluation of On-Chip Microprocessor Cache Memories", Proc. 11'th Ann. Symp. on Computer Architecture, June, 1984, Ann Arbor, Michigan, pp. 158-166. IEEE Computer, 17, 1, January, 1984, pp. 6-22.

[3] Mark Hill, "Aspects of Cache Memory and Instruction Buffer Performance", Ph.D. Thesis, Computer Science Division, EECS Department, University of California, 1987, in preparation.

[4] Alan Jay Smith, "Sequential Program Prefetching in Memory Hierarchies", IEEE Computer, 11, 12, December, 1978, pp. 7-21.

[5] Alan Jay Smith, "Cache Memories", Computing Surveys, 14, 3, September, 1982, pp. 473-530.

[6] Alan Jay Smith, "CPU Cache Memories", to appear in *Handbook for Computer Designers*, ed. Flynn and Rossman.

[7] Alan Jay Smith, "Cache Evaluation and the Impact of Workload Choice", Report UCB/CSD85/229, March, 1985, Proc. 12'th International Symposium on Computer Architecture, June 17-19, 1985, Boston, Mass, pp. 64-75.

[8] "CPU Cache Consistency with Software Support and Using "One Time Identifiers"", Proc. Pacific Computer Communication Symposium, Seoul, Republic of Korea, October 22-24, 1985, pp. 142-150.

[9] Alan Jay Smith, "Bibliography and Readings on CPU Cache Memories", February, 1986. Computer Architecture News, 14, 1, January, 1986, pp. 22-42.

[10] Alan Jay Smith, "Design of CPU Cache Memories", Proc. IEEE TENCON, Seoul, Korea, August, 1987 (Invited Paper), p. 30.2.1-30.2.10. Also available as Computer Science Division Technical Report UCB/CSD 87/357.

[11] Alan Jay Smith, "Line (Block) Size Selection in CPU Cache Memories", IEEE Transactions on Computers, C-36, 9, September, 1987, pp. 1063-1075. (UC Berkeley CS Report UCB/CSD85/239, June, 1985)

[12] Paul Sweazey and Alan Jay Smith, "A Class of Compatible Cache Consistency Protocols and Their Support by the IEEE Futurebus", Proc. 13'th Ann. Int. Symp. on Computer Arch., Tokyo, Japan, June, 1986, pp. 414-423.

Alan Jay Smith was born in New Rochelle, New York, USA. He received the B.S. degree in electrical engineering from the Massachusetts Institute of Technology, Cambridge, Massachusetts, and the M.S. and Ph.D. degrees in computer science from Stanford University, Stanford, California, the latter in 1974.

He is currently a Professor in the Computer Science Division of the Department of Electrical Engineering and Computer Sciences, University of California, Berkeley, California, USA, where he has been on the faculty since 1974, and was vice chairman of the EECS department from July, 1982- June, 1984. His research interests include the analysis and modeling of computer systems and devices, computer architecture, and operating systems. He has published a large number of research papers, including one which won the IEEE Best Paper Award for the best paper in the IEEETC in 1979. He also consults widely with computer and electronics companies.

Dr. Smith is a senior member of the Institute of Electrical and Electronic Engineers, and is a member of the Association for Computing Machinery, the Society for Industrial and Applied Mathematics, the Computer Measurement Group, Eta Kappa Nu, Tau Beta Pi and Sigma Xi. He was chairman of the ACM Special Interest Group on Operating Systems (SIGOPS) from 1983-1987, is on the board of directors of the ACM Special Interest Group on Measurement and Evaluation (SIGMETRICS), was an ACM National Lecturer (1985-6) and an IEEE Distinguished Visitor (1986-7) and is an Associate Editor of the ACM Transactions on Computer Systems (TOCS).

Design Considerations of the GMICRO/100

Osamu Tomisawa, Toyohiko Yoshida, Masahito Matsuo, Toru Shimizu, Tatsuya Enomoto

LSI Research and Development Laboratory, Mitsubishi Electric Corporation
4-1, Mizuhara, Itami, 664 Japan

Abstract

The 32 bit microprocessor GMICRO/100 is based on the TRON architecture specification. The chip will be used in a small system that does not require a memory management function. The GMICRO/100 supports variable length bit field instructions in full option so that the chip can handle bitmap operation at high speed. The chip has a 5-stage pipeline scheme. A dynamic branch prediction mechanism was chosen in order to reduce the performance degradiation caused by branch instructions. The effect of dynamic branch prediction was evaluated by two bench mark tests. The results of the bench mark showed improvements of 5 to 10 percent with the branch prediction scheme.

Key Words

Microprocessors, Microprocessor Chips, Computer Logic, BTRON

1. Introduction

There are several 32bit microprocessors being developed based on the TRON architecture specification [1],[2] proposed by University of Tokyo associate professor Ken Sakamura. The GMICRO/100 is one of them. Utilizing the same architecture as the other 32 bit microprocessors, allows them to be software compatible with each other. This paper describes features of the GMICRO/100 and some considerations made on the design of the chip focusing on the pipeline and dynamic branch prediction scheme.

2. Design Strategy

High performance, specifically high speed operation is a very important objective of the GMICRO/100. A pipelining scheme has been adopted to meet this requirement in conjunction with a dynamic branch prediction mechanism. By using a 1.0 micron double metal CMOS process, the clock frequency is predicated to be more than 20 MHz, with a target performance of 4 to 5 MIPS(Million Instruction Per Second).

One of the most appropriate applications of the GMICRO/100 is predicted to be the future personal workstation, BTRON with real memory system, where the cost of a microprocessor is an important issue. Hence the die size has to be as small as possible. Another potential application of this chip is in embedded industrial control equipment that houses ITRON.

The instruction set implemented in GMICRO/100 is based on TRON Level 1 specification. However, the instruction set was optimized for the above-mentioned applications. Instructions related to a memory management unit were rejected, while enhanced bitmap instructions in the level 2 specification were included.

The GMICRO/100 does not have on chip MMU, FPU nor cache. This means that the die size can be made relatively small and gives a potential of being used as a core processor for a cell-based design methodology. It also has the potential for application specific processors that integrate peripheral functions on the same chip. The specification of GMICRO/100 is summarized in Table 1.

Table 1 Features of GMICRO/100

CLOCK	20 MHz
PERFORMANCE	4-5 MIPS
MEMORY PROTECTION	2 LEVEL
GENERAL PURPOSE REG.	16
PROCESS	1 μ m CMOS
	2-LEVEL METAL
TRANSISTORS	300K

3. Architectual Features

There are 5 levels in TRON architecture specification: level L0, L1, L2, LX and LA [2]. The GMICRO/100 implements the instruction set based on level L1 [3]. Since predicted application systems of the GMICRO/100 are supposed to have a real memory system instead of a virtual memory, some instructions related to MMU (memory management unit) function have been deleted. Hence, the instruction set is called L1R where R stands for real memory system. The GMICRO/100 does not support memory protection for each page. However, 2-level ring protection is provided using the MSB (most significant bit) of an address.

On the other hand, the GMICRO/100 supports some higher level instructions from L2, specifically for enhanced support of bitmap processing. A system that has a bitmap display can be constructed without using a specific graphic processor.

The typical higher level instructions supported by GMICRO/100 are for variable-length bit field manipulations. The following instructions with full options are supported:

1) BVMAP: Bitmap operation
2) BVCPY: Bitmap transfer
3) BVPAT: Bitmap operation for repeated pattern
4) BVSCH: Search for "0" or "1"

A variable length bit field is specified by base address, offset and field width. The address of a specific bit in a bit field is base address + offset/8. Bitmap data can be calculated or transferd by the instructions BVMAP, BVCOPY and BVPAT so that high speed window manipulation can be performed. These instructions in the TRON specification can be used for a color scale of 1, in other words, one dot in the bitmap display is expressed with one bit, hence 8 dots are expressed by 1 byte. In bitmap displays where the lower address is displayed on the left side, dots having smaller bit number are displayed in the left side (bit-dot polarity is positive). The GMICRO/100 uses so called big-endian, bit numbering, it has a positive bit-dot polarity.

Instructions BVMAP and BVCOPY can handle the case where the source and destination in bitmap display overlap each other. If the operation proceeds in one direction only, say from a lower offset to a higher one, and if the source address is lower than the destination address, the source data has to be saved in order to avoid the source data being destroyed by overwriting. This reduced the operation speed significantly. However, the BVMAP and BVCOPY instructions have an option that specifies both the forward and backward operations. The direction can be specified as /F and /B options in GMICRO/100. An example of this operation is shown in Fig.1(a)-(c). Here

Fig.1 Example of Bitmap Operation
  (a) No overlap
  (b) Overlap (Src address
     is larger than Dest)
  (c) Overlap (Dest assress
     is larger than Src)

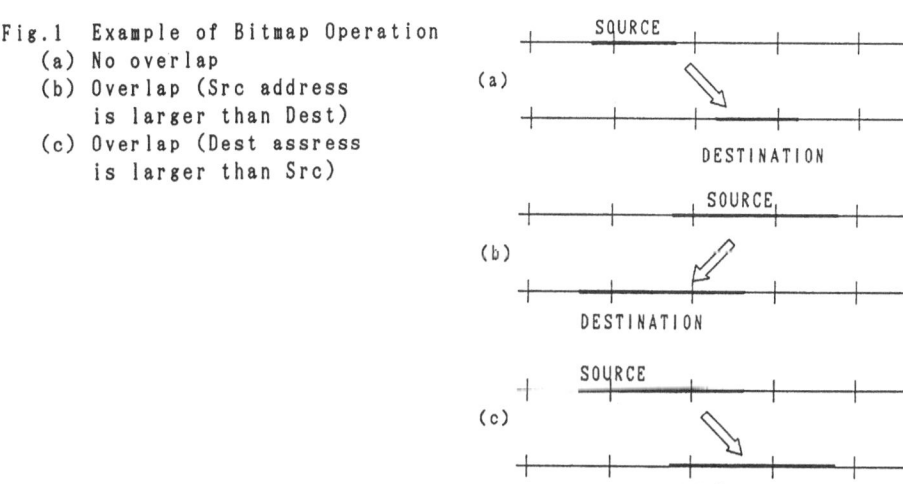

the address increases as you move to the right. Fig.1(a) shows the case having no overlap of source and destination data. When the address of source is larger than the address of destination, as shown in Fig.1(b), the operation has to proceed from the smaller offset. This is done by specifying the /F option. This can be used, for example, when the bitmap data is moved toward the left by deleting a character made of bitmap data. On the other hand, if the bitmap data is required to be moved toward the right, the address of source is smaller than the address of the destination as shown in Fig.1(c). This situation can be handled by proceeding the operation from the larger offset by simply specifying the /B option. Since GMICRO/100 has a microprogram for each high level instructions, higher performance can be expected compared to conventional processors where the bitmap data is manipulated by a combination of high level instructions.

4. Micro-Architecture

4-1 Pipelining

Pipelining is one of the most efficient technologies for implementing a high speed microprocessor. After evaluation of several pipeline configuration by simulation [4], a 5-stage pipeline, as shown in Fig.2, was adopted for GMICRO/100. Basically, at least 2 clocks are required for 1 pipeline stage. At the instruction fetch stage, an instruction code comprising 4 bytes is fetched in 2 clock period from a memory. Most of the fetched instructions including all the short format instructions are decoded in 2 clock period. The address calculation stage calculates one address in 2 clocks. Memory indirect addressing or index addressing obviously require more than 2 clocks. The operand fetch stage gets the maximum 4 byte operand at one time from a memory. The execution stage requires 2 clocks for 1 arithmetic or logic operation and an additional 2 clocks for storing data into the memory.

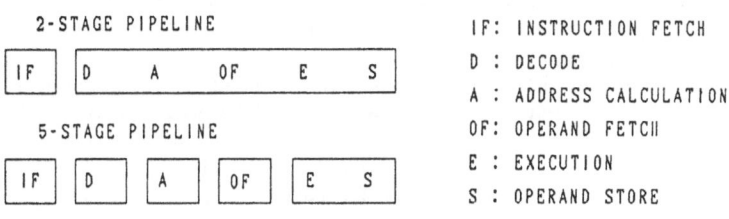

Fig.2 5-Stage Pipeline Structure

4-2 Dynamic Branch Prediction

Since the GMICRO/100 uses a multi-stage pipelining scheme, performance loss caused by branch instruction has to be improved [5]. According to the references, the branch instructions is approximately 20 percent in average program [6]. A dynamic branch prediction scheme was adopted for the GMICRO/100. Basically, branch prediction is treated at the decoding stage, rather than the execution stage, in order to prefetch the branch destination instruction as early as possible.

Branch instructions in the TRON specification can be divided into the following four categories:

1. Instructions for which both the branch condition and branch destination are static: BRA(Branch always), BSR(Branch to subroutine) etc.
2. Instructions for which the branch condition is dynamic while the branch destination is static: Bcc(Branch conditionary), ACB(Add compare and branch) , SCB(Subtract compare and branch) etc.
3. Instructions for which the branch condition is static while the branch destination is dynamic: RTS(return from subroutine), EXITD(Exit and deallocate parameters), TRAPA(Trap always), REIT(Return from EIT), JMP(Jump) etc.
4. Instructions for which both the branch condition and branch destination are dynamic: TRAP(Trap conditionally) etc.

Here the term static indicates that the condition or destination can be determined at compiling time, while dynamic refers to as those determined at run-time. The branch instructions that can be handled by the dynamic branch prediction mechanism are referred to as pre-branch instructions and they are BRA, BSR, Bcc, ACB and SCB. This is summarized in Table 2.

Table 2   Prebranch Instructions

CONDITION / DESTINATION	STATIC	DYNAMIC
STATIC	BRA BSR	Bcc,ACB SCB
DNAMIC	RET	TRAP

The dynamic branch prediction mechanism works as follows. Branching is always assumed to occur for instructions BRA, BSR, ACB and SCB. Obviously this prediction for BRA and BSR is always correct. As for the instructions, ACB and SCB, the probability of branching is usually very high.

Branch prediction for Bcc is determined according to the history of this instruction executed in the past. If branching has occurred for a Bcc instruction at a certain address, then the next Bcc instruction (at the address of which the lower 8 bit coincide with the previous Bcc instruction) is predicted to branch. This prediction is performed by looking at the branch prediction table that stores past records of branching in latches. The most recent result is stored at a branch prediction table by using a direct mapping scheme. The initial values of the branch prediction table are all "0" which means branching will not occur. When a Bcc instruction branches, the table is set to "1" during the execution stage.

When a Bcc instruction is predicted to be non-branching at the decoding stage, the next program counter value is calculated by adding the address of the Bcc instruction and the instruction length. On the other hand, when the Bcc instruction is predicted to branch, the next program counter value is calculated by adding the address of the Bcc instruction and branch displacement so that the branch destination instruction can be fetched. Figure 3 shows the dynamic branch prediction mechanism. Reduction of pipeline overhead by introducing dynamic branch prediction mechanism is shown in Fig. 4.

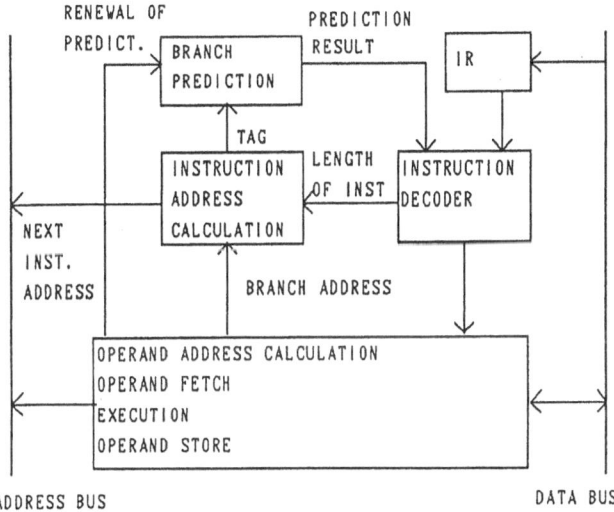

Fig.3 Dynamic Branch Prediction Scheme

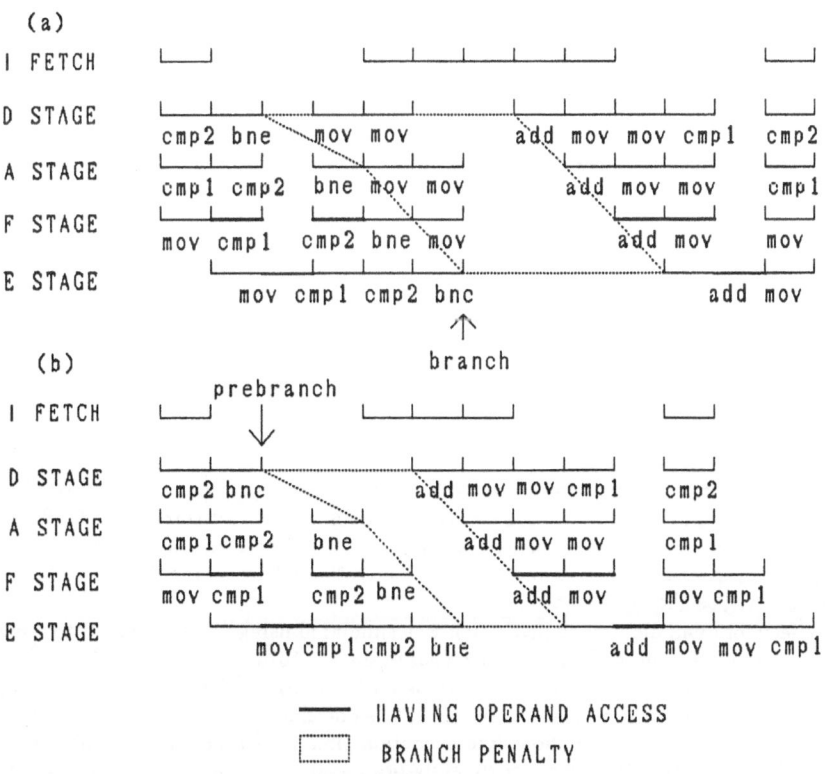

Fig.4 Reduction of Pipeline Overhead by Branch Prediction
(a) No Branch Prediction
(b) With Branch Prediction

4-3 Hardware Configuration

Figure 5 shows a functional block diagram of the GMICRO/100 CPU chip. The chip is organized as twelve logical units with each unit assigned a task in the fetching and execution of each instruction. The twelve units are the instruction fetch unit, the instruction decode unit, the microprogram ROM, the branch prediction unit, the addressing mode decode unit, the two address and data execution control unit, the two arithmetic units for addressing and PC calculation, the arithmetic and logic unit, and the two bus interface units. The units are pipelined and parallel execution of the instruction stream can be allowed by this arrangement.

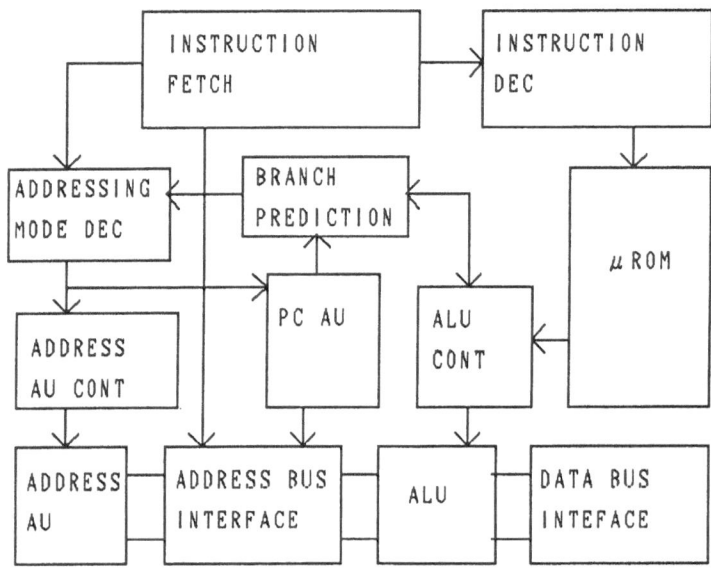

Fig.5   Block Diagram of GMICRO/100

5. Evaluation

Benchmark test has been done in order to evaluate the performance of the GMICRO/100. The benchmark programs used were the sieve of Eratosthenes [7] and Dhrystone [8]. The function of GMICRO/100 was described by using PL/I and GPSS (General Purpose Simulation System). The hit ratio for instructions Bcc and BRA was investigated by simulation and the result was around 75 percent as shown in Table 3.

The effects of dynamic branch prediction was simulated using the sieve of Eratosthenes. The simulation results is shown in Table 4. The initial value was 10H. Here the performance is normalized by the case of 2-stage pipeline that contains an instruction fetch stage and other operation stage. The performance improvement of 10 percent has been achieved by introducing the dynamic branch prediction scheme. Fig.6 shows the execution time as a function of number of executed instruction. The execution time is approximately proportional to the number of executed instructions.

The similar simulation was also done by using Dhrystone benchmark. The original source program was written in ADA. This was translated to Pascal and compiled using an off-the-shelf Pascal compiler. Then the assembler codes were modified into GMICRO/100 assembler code.

Table 3 Hit Ratio of Branch Instructions

| | SIEVE OF ERATOSTHENES | | DHRYSTONE | | | |
| | INITIAL 40H | | 1st CYCLE | | 2nd CYCLE | |
	EXEC	HIT	EXEC	HIT	EXEC	HIT
Bcc(taken) Bcc(not taken)	224 66	189 31	9 18	1 14	9 18	5 14
TOTAL	290	220	27	15	27	19
HIT RATIO(Bcc)	75.9 %		55.6 %		70.4 %	
BRA BSR	33 0	33 0	10 15	10 15	10 15	10 15
GRAND TOTAL	323	253	52	40	52	44
HIT RATIO (TOTAL)	78.3 %		76.9 %		84.6 %	

Table 4 Effect of Dynamic Branch Prediction
(Initial value is 10H)

| | RELATIVE PERFORMANCE | | IMPROVEMENT |
	WITHOUT BRANCH PREDICTION	WITH BRANC PREDICTION	RATIO
2-STAGE PIPELINE	1.00	1.02	1.02
5-STAGE	2.22	2.45	1.10

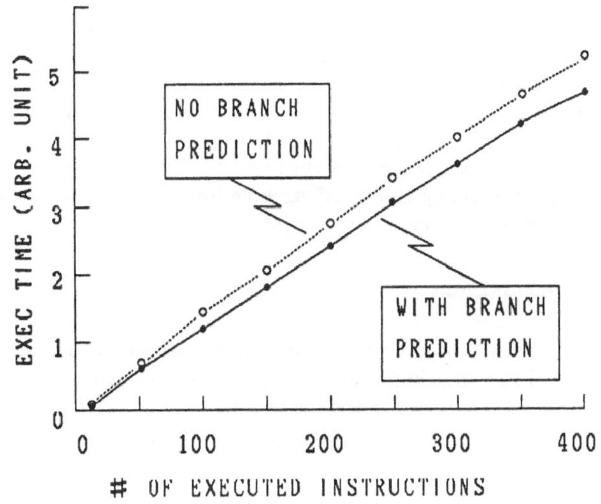

Fig.6
Effect of Dynamic Branch
Prediction
(Benchmark by the Sieve
of Eratosthenes)

The code was optimized by hand using the algorithmic methodologies, in other words, methods without using any heuristic approach. The optimization technics used here includes replacement of instructions to the better GMICRO instructions. For example, instructions needed for operation on different data sizes was replaced by the GMICRO/100 instruction that performs the sign extension and operation with single instruction. Re-ordering of the code was also done for the purpose of reducing the pipeline conflicts. Since the GMICRO/100 has 16 registers, the allocation of registers was improved. This kind of optimizations is expected to be obtained also by compiler/optimizer.

Figure 7 shows the results of the benchmark at each optimization level. The performance predicted by the Dhrystone benchmark improved approximately two times with the optimizations. The performance improvement of 5 percent due to dynamic branch prediction can be seen at all optimization levels.

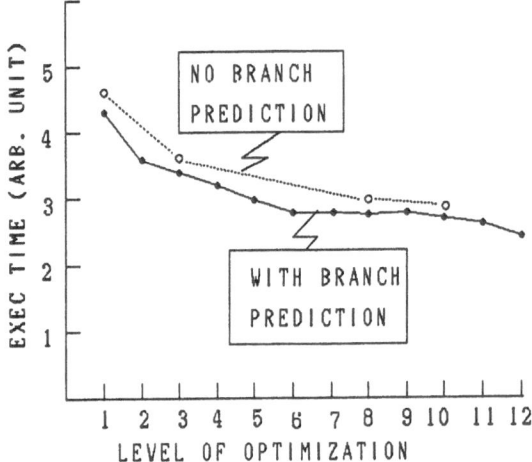

Fig.7 Effect of Dynamic Branch Prediction
(Benchmark by Dhrystone)

6. Conclusion

The TRON architecture specification level L1R has been chosen for the 32 bit microprocessor GMICRO/100. The effects of the dynamic branch prediction scheme was investigated by benchmark tests. The results of the sieve of Eratosthenes showed 10 percent improvement. The Dhrystone code was optimized in several levels by hand, and 5 percent improvement due to dynamic branch prediction was obtained for all the optimazation levels. Since the chip does not have on-chip MMU, cache nor the associated instructions, the die size can be made relatively small. The chip supporting enhanced variable bit fields will be succesfully used for the high performance workstations with real memory system.

Acknowledgment

The authors would like to appreciate associate professor Ken Sakamura for helpful discussions. We would like to acknowledge the GMICRO members at Hitachi Ltd. and Fujitsu Ltd. for their useful comments. We also wish to thank Drs. K. Shibayama, H. Nakata and all the design engineers involved in this projects at Mitsubishi Electric Corp.

References

[1] K. Sakamura: "Architecture of VLSI CPU in the TRON Project", 2nd TRON Project Symposium, TRON Association, March 1987.

[2] K. Sakamura: "Architecture of the TRON VLSI CPU",IEEE Micro April 1987, pp.17-31

[3] T. Enomoto: "A 32 bit microprocessor based on TRON specification", 2nd TRON Symposium, TRON Association, March 1987.

[4] T. Yoshida, etal.:"Branch prediction in a pipelined microprocessor", WGMIC, Information Processing Soc., March 1987 (in Japanese)

[5] J. K. F. Lee, etal.:"Branch Prediction Strategies and Branch Target Buffer design", IEEE Computer, Vol.17, No.1, 1984, pp.6-22.

[6] J. A. Lukes,"HP Precision Architecture Performance Analysis", HP Journal, August 1986, pp.30-39.

[7] J. Gilbreath, etal. "Eratosthenes Revisited Once More through the Sieve", BYTE, January 1983, pp.283-326.

[8] R. P. Weicker, "Dhrystone: A Synthetic System Programming Benchmark", Communications of the ACM, Vol.27, No.10, October 1984, pp.1013-1030.

Osamu Tomisawa received the B. S. and M. S. degrees in electronic Engineering from Kyoto University, Kyoto, Japan, in 1969 and 1971, respectively. He received Ph.D degree in electrical engineering in 1980 from Osaka University, Osaka, Japan. He joined Mitsubishi Electric Corporation in 1971, Since then he has been working on logic LSI/VLSI design. In 1980, he stayed one year at Univesity of California, Berkeley as a visiting scholar, where he was involved in the research of VLSI computer architecture. He is currently a manager of Advanced Microprocessor Group in LSI Research and Development Laboratory, Mitsubishi Electric Corp. Dr. Tomisawa is a member of IEEE and the Institute of Electronics, Information and Communication Engineers of Japan.

Toyohiko Yoshida was born in Kyoto, Japan, on April 29,1957. He received his B.E. and M.E. degrees, both in electronics engineering, from Kyoto University, Kyoto, Japan, in 1981 and 1983, respectively. He joined Mitsubishi Electric Corporation in 1983. Since then, he has been engaged in research and development of microprocessor design at LSI Research and Development Laboratory. Mr. Yoshida is a member of the Institute of Electronics,Information and Communication Engineers of Japan.

Masahito Matsuo was born in Hyogo, Japan, on March 28, 1961. He received his B.E. and M.E. degrees, both in electrical engineering, from Osaka University, Osaka, Japan, in 1983 and 1985, respectively. He joined Mitsubishi Electric Corporation in 1985. Since then, he has been engaged in research and development of microprocessor design at LSI Research and Development Laboratory.

Toru Shimizu was born in Tokyo, Japan, in June 1958. He received the B.S., M.S. and Ph.D. degrees in computer science from University of Tokyo in 1981, 1983, and 1986, respectively. He joined Mitsubishi Electric Corporation in 1986. Since then, he has been engaged in research and development of a 32-bit microprocessor in Advanced Microprocessor Development Department, LSI Research and Development Labratory. Dr. Shimizu is a member of ACM, IEEE, the Institute of Electronics, Information and Communication Engineers of Japan, and Information Processing Society of Japan.

Tatsuya Enomoto was born in Hyogo, Japan, on January 12, 1940. He received his B.S. and Ph.D. degrees, both in electronics engineering, from the University of Tokyo, Tokyo, Japan, in 1962 and 1980, respectively. He joined Mitsubishi Electric Corporation in 1962. From 1962 to 1977, he was engaged in wafer process engineering of MOS integrated circuits at Kita-Itami Works. Since 1977, he has been engaged in research and development of VLSI process technologies,gate array design, and advanced microprocessors at LSI Research and Development Laboratory. Dr. Enomoto is a member of the Institute of electronics, Information and Communication Engineers of Japan and the Japan Society of Applied Physics.

Outline of GMICRO/200 and Memory Management Mechanism

Katsuaki Takagi, Tadahiko Nishimukai, Kazuhiko Iwasaki
Central Research Laboratory, Hitachi Ltd.
Kokubunji, Tokyo,185 Japan

Ikuya Kawasaki, Hideo Inayoshi
Musashi Works, Hitachi Ltd.
Josuihon-cho, Kodaira, Tokyo,187Japan

ABSTRACT

This paper outlines the 32-bit microprocessor GMICRO/200 and its memory management mechanism on chip. This microprocessor's target performance is 6 MIPS. To achieve this performance, a 6-stage pipeline, 5-unit distributed processing, 1-kbyte instruction cache, 128-byte stack cache, and 16-byte branch prediction table are used. The virtual memory management mechanism defined by the memory management unit (MMU) is 2-level paging with dual regions. the translation look-aside buffer (TLB) has 32 entries. It translates logical address within one machine cycle (50 ns) to physical address. The pipeline of the address translation and the external bus access cancels address translation delay.

KEY WORDS

Memory Management Unit, Microprocessor, Cache Memory, Translation Look-Aside Buffer, Dynamic Address Translation

1. INTRODUCTION

GMICRO/200 is a high-performance 32-bit microprocessor which has been developed using the standard architecture defined by TRON(*) project.

Microprocessor performance has improved rapidly with the development of VLSI technology[1][2][3]. However, improved performance can no longer be expected from process technology alone. One approach to achieve high performance is to take advantage of the high density of VLSIs. Specifically, this approach involves: (1) distributed processing (2) pipeline architecture (3) cache memory on chip.

---

* TRON : The Real time Operating system Nucleus
   TRON project is headed by Prof. Ken Sakamura of the University of Tokyo

The GMICRO/200 uses a 6-stage pipeline, 5-unit distributed processing, 1-kbyte instruction cache, 128-byte stack cache, and 16-byte branch prediction table to achieve high performance with 1.0-micron CMOS process. The target performance is 6 MIPS measured in EDN benchmark programs at a 20-MHz clock rate.

Another feature of GMICRO/200 is on-chip memory management Unit (MMU) adapted to this microprocessor's linear addressing capability. The logical address space defined by this MMU is divided into two regions. Each region is managed by a two-level paging algorithm whose page size is 4 kbytes.

The address translation buffer (TLB) has 32 entries. TLB translates the input logical address into a physical address in one machine cycle (50 ns at 20-MHz operation). Moreover, instruction prefetch and operand access occurs alternately, address translation delay is cancelled by the pipeline operation.

This paper clarifies the GMICRO/200 specifications, chip architecture, and the address translation mechanism.

2. GMICRO/200 SPECIFICATIONS

2.1 Design Targets

GMICRO/200 is the name of a 32-bit microprocessor that satisfies TRON specification[4]. This microprocessor's major target application is engineering workstation systems. To enhance this feature the following co-processor and peripheral LSIs are being designed and developed in the GMICRO group: 1. Floating Point Unit (FPU) 2. Direct Memory Access Controller (DMAC) 3. Interrupt Request Controller (IRC) 4. Cache Chip 5. TAG RAM and so on.

Design specifications are as follows:

(1) High performance

The target performance of the microprocessor is 6 MIPS measured in EDN benchmark programs.

(2) High level instructions for graphic operation

Bit-map and bit-field instructions are integrated for use in high-speed graphic operation.

(3) Virtual memory

It will become essential to use virtual memory in engineering workstation because of its large data size and a multiple process environment. So the memory management unit is integrated in GMICRO/200 .

(4) New co-processor interface

The CPU alone may be insufficient for several applications such as high-speed graphic operation and mass data operation. To enhance system performance, a new co-processor interface and corresponding instructions are integrated.

2.2 Instruction Set

The GMICRO/200 instruction set includes L1 and L2 levels and part of the LA specifications specified by the TRON project.

The instruction set is specified hierarchically by TRON project as follows:

LO specification   ----- essential
L1R specification ----- real memory
L1 specification   ----- virtual memory (basic)
L2 specification   ----- virtual memory (enhanced) and coprocessor
LX specification   ----- will be included in 64-bit processor
LA specification   ----- depends on implementation
LV specification   ----- depends on company

LO and L1 specifications are included in GMICRO/200 in consideration of instruction usage frequency and chip integration. Part of the L2 specification is integrated concerning the memory management unit and co-processor interface.

The GMICRO/200 instruction set is shown in Table 1. There are totally 123 instructions.

2.3   Virtual Memory

2.3.1 Linear addressing

GMICRO/200 adopts linear addressing, where 4-Gbyte space can be accessed.

In segment addressing, processing clusters called segments are specified by a segment register. Linear access is possible only within the scope of the segment. Since a segment is processed as one object, invalid access can be prevented easily. However, programs are responsible for modifying segments. Furthermore, it is difficult to manipulate data larger than the segment size.

By contrast, linear addressing places no constraints on data size or data structure. Thus software does not need to know this. Linear addressing is better than segment addressing for applications requiring real-time processing or graphic systems using huge data. However the data protection mechanism must be considered carefully.

The GMICRO/200 uses linear addressing because of its data manipulation flexibility and high-speed access. Data protection is performed by on-chip memory management unit.

2.3.2 Some considerations regarding linear addressing virtual memory

Virtual space structure fit to linear addressing is as follows:

(1) The same space should be accessed by different types of access.

This is needed to prevent the difficulty of data transfer between spaces.

(2) address translation/protection by page

In linear addressing, software can construct any data structure knowing only the page boundary.

(3) A common area should exist for multiple spaces

For multiple spaces, user areas are multiplexed however system program must be accessed commonly.

Table 1 GMICRO/200 Instruction Set

(1) Move operations

| MOV | MOVU | LDM | STM | MOVA | PUSH | POP | PUSHA |

(2) Compare/Test Instructions

| CMP | CMPU | CHK |

(3) Arithmetic operations

| ADD | ADDU | ADDX | SUB | SUBU | SUBX | MUL | MULU |
| MULX | DIV | DIVU | DIVX | REM | REMU | NEG |

(4) Logical operations

| AND | OR | XOR | NOT |

(5) Shift operations

| SHA | SHL | ROT | SHXL | SHXR | RVBY |

(6) Bit operations

| BTST | BSET | BCLR | BNOT | BSCH |

(7) Fixed length bit field operations

| BFEXT | BFEXTU | BFINS | BFINSU | BFCMP | BFCMPU |

(8) Variable length bit field operations

| BVSCH | BVMAP | BVCPY | BVPAT |

(9) Decimal operations

| ADDD | SUBD | PACK | UNPK |

(10) String operations

| SMOV | SCMP | SSCH | SSTR |

(11) Queue operations

| QINS | QDEL | QSCH |

(12) Branch operations

| BRA | Bcc | JMP | JSR | BSR | ACB | SCB | ENTER |
| EXTD | RTS | NOP | PIB |

(13) Multiprocessor operations

| BSETI | BCLRI | CSI |

(14) Control space/physical space operations

| LDC | STC | LDPSB | STPSB | LDPSM | STPSM | LDP | STP |

(15) Instructions for operating system

| JRNG | RRNG | TRAPA | TRAPcc | REIT | WAIT | LDCTX | STCTX |

(16) MMU operations

| ACS | MOVPA | LDATE | STATE | PTLB | PSTLB |

(17) Co-Processor operations

COP_CTL	COP_Bcc	COP_LDI1	COP_LDI2	COP_STI1	COP_STI2
COP_RESTORE		COP_SAVE	COP_LDMI	COP_STMI	COP_CMP1
COP_TST	COP_LIMIT		COP_MISC	COP_LD	COP_ST
COP_LDM	COP_STM	COP_UO	COP_BOP	COP_VOP1	COP_VOP2

(18) Debug operations

| DBG | RTD |

2.3.3 Logical address structure of GMICRO/200

Considering the above constraints, the space structure depicted in Figure 1 is used. There are two regions, shared and unshared, and two-level paging is used.

The logical address is constructed from region specifier R, section index SX, page index PX and OFFSET field.

According to the region specifier R, the 4-Gbyte address space is divided into the shared region (R = 1, negative region) and the unshared region (R = 0, positive region). These regions are managed independently. The section index SX divides each region into 4-Mbyte sections. The section is the intermediate processing unit which makes region management possible by using multiple page tables. The page index PX divides each section into 4-kbyte pages, where a page is the minimum processing unit of managing memory. The OFFSET field designates the offset within a page.

Each process can use the unshared region (R = 0) independently. There is only one shared region (R = 1) where operating system or common data exist. As explained in this section, GMICRO/200's logical address structure is suitable for linear addressing, where only unshared regions are multiplexed.

The logical address space can be expanded to 64-bit address with consistency to the instruction set of TRON specification. This is done by taking the region specifier R as sign bit of logical address. The image of the expansion to 64-bit address space is shown in Figure 2.

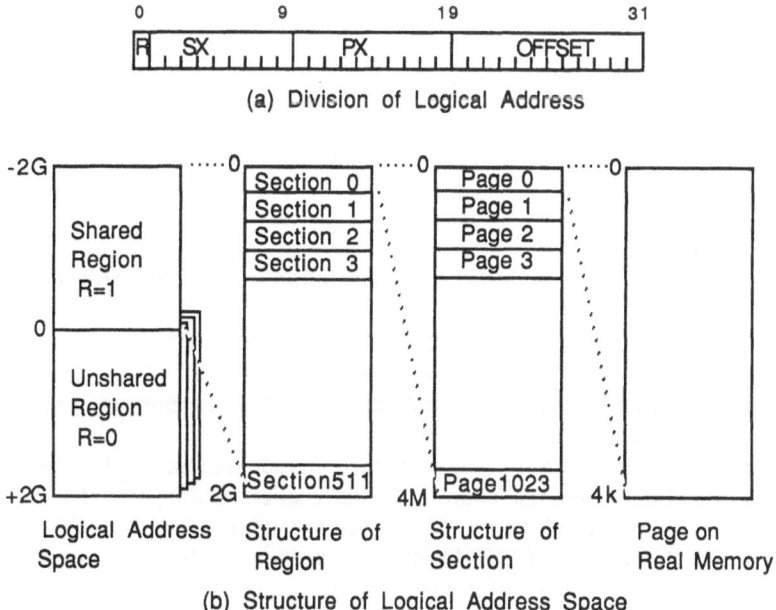

(a) Division of Logical Address

(b) Structure of Logical Address Space

Figure 1   Division of Logical Address and Space Structure

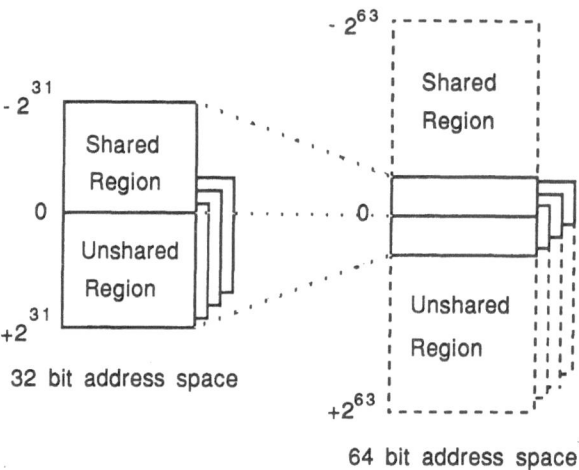

-2^{63}

Shared
Region

-2^{31}

Shared

Region

0

Unshared

Region

$+2^{31}$

32 bit address space

0.

Unshared

Region

$+2^{63}$

64 bit address space

Figure 2   Continuation to 64 bit Address

2.4 Specifications of the Memory Management Mechanism

2.4.1 Address translation process

The address translation process of the GMICRO/200 is shown in Figure 3. At first, either the shared address translation base (SATB) register or the unshared address translation base (UATB) register is selected according to region specifier R. These registers indicate the top address of section table ST. Within the section table, the entry designated by section index SX includes the top address of page table PT.   Same as ST, the entry designated by page index PX includes page frame number PFN. The page frame number indicates the upper 20 bits of physical address. The physical address is derived by concatenating the page frame number and offset.

2.4.2 Registers

The registers concerned with address translation are PSW, UATB, and SATB. These registers are shown in Figure 4.

PSW is used to set up processor states.   The field of RNG, AT, and PRNG is used in address translation.   RNG shows the current ring number, PRNG stores the previous ring number, and AT indicates whether or not address translation should be performed.

SATB specifies the section table for the shared region.   The section table base (SATB) designates the top address of the section table.   The length L of the section table shows the valid extent of the section table. For L = 00, 01, 10 and 11, the section table size is 2 kbytes, 1 kbytes, 256 bytes and 64 bytes, respectively. The direction D of table validity designates whether the upper or lower address of the section table is valid when the section table size is limited. Page in (PI) indicates whether or not the section table exists in the main memory.

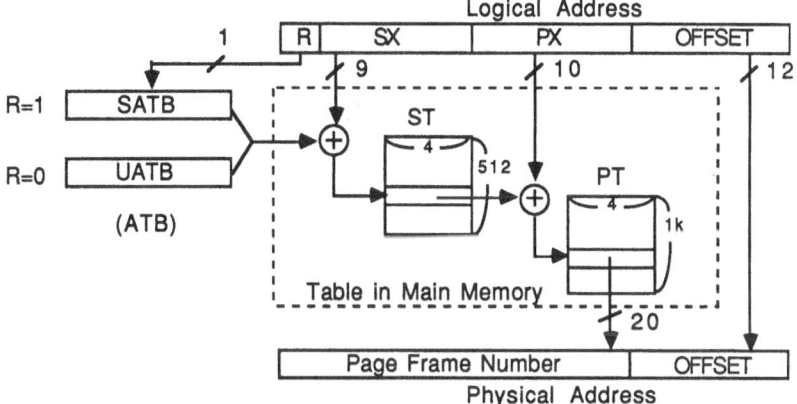

Figure 3 Address Translation Process

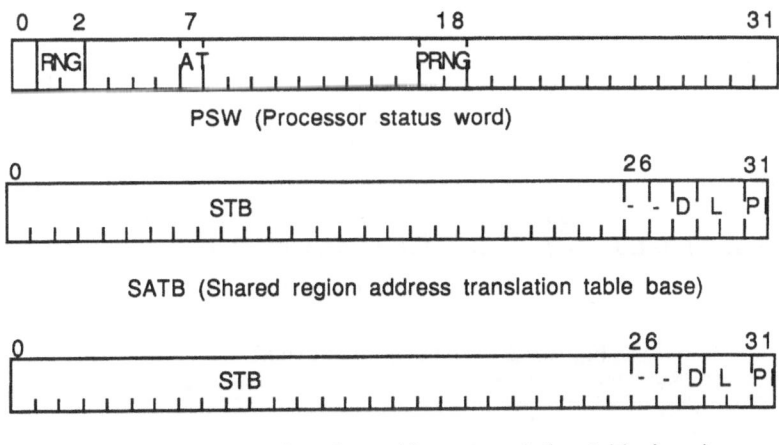

PSW (Processor status word)

SATB (Shared region address translation table base)

UATB (Unshared region address translation table base)

Figure 4 Address Translation Register

UATB specifies the section table for the shared region. The meaning of the fields is exactly the same as for SATB.

2.4.3 Descriptor

The descriptor formats of the address translation table (section table and page table) are shown in Figure 5.

STE is the descriptor for the section table. Page table base (PTB) designates the top address of the page table. The length L of page table and the direction D of table validity are similar in meaning to those of the SATB/UATB except that for L = 00, page table size is 4 kbytes. Address translation exception is defined for D=1 and L=01 Page in (PI) indicates whether or not the page table exists in the main memory.

PTE is the descriptor for page table. Page frame number (PFN) indicates the page number of the main memory, that is, the upper 20 bits of the physical address. Operating system can use the operating system field (0S) at any usage. Referenced bit (R) and modified bit (M) indicate the page was referred and modified respectively. Read level (RL) indicates the ring number with which the page is read. Access level (AL) has the similar meaning to RL for access of writing and executing. T indicates protection type for writing and executing. The first bit of T shows writing permission and the second bit shows executing permission. The ring level with which access is permitted is as follows:

reading level =< RL

writing level =< min (RL, AL)

executing level =< max (RL, AL)

When T = 00 and AL = 01, 10, 11, the address translation exception will occur. Non-cacheable (NC) indicates the changing of the page to be inhibited. Page in (PI) indicates whether or not the page exists in the main memory.

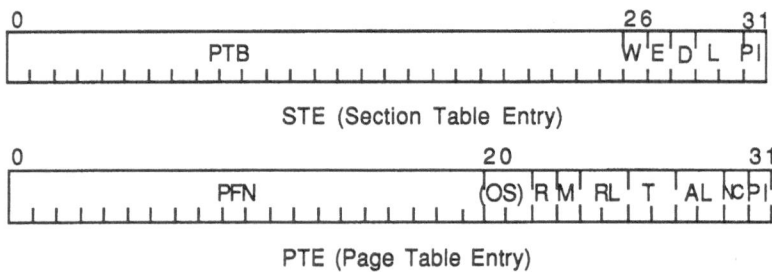

Figure 5   Descriptor Format

3. CHIP DESIGN

3.1 Distributed Processing and Pipeline

GMICRO/200 is constructed from 6 units as shown in Figure 6. These units are the instruction prefetch unit, instruction decode unit, control unit, execution unit, memory management unit, and input/output unit. Each unit is event

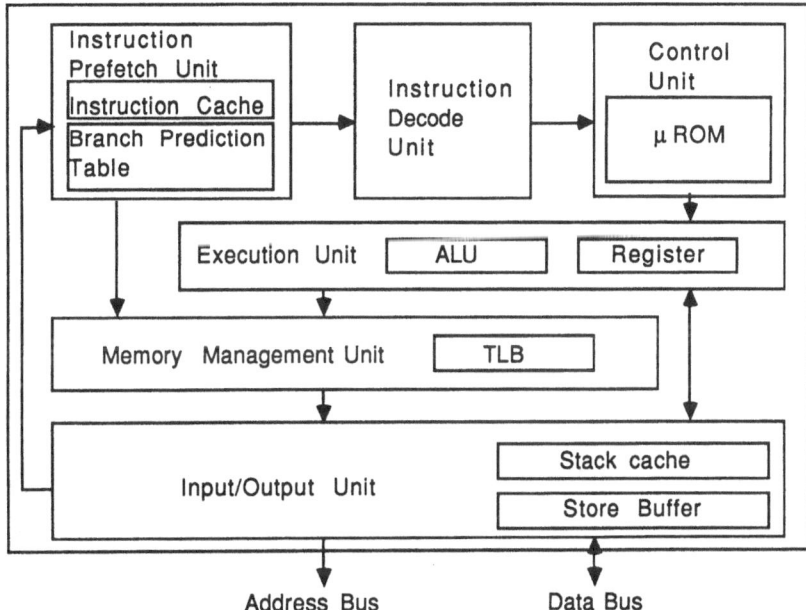

Figure 6   Block Diagram of Gmicro/200

driven. This makes distributed processing and pipeline operation possible.   The maximum number of pipeline stages is six. These stages are instruction fetching, instruction decoding, effective address calculations, executing, address translating, and store buffer.

3.2 Internal Caches

The instruction cache has 64 entries with 28-bit associative array and 128-bit data array. The prefetched instruction is set by a first-in first-out algorithm.

The stack cache is prepared for fast stack operation such as subroutine calls. It has 32 entries with 37-bit associative array and 32-bit data array.   Data are taken in stack cache at stack operation addressing mode. Entry contents are exchanged by a first-in first-out algorithm.

A branch prediction table is effective in a program with loop operation. It has 4 entries with 34-bit associative array and 62-bit data array. Entry contents are exchanged by a first-in first-out algorithm only when the branch operation is executed .

3.3. Memory Management Unit

The memory management unit is constructed from table searching hardware and address translation buffer (TLB). The structure of the memory management unit is shown in Figure 7 .The registers SATB and UATB can be

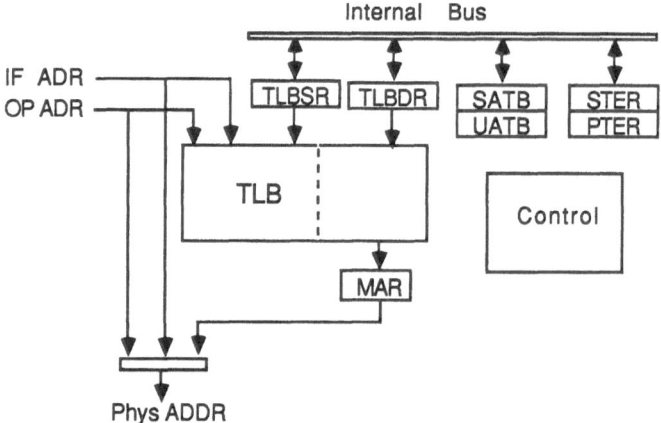

Figure 7   Block Diagram of Memory Management Unit

indicated by instruction. Other registers are accessed by microprogram only. STER and PTER respectively hold the section table entry and the page table entry. TLBSR and TLBDR are used for TLB operation. MAR latches the physical address read out of TLB.

A block diagram of TLB and its peripherals is shown in Figure 8. Two address buses input to TLB, instruction prefetch address and operand address. The selector is controlled as operand address has higher priority.

TLB structure is shown in Figure 9 TLB has 32 entries. The associative array has 20-bit logical address field, an entry validity bit, and an LRU bit for entry exchange control. The data array has 20-bit physical address field, 9-bit protection information field, a modify bit M, and a non-cacheable bit NC. Protection information is constructed from three fields with three bits, RA, WA, and EA. Each field has 2-bit ring level and an enable bit. M and NC bits are copies of those of the page table entry.

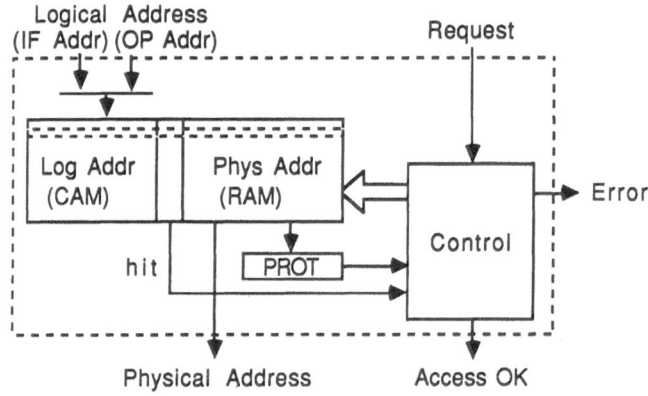

Figure 8   Block Diagram of TLB and its Peripheral

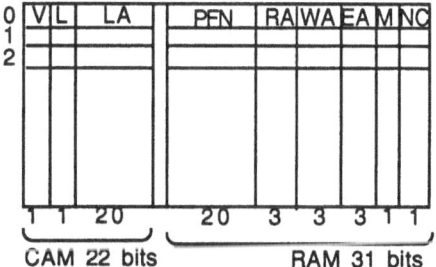

Figure 9   TLB Structure

TLB is searched with logical address for entries with V = 1. When the address is matched, the contents of the data array are read. The access right is then checked with the protection information field. TLB entries are exchanged by a pseudo-least recent used algorithm in the dynamic address translation routine.

TLB translates a logical address to a physical address in one machine cycle. The cancelling mechanism of address translation time is shown in Figure 10. External bus is assumed to operate in two machine cycles. In the first cycle, TLB translates a prefetch address. Prefetch is executed in the second and third cycles. In the third cycle, TLB translates the next operand address. Thus in the fourth cycle, operand access can be performed continuing to the prefetch cycle. In this way, translation time is hidden in external bus access time.

When the logical address cannot be detected or a protection error is detected, TLB miss occurs and the microprogram jumps to the dynamic address translation (DAT) routine. There are three cases which cause entry into the dynamic address translation routine: (1) No entry is detected to match the logical address to be searched. (2) Access is not permitted. (3) In write access,

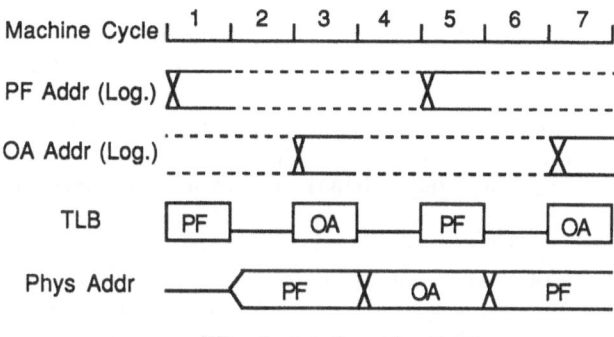

PF: Instruction Pre-Fetch
OA: Operand Access

Figure 10   TLB Pipeline Operation

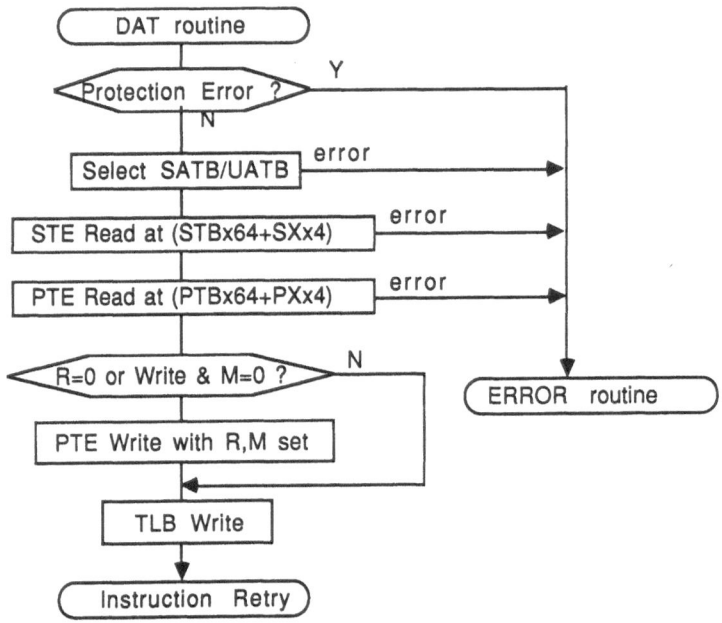

Figure 11   DAT Routine Flow

the M bit in TLB is cleared. DAT routine flow is shown in Figure 11. The information of descriptor fetched by DAT routine is set into TLB entry by a pseudo-LRU algorithm. After the DAT routine finishes, the instruction is restarted.

4. CONCLUSION

The GMICRO/200 has a powerful instruction set including co-processor instructions. Target performance is 6 MIPS in EDN benchmark programs. To obtain high performance, 5-unit distributed processing, 6-stage pipeline, 3 internal caches as instruction cache, stack cache, and branch prediction table, 20 MHz of machine cycle, and 2 machine-cycle memory bus protocol, are incorporated. To support the virtual memory necessary for engineering workstations, a memory management unit is adopted. This memory management unit's specifications are designed to fit for the instruction set's linear addressing ability. TLB has 32 entries and translates a logical address to a physical address in one machine cycle. Address translation and external bus access are executed as a pipeline, so that address translation time is hidden in bus access time. The GMICRO/200 family including co-processors and peripheral LSIs are being developed. A high-performance graphic processing system may be constructed using the GMICRO/200 family.

5. ACKNOWLEDGEMENTS

The authors would like to thank Prof. Ken Sakamura of the University of Tokyo for leading the TRON project, and the members of the GMICRO group, Fujitsu Ltd.,and Mitsubishi Electric Corp, for their cooperations.

References

[1] L. Kohn, "A 32 b Microprocessor with Virtual Memory Support", Digest ISSCC 81, 1981
[2] D. MacGregor, D. Mothersole, B, Moyer,"The Motorola MC68020", IEEE MICRO, pp101, Aug. 1984.
[3] K. A. El-Ayat, R. K. Agarwal, "The Intel 80386 - Architecture and Implementation", IEEE MICRO, pp4, Dec. 1985.
[4] K. Sakamura, "Architecture of the TRON VLSI CPU", IEEE MICRO, pp17, Apr. 1987.

Katsuaki Takagi is a senior researcher of Central Research Laboratory, Hitachi Ltd. He is engaged in research and development on microprocessor and its memory management technique. He received a B.S. and a M.S. degrees in electronics engineering from Nagoya University in 1972 and 1974 respectively.

Kazuhiko Iwasaki is a researcher of Central Research Laboratory, Hitachi Ltd. He has been engaged in research on architecture and logic design, and testing methodology for microprocessor VLSI. He won 1985's paper award from the Institute of Electronics, information and communication engineers of Japan. He received a B.S. and a M.S. degrees in computer and information science from Osaka University in 1977 and 1979 respectively.

Ikuya Kawasaki is an engineer in the Microcomputer Engineering Dept. at Musashi Works, Hitachi Ltd. He is presently engaged in development of 32-bit microprocessor of TRON specification. He received a B.S. in Electrical Engineering from The University of Tokyo in 1980 and a M.S. from the University of Washington in 1982.

Tadahiko Nishimukai is a senior researcher of Central Research Laboratory, Hitachi Ltd. He is currently engaged in research and development on high end microprocessor. He received a B.S. and a M.S. degrees from the University of Tokyo in 1972 and 1974 respectively.

Hideo Inayoshi is a senior engineer of the Microcomputer Engineering Dept. at Musashi Works, Hitachi Ltd. He is presently engaged in development of 32-bit microprocessor and peripherals He received a B.S. and a M.S. in applied physics from the University of Tokyo in 1969 and 1971 respectively.

Architecture Characteristics of GMICRO/300

Matao Itoh

Microcomputer Development Division, Semiconductor Group, FUJITSU LIMITED
1812-10 Shimonumabe, Nakahara-ku, Kawasaki, 211 Japan

ABSTRACT

Two major architecture characteristics of G micro /300 are described.
LSID(LOGICAL SPACE IDENTIFIER)support is very effective for multi-job,
multi-task applications. LSID is controlled by software, and this is more
efficient than by hardware control that is normally used in general purpose
mainframe.
New decimal instructions are defined as LEVEL2 TRON architecture, and they
make COBOL programs run more than three times faster and be more than three
times smaller in code size.

KEY WORDS

Logical Space Identifier, Signed decimal,

INTRODUCTION

Recently application areas of microprocessors have become very wide. Gmicro
family will cover from lap-top personal computers to high-end mini-computers.
Gmicro /300 is the high-end machine of Gmicro family, and will be used for
engineering workstations, servers, minicomputers and business workstations. It
is carefully designed to support some of LEVEL2 functions of TRON architecture
adequate for such applications.

Two major architectures are supported by G micro /300. 1st is efficient support
architecture of multi virtual memory , and 2nd is signed decimal arithemetic
instructions support which is suitable for COBOL language. This paper will
discuss these two architectures.

1. Multi Virtual Memory Enhancement

1.1. LOGICAL ADDRESS

Multi virtual memory is supported by LEVEL1 TRON architecture. Figure-1 shows
logical address format, and virtual memory configuration. Logical address is
translated to physical address by two address translation tables.

LOGICAL ADDRESS(32BIT)

R: REGION IDENTIFIER

VIRTUAL MEMORY CONFIGURATION

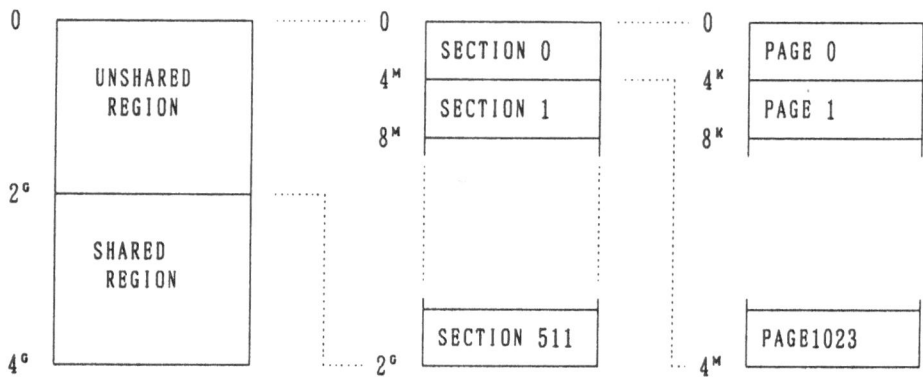

FIGURE-1

 4G Byte logical address space is divided into two 2G Byte regions, and each
region is divided into 512 4M Byte sections. A section is divided into 1024 4K
Byte pages. The translation between logical address space and physical address
space is done by a unit of 4k byte page .

1. 2. MULTI VIRTUAL MEMORY

 For the unshared regions, multiple address spaces can exist simultaneously.
But, for the shared region there can not exist more than one address space
because it is the common address area for all address spaces. Figure-2 shows
multi virtual address space configuration.

 Address translation is done by TLB(Translation Lookaside Buffer) and address
translation feature. TLB has logical address and physical address pair entries,
therefore, logical address is translated into physical address very quickly.
 Each unshared region has its own address translation tables designated by
UATB. So, normally, if UATB is newly loaded , all the TLB entries are no longer
valid and all the entries must be purged.
 Under the workstation server, or minicomputer environment, multi-job, multi-task
capabilities are essential. Under such applications, reloading of UATB are more
frequent than under normal workstation applications. On such applications TLB
purge may degrade the performance.

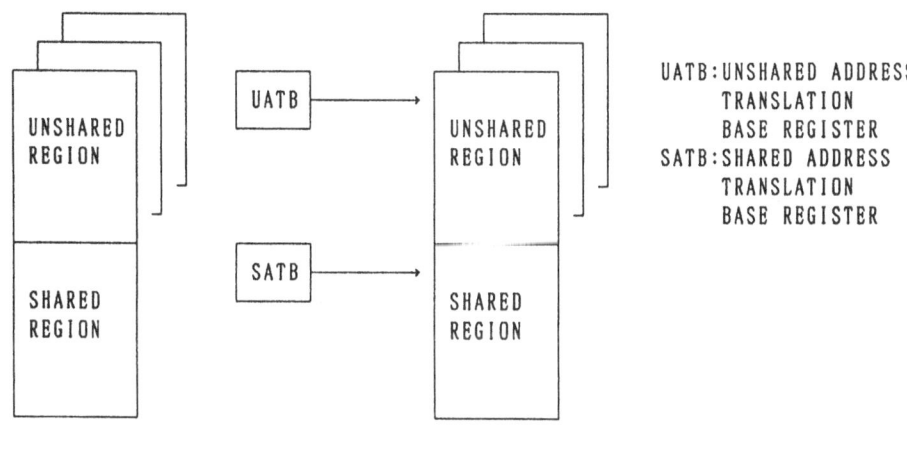

FIGURE-2

1.3. MULTI VIRTUAL MEMORY ENHANCEMENT

G ᴍɪᴄʀᴏ /300 supports LSID feature so as not necessarily to purge TLB when UATB is loaded.

LSID Register is LEVEL 2 architecture and identifies logical address space. Figure 3 shows LSID and UNSHARED REGION relation. LSID is 12bits, so identifies up to 4096 unshared regions. G ᴍɪᴄʀᴏ /300 TLB has 64 entries and each entry includes logical address, LSID, and physical address. Therefore, region switch changes the value of LSID, and loads new entry to UATB, and does not necessarily purge TLB because LSID of TLB ENTRY is differrent.

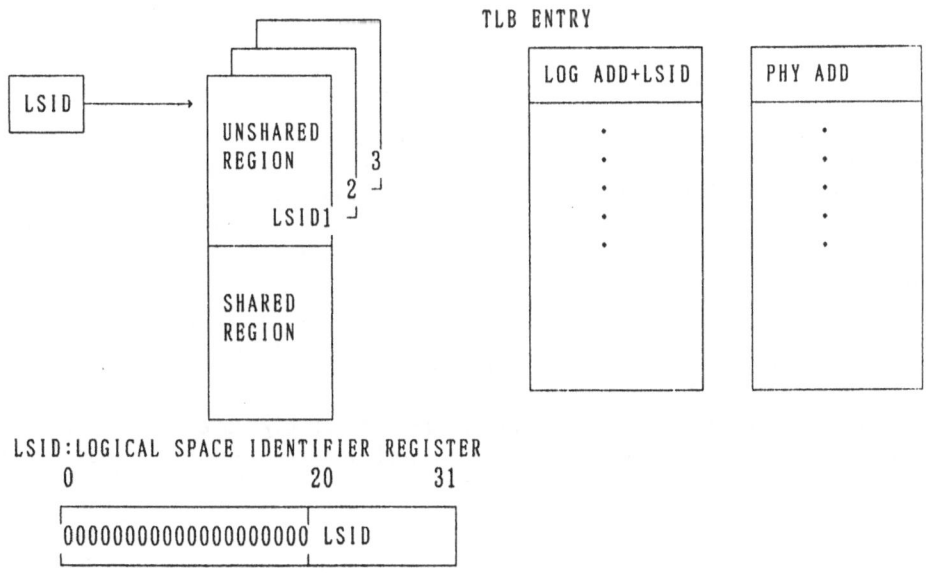

FIGURE-3

LSID register and UATB register are mutually independent registers, and changing the contents of UATB does not affect the contents of LSID register. To control the correspondence between UATB and LSID is done by software. The reason for software control, as opposed to hardware control as usually used in case of general purpose main frame, is that under servers, or minicomputers applications many small jobs are opened and killed shortly, and differrent unshared region may be assigned to the same contents of UATB, therefore, hardware can not control the correspondence between LSID and UATB.

1. 4. COMPATIBILITY

GMICRO /300 is upward compatible of GMICRO /200 which does not support LSID.

2. DECIMAL ARITHEMETIC ENHANCEMENT

Microprocessors have now been used in business workstations. In business applications, COBOL programs are widely used. But normal microprocessor architectures do not consider COBOL programs, and they have only poor decimal instruction sets. Hence, we decide that G MICRO /300 support LEVEL2 decimal instructions. LEVEL2 decimal instructions are carefully selected so as to support COBOL programs efficiently with reasonable hardware.

2. 1. ENHANCING POINTS OF LEVEL2 DECIMAL INSTRUCTIONS

The following points are considered to make LEVEL2 decimal instructions.

    ① Signed decimal ADD/SUB instructions
    ② Decimal-complement instructions
    ③ Decimal compare instructions
    ④ Decimal number check
    ⑤ 4digits PACK/UNPACK instruction

Signed decimal support is essential to run COBOL programs efficiently. But, instead of supporting variable length arithemetic, we have decided to support fixed length arithmetic instructions and to realize variable length arithemetic by the sequence of instructions. If variable length arithemetic is supported by decimal instructions, handling of interruptions and page fault exception will be very complicated and inefficient.

2. 2. LEVEL2 decimal instructions explanation

The following 15 instructions are supported for high speed COBOL execution. 11 instructions are newly defined as LEVEL2 instructions and 2 instructions have optionally been enhanced.

TABLE 1

		LEVEL1	LEVEL2
ADDX	ADD DECIMAL WITH EXTENTION	○	
DCADD	DECIMAL CALCULATE ADD		○
DCADDU	DECIMAL CALCULATE ADD UNSIGNED		○
SUBDX	SUBTRACT DECIMAL WITH EXTENSION	○	
DCSUB	DECIMAL CALCULATE SUBTRACT		○
DCSUBU	DECIMAL CALCULATE SUBTRACT UNSIGNED		○
DCX	DECIMAL CALCULATE WITH EXTENSION		○
DCADJ	DECIMAL CALCULATE ADJUST		○
DCADJU	DECIMAL CALCULATE ADJUST UNSIGNED		○
DCADJX	DECIMAL CALCULATE ADJUST WITH EXTENSION		○
DCCMP	DECIMAL CALCULATE COMPARE		○
DCCMPU	DECIMAL CALCULATE COMPARE UNSIGNED		○
DCCMPX	DECIMAL CALCULATE COMPARE WITH EXTENSION		○
PACK	PACK	○ H, W →B	○ W →H
UNPACK	UNPACK	○ B →H, W	○ H →W

B:BYTE H:HALF WORD W:WORD

Above 15 instructions operate as followings.

TABLE 2

ADDX	dest+src+X flag ⇨ dest;

DCADD	if (sign of dest = sign of src)
	    then [dest + src ⇨ dest;
	                         0 ⇨ F flag;]
	    else [dest - src ⇨ dest;
	                         1 ⇨ F flag;]
	    sign of dest ⇨ sign of dest;

DCADDU	dest+src ⇨ dest; 0 ⇨ F flag;
SUBDX	dest-src-X FLAG ⇨ dest;

DCSUB	if (sign of dest = sign of src)
	    then [dest - src ⇨ dest;
	                         1 ⇨ F flag;]
	    else [dest + src ⇨ dest;
	                         0 ⇨ F flag;]
	    sign of dest ⇨ sign of dest;

(Table continued on following page)

TABLE 2 (continued)

| DCSUBU | dest-src | ⇒ dest; |
| | | 1 ⇒ F flag; |

DCX	if (F flag=0)	
	then [dest+src+X flag ⇒ dest;]	
	else [dest-src-X flag ⇒ dest;]	

DCADJ	0 - src	⇒ dest;
	if (sign of src =(+))	
	then	[(-) ⇒ sign of dest;]
	else	[(+) ⇒ sign of dest;]

| DCADJU | 0 - src | ⇒ dest; |

| DCADJX | 0 - src -X FLAG | ⇒ dest; |

DCCMP	if (sign of src2 = sign of src1)	
	then [src2-src1	⇒ flag set;]
		1 ⇒ F flag;
	then [src2+src1	⇒ flag set;]
		0 ⇒ F flag;

| DCCMPU | src2-src1 | ⇒ flag set; |
| | | 1 ⇒ F flag; |

DCCMOPX	if (F flag=0)	
	then [src2+src1+Xflag ⇒ dest;]	
	else [src2-src1-Xflag ⇒ dest;]	

PACK	UNPACD DATA	⇒ PACKED BCD
	HALFWORD	→ BYTE
	WORD	→ BYTE, HALFWORD

UNPACK	PACKED BCD	⇒ UNPACKED DATA
	BYTE	→ HALFWORD, WORD
	HALFWORD	→ WORD

2.3. EFFECTS OF LEVEL2 DECIMAL INSTRUCTIONS

Table 3 shows the hand compiled result of some of typical COBOL statements.
The result shows that the support of new decimal instructions makes COBOL
programs run more than three times faster and be more than three times smaller
in code size.
COBOL compiler normally translates COBOL statement into library procedure
under microprocessor architectures. But, new decimal instructions may give
chances to COBOL compiler to translate into in-lines. In that case performance
enhancement will be much greater.

TABLE 3

		INSTRUCTION STEPS	
		WITHOUT LEVEL2 DECIMAL INSTRUCTIONS	WITH LEVEL2 DECIMAL INSTRUCTIONS
ADD	S9(6) =S9(6) +S9(4)	63 (1.0)	22 (0.35)
	S9(16)=S9(14)+S9(14)	112 (1.0)	38 (0.34)
COMP	IF S9(8) =S9(8)	36 (1.0)	9 (0.25)
	IF S9(4)c=S9(4)c	38 (1.0)	6 (0.16)
	TOTAL	249 (1.0)	75 (0.30)

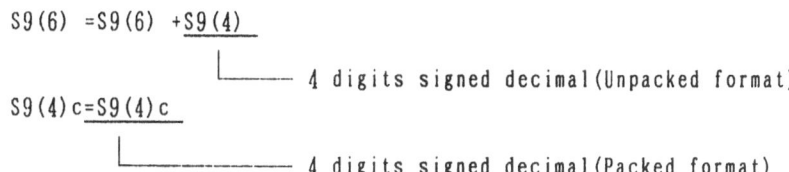

S9(6) =S9(6) +S9(4)

└─── 4 digits signed decimal(Unpacked format)

S9(4)c=S9(4)c

└──── 4 digits signed decimal(Packed format)

3. CONCLUSIONS

(1) LSID (LOGICAL SPACE IDENTIFIER)support is very effective for multi virtual memory support, because TLB is not necessarily purged when virtual memory switched.

(2) Software LSID control is better than hardware control under which many small applications run simultaneously.

(3) New decimal instructions make COBOL run more than three times faster.

(4) New decimal instructions make COBOL be more than three times smaller in code size.

I acknowledge that we are indebted to special and precious advices concerning G micro /300 functions from PROF. KEN SAKAMURA, Department of Information Science, Tokyo University and G$_{MICRO}$ members of HITACHI LIMITED and MITSUBISHI ELECTRIC CORPORATION.

MATAO ITOH is a manager of G$_{MICRO}$ /300 logic design
group at Microcomputer Development Division, FUJITSU
LIMITED in KAWASAKI. He received his BA in electronics
from Tokyo University in 1970.

Pipeline Structure
of Matsushita 32-bit Microprocessor

Tokuzo Kiyohara, Masashi Deguchi, Takashi Sakao

Central Research Laboratories, Matsushita Electric Industrial Co., Ltd.
Yagumo-nakamachi, Moriguchi, Osaka, 570 Japan

ABSTRACT

We have been designing a virtual memory support model with performance of more than 6MIPS, which is one model of the Matsushita 32-bit microprocessor series based on TRON CPU specifications. In this paper, our approaches for high performance and virtual memory support (i.e., on-chip cache memory and address translation buffer implementation, pipeline structure, and speed-up of branch instructions) are introduced. It developed, through performance evaluations, that this model achieves 7-9MIPS at a 20MHz clock rate.

KEY WORDS

TRONCHIP, Pipeline, Cache memory, Address Translation Buffer, Branch.

1. INTRODUCTION[1],[2],[3]

In the field of high performance personal computers and workstations, large scale development in high level languages is increasing from the software productivity; virtual memory will be indispensable in the 1990's, and the demand for microprocessor performance is increasing remarkably. Therefore, we have been designing a virtual memory support model with performance of more than 6MIPS, which is one model of the Matsushita 32-bit microprocessor series based on TRON CPU specifications.

For the target of high performance, the high-speed execution of the basic instructions which are frequently used in a compiled program and efficient support of virtual memory are very important. Especially in high level languages, the reference frequency for the stack frame is very high. For this reason, we should increase the speed of not only register-to-register instructions but also memory-to-register instructions. Therefore, the first design concept of this model is one clock execution of register-to-register instructions and memory-to-register instructions of short format, such as ADD and SUB, and speed-up of branch instructions.

For one clock execution of register-to-register instructions and memory-to-register instructions, our main approaches are pipelining and wide bus bandwidth, which is achieved by two high-speed split buses for instruction and data, and fast on-chip implementation of cache memories and an address translation buffer. In particular, the major problems in virtual memory support were address translation overhead reduction and efficient instruction restart mechanism after a page fault.

One clock execution of memory-to-register instructions can be achieved in the on-chip cache memory hit case; in the miss case, moreover, the execution of memory-to-register instructions requires some clocks, but a high hit ratio cannot be expected because of the capacity limit. So, an additional pipeline stage is inserted to access the external bus. This insertion achieves two clock execution of memory-to-register instructions even in the miss case.

For the speed-up of branch instructions which are the cause of performance degradation in the pipeline, our main approaches are reduction and variation of the number of pipeline stages, and a multiple instruction streams method with branch target prefetch.

These approaches achieve 7-9MIPS performance at a 20MHz clock rate, under EDN proposed benchmark programs, and the same branch instructions performance as the branch prediction approach.

After describing the implementation and performance evaluation results of on-chip cache memories and the address translation buffer in Chapter 2, Chapter 3 presents the pipeline structure and behavior. Chapter 4 presents the speed-up of branch instructions. Chapter 5 is the summary.

2. ON-CHIP CACHE MEMORIES AND ADDRESS TRANSLATION BUFFER

The on-chip cache memory is logical and is split into the instruction cache(I-Cache) and data cache(D-Cache). On-chip cache memory is fast in itself, and specialized buses for I-Cache and D-Cache reduce the overhead of access conflict between instruction and data; one clock execution of memory-to-register instructions is achieved.

The on-chip address translation buffer is unified with instruction and data, and performs concurrently with the D-Cache. Thus, if a D-Cache miss occurs, an address translation delay can be avoided.

There are some on-chip advantages and disadvantages for the cache memory and address translation buffer. The advantages are the capability of complex address mapping method, such as full associative, and additional local buses cost-effectiveness. The disadvantage is the small capacity because of the chip-size limitation. For that reason, the performance evaluations of the cache memory and address translation buffer are required.

-EVALUATION SYSTEM

We used the performance evaluation system, which is shown in Fig.1, and the real-time trace system, which is shown in Fig.2. The performance evaluations consist of two parts, static analysis and dynamic analysis. Static analysis depends on the results of the compiler and assembler. Dynamic analysis depends on the traces which are the workstation's memory reference histories.

The real-time trace system monitors the CPU chip-bus of the workstation, and stores the information on the chip-bus into trace memories per a memory reference. The trace memory performs real-time trace up to 1×10^6 memory references.

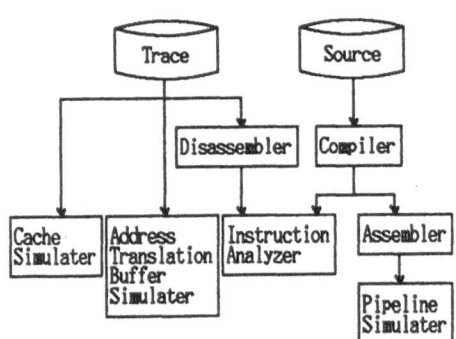

Fig.1 Performance evaluation system

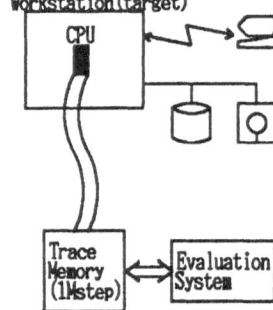

Fig.2 Real-time trace system

-ADDRESS TRACE

The real-time address trace is stored with access attributes. Thus, it is possible to distinguish between instructions and data. As the result of analysis, it became clear that the working set of instructions is especially small.

Fig.3 shows the address reference histories. This data is a part of the history of the C-compiler on the UNIX. The working set of only instructions or of only data is remarkably smaller than one of instructions and data mixed. We used the MC68010(Motorola) as the CPU instead of TRON CPU.

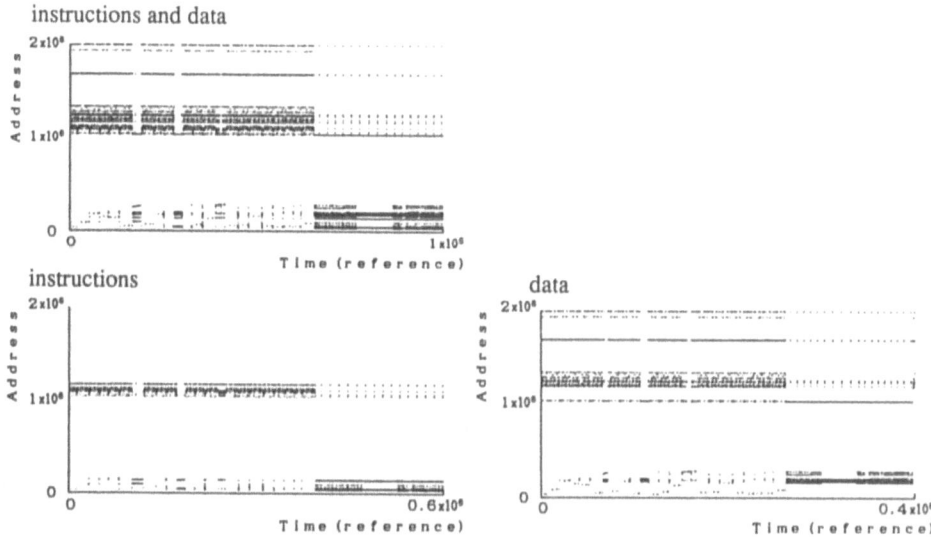

Fig.3 Address reference histories

-CACHE SIMULATION

There is no bad effect of the split implementation for bus-neck resolve, compared with the unified implementation, and the hit ratio increases in the I-Cache.Because of the small capacity, there is no performance difference between logical and physical cache implementation. In logical implementation, moreover, there is no performance advance from logical space ID(LSID) which identifies the logical spaces of multiple virtual memory and avoids cache flush in context switch.There are performance differences among address mapping methods(direct, 2way, 4way) only in the D-Cache.

Fig.4 shows a plot of the hit ratio versus the cache size in address mapping methods(direct, 2way, 4way) for the unified implementation and the split implementation.

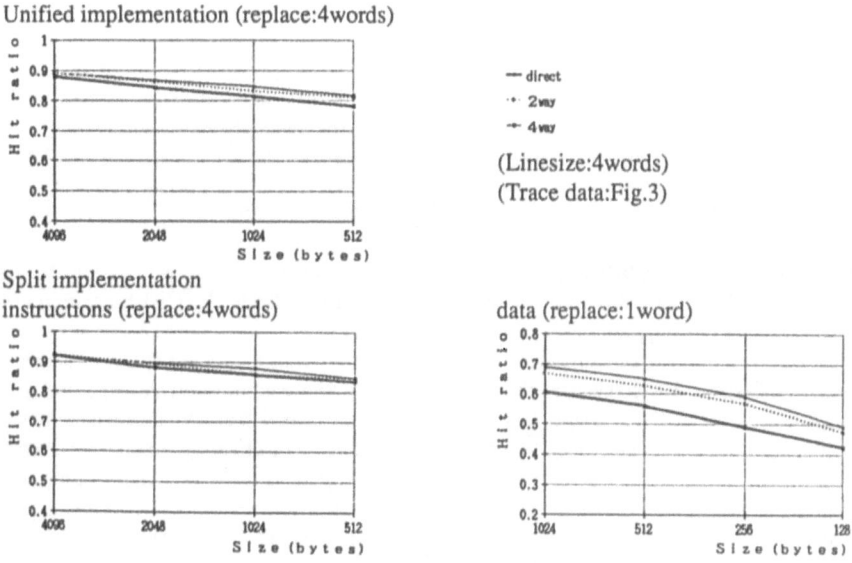

Fig.4 Cache hit ratio versus size

-ADDRESS TRANSLATION BUFFER SIMULATION

In the same total capacity, the performance difference between the unified implementation and the split implementation is slight. In small capacity, however, the unified implementation is better.In address mapping methods, the performance increases in the order: direct, 2way, and 4way. There is no performance difference between 4way and full.

Fig.5 shows a plot of the hit ratio versus the address translation buffer size in address mapping methods(direct, 2way, 4way, full) for the unified implementation and the split implementation.

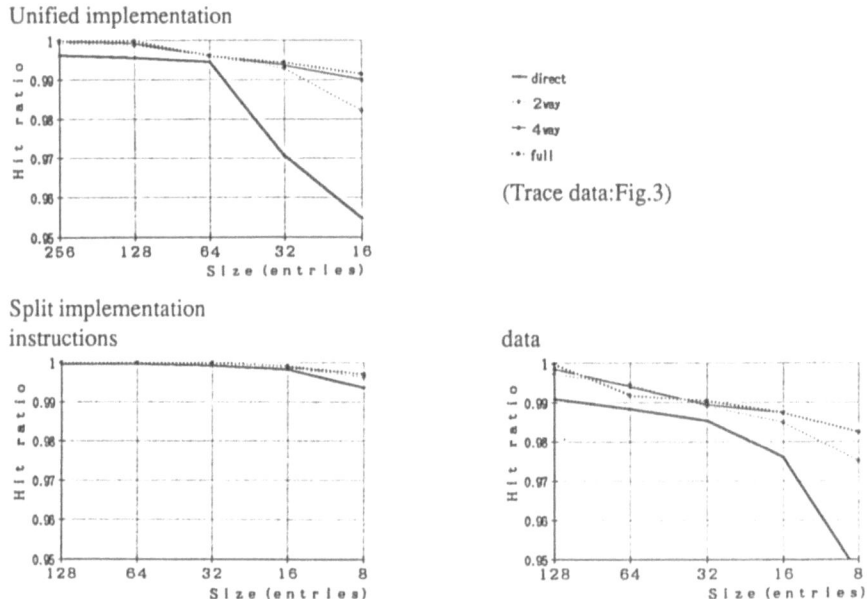

Fig.5 Address translation buffer hit ratio versus size

3. PIPELINE WITH OPERAND PREFETCH

-PIPELINE

A typical pipeline performs a number of operations sequentially(Fig.6). The typical sequence consists of instruction fetch, decode, operand address generation, operand fetch, execution, and operand write.

In this model, operand address generation, operand address translation, and operand fetch are implemented as an additional concurrent stage of the main pipeline, which consists of instruction fetch, decode, and execution. The number of pipeline stages is reduced to the minimum for the speed-up of branch instructions.

For the synchronization between pipeline stages, there are many queues such as the operand buffer(OB) for prefetched memory operands, and the EX-command buffer(EXCB) for variation of the number of instructions in the pipeline.

Fig.7 shows this model's pipeline. The pipeline stages consist of the IF-stage, DEC1-stage, DEC2-stage, OA-stage, OF-stage, EX-stage, and the BUS(read and write)-stages.The OA-stage and OF-stage perform concurrently with the DEC2-stage. Instruction fetch is performed in the IF-stage which includes the I-Cache. Decode is performed in the DEC1-stage and DEC2-stage. When memory references are required, operand address generation is performed in the OA-stage, and operand fetch and address translation are performed in the OF-stage which includes the D-Cache and address translation buffer. If a D-Cache miss occurs, the BUS(read)-stage is inserted to read the miss data from the external bus. This achieves two clock execution of memory-to-register instructions in the D-Cache miss case. Execution is performed in the EX-stage. The pass of EXU means the execution of instruction. Operand write is performed in the BUS(write)-stage.

When operands need memory reference, operand address generation and translation are performed before execution. Therefore, the whole environment, data and translated write-address, is guaranteed before execution starts. Thus, it's possible to check before execution if page faults occur. This reduces the amount of hardware for the restart mechanism. And the instructions which require no memory references, such as register-to-register instructions, don't pass over the OA-stage and OF-stage. This expands the data bus bandwith.

The TRON CPU instruction set is a 2-operand instruction. This instruction format is based on 16-bits(half word), and after the first half word decoding it enables the start of the source operand access. Thus, the next operand prefetch can be performed concurrently with decoding. Therefore, the instruction set assists the operand prefetch.[1],[3]

IF →DEC →OA →OF →EX →OW

IF: Instruction Fetch
DEC:Decode
OA: Operand Address Generation
OF: Operand Fetch
EX: Execution
OW: Operand Write

Fig.6 Typical pipeline stages

IF →DEC1 →DEC2 ─────────→EX →BUS(w)
                └→OA →OF ─────────→
                        └→BUS(r)─┘

IF: Instruction Fetch
DEC1: Decode
DEC2: Decode
OA: Operand Address Generation
OF: Operand Fetch
BUS(r):Operand Fetch(external bus)
EX: Execution
BUS(w):Operand Write(external bus)

Fig.7 Pipeline stages of this model

-STRUCTURE

This model consists of five units: IFU, OPU, OFU, EXU, and BTU(Fig.8). There are many queues between units for synchronization. Each unit's function is described below.

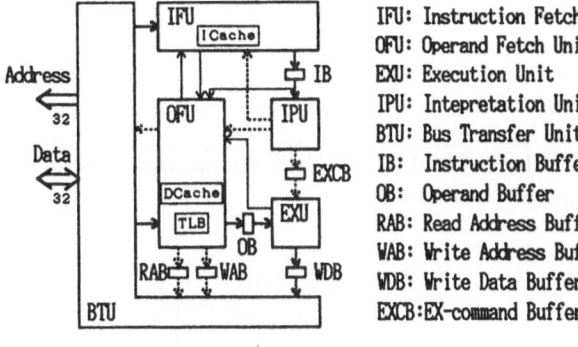

IFU: Instruction Fetch Unit
OFU: Operand Fetch Unit
EXU: Execution Unit
IPU: Intepretation Unit
BTU: Bus Transfer Unit
IB: Instruction Buffer
OB: Operand Buffer
RAB: Read Address Buffer
WAB: Write Address Buffer
WDB: Write Data Buffer
EXCB:EX-command Buffer

Fig.8 Pipeline structure

IFU (Instruction Fetch Unit)   :IF stage

This unit prefetchs the instruction streams and stores them into the instruction buffer(IB). The IF-command from the IPU controls the sending of instructions to the IPU through the instruction buffer(IB), and displacements and immediates to the OFU.

This unit includes an instruction cache(I-Cache).

IPU (Interpretation Unit)   :DEC1 and DEC2 stages

This unit decodes the instruction stream and generates the command stream. There are three kinds of commands: IF-commands which control the IFU, OF-commands which control the OFU, and EX-commands which control the EXU.

The EX-command is sent through the EX-command buffer(EXCB). If the EX-command needs the memory operand, this unit checks the OFU operand prefetch status to synchronize, and sends the EX-command to the EXU after the synchronization.

If the next OF-command needs a register to generate the operand address, this unit checks the existence of the already decoded EX-command which will modify the register. If there is an EX-command which modifies the register, this unit delays the OF-command until the EX-command is completed. (register conflict)

OFU (Operand Fetch Unit)   :OA and OF stages

This unit generates the operand address, translates the logical address to a physical address, and prefetches the memory. According to the OF-commands from the IPU, it sends data to the operand buffer(OB), read-addresses to the read address buffer(RAB), and write-addresses to the write address buffer(WAB).

This unit includes a data cache(D-Cache) and address translation buffer. If a D-Cache miss occurs, an external read bus cycle is inserted, and thus the next OF-command can perform concurrently on the OFU.

An additional use of the D-Cache is to check for memory conflict. When an write-address is translated, the corresponding D-Cache entry is marked. When the memory-write performed by the BTU, the mark is reset. Thus, if the referenced entry is marked, it means that there is a preceding memory write request which has not yet been completed. This mechanism assures the consistency of changes of read-write sequences. (memory conflict)

EXU (Execution Unit)   :EX stage

Only this unit can modify the resources; that is, this unit's execution only means the instruction execution, and for that reason it includes many resources(register, PSW, SP etc).

According to the EX-command from the IPU, it performs the operation from registers or prefetched data, and stores the results in a register or memory. When memory-write is required, this unit requests the BTU.

BTU (Bus Transfer Unit)   :BUS(read and write) stages

This unit performs data transfers between the internal units and external resources such as a memory or I/O. The IFU and OFU request read bus cycles, and the EXU requests write bus cycles. Only this unit isn't controlled directly by the IPU.

This unit has a write data buffer(WDB). The EXU regards writing of this buffer as the completion of operand-write, and accepts the next EX-command.

-BASIC PIPELINE BEHAVIOR

Fig.9 shows the flow of the continuous execution of register-to-register instructions. In this case, the number of pipeline stages is four, and the pipeline rate is one clock per instruction.

Fig.10 shows the flow of the continuous execution of memory-to-register instructions in the D-Cache hit case. In this case, the number of pipeline stages is five, and the pipeline rate is one clock per instruction.

Fig.11 shows the flow of the continuous execution of memory-to-register instructions in the D-Cache miss case. In this case, the number of pipeline stages is six, and the pipeline rate is two clocks per instruction. The update of the D-Cache requires one clock at the OF-stage.

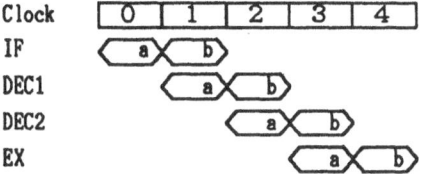

Fig.9 Typical pipeline flow of the continuous execution of register-to-register instructions.

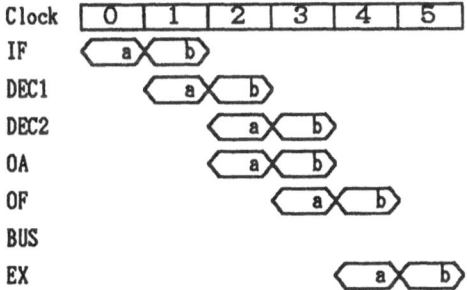

Fig.10 Typical pipeline flow of the continuous execution of memory-to-register instructions in the D-Cache hit case.

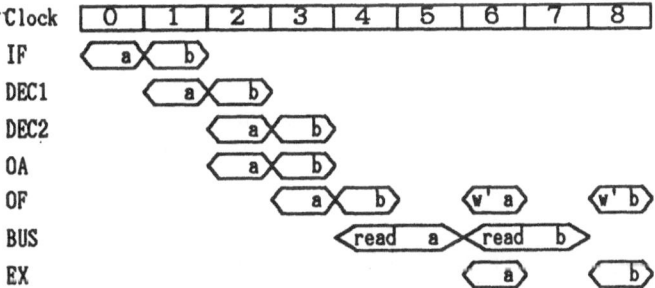

Fig.11 Typical pipeline flow of the continuous execution of memory-to-register instructions in the D-Cache miss case.

-PIPELINE INTERLOCK

There are some cases which cause incorrect execution because of pre-execution in pipelining. In those cases, pre-execution must be suppressed to guarantee the correct execution.

-REGISTER CONFLICT (REGISTER INDIRECT)

When a register is required to generate the operand address and there are some preceding instructions which will modify the register in the pipeline, the address generation must be delayed. IPU performs this check and control.

-CONDITION CODE

Conditional branches must be delayed until the last instruction is completed. IPU delays the IF-command for the branch until then.

-MEMORY CONFLICT

Memory prefetch can't be performed until the preceding memory-write is completed, because the read-address might be the same as the write-address. But this model checks for operand conflict with the D-Cache, and changes the order of read-write sequence to speed-up.

-I/O(non-cache area)

For I/O references, the access itself is important. Thus, it is impossible to change the frequency and the order of read-write accesses. Therefore the speed-up techniques for normal memory access are inhibited. First, caching data changes the frequency of reference. Therefore, caching data should be inhibited. Second, data prefetching causes the I/O data to be abandoned when EIT occurs, so the I/O read must be delayed until the corresponding instruction's execution is guaranteed. Third, an operand conflict check changes the read-write sequence, so the I/O read is delayed until the preceding I/O write is completed.

4. SPEEDUP BRANCH INSTRUCTIONS[4]

Performance degradation from branch instructions is a major problem in pipelining. Therefore, for the speed-up of branch instructions we reduce and vary the number of pipeline stages to speed the pipeline reload penalty, and select three other approaches.

-Preceding branch for unconditional branch instructions

Branch is performed on the OFU and IFU as soon as unconditional branch instructions are decoded because of no requirement for condition check.

-Multiple instruction streams for conditional branch instructions

A branch target instruction is precedingly prefetched on the I-Cache. Therefore, in the condition code wait, the status of the mainline instruction is decoded, and the status of the branch target instruction is prefetched. In that way, speed-up after a condition check can be achieved.

-Branch condition check on decode stage

The condition check is performed on the IPU, not on the EXU. Therefore, the instruction of the mainline or branch target can continue as soon as the last instruction is completed.

Those approaches achieve the same performance level as the branch prediction approach with only taken/not taken information and 70% prediction success probability as the result of performance evaluation.

5. CONCLUSION

We have described our implementation approaches for cache memory, address translation buffer, pipeline, and branch instructions.As the result of performance evaluation, it develops that 7-9MIPS performance at a 20MHz clock rate, under EDN proposed benchmark programs.

ACKNOWLEDGMENTS

We thank Dr.Ken Sakamura for his discussion.

REFERENCES

[1]K.Sakamura,"Architecture of the TRON VLSI CPU,"IEEE Micro, April 1987,pp.17-31.
[2]T.Kiyohara,M.Deguchi,T.Sakao,"A Study of Microprocessor Implementation Based on TRON Specifications,"Proc.Third TRON Symp.,March 13, 1987, pp.34-39.(in japanese)
[3]K.Sakamura,"Architecture of VLSI CPU in the TRON Project,"Proc.Third TRON Symp.,March 13, 1987, pp.1-33.
[4]J.K.Lee,A.J.Smith,"Branch Prediction Straregies and Branch Buffer Design,"IEEE COMPUTER, Vol.17,No.1, January 1984, pp.6-22.

Tokuzo Kiyohara was born in 1957, in Osaka, Japan.He recieved B.E. and M.E. degrees from Kyoto University in 1980 and 1982. After joining Matsushita Electric Industrial Co., Ltd. in 1982, he has been engaged in the development of the VLSI processor and application systems at Central Research Laboratry.He is a member of IECEJ and IPSJ.

Masashi Deguchi was born in 1950, in Osaka, Japan.He recieved B.E. and M.E. degrees from the Nagoya Instite of Technology in 1974 and 1976. After joining Matsushita Electric Industrial Co., Ltd. in 1976, he has been engaged in the development of the VLSI processor and application systems at Central Research Laboratry.He is a member of IECEJ.

Takashi Sakao was born in 1945, in Fukuoka, Japan.He recieved B.E. degree from Osaka University in 1968. After joining Matsushita Electric Industrial Co., Ltd. in 1972, he has been engaged in the development of the VLSI processor and application systems at Central Research Laboratry.He is a member of IECEJ and IPSJ.

TX Series Based on TRONCHIP Architecture

Keiji Namimoto, Tai Sato, Akira Kanuma

Semiconductor Device Engineering Laboratory, Toshiba Corporation
580-1, Horikawa-cho, Saiwai-ku, Kawasaki, 210 Japan

Abstract

The general development philosophy is described for our TX series which consists of a basic core processor, higher performance ones and superintegrated autonomous derivative processors. All these processors are designed on the single TRONCHIP architecture. The core processor TX1 is designed to be widely used for controllers of highly intelligent machines. The TX1 pipeline structure and its performance simulation are discussed intensively, which endorse more than five MIPS. The higher performance processor TX3 contains a memory management unit and 16K byte cache memory on chip and achieves over ten MIPS including basic floating-point instructions. As the first example of TX series superintegration, an organization of LAN processor is discussed which integrates a Token Ring controller logic, high speed RAM and TX1 as a network processor. Lastly, our basic idea is described for the application support systems which include a real-time OS nucleus.

Key Words

Microprocessor, TRONCHIP, Pipeline, Local Area Network, Super Integration.

1. Introduction

We had studied to design a new 32-bit microprocessor which has an original architecture for several years. It was possible to design competitive processors for 1990's by ourselves only in technical point of views. But one of severe problems was a shortage of marketing ability to spread our original processors in the world only by ourselves. Meanwhile, Dr. Ken Sakamura announced his concept for a new microprocessor in the TRON project few years ago [1]. He had declared that his TRONCHIP architecture is opened to everyone, in free of charge in principle [2].

We had decided to join the TRONCHIP subproject this spring under the long-term company policy and to develop a series of TRONCHIP microprocessors, named TX series which have enough performance to compete with the existing 32-bit microprocessor in 1990's. Our original microprocessors are designed on the advanced CMOS VLSI technology. The TX series has been expanding from a basic processor to high performance ones. Three processors in the TX series are described hereinafter. They are a basic core processor TX1, a high performance TX3 and a communication control processor TRL1 for Token Ring LAN. The application system is introduced briefly, which is common to these processors because they have the same TRONCHIP architecture.

2. Development Philosophy

TOSHIBA has been developing 1990's VLSI chip family based on TRON-CHIP architecture. Figure 1 shows the basic idea of the TX series. There are two major products stream in the TX series. One is a higher performance microprocessor stream and the other is a super-integrated autonomous processor stream. The start product of the higher performance microprocessor stream is a 32-bit core processor based on TRONCHIP <<L1>> level specification [3] and it is called TX1. TX1 is designed suitable for built-in machine control, and it has no memory management unit(MMU) and no cache. The second product of this stream is a high performance 32-bit microprocessor based on TRONCHIP <<L2>> level specification and it is called TX3. TX3 is fully upward compatible (that means object code compatible and pin compatible) with TX1, and it has on chip MMU and large cache. TX3 is designed suitable for CPU of personal computer or engineering work station. And as next product of this stream, we are planning to develop more powerful microprocessor. Since all these microprocessors are upward compatible in object code and pin assignment , user can select the most suitable MPU from one of the TX series microprocessors in accordance with his target system and can easily upgrade the MPU if it is needed. Another products stream consists of super-integrated autonomous processors that integrated TX1, some other controllers and so on. As one example of product in this stream, there is a token ring LAN processor that is called TRL1. TRL1 includes a TX1, a token ring LAN controller, a programmable interrupt controller/timer and a 4Kbyte RAM.

Figure 2 shows one example of TX series hardware system. It consists of TX1/TX3 as main MPU, clock generator (CG), interrupt controller/timer (ICT), direct memory access controller (DMAC), memory, and several super-integrated autonomous processors. (Note that CG, ICT and DMAC are also developed by TOSHIBA, but not mentioned in this paper.) Since all processors in the TX series hardware system are united under the TRONCHIP architecture, same software developing tools can be used.

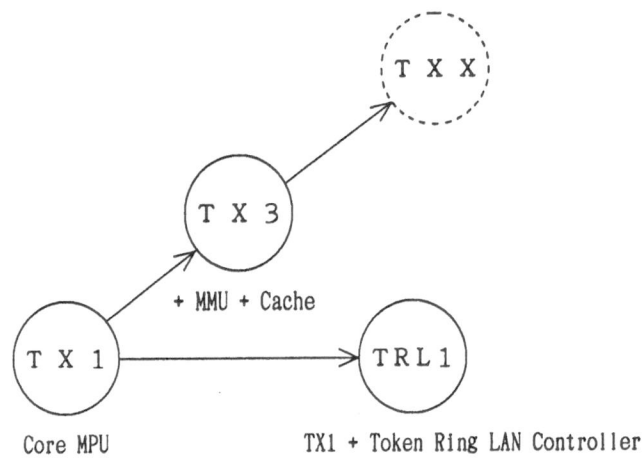

Fig.1 TX Series Processors

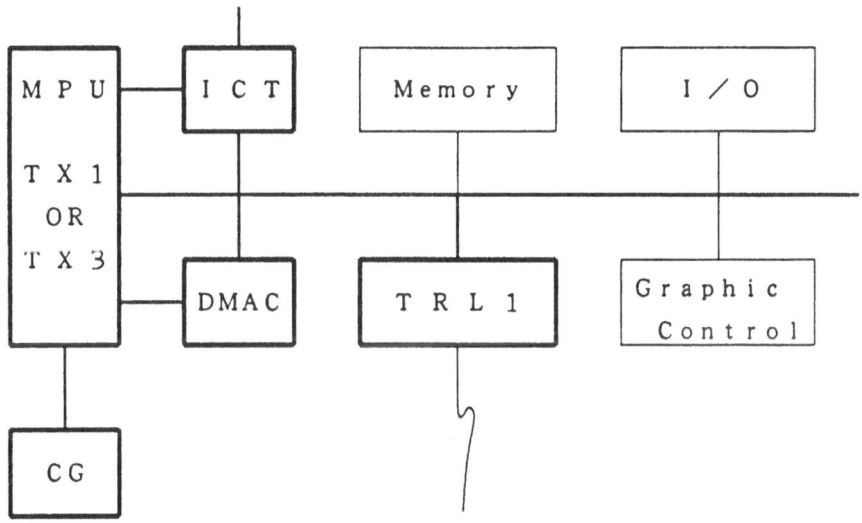

Fig.2 TX Series Hardware System

3. Outline of TX series MPU specification

The abstract of TX1 and TX3 specification is shown in Table 1. Main application target of TX1 is the controller in highly intelligent machine such as laser beam printer, facsimile, NC machine, industrial robot and so on. TX1 has 88 instructions of TRONCHIP specifications and executes basic instructions in 2 cycle, that is 80nsec at 25MHz. The average performance of TX1 is more than 5 MIPS. TX1 will be fabricated by using 1.0 um CMOS technology, containing 400K transistors, and packaged in a 135 pin PGA.

On the other hand, the application target of TX3 is the personal-computer and engineering work station. TX3 has about 130 instructions including decimal and IEEE floating-point instructions. As salient features, TX3 contains memory management unit (MMU) to support paged virtual memory system and 8Kbyte cache memories for both instruction and data to achieve high performance. TX3 executes basic instruction in only 1 cycle, that is 30nsec at 33MHz and the average performance is about 10MIPS. TX3 will be fabricated by using 0.8um CMOS technology, containing about 1M transistor and packaged in a 135 pin PGA that is the same package of TX1.

Table 2 shows the fundamentals of TX1 architecture. The logical architecture of TX1 is defined according to TRONCHIP <<L1>> level specification. A debugging support function and physical structure of TX1 adopts proprietary specification of the TX series. One of the features of the proprietary specification is the strong debugging support functions. There are three major types of on-chip debugging aids that are address trap break, execution step break and flow trace. Address trap break is the function that causes debug exception when breakpoint address is accessed. Execution step break is the function that causes single step, double step and so on. Flow trace is the function to record latest two branch addresses. By using these functions, user can easily debug his software. Another feature of the proprietary specification is testability. It includes self-test by using signature analysis and diagnosis microprogram.

Table 1 TX1 and TX3 Outlines

Microprocessor	TX1	TX3
Target System	Controller	Work station
Performance	5MIPS(peak12.5MIPS)	10MIPS(peak33MIPS)
Clock Frequency	25MHz	33MHz
Min. Bus cycle	2cycle access	2cycle access 1cycle burst
Process Technology	1.0 μm	0.8 μm
Number of Transistors	0.4M	1M
Package	135 pin PGA	135 pin PGA
Number of Instructions	88	130
Decimal	no	yes
Floating-point	no	basic arithmetic
MMU	no	2level paging 4level ring protection
TLB	no	32entries
Cache	no	Inst. cache 8Kbyte Data. cache 8Kbyte
Number of Pipeline Stage	6	6

Table 2 TX1 Architecture

Registers	General Register	32bits×16
	Program Counter	32bits× 1
	Prossor Status Word	32bits× 1
	Pointer	32bits× 6
	Base Register	32bits× 3
	Control Register	32bits× 2
	Debug Register	32bits×12
Memory	Logical Space	8bits ×4G(2^{32})
EIT	Vector methed	15 levels priority

▨ : TX1 Proprietary Specification

Figure 3 shows the pin signals of TX1 and TX3. There are 32 pins for each address bus(A0-A31) and data bus(D0-D31) and zone signals (ZN0#-ZN3#) to indicate byte enable of data bus. As for bus control signals, there are address strobe signal(AS#) and data strobe signal (DS#) to indicate the data enable of address bus and data bus. Bus cycle start signal(BCS#) and bus cycle end signals(BCE0#,BCE1#) indicate first bus cycle and last bus cycle, and BCE0# and BCE1# control 8/16/32 bit dynamic bus sizing. Bus attribute signals (BAT0-2,R/W#) show the type of the bus cycle such as instruction read, operand read/write from memory space or control space and interrupt vector read. Minimum bus cycle of TX1 and TX3 consists of two clocks. TX3 also supports burst data transfer that is used to transfer one line data of the cache memory and it is controlled by BRSTR# and BRSTA#. In order to handle a variety of interrupt, there are 6 interrupt input signals that are reset(RESET#),non-maskable interrupt(INTR#) and 4 maskable interrupt signals(IRP0#-IRP3#) in which 15 priority levels are encoded.

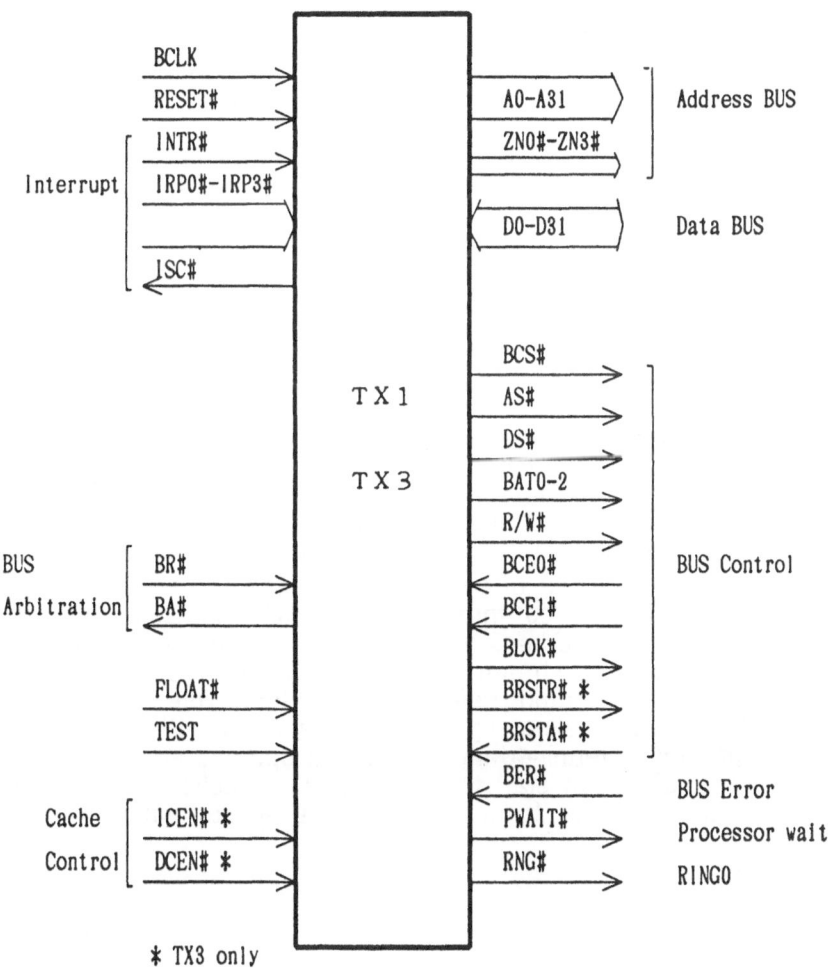

Fig. 3 Pin Signals of TX1 and TX3

4. TX1 Processor

TX1 consists of four blocks; the instruction fetch unit (IFU), the decode unit (DCU), the operand management unit (OMU), and the execution unit (EXU). These four blocks are coupled loosely. They operate independently and communicate in 'shake-hand' manner. This structure was taken because the TRON instruction set has highly functional instructions and complicated addressing modes such as an 'additional mode'. A tightly coupled structure doesn't work efficiently under these conditions. A loosely coupled structure requires less logics to control the whole chip, and allows modular design of each block, which reduces the development time of the whole circuit.

The block diagram of TX1 is shown in Fig. 4. Some features of the four blocks are described below.

IFU (Instruction Fetch Unit) prefetches instruction codes and stores them into an instruction buffer, the size of which is 16 bytes. This size was determined in consideration of the simulation results which is discussed later. Instruction codes are read out by 2 or 4 bytes at a time from the instruction buffer and sent to DCU.

DCU (Decode Unit) decodes instruction codes, and generates operand addresses and a start address of micro-program which executes a machine instruction.

It has a three input adder to generate an address of an additional addressing mode. It performs unconditional branches and a part of conditional branches prior to the execution by EXU. This reduces the execution time of branch instructions, and it is very efficient to improve the performance. DCU generates the branch target address in the same way as operands and sends it to IFU. Then IFU purges the instruction buffer and starts to prefetch the target instruction. Conditional branch instructions are also performed by DCU in the same manner.

OMU (Operand Management Unit) controls memory accesses and prefetches operands. It has a 32 byte operand buffer (16 byte each for data and address) for prefetched operands and those to be stored. It performs operand size transformations between 8 or 16 bit data and 32 bit one. This hides the difference of operand sizes from EXU.

EXU (Execution Unit) executes instructions with controlled by microprograms. It has an ALU, a barrel shifter, several working registers and two busses.

TX1 has two streams of pipeline as shown in Fig. 5. One of them is a stream of operation codes through IFU, DCU and EXU. Instruction fetch, decode, microprogram address generation and execution are performed by this pipeline. The other is a stream of operands through DCU and OMU. Operand address generation, operand prefetch, and operand write are performed by this pipeline. These two pipelines operate asynchronously. Since a start address of a microprogram is determined independent of operand address generation and operand fetch, EXU can start to execute an instruction before operands are fetched. This is effective for the instruction execution which needs a preprocess.

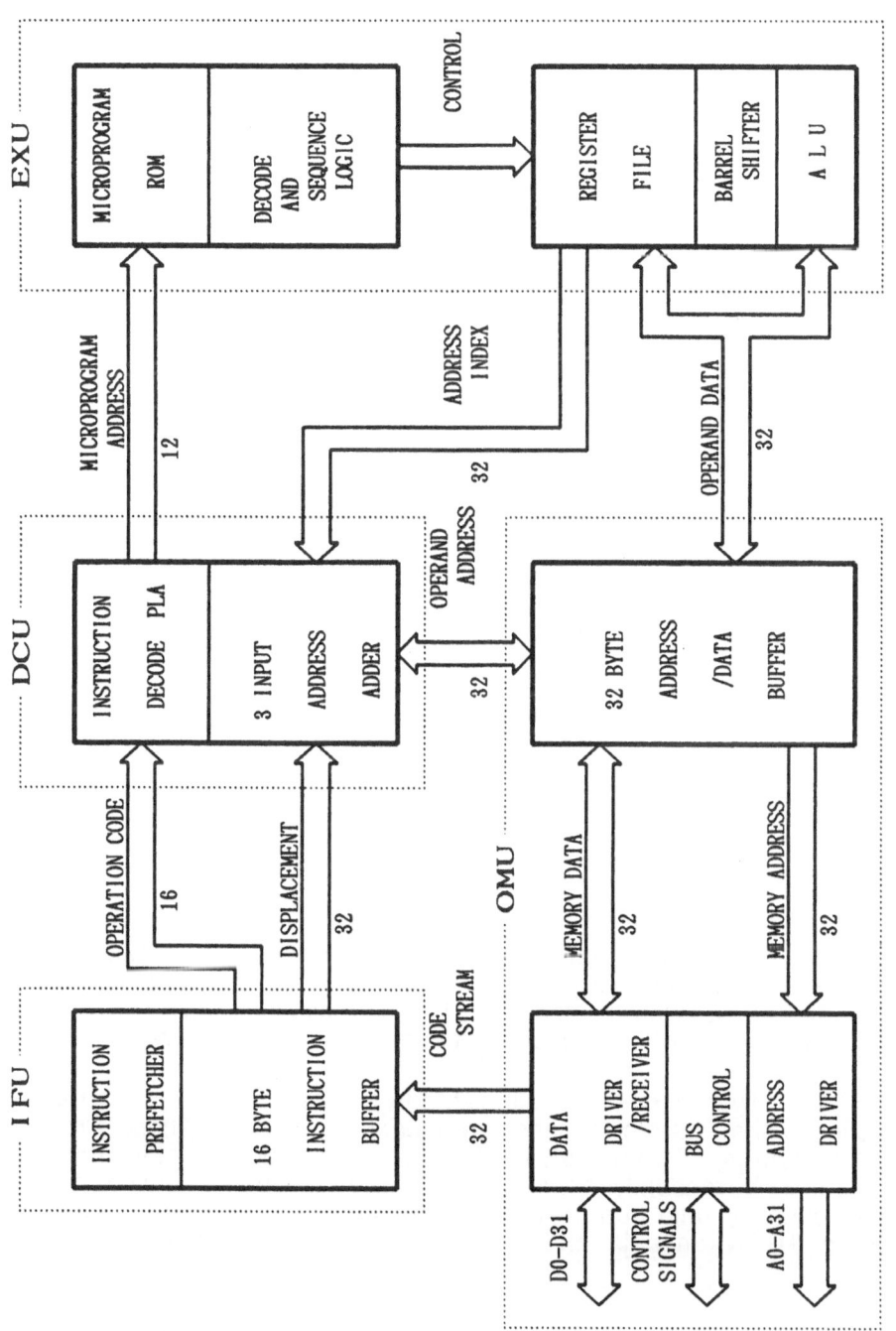

Fig. 4 TX1 Block Diagram

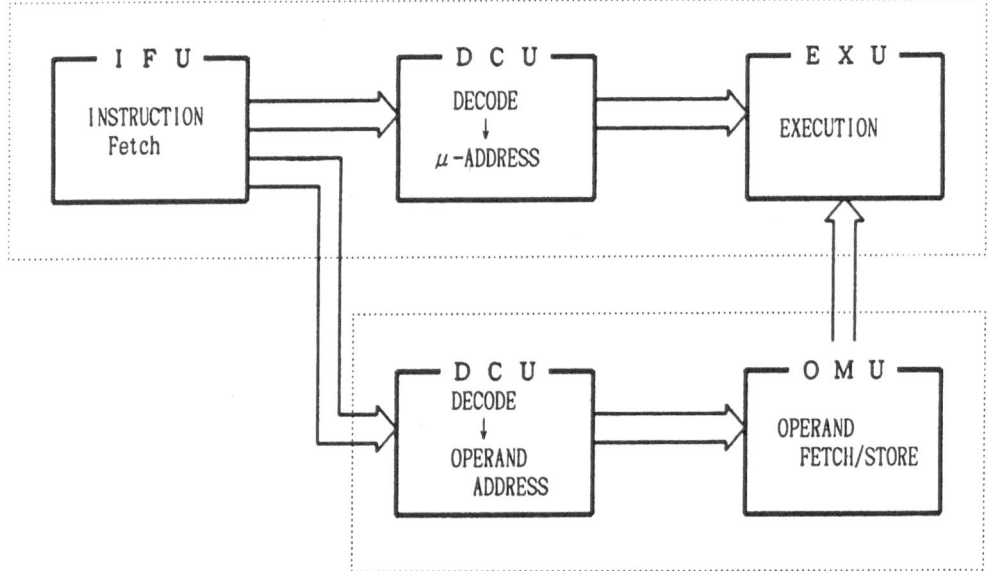

Fig. 5 TX1 Pipeline Scheme

An example of instruction executions is described here. The model is shown in Fig. 6. Suppose that the sequence of instructions is as follows.

```
        NOT @abs:16
        JMP LBL
            ⋮
            ⋮
LBL     ADD Rn, Rm
```

Since an unconditional branch, JMP, is performed by the decode unit (DCU), the instruction fetch unit (IFU) can start to prefetch the target instruction before the JMP instruction is executed by the execution unit (EXU). This suppresses the disturbance of pipeline stream, and it is effective to achieve high performance.

The TX1 hardware model was simulated to evaluate the physical structure and to estimate the total performance by means of GPSS (General Purpose Simulation System [4]). Two models were used for the sequence of instructions. One of them is a randomly generated instruction sequence based on the instruction frequency ratio published by Intel Corp. [5]. Intel instructions were converted to TRON ones in one-to-one manner. For example, Intel store instruction

```
    MOV  M, R
```

was converted to TRON

```
    MOV:S  Rn, @(disp, Rn)
```

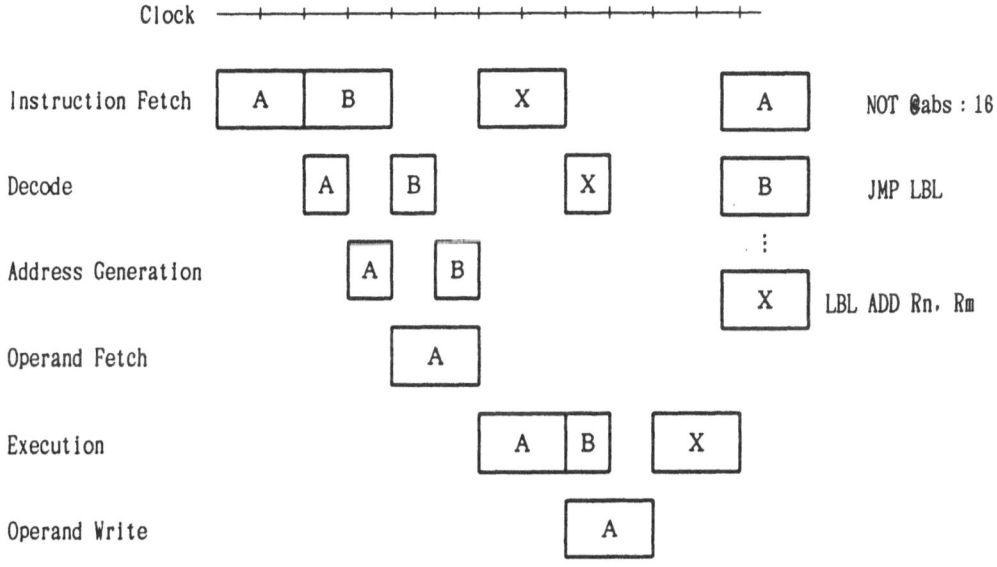

Fig.6 Pipeline Operation

instruction. In this case, the length of a displacement and an immediate data operand was fixed to 16 bits or 32 bits. The other is a real instruction sequence which was obtained by tracing a benchmark program called 'Sieve of Eratosthenes'.

In this paper, only the relation between the performance and the size of the instruction buffer is discussed briefly. The simulation results are shown in Fig. 7 and Fig. 8.

Figure 7 shows that TX1 performs 5.2 ~ 5.4 MIPS for randomly generated data and 6.1 MIPS for a benchmark program if the size of the instruction buffer is 16 bytes or more.

Figure 8 shows the wait occurrence ratio of the decode unit (DCU). Such a wait occurs when a displacement or an immediate data does not exist in the instruction buffer. The ratio becomes high when the size of the instruction buffer is small. It lowers the performance as shown in Fig. 7.

In addition to these, the availability and wait status of each block were examined. They also show that the size of the instruction buffer is needed to be 16 bytes or more. But larger size than needed is harmful because wasteful prefetches increase. The size was determined to be 16 bytes in consideration of these results. In this case, TX1 was proved to perform more than 5 MIPS which is the target. In this simulation, branch instructions are modeled to be executed by the execution unit (EXU). That is, when a branch instruction reaches EXU, the instruction buffer is purged, and then the branch target instruction fetch starts. In reality, branches are performed by DCU before the instruction reaches EXU as mentioned before. Therefore, the performance will be improved compared with the simulation results.

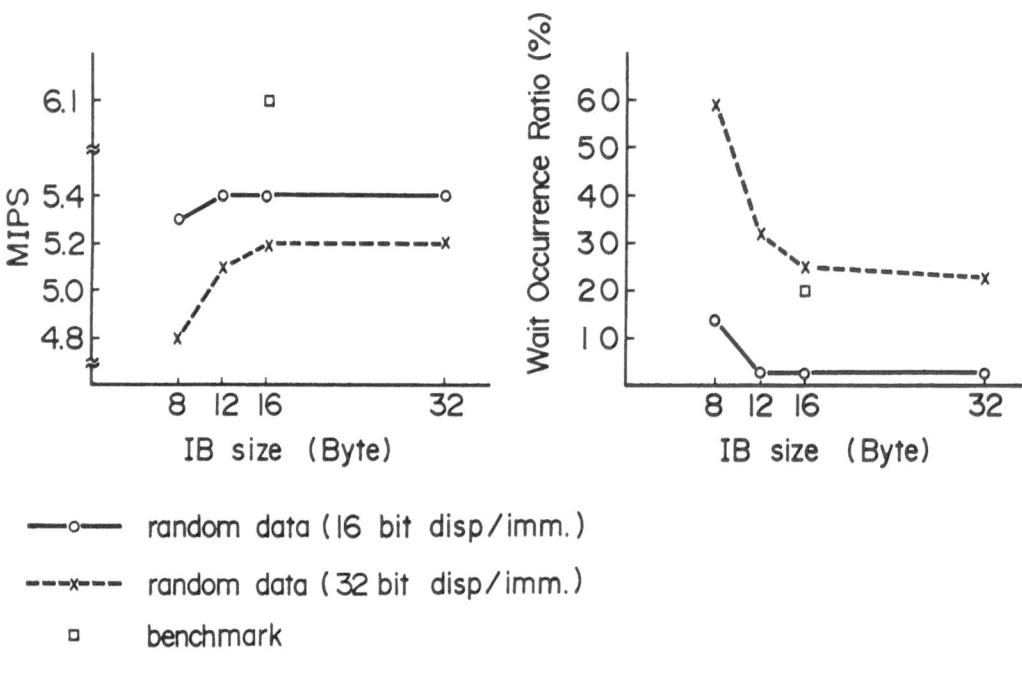

—o— random data (16 bit disp/imm.)

---x--- random data (32 bit disp/imm.)

□ benchmark

Fig. 7 MIPS   **Fig. 8 DCU Wait Occurrence Ratio**

5. TX3 Processor

TX3 is fully upward compatible with TX1. TX3 has many advanced features that do not appear in TX1. One of these advanced feature is the high performance that is twice as fast as that of TX1. Figure 9 shows a rough image of TX3 block diagram. TX3 consists of four units and two large caches. They are Instruction Prefetch & Decode unit, Instruction Issue unit, Memory management unit, Execution unit, Instruction cache and Data cache. In order to achieve high performance, several advanced architectural techniques are adopted.

Large cache
TX3 has two large caches, 8Kbyte for instruction and 8Kbyte for data. To have this split type caches on the chip, TX3 can not only shorten memory access time from more than two cycles to only one cycle (30ns), but also increase bus band-width to the double compared with TX1.

Pipelined execution and fast branch technique
TX3 has four units as shown in Figure 9, and each unit can operate in a pipeline fashion. TX3 can execute a basic instruction in only one cycle (which is 30ns at 33MHz clock rate), so the peak performance will reach 33MIPS. In the instruction Prefetch & Decode unit, there is some branch prediction mechanism that can decrease the performance degradation due to pipeline disturbance at a branch instruction execution. We are also planning to implement instruction buffer in the Instruction Issue Unit. This loop buffer can reduce the penalty of a branch to almost zero in case of short branch distance.

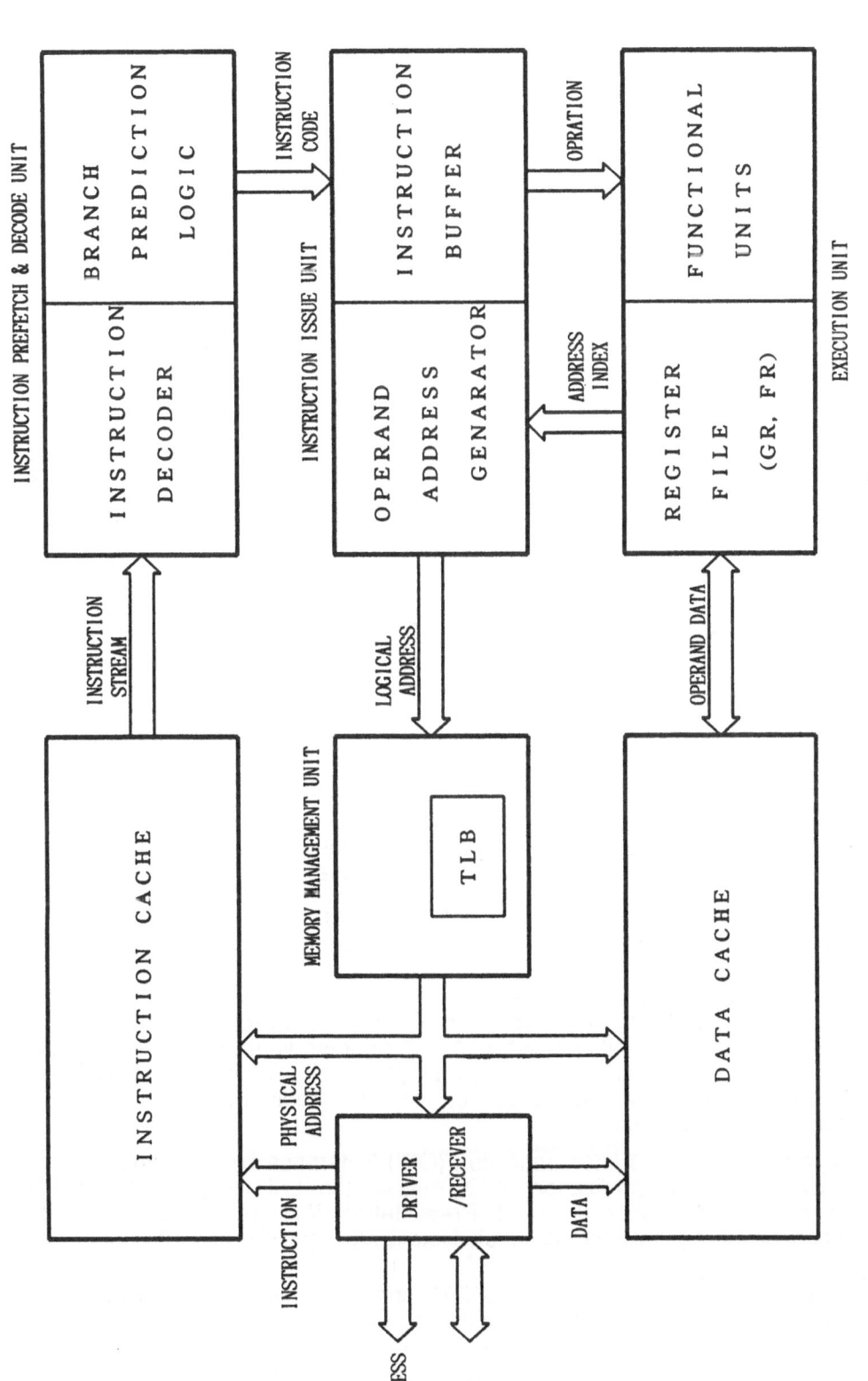

Fig. 9 TX3 Block Diagram (rough image)

Dedicated-functional Logic

In the Execution Unit, there are ALU, Barrel Shifter, Decimal Adder and Floating-point Executing logic and so on . These dedicated-functional logic enable TX3 to execute not only a basic instruction only one cycle, but also decimal and floating instructions very fast under microprogram control.

6. TRL1

The TRL1 is a protocol engine for the token ring local area network fully compatible with the IEEE Std 802.5 Token-Passing Ring Access Method [6]. The maximum bit rate supported is 16 million bit per second. The super-integrated TRL1 includes a 32-bit core processor TX1, a token ring LAN controller, a programmable interrupt controller/timer and a 4k-byte shared memory (RAM).

The integration of these subsystem components into a chip reduces the system cost. And it makes faster the data transfer between those components, which results in producing a high performance LAN control LSI [7]. The super-integration design method can reduce the time and cost for the development of the TRL1 and it facilitates the development of a LAN control LSI family which also includes protocol engines for CSMA/CD and Token Bus protocols. In the LAN control LSI family the communication software higher than 1.5th layer of the OSI model is the same. And the LAN control LSI family and the TX series processors share the same tools for the higher layer software development.

A token ring consists of a set of stations serially connected. And data circulate on the ring in the same direction. It uses a token passing on the ring to control the communication between the stations. And only the station which has obtained a token can transmit data on the network. There is no collision on the network and it results in highly efficient communication capability even on a heavy traffic network [8].

In order to connect a host system to the token ring LAN , only the FBM (Frame Buffer Memory), the PM (Protocol Memory), the system bus interface and the medium interface are needed besides the TRL1, which reduces the number of components for a communication system compared with conventional ones (Fig 10). The FBM is a memory to hold communication data shared by TX1 and LANC (LAN controller) in the TRL1 and the host system. The FBM bus interface consists of 32-bit data lines, 32-bit address lines and several control lines, which are fully compatible with the TX series bus. Therefore, if the system bus is the TX series bus, simple tristate buffers can be used to separate the FBM bus from the system bus. The PM is a local protocol memory which has the interface of 16-bit data lines, 16-bit address lines and several control lines. The TRL1 has also the ring network interface which consists of two data lines and several control lines to connect with the medium interface which can be attached to the ring directly.

The Open Systems Interconnection (OSI) Reference Model of International Organization for Standardization (ISO) defines the LAN protocol with seven layers, namely Application (layer 7), Presentation (layer 6), Session (layer 5), Transport (layer 4), Network (layer 3), Data Link (layer 2), and Physical (layer 1).

In conventional LAN systems the LAN controller could only deal with up to the medium access control (MAC) sublayer of the data link layer, and the host processor had to deal with Logical Link Control (LLC) sublayer of the data link layer and upper layers, which could be a heavy load for the host processor.

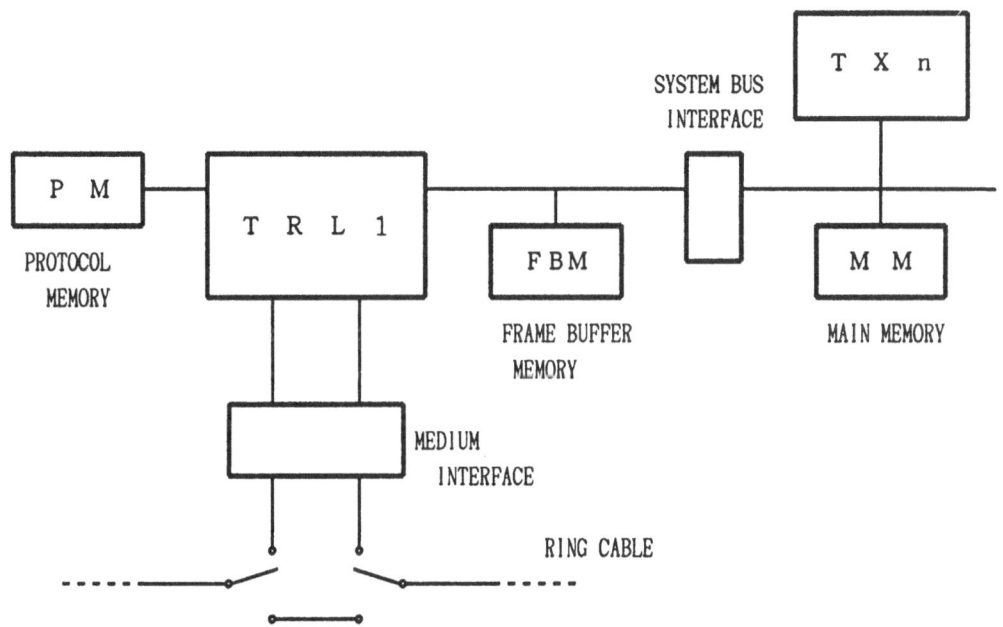

Fig. 10 Token Ring LAN System Organization

The TRL1 can deal with up to the transport layer or the application layer, integrating the TX1, which is appropriate for processing the communication protocols for those layers efficiently, and the LAN controller, which is the MAC protocol engine for the token ring. It lessens the communication load of the host processor. Furthermore, its parallel processing of multiple layers serves to the high speed communication response.

The TRL1 is divided into seven functional blocks which are the core processor (TX1), a LAN controller (LANC), a programmable interrupt controller/timer (ICT), a 4k-byte RAM (IM), an internal bus arbiter (ARB), a TX bus interface (TBIF) and a PM controller (PMC) (Fig 11). The TX1 is described before. The LAN controller is the MAC protocol engine which implements the IEEE 802.5 MAC protocol. The programmable interrupt controller/timer enables TX1 to respond quickly to the interrupts which frequently occur from a LANC. The 4k-byte RAM is shared by the TX1 and the LAN controller. It contains instructions and data for TX1 to provide high speed accessibility to TX1 and assure TX1 of its high performance.

The TRL1 features are summarized as follows:

1.) An integrated 32-bit core processor TX1 (5MIPS,25MHz) reduces the communication load of host CPU.

2.) An integrated token ring LAN controller executes MAC protocol functions fully compatible with the IEEE Std 802.5 Token Ring Access Method.

3.) An integrated programmable interrupt controller/timer enables TX1 to respond quickly to the interrupts which frequently occur from a LANC.

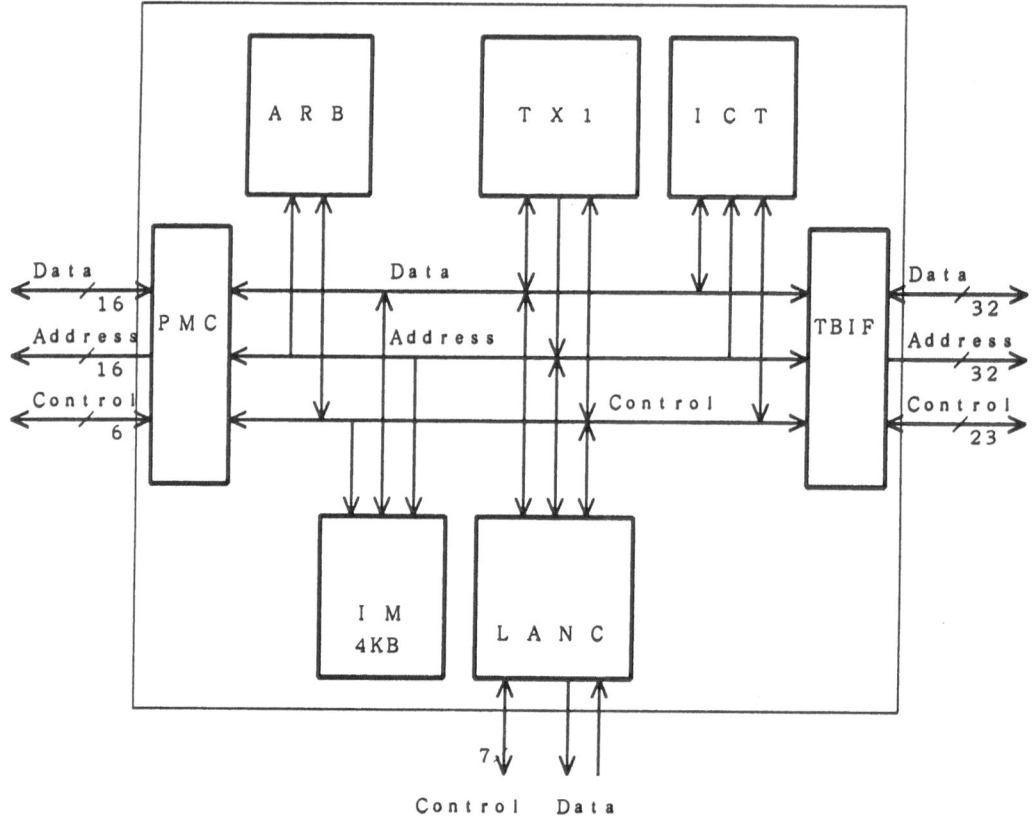

Fig. 11 TRL1 Block Diagram

4.) An integrated 4k-byte shared memory which contains instructions and data for TX1 provides high speed accessibility from TX1 and assures TX1 of its high performance.

5.) TRL1 has the TX series bus interface which enables TRL1 to connect directly to the TX series bus.

7. Development support system

This section will describe the TX1 support system. Further extension to TX3 and upgrade is expected.

Circuit schematics operating at 25MHz that includes TX series LSI's, various memories and standard peripherals will be submitted as typical hardware system configurations. TX series includes TX1 MPU, clock generator (CG), interrupt controller/timer (ICT) and DMA controller (DMAC). Memory subsystem includes no wait SRAM, no wait EPROM, interleaved DRAM. We will also offer design idea of parity generation/check and ECC for improvement of system integrity. I/O subsystem includes basic I/O such as RS232C and Centronics interface, 32 bit parallel I/O and standard data transfer protocol such as SCSI

Host System

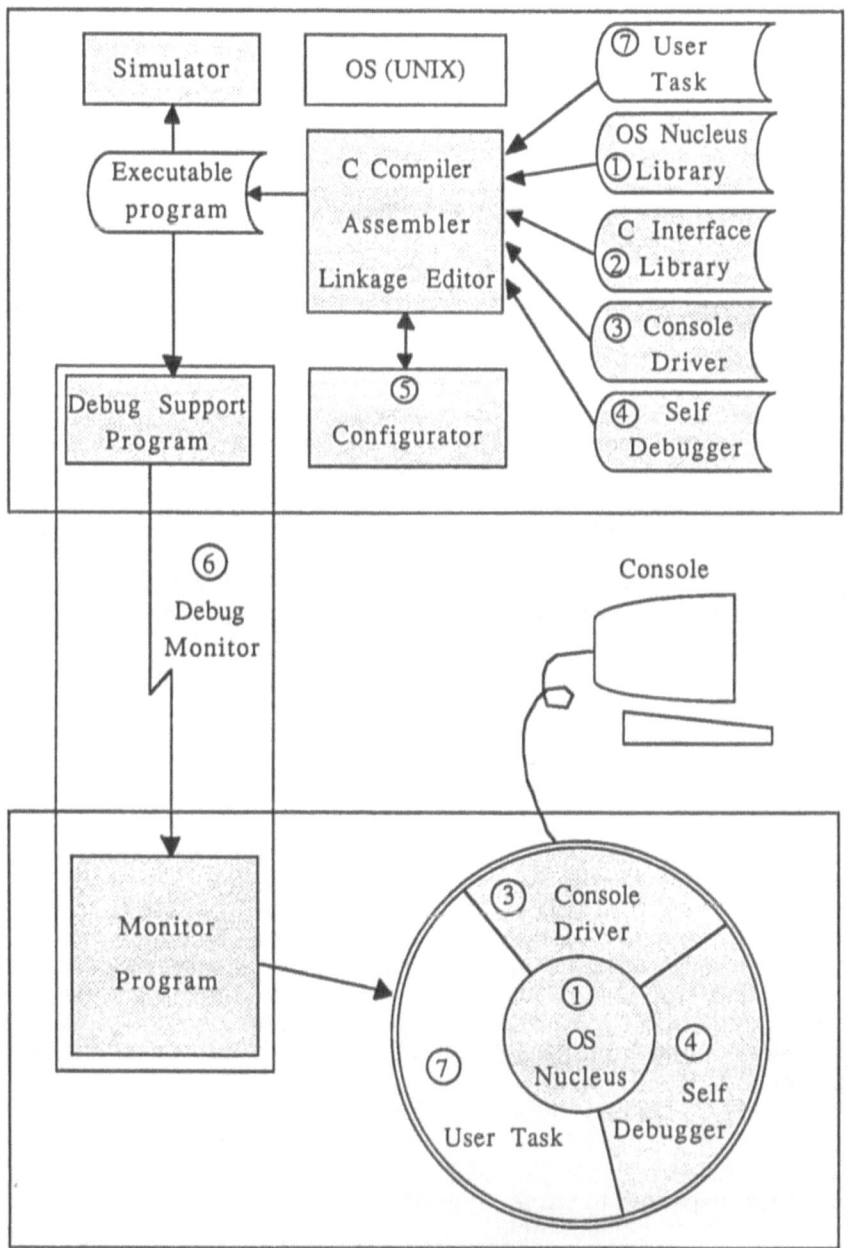

Target system

Fig. 12 Software Development Support System

and GPIB. We will also offer a design example of standard bus interface as a system bus. Users can design their own hardware systems using these design informations.

As a part of software paradigm of TX1, we are developing a real-time OS nucleus, self debugger, console driver, auxiliary I/O drivers. The real-time OS nucleus is based on ITRON/CHIP specification. It supports primitive system calls. In order to support C language level application coding, we will offer C language interface library. A software configurator will be offered on a host system to generate a final application software composed of OS nucleus, supporting utilities and user tasks.

As for programming tools, C compiler, assembler, linkage editor, librarian and simulator will be supplied on the UNIX* system at first step. The C language is based on the UNIX System V Portable C Compiler. It generates codes using TX1's additional mode and functional instructions. The assembler is based on the TRONCHIP assembler specification and the IEEE 694 Assembler Directives. It selects the most appropriate instruction format to generic mnemonics in source programs. Object module format used here is based on the IEEE 694 (MUFOM) with several extensions. The linkage editor does linkage processing of object files and library files. It also generates various vector tables and context blocks specified by system configuration language. The librarian manages object module library. The simulator simulates TX1's operation on a host computer. It provides assembler level debugging environment. User can specify his hardware configuration using system environment language.

A debug monitor and an emulator system will be provided for system debugging under real-time operating environment. These systems have the same human interface as the simulator.

8. Conclusions and future extensions

TX series design philosophy are presented. Entry level processor TX1 is designed to perform more than 5MIPS. Instruction prefetch buffer size of 16 bytes was determined optimal considering the pipeline structure used.

TX3 includes 16K byte split cache memory and on chip MMU. They reduce the overhead in time and components counts of the memory system. Basic instruction cycle time is one machine cycle. Branch penalty should be minimized to match this high speed. An instruction buffer will be implemented. TX3 is upward compatible to TX1 in instruction repertoire and pin configuration. Thus we can easily migrate from simple controllers to complex computers using the same model.

TX1 software support tool includes OS nucleus based on ITRON specification.

Token Ring LAN Processor proved the core processor concept of TX1. More Peripherals are expected to come. This unified architecture reduces design support system overhead considerably.

Ever increasing demand of higher speed and more functionality requires careful analysis of the system performance. Among them, memory hierarchy and pipeline break are importants factors to be considered and will be reported elsewhere.

Extensibility of TRON architecture allows easy migration from 32 bit to 64 bit MPU. Also more powerful and functional MPU and peripherals and support systems are planned and they conform the TRON architecture.

---

* UNIX is the name of operating system developed by AT&T.

References:

[1] K.Sakamura,"Development of TRON Chip:A single chip VLSI computer architecture in the 1990's",Proceedings of IFIP VLSI 85.

[2] K.Sakamura,"ITRON Real-Time Operating System: Architecture and Future Perspective," paper, Computer Architecture Study Group, Information Processing Soc. Japan, 61-1, 1986, pp1-12(in Japanese).

[3] K.Sakamura,"Architecture of the TRON VLSI CPU", IEEE Micro, Vol. 7, No. 2, April 1987, pp.17-31.

[4] S.Greenberg, "GPSS Primer", John Wiley & Sons,Inc., N.Y.,1972.

[5] Intel, "INTEL iAPX286 and Motorola 68020 Compared in High-end System Applications", Intel Application Note, Feb. 20, 1985.

[6] IEEE, "An American National Standard IEEE Standards for Local Area Networks: Token Ring Access Method and Physical Layer Specifications", IEEE, 1985.

[7] G.T.Almes and E.D.Lazowska,"The behavior of Ethernet-like Communication Ring", Proc. Local Area Comm. Network Symposium, Mitre Corp., May 1979, pp.47-61.

[8] A.V.Nadkarni, S.T.Chanson and A.Kumar,"Performance of Some Local Area Network Technologies", Digest of Papers, Compcon Spring 83, Feb. 1983, pp.137-141.

Keiji Namimoto is a senior manager of Advanced Microprocessor Technology Department at the Semiconductor Device Engineering Laboratory of Toshiba Corporation. He received his Master degree in electrical engineering from Waseda University in 1963.

Tai Sato is a chief specialist at Advanced Microprocessor Technology Department of SDEL, Toshiba. He joined Toshiba R & D Center in 1967. Since then he has been engaged in MOS LSI design. Now he is in charge of microprocessor system design.

Akira Kanuma is a senior specialist at Advanced Microprocessor Technology Department of the Semiconductor Device Engineering Laboratory in Toshiba Corporation. He joined Toshiba in 1974. Since then he has been engaged in research and developmental design of microprocessors and dedicated processors.

List of Contributors

The page numbers given below refer to the page on which contribution begins.

Keywords Index

TRON TOTAL ARCHITECTURE

Designed by Ken Sakamura

New Computer Systems Construction

In TRON (The Realtime Operating system Nucleus) project, we try to build new computer systems architecture by foreseeing the technological breakthroughs in the future together with the demands on computer systems and then designing new systems accordingly. We feel the existing computer systems have many problems not fit for the future.

The Objectives of the TRON Project

The TRON project aims to support a society structure where computers are used in every conceivable places and where these computer systems talk to each other without difficulty. The TRON project supports such vision of future society by providing methodology of how to build such computer systems and plan for acceptance of the computer systems by the society. The reason the TRON project covers many fields is to realize such environment.

The 21st century will come within two decades. It is certain that the number of computers used then will be much larger than today's figure. Because the computer will be used very widely, any problem associated with it, however small, should be eliminated as soon as possible. Not all the criticisms about today's computer systems are about technical matters but are about socioeconomical matters as well. Hence, the preparation for eliminating or reducing the problems of the computer systems in the future must be planned in a very broad context.

TRON Subprojects

The TRON project covers many fields of computer system construction and application. Activities of the TRON project are divided into subprojects. The following software subprojects are running currently; ITRON (Industrial-TRON) for embedded computer systems, BTRON (Business-TRON) for workstations, CTRON (Central-TRON) for large file and communication servers, and MTRON (Macro-TRON) for distributed control of TRON computer systems in a large network. The TRON VLSI CPU CHIP subproject to design VLSI microprocessor which can support various TRON systems is also underway.

The Features of the TRON Project

The TRON computer systems are designed as hierarchy of system layers. The TRON project provides specifications for interfaces among these layers. However, the realization of each layers is left to each implementor. While following the TRON Design Guideline, each implementor can freely compete in creating a concrete computer system based on the general TRON concept and specifications.

The TRON computer systems has the data compatibility and the program compatibility. In addition, the TRON computer systems have man-machine interface compatibility, which has rarely been discussed before.

The man-machine interface compatibility together with other TRON design principles have make it possible to use uniform design principles in computer systems and application design. These principles are valid for all TRON-based computer systems.

TRON Association

TRON Association is an organization to provide a forum for discussions about the future computer systems among TRON project members and any interested parties. Please contact the address below if you are interested in joining the TRON Association. Annual membership fee is 500,000 YEN.

TRON Association
c/o JEIDA 5-8, Shiba-koen 3 chome
Minato-ku, Tokyo 105 JAPAN
PHONE: 03-433-1922
FAX: 03-433-2003